JUMPSTART365
(daily devos to start your day with God)

beth jones

JUMP START 365
Daily devos to start your day with God
by Beth Jones

Published by Beth Jones Ministries
2500 Vincent Ave.
Kalamazoo, MI 49024
269.324.5599

Produced by
Blaze Publishing House
BPH is a division of Ministry Solutions, LLC
P.O. Box 184
Mansfield, TX 76063
817.791.4388
www.blazepublishinghouse.com

ISBN-13: 9781933433172

presented to

_____

by

_____

on this date

_____

(acknowledgments)

behind every book are the dear-hearted family and friends
who contributed love, prayers, encouragement, time,
laughter and hard work to make it possible.
i would like to thank these wonderful people:

my husband - jeff
my kids - meghan, annie, luke, eric
my mom and sisters - carol, rhonda, kelly, michelle
the staff and congregation at valley family church
praying friends - too many to name,
but the Lord knows who you are
all the jump start daily e-devo readers
the jump start daily e-devo editor - janelle zander
the jump start 365 book editors - kent and laura-lee booth
editing & proofing - dawn eustice

and most importantly:

i thank the Lord for His goodness and His Words.
they are living and active.
they are able to effectually work within us
they are spirit and life...
and they are true!

"I love Beth's books and am so excited about her new *Jump Start* devotional. We are always looking for relevant material for the young women we serve at Mercy Ministries; material that is written in a language they understand, so they can connect with Jesus right where they are. I am confident this new book will be a great tool. We've used Beth's other books at our Mercy homes for many years, and we definitely plan to have her *Jump Start 365* devotional available in all of our libraries."

Nancy Alcorn, Founder and President
Mercy Ministries International — Nashville, TN

"Beth has a very creative and innovative way of expressing substantive and eternal truths. I've found encouragement, wisdom, and helpful challenges within her writings. Every day that starts with reflection upon the wisdom of God is going to be a better day, and I know you'll be enriched by Beth's writings."

Tony Cooke
Tony Cooke Ministries — Tulsa, OK

"Thank you so much for the devotions. They reach us at Living Faith International Church in Indonesia. They have been encouraging and very useful in preparing my messages."

Rev. Steve Laidlow, Senior Pastor
LFIC — Jakarta, Indonesia

"I really enjoy Beth's fresh approach to the Word of God using expressions that we are so familiar with in this generation. These devotions are a blessing to the Body of Christ."

Jan Wright, Vice-President of Ministério Verbo da Vida
RHEMA Brazil

"As an on-the-go professional, Beth Jones' daily devotions are just what I need to start each day. She begins with a Scripture, then a straight-forward, straight-to-the heart message that is easy to remember throughout the day. The concluding prayer is laced with Scripture and a wonderful way to "lock-in" the truths from the day's devo. I highly recommend it to anyone looking for a spiritual jump start to their day."

Tanya Baker, Elementary Music Teacher
Church on the Move — Tulsa, OK

"In *Jump Start 365*, my close friend Beth Jones provides some clear direction and purpose for every day of the year. This isn't pie-in-the-sky philosophy. Beth has a gift for speaking the truth poignantly and directly into the lives of so many women right where they are, and helps them get where they need to be. I can't promise this book will make you skinny, rich or look 15 years younger (sorry, ladies); but Beth's wisdom and words in these pages will definitely help you discover the path toward the true success God has in store for you each day!"

"Cathy and I absolutely love Beth's devotionals. Each one inspires hope, confidence and a spiritual stamina to win the day!"

"I have received Beth's devos since the beginning, and they are my quick favorites. I liked them so much I encouraged the staff to sign up. They are always timely and relevant and easy to share with the kids."

"Beth Jones' daily devo has proven to be one of the best and most reliable sources for a good 'shot in the arm' of the Jesus Truth serum. Freedom awaits the careful listener to this humble servant of God."

"I read the *Jump Start* devotions every day. They are the perfect way to start my day before it gets hectic! I frequently send them to friends and family members. Thanks for keeping my daily focus in the right direction."

"Beth's anointing to share God's Word in a culturally-relevant manner has given me a true jump start to my day. It has not only blessed me, but others I come in contact with throughout the day and week."

Tori Root, Owner
Jewelry by Tori

"Your devotional everyday is so 'down to earth.' I often send them to my son and daughter. Your way of teaching is so universal and reaches all generations, so real and relevant and easy to understand!"

Mindy Johnson
Mom

"I have been blessed over and over by the *Jump Start* daily devos. I love the "real" style they are written in. It's amazing how many times the daily topics have been just what I needed."

Sheryl Hopkins, Pastoral Assistant
Victory Church

"I love the daily devos and look forward to them every day! When I get to work in the morning, reading my daily devo is one of the first things I do to get my day going in the right direction."

Stacy Caudill, Senior Registered Associate
Raymond James and Associates

"Just when I think I can no longer stand alone, God will speak to me through the *Jump Start* daily devotionals—so strong, you know it's Him. First thing each morning, I'm able to read them and know that God heard my prayers on the drive in, and I already have an answer! God is good!"

Dorothy Bennett, RN, MBA
Director of Nursing Services/Quality Improvement

"Short and sweet. The devos are a great way to start the day, filled with practical, relevant messages and a quick Bible verse to put into your heart and ponder for the rest of the day. Pastor Beth knows just what I need to hear. Whether it's about restoring my marriage, helping raise my kids or just being a better person, her prayers help me feel encouraged and blessed every day."

Melissa Rito Bibler
Homemaker/Business Owner

"Your daily devotionals have made an impact and change in my life, for sure. In the tough times we are facing in this economy, and in my specific business; it's amazing that on the days I seem to be down the most, your devotion is the exact word I needed to hear that moment, that day. I have been truly blessed and encouraged by them."

Donnie Brumley
Sureway Transportation

"*Jump Start* is like a supercharged daily soul-booster that connects powerful Biblical truths with everyday realities. It's invigorating, energizing and inspiring!"

Dr. Jennifer Palthe
Western Michigan University

"I am up very early in the morning and am eager to get a jolt of your *Jump Start* to begin the day with a positive reinforcement! Thanks a bunch for keeping me motivated, so I don't lose hope."

Jolly Sinha, Official Title "Expat Wife"
Sydney, Australia

"I really like how Beth takes passages from the Bible and either explains them, gives examples from her personal life as to how the Bible has taught her, or gives us a challenge or something to think about. I cannot tell you how many times the devo [for the day] spoke directly to me and gave me peace of mind."

Cecelia Tarchalski, Retired Teacher

"Many of the *Jump Start* devotionals have just hit the mark for me in my season. I have cut and pasted many words of practical, timely wisdom [to my students] that I know will bless them or speak to their situations. Beth focuses on issues we all live with, day in and day out."

Anne K. Hartzfeld
Educator

"I am always so encouraged by the daily *Jump Start* devotions. They give me a great source of encouragement and are just what I need to start my day!"

Amanda Regnerus, Director of Client and Channel Development
US Signal Company

"*Jump Start* is another tool for spreading the Good News! I often forward them to a Believer friend or colleague that needs a lift. They are full of REAL LIFE words that speak to everyone!"

Karen Fulton, RN, MSN, Administrative Director
Neurological Practices & Services
Borgess Brain and Spine Institute

"Beth's devos are right on. My daughter got me started on her daily devotionals, and I love every word. I am so excited about them. I enjoy forwarding them on to friends at work and relatives."

Jeanne Van Eerden
Real Estate Broker

"I have been getting encouragement, confirmation, knowledge and wisdom from the very first time I subscribed to this daily devotional. I have forwarded many messages on to people I know in the business world, as well as close family and friends. I am amazed at the high percentage of messages that apply directly to my life each and every day! Thank you and God bless."

Al Balko
Message Marketing

"I look forward to Beth Jones' daily *Jump Start* devos every morning; they are written in a way I totally relate too! Through these devotions, God speaks directly to my heart enabling me to overcome everyday struggles with His Word and prayer."

Deb Harbert
Homemaker

"My husband and I enjoy starting our workday with your thoughtful analysis of God's Word. It's amazing how two people can read the same thing and have it speak unique thoughts to each of us. Thank you for sharing your gift of understanding and for enlightening our days."

Ann & John Wiedlea
Automation Plus

DAY 1

(some things are worth fighting for)

"For our struggle is not against flesh and blood, but against the rulers, against the authorities, against the powers of this dark world and against the spiritual forces of evil in the heavenly realms."
Ephesians 6:12, NIV

Some things are worth fighting for! Our faith is one of those things.

What are you fighting for? Who are you fighting for? Why are you fighting?

Three things you should fight for:

- **Your spiritual freedom.** Jesus fought and won the ultimate battle by completely defeating the devil on the cross. Now, it's our job to enforce Satan's defeat by being strong in the Lord. So, let's fight the temptation to get weary, lazy and complacent in our faith.
- **Others' spiritual freedom.** Our fight of faith goes to another level when we choose to put the spiritual interests of others ahead of our own personal desires. It's a battle to resist the temptation to be selfish and to be concerned only about our own spiritual condition. It takes brave, unselfish soldiers of Christ to fight for others—pushing through the pain of persecution to lead them to Christ and help them grow in their faith and to equip and train them for God's army. *(John 15:13)*
- **The blessed life.** While Jesus already bought and paid for us to be blessed with every spiritual blessing and while it is His will that we prosper *(3 John 1:2)*, we have to engage in the fight of faith to possess these things. We have an enemy who wants to steal, kill and destroy everything God wants for us *(John 10:10)*. We need to fight the fight of faith to experience the blessed life Jesus provided.

Some, mistakenly, think it's easy to be a Christian. Others assume God is like a sovereign, jolly-old candy man who drops blessings from heaven at will. Neither is true. It takes grit, perseverance, intentionality, and a proactive attitude of faith to lead a victorious, blessed Christian life. We have to use the weapons of our warfare to enforce Satan's defeat, so we can "possess the land" in every area of our lives.

Read It! Ephesians 6:10-17

Speak It! "Father, I've been too passive. Help me determine the things worth fighting for. I ask You to help me use every weapon at my disposal to enforce Satan's defeat and possess the land. In Jesus' Name. Amen."

DAY 2

(me, myself and I)

"He that speaketh of himself seeketh his own glory: but he that seeketh his glory that sent him, the same is true, and no unrighteousness is in him."
John 7:18, KJV

"I think I'm great, I think I'm grand... I go to the movies, and I hold my hand." Ever heard that little ditty? Now, there is someone who is impressed with themselves!

Newsflash: it's about Jesus! Not us.

So, who have you been talking about lately? You or Him? When we spend too much time speaking about ourselves, we are seeking our own glory. Bitter pill, isn't it? It's ugly. But, let's look at it.

When we want the focus of our words to originate with us and to be about *our* greatness—our never-before-thought-of ideas, our look-I-have-amazing-talent, our give-me-a-PhD-for-my-brains; our fascinating, make-a-movie-about-my-life stories, our award-winning sense of humor, our WWF-brute strength, our incredible-Disney®-wants-me creativity, our stupendous let-me-speak-to-the-nations teaching gift, our unbelievable American-Idol-has-nothing-on-me musical talent, our cover-of-the-magazine good looks, our draft-me-now athletic prowess, or our I am the entrepreneur-of-the-year biz whiz'—we have BIG pride issues!

So, let's talk a lot less about us and a lot more about Him. Let's seek His glory! When people leave an encounter with us, our goal shouldn't be for them to say, "Wow, isn't he (or she) amazing?" The goal should be something like, "Wow, what an amazing God they know! I wonder if I could know Him?" or "Wow, the Lord sure is living big in them. I'll bet He'd help me, too!"

He must increase, and we must decrease *(John 3:30)*.

Read It! Proverbs 6:16-17; 25:27; 27:2

Speak It! "Father, help me to get over myself. You must increase, and I must decrease. I want to seek Your glory. You are the One worthy of attention and praise. Help me speak less about me and more about You. In Jesus' Name. Amen."

DAY 3

(mouth guard)

"Obscene stories, foolish talk, and coarse jokes—these are not for you.
Instead, let there be thankfulness to God."
Ephesians 5:4, NLT

I was following a few pastors on Twitter® but had to delete them because of their constant use of the phrase: "holy crap." I just couldn't reconcile the idea of a spiritual leader being so comfortable using this combination of words on a regular basis. In fact, this Twitter® situation made me evaluate my own choice of words.

Words are tools. They can do so much to encourage, strengthen, refresh, exhort and correct people. We need to use them in wise, creative, relevant and redemptive ways! We live in a culture that is very loose with their words. That's just the way of the world. But, that shouldn't be the way of a Christ-follower, should it? I'm all for having fun, being hip, culturally relevant and "with it," but if our words move into the carnal, obscene, foolish, coarse, crude or spiritually unproductive realm, we need to re-evaluate. We should be more concerned with pleasing the Lord, right? This should be the case for *all* Believers—but especially Christian leaders who have a responsibility to set an example for those who follow.

Done a personal inventory of your words lately? Might not hurt...or then again, it might hurt a lot! Here are some things to consider:

- **Words can grieve the Holy Spirit**. I don't want to grieve the Holy Spirit; I need all the help He will give me. I need His anointing to speak, write and do what He's called me to do. So, the laugh or attention I might get by using unwholesome words is not worth grieving the Holy Spirit *(Ephesians 4:29-30, NIV)*.

- **Words can get you in trouble.** Ever been "hung by the tongue"? Words can get us into trouble *(Proverbs 17:20, NIV)*. Sadly, too many people have caused their own trouble—wrecked relationships, a demotion on the job, wayward kids, financial ruin—simply because they lacked discipline with their mouth. What a price to pay!

- **Words reveal rebellion.** Quit being a rebel, trying to impress people with your carnal words. It'll never take you where you want to go. You know when you're being rebellious, so call yourself on the carpet right now and make a decision to quit using certain words or phrases that feed into it. *(Proverbs 10:32, TLB)*

Read It! Psalm 141:3, MSG and Ephesians 5:3-5

Speak It! "Father, I'm sorry. I ask for Your forgiveness and help. Let me not use words that do not honor You. I ask You to put a guard on my mouth to only to speak words that please You and help people. In Jesus' Name. Amen."

DAY 4

(the "get it" factor)

"The hand of the diligent will rule,
but the slothful will be put to forced labor."
Proverbs 12:24, AMP

Who gets to rule? The diligent person. Who gets the promotion? The diligent worker. *(Proverbs 22:29, AMP)*

Who gets demoted? The lazy, slothful person. Who goes broke? The lazy bones. *(Proverbs 10:4, NIV)*

Big question. Are you diligent? Are you a hard worker? Are you persistent in your efforts? Do you work smart? The diligent person will always rise to the top, can spin more than one plate, and is able to keep pace. A diligent person is a "get 'er done" type of worker who has the "get it" factor.

Being diligent also requires wisdom. It's not wise to be persistent in working on the wrong thing. The diligent person knows how to use wisdom and understanding to work smart—and there is a difference between working hard and working smart. Anyone can go 100 m.p.h. and get nowhere; that kind of diligence is of no real value. The kind of person who adds value to the organization, company, business or church is the diligent person who works smart and actually accomplishes the task at hand. This type of person has the good judgment to know what to work on and when to do it. They have the "get it" factor in their favor.

Trust me. Employers are looking for diligent people who know how to exercise wisdom and understand how to work smart. They want people who "get it" and who can "get 'er done!" The hand of the diligent will definitely rule. Those who are lazy, foolish, wasteful, unwise and lack good judgment will definitely not be promoted or prosper.

Which one are you? I hope you make a prayerful decision to seek the Lord on how to be diligent in the opportunities God has set before you. In time, you will rule!

Read It! Proverbs 10:4-5, NLT

Speak It! "Father, I ask You for wisdom and understanding, so my diligence produces real, tangible results. I don't want to be lazy or waste time on things that are not important or valuable. Help me to add value to the organization, company, business, church or group I work with and for. I trust You and know that if I am diligent and work smart in all that I do, I will rule in life. Help me to be that kind of worker. In Jesus' Name. Amen."

DAY 5

(finish strong)

"...so that I may finish my race with joy..."
Acts 20:24

Years ago, my husband ran the Chicago Marathon. The kids and I were at the finish line ready to cheer him on to victory. It was such a moving experience to watch all those runners come across the finish line. Some people got a sudden burst of energy and raced past the line; others limping, cramping and practically crawling to the end. But, for sure, all of them were beside themselves with happiness—and relief—when they got to the finish line.

We stood in the bleachers and watched for Jeff. When we saw him hit the last 100 yards, we started screaming, "You can do it! Way to go, Jeff! Keep running! You're the man! You did it! Go...go...go...! You can do it!" What joy there was for him—and for us—as he finished that marathon.

I know the Lord is watching us from the grandstands of heaven. He's aware of what mile marker we're at, and I have no doubt He and all the angels are cheering us on to victory. I hope today you hear the Lord calling your name, "C'mon, dear one. You can do it! Keep running! You're almost there! Don't quit! Stay strong. Keep the faith. Hold fast to your confession. Keep going! You'll make it! C'mon, finish strong! Great joy awaits you!"

If you're like me, you've been running your own "marathon." It's always something, isn't it? A project in progress...and another waiting in the wings. Deadlines. Details. Maybe you're going through a struggle, a difficult time or facing the trial of your life? Or, you might be consumed with school, work or meetings? Pressure's mounting. Responsibilities seem overwhelming. Maybe you have a baby on the way—or on the other end of the spectrum, kids moving out? A 1,000 things on your "to-do" list, and the clock just keeps ticking. Just keep your eye on the prize. You can make it. You're almost to the finish line. Stay focused and finish strong! The last lap of the race is the hardest and most important. Your finish line is in sight—even though your body may be tired, your mind may be weary and your muscles may be screaming. Hang in there, even if you want a breather and if you desperately crave rest. Don't quit too soon. Fight the fight of faith and stay strong to the end. It will be worth it. May the Lord give you a supernatural burst of energy and a deposit of great grace, so you can finish strong and hit the finish line with joy. You can do it!

Read It! 1 Corinthians 9:24, 2 Timothy 4:7 and Hebrews 12:1

Speak It! "Father, with Your help, I will finish my race in this season! I will finish strong and with joy. Thank You for Your grace to run my race! In Jesus' Name. Amen."

DAY 6

(debbie downer & friends)

"In everything you do, stay away from complaining and arguing so that no one can speak a word of blame against you."
Philippians 2:14-15a, TLB

Recently, a friend of mine said someone asked her about the cross necklace she wore. They asked, "Is that necklace just for decoration or are you really a Christian?" Fortunately, she really is a Christian. But, what an interesting question to be asked, eh? Why did that question even come up?

Likely, it's because there are plenty of pretend Believers who wear the Christian "decorations" but don't have anything to back it up. Worse, there are too many Debbie Downers, Eeyores and Schleprocks who claim to be Christians but their habit of complaining, negativity and grumbling completely invalidates their Christian testimony. How sad is that?

Just what kind of Christians are people looking for these days? Real ones! Would you like to stand out in this dark, crooked, stubborn world? Would you like people to take your faith in Jesus Christ seriously? How about extending a beacon of hope and the Word of Life to people who are lost, empty and living in confusion, hurt and pain?

It starts with your mouth. Instead of complaining, murmuring, fault-finding and arguing like everyone else, how about expressing gratitude, thankfulness, encouragement, hope, faith and a positive attitude? You can make a difference today at your job, school, neighborhood, surroundings or home.

When a Debbie Downer starts to grumble that it's Monday, why not say, "Hey, Debbie, this is the day the Lord has made! It beats being dead." Next time Eeyore murmurs about the price of gas, why not say, "Praise God, Eeyore, you have a car! It sure beats riding a donkey." Or, when Schleprock finds fault with the boss or complains about his job, why not say, "Hey, Schlep, you should be happy to have a job. It beats living under a bridge."

No one likes to be around the Debbie Downers, Eeyores or Schleprocks of this world, so don't be one! Instead, be a real Christian who changes the atmosphere in our part of this dark world by being a positive, hopeful, faith-filled person.

Read It! Philippians 2:14-16

Speak It! "Father, help me to stop complaining, fault-finding, arguing, murmuring and grumbling. I want to be a real Christian. I ask You to help me infuse my world with the positive, hopeful, faith-filled reality of Jesus Christ and the Word of Life! In Jesus' Name. Amen."

DAY 7

(wisdom from above)

"Do you want to be counted wise, to build a reputation for wisdom? Here's what you do: Live well, live wisely, live humbly. It's the way you live, not the way you talk, that counts."
James 3:13, MSG

It's easy to tell—in a quick hurry—when we are operating in God's wisdom or in the wisdom that comes from our own selfish ambition, pride and the enemy's influence. Been irritated lately? Frustrated with all the people who don't agree with you? Read on...

When we operate in God's wisdom, it's easy to get along with people. Look at the characteristics of godly wisdom: there is a desire to get along with others rather than the desire to look for a fight.

One version of the Bible says it this way, *"But the wisdom that is from above is first pure, then peaceable, gentle, willing to yield, full of mercy and good fruits, without partiality and without hypocrisy," (James 3:17).* Wisdom from above is pure, peace-seeking, gentle, willing to reason, full of mercy, impartial, sincere and genuine. Godly wisdom treats others with dignity and honor. Wisdom from above doesn't have a selfish "agenda."

Wisdom from "below" is hot-tempered, rude, mean-spirited, selfish, hypocritical, unfair or bigoted. Look at a few other verses of this same passage in James: *"Mean-spirited ambition isn't wisdom. Boasting that you are wise isn't wisdom. Twisting the truth to make yourselves sound wise isn't wisdom. It's the furthest thing from wisdom—it's animal cunning, devilish conniving," (James 3:14-15, MSG).*

When we operate in God's wisdom, God can actually bless our endeavors. We may not see eye-to-eye on everything with everyone, but we can agree to disagree without being disagreeable. If we do the hard work of getting along with one another, we can develop a healthy, robust community that is congruent with the Lord's heart and purposes.

In this day and age, it's obvious that we need God's wisdom more than ever. May we seek Him and His wisdom in a greater way and may the fruit of the wisdom that comes from above be evident among us.

Read It! Proverbs 8

Speak It! "Father, help me operate in the wisdom that comes from above. Help me resist the temptation to operate in the wisdom that originates in deceit, my own selfishness and in the devil's motivations. I thank You in advance for the good fruit that comes from godly wisdom! In Jesus' Name. Amen."

DAY 8

(the God you don't know?)

"Christ is the visible image of the invisible God. He existed before God made anything at all and is supreme over all creation."
Colossians 1:15, NLT

Ever wondered what God was really like? A lot of people really don't know the God of the Bible. They have all kinds of ideas about what God is like—based mostly on human opinion, personal experiences or religious traditions—but not always based on a real Biblical revelation. What about you? Do you really know God—the Father, the Son and Holy Spirit? Fortunately, God is not mysterious or in hiding; He has openly revealed Himself.

Jesus is the VISIBLE image of the INVISIBLE God! If you want to know what God is like, look at Jesus *(John 14:9)*. Study His life. Listen to His words. Follow His actions. Jesus perfectly revealed the Father God to humanity. When we look at everything Jesus said and did, we get an accurate picture of the character, heart and operations of God Almighty. Here are just a few things:

- **He always did good things for people** *(Acts 10:38)*.
- **He rebuked people who worshiped their traditions more than God** *(Mark 7:7-9)*.
- **He always showed mercy to the humble** *(Matthew 9:13)*.
- **He healed everyone that came to Him in faith** *(Luke 6:19)*.
- **He didn't appreciate unbelief** *(Matthew 14:31)*.
- **He loved and blessed kids** *(Matthew 19:14)*.
- **He lived by faith in God's Word and told us to do the same** *(Matthew 4:4)*.
- **He had more joy than anyone else and showed us it's possible to rejoice always** *(Hebrews 1:9)*.
- **He never sent tragedy, calamity or sickness to teach someone a lesson** *(John 10:10)*.
- **He always turned impossible situations into possibilities** *(Matthew 19:26)*.
- **He loved sinners** *(Luke 7:34)*.

God ISN'T the harsh, angry ogre many have made Him out to be. He DOESN'T "send" evil to teach, humble or get the attention of His children. God ISN'T mysterious. His real character is love. All of His intentions toward His people are full of mercy, compassion, patience, graciousness, faithfulness and truth.

Read It! Hebrews 13:8

Speak It! "Father, thank You for revealing Your Son, Jesus to us! Engrave the reality in my heart that Jesus is the visible image of the invisible God. You are a good God and always have been. Help me to be more like You to this world. In Jesus' Name. Amen."

DAY 9

(a toothless roar)

*"Be sober, be vigilant; because your adversary the devil
walks about like a roaring lion, seeking whom he may devour.
Resist him, steadfast in the faith..."*
1 Peter 5:8-9

We have an enemy who *walks about* like a roaring lion seeking whom he may devour. Notice, he is *not* a roaring lion; he just tries to *act* like one. The reality is: he has a toothless roar.

That's because Jesus completely defeated the devil, disarmed and defanged him! Jesus has given us the authority of His Name to enforce Satan's defeat. So, stand strong in Christ and let the enemy know he MAY NOT devour you.

Has the enemy been roaring in your ear? Enforce his defeat! Here are a few reminders:

- **Satan is defeated.** Jesus completely disarmed the devil and the host of hell *(Colossians 2:15)*. He has armed us with spiritual weapons that have divine power. We need to know our position as victors through Jesus Christ.
- **You have authority.** Not only did Jesus completely defeat Satan through the cross, He gave us the authority to use His Name to enforce Satan's defeat *(Luke 10:19)*. Use it!
- **Yield to the Greater One.** No matter what the enemy throws against us, the Greater One lives in us *(1 John 4:4)*. And, because of that, His power in and through us is greater than anything we face!
- **Remember, you win.** Not only did Jesus defeat Satan on the cross and give us His authority to exercise now, but He will ultimately crush Satan once and for all *(Romans 16:20)*. Jesus is Lord! He won—and we win!

Forget what the devil is doing, focus on what God is doing. Don't forget, God is still the Creator of the universe and Jesus is still Lord. The Holy Spirit is still the Greater One. The Lord is searching the whole earth to show Himself strong on our behalf *(2 Chronicles 16:9)*.

Read It! Deuteronomy 32:30

Speak It! "Father, I thank You that Jesus completely defeated the devil on the cross. You disarmed Satan, and You have armed me. I declare that the Name of Jesus, the blood of Jesus and the Word of God dominate my life, and I enforce the devil's defeat. He may not devour me; I resist him and I stand strong in the faith. I thank You that Your eyes find me, and You show Yourself strong in my life! In Jesus' Name. Amen."

DAY 10

(eclectic playlist)

"You are my hiding place; You shall preserve me from trouble;
You shall surround me with songs of deliverance."
Psalms 32:7

There's just something about music. It's amazing how certain songs can instantly take us back to a time and place, isn't it? It's so interesting the way certain melodies or words can put us into a worshipful attitude, a melancholy mood, or an adrenaline-filled mindset.

The Lord gave us a wonderful gift when He gave us music. The blend of various lyrics, instruments, tempos, beats and rhythms get into our spirit, soul and body.

These days, we don't have to listen to an 8-track, album or CD by one band with one sound. With the advent of MP3 players and iTunes®, we have the ability to create our own unique, personalized, customized playlists full of eclectic genres.

I have several "go-to" playlists I play when I want some help getting into a groove. I have my "fresh worship," "heartfelt worship," "moving songs," "oldies," "love songs," playlists...and one of my favorite's, the "fun and funky" playlist.

The "fun and funky" playlist is perfect for a Monday morning or those moments when I need a boost or shot in the arm. These are my "songs of deliverance," and they help me rise into a place of joy, victory, praise, joy and freedom. The funny thing is this list has the weirdest, ever-changing mix of musical genres. Some are high-energy worship songs; some are good, old-fashioned, gospel-tent-revival songs; some are just fun, clean, secular songs that fire me up. I can't put my finger on it, but this eclectic playlist just gets me going. Who knew the combo of "Weapons of our Warfare" and "The Cupid Shuffle" could bring such joy to my soul and spirit.

How about you? What's on your playlist? Do you have your eclectic playlist full of "songs of deliverance"? The Holy Spirit knows what songs, melodies and words will renew your mind, lift your spirit and bring you into a place of victory and joy. May the Lord help you to create the customized playlists you need. He will surround you with songs of deliverance!

Read It! Psalm 40:3

Speak It! "Father, I thank You for the gift of music. I know You will surround me with songs of deliverance. You know the songs that will fire me up. So, I ask for Your help in creating some customized, eclectic playlists that bring me into a greater place of praise, joy, worship, freedom and victory! In Jesus' Name. Amen."

20

DAY 11

(what to do about a pandemic?)

"There shall no evil befall you, nor any plague or calamity
come near your tent."
Psalm 91:10, AMP

One night, we went out for dinner and got to talking with our waitress. We quickly realized this dear girl lived in absolute fear. She must have said, "I am so afraid...," over a dozen times in our short exchange. We tried to allay her fears as we talked with her about knowing Jesus. At the end of our meal, we explained that when Jesus is our best friend and the Lord of our lives, He not only forgives us of our sin, but also gives our hearts peace, freedom from fear and the promise of protection. She was so bound by fear, I'm not sure how much she really received. It was a sad reminder that without a vital relationship with Jesus and the knowledge of His Word, people have no real security or solid rock on which to stand on in time of crisis or national fear.

Times like these were made for faith-filled Christians! When the world is freaking out about the swine flu and a host of other things, Christians who know their God can be a welcomed source of hope and encouragement. We can let those living in fear, panic, unrest and anxiety know about our faithful Jesus. We can share God's promises, the power of the blood of Christ, the mercy of God and the Jesus who still saves, protects, heals and restores.

If Jesus is Lord of our lives, there's no time to be in fear or panic. This is our time to shine the light. We were born-again for this! Remember, Isaiah told us to arise and shine. It's no mystery; the world is going to get darker, but the light of Christ on and in us is going to get brighter. *(Isaiah 60:1-2, NIV)*

In these days, we Believers can—and should—reach out to those around us with faith, hope and compassion. Let's share the reality of the love of Jesus and the power of His Word. People need the peace, protection and power Jesus offers. Be strong and shine the light. *(Daniel 11:32, AMP)*

Now, if you've been watching too much news and have felt the fear of sicknesses and diseases trying to take hold of your mind, get a grip on God's Word—today. As Believers, I'm not suggesting we go into denial about reality, but I am suggesting we let the Truth—the Word of God—trump reality. As we all follow the Lord, we can rest in the Truth that no evil shall befall us and no plague or calamity will come near our dwelling. Let's declare it today.

Read It! Psalm 91 and Mark 16

Speak It! "Father, thank You for Your mercy and power. I agree with Your Word that no evil shall come near me—no plague, disease, flu, pandemic or calamity. My home, family and children are covered by the blood of Jesus. Thank You for Your divine protection and wisdom. In Jesus' Name, Amen."

DAY 12

("the omni factor")

"Wisdom and knowledge will be the stability of your times..."
Isaiah 33:6

In this uncertain world, where pressure, deadlines, job loss, anxiety, depression and changing headlines are common occurrences, is there any real hope for stability?

Absolutely! When we walk in knowledge and wisdom. We can rest in the knowledge and wisdom that comes from what I call "the omni factor."

- **God is omniscient.** We don't have to know everything—He does. If we will spend some time with Him, He'll give us revelation knowledge and wisdom, so we know what to do and when to do it.
- **God is omnipresent.** We don't have to be everywhere—He is. If we'll follow the Lord, He'll make sure we are in the right place at the right time. *(Proverbs 15:3)*
- **God is omnipotent.** We don't have to be all-powerful—He is. God has all the power we need! As we believe and cooperate with His Word, He'll use it on our behalf. *(Matthew 19:26)*

If we're looking for stability in this unstable world, let's soak ourselves in the knowledge and wisdom that comes from "the omni factor."

Read It! Amos 4:13

Speak It! "Father, thank You for stability! Fill me with the knowledge and wisdom I need to rest in all the realities of the 'Omni Factor.' In Jesus' Name. Amen."

DAY 13

(the name)

"Therefore God exalted Him to the highest place and gave Him the name that is above every name, that at the name of Jesus every knee should bow, in heaven and on earth and under the earth, and every tongue confess that Jesus Christ is Lord, to the glory of God the Father."
Philippians 2:9-11, NIV

I was having a nice little prayer time on the treadmill one day, and it hit me in a fresh way: "Jesus is the Name above ALL names!"

We sing it. We know it. We pray it. But, perhaps, like me—you need a fresh reminder of this truth.

Jesus really IS the Name above ALL names. If someone has a name, Jesus is above them. If something has a name, Jesus is above it.

These days, everyone and everything has a name, doesn't it? Think about it. The President. The Senate. CNN®. The pastor. The athlete. The idiot. The jerk. The crazy aunt. The recession. The swine flu. The economy. The stock market. Hollywood. Fear. Terror. Democrat. Republican. Cancer. Strife. Anger. Bitterness. Hatred. Jealousy...and so much more.

But, Jesus is the Name above all of those names. He trumps them all! His Name has all power in heaven and earth. And the big bonus? He has given us the authority to use His Name. He has deputized us with the "power of attorney" to pray, say, decree, declare, bind, loose and operate in the authority that His Name carries as we walk with Him in the light of His Word.

Wow! Think about the power of Jesus' Name.

Let's decree the Name of Jesus over our life today.

Read It! Matthew 18:20, John 14:13-14, John 15:21 and John 16:23-24

Speak It! "Father, thank You for the Name of Jesus! Jesus, I am so glad You humbled Yourself, came to this earth, fulfilled Your mission, and now You are highly exalted and have been given the Name above all names. Thank You for giving us the authority to use Your Name to walk in Your Word, to overcome the enemy, to live the life You have called us to live and to preach the good news about knowing You. Today, I declare and decree the Name of Jesus over my life and every 'name' that has tried to come against me. Jesus is the Name above: _____. (List any 'names' that have been trying to usurp His authority in your life.) Thank You for it! In Jesus' Name. Amen."

DAY 14

(hard choices)

"For the word of God is living and powerful, and sharper than any two-edged sword, piercing even to the division of soul and spirit, and of joints and marrow, and is a discerner of the thoughts and intents of the heart."
Hebrews 4:12

It's not always easy being a Christian. Sometimes, we have to make hard choices—choices to obey God instead of our flesh, our friends, our desires or our preferences. There is only one way to make right choices and that is to let the Word of God be the divider.

Sometimes, it's a challenge to discern the right thing to do. Our soul and spirit are so closely linked that we need a strong divider to help us discern God's will and desire in a matter. Our soul—our mind, emotions and will—wants one thing, but in our spirit—our heart—we sense God wants something else. The only thing that can truly divide between soul and spirit is the Word of God. Siding with God's Word is always a safe guide.

Too many Believers follow logic, reason, pros and cons, past experience, their desires and circumstances to make decisions and totally overlook the most important guidance tools of all—God's Word and His Spirit. Natural things are not sufficient to divide between soul and spirit, but God's *living* Word is.

How does this work in real life? If we're facing a tough decision or having a hard time hearing God's voice because our soul is screaming, the Word will help us to discern the right decision to make. Some of the more common choices God calls us to make have to do with things our soul desires: the lust of the flesh, lust of the eyes and the pride of life. This includes choices about following God's plan for our life instead of our own plan—friendships, choices about partying, living with a boyfriend/girlfriend, premarital sex, doing drugs, being a slave to addictions, porn, greed, materialism, gossip and ego—just to name a few.

We shouldn't try to figure it out on our own or go with logic and reason. Instead, we need to dive into the Word and let it divide between our soul and spirit. We can trust God's Word to light our path. He will speak to us through His Word and give us the precise direction we need. Then, He'll give us the grace to follow through. We can make hard choices—and we must! We can do so when we choose to absolutely live by the living Word of God.

Read It! Deuteronomy 30:19 and Matthew 4:4

Speak It! "Father, I thank You for Your Word. I'm facing some hard decisions, and need to hear from You. Thank You that Your Word is a safe guide and a reliable divider. Help me spend extra time in Your Word, so I can hear Your voice. I choose to follow You as I make hard choices. In Jesus' Name. Amen."

DAY 15

(you are an original)

"Thank You for making me so wonderfully complex! Your workmanship is marvelous—and how well I know it."
Psalm 139:14, NLT

You are a one-of-a-kind! You don't have to be like everyone else. You don't have to go along with the crowd. You have not been made like any one else. You are an original!

Be encouraged today...

- **You are not a mistake.**
- **You are a special person.**
- **You are gifted.**
- **You are highly favored.**
- **You are complex.**
- **You are more intelligent than you realize.**
- **You are full of creative potential.**
- **You are extremely good looking.**
- **You are unique.**
- **You are marvelous.**
- **You are accepted.**
- **You are created in His image.**
- **You are an original.**
- **You are loved.**

Let me remind you of an old saying: "God don't make no junk." Today, throw caution to the wind and just be that one-of-a-kind, original person God has created you to be!

Read It! Isaiah 43:7

Speak It! "Father, thank You. I needed that today. It's nice to know that You love, accept and care about me. I am glad that You have made me to be a one-of-a-kind person with unique and complex traits. Help me to relax and be free to be the person You have created me to be! In Jesus' Name. Amen."

DAY 16

(put a sock in it)

"'No weapon formed against you shall prosper, and every tongue which rises against you in judgment you shall condemn. This is the heritage of the servants of the Lord, and their righteousness is from Me,' says the Lord."
Isaiah 54:17

Ever wanted to tell a loud-mouthed, critical, judgmental, obnoxious, arrogant person you know to "put a sock in it"? Well, now you can. Permission granted.

True, there will always be loudmouths, critics, people with agendas who do not approve of us—our life, our choices, our faith, our ministry, our church, our existence. Accept it. In fact, we should consider this type of persecution as a compliment from the devil.

So, what do we do when people come against us and the plan of God for our lives? There are several things we can do:

- **Evaluate.** Before we go on the offensive, evaluate. Ask ourselves, "Is there any truth to the things people are saying?" Sometimes, the truth of criticism hurts. But, if we are brutally honest with ourselves, we can sometimes find the silver lining in a judgmental comment and find areas where we can make adjustments.
- **Condemn.** Yes, that's right! Isaiah 54:17 gives us permission. We can tell the hypocrites who come against us to "put a sock in it!" We can—and should— refute those who lie and come against us. We have permission to show them to be in the wrong—not to condemn them, but their words, lies and untruths. We can—and should—speak the truth in love and set the record straight when people come against us and the plan of God.
- **Love.** On top of all these things, we need to put on love! Love never fails. Love our enemies and pray for them. Over the years, when people have come against us or the work of God in and through our church, we made a decision to walk in love. At times, we had to be bold and "condemn" misinformation or blatant lies by speaking the truth in love; and at other times, we said nothing and simply prayed for them. We asked the Lord to bless our opponents and to fill their lives with His love. We chose to pray those prayers by faith, because we know that love never fails. Now, let's make that choice today, too.

Read It! Matthew 16:19

Speak It! "Father, I am so thankful that no weapon that comes against me shall prosper. I praise You for the blood of Jesus and the Name of Jesus. I thank You that I stand perfect and complete in Your will. I will condemn every tongue that rises against me in judgment and choose to speak the truth in love. Your plans and purposes shall prevail! I bind the enemy's plans, and I loose the power of God in my life. In Jesus' Name. Amen."

DAY 17

(could God call little 'ole me?)

"But then something happened! For it pleased God in His kindness to choose me and call me, even before I was born! What undeserved mercy!"
Galatians 1:15, NLT

Ever feel so inadequate that you are positive the Lord cannot use you? I did. But then God...

I came to Christ between my freshman and sophomore year of college. During spring break of 1979, I started in ministry, evangelizing. It was my first ministry experience, and I was a "green" Christian; but my group and I talked to hundreds of kids about the Lord on Daytona Beach. It was only a few years earlier that I had been just like them—lost without Christ, partying on the beach my senior year of high school. But, there I was "preaching on the beach," launching into what would become a wonderful journey of ministry. I was hooked; I loved evangelism. There was nothing more exhilarating than leading someone to Jesus.

Now, decades later, I still feel the same way. There's nothing like being in God's will and walking in the calling and purpose for which He created me.

How about you? What have the past 20 years looked like for you? What will the next 20 years hold? Do you wonder if God has called you to something and you just need a little encouragement and exhortation? Here are a couple of "calling observations" to encourage you in your pursuit of God's purpose for your life:

- **God delights in using imperfect people.** He uses the weak to confound the wise *(1 Corinthians 1:27)*. This is comforting. God uses flawed, insecure, unknown, dysfunctional, addictive, ordinary people who will dare to believe Him to do great things. We don't have to wait to become perfect; we can start serving God now. I don't know any perfect Christians—or ministers—but I do know a lot of people who have yielded their lives to Jesus and have received His forgiveness and empowerment to do mighty things.

- **Don't compare yourself with others.** We can always find people who are better at everything than we are. Comparing ourselves is a recipe for defeat. Let's be confident in who God made us to be and take joy in NOT being like others. Who wants to be a "carbon-copy"? We each have a unique flavor and gift to offer the world. So, let's be the creative, one-of-a-kind people God has created us to be.

God calls normal, average, everyday people, and He can use little 'ole you.

Read It! John 15:16

Speak It! "Father, thank You that You've called me to Your kingdom for such a time as this! Thank You for calling normal, average, everyday people! Help me be the person You've called me to be. In Jesus' Name. Amen."

DAY 18

(God doesn't move a parked car)

"Go..."
Matthew 28:19

A lot of Believers are waiting for the Lord to say, "Go," when the reality is, He already has. Jesus said, "Go," and He meant it. Sometimes, we waste so much time asking the Lord to tell us what to do; when really, He's already told us to "go into all the world and preach the Gospel." Many Christians spend too much time "waiting on the Lord;" when in reality, He is waiting on them. The ball isn't in God's court; Jesus put the ball in our court when He said, "Go." So, unless the Lord specifically tells us to stop, He has already said, "Go,"—so let's do it! Oh, yeah, it will require faith, and you will probably have to make big sacrifices...for a while.

But, faith it. By faith, we have to do something. God doesn't move a parked car. While God wants to use all of us, He needs our cooperation with Him. He needs us to take some steps of faith, and then He'll show up to bless, maximize, multiply and use the little bit we give Him. God has given all of us at least one gift. Let's discover what ours is and start using it.

So, what do you have? A gift for organizing? Singing? Listening? Speaking? Writing? Creating? Designing? Working with kids? Teens? Elderly? God never asks us to use what we *don't* have; He always uses what we *do* have! If we sit still and never take any steps of faith to move in the direction of God's leading, He doesn't have anything to work with. Once we start doing something, the Lord can fine-tune our gifts and calling and position us right where He wants us.

- **Focus.** True, God doesn't move a parked car; but He also can't use a car going in 10 different directions. It's easy to get so full of vision and dreams and end up doing too many things. But, it only dilutes our usefulness. Instead, let's focus on our sweet spot, doing one or two things well. Once we pray and get what we believe is His direction, then stay focused and start moving forward. Become an expert at something and do it well.

- **Finish.** The Lord wants us to run our race and finish our course. In the end, it's our job to be faithful to the finish. When we keep our eyes on eternity and trust God to lead, guide and use us, we'll have a great sense of satisfaction and peace, knowing that we have lived lives worthy of Him. Let's stay faithful, and one day we'll hear those important words: "Well done, good and faithful servant."

Read It! 1 Chronicles 28:20

Speak It! "Father, help me to 'go' do something, to stay focused and to be faithful until the finish. In Jesus' Name. Amen."

DAY 19

(voices)

"...'Man shall not live by bread alone, but by every word that proceeds from the mouth of God.'"
Matthew 4:4

Recently, Jeff and I, along with several other pastors, had the opportunity to spend a few hours with Oral Roberts. I have always respected Oral Roberts, although I had not previously been a big follower of his, other than I remember his TV show as a kid, loved his classic book, *The Miracle of Seed Faith*; and our oldest daughter, Meghan, was born in the hospital he founded, formally called, City of Faith. No matter what people do or don't think about Oral Roberts, no one can deny the Lord has used him in unique ways, starting with his massive tent crusades, which launched a national TV healing ministry and later the founding of a university that has blessed millions.

After our visit, I have even more respect for Oral Roberts than ever. He's a Jesus-focused, compassion-filled, humble man. For the first 15 minutes of our time together, he told us about his testimony and ministry. Then, we each had the opportunity to ask him a question. Mine was: "If you were 50 years old and had it to do over again, what would you do differently; and what would you recommend to people like us who are in that season of life and ministry?" His answer was refreshing, honest and loaded with the wisdom that only comes from experience. He said, "I wouldn't do anything different. I have always made it my goal to hear from God—to hear His voice and obey Him. I purposed to do that during my whole life and ministry, and I wouldn't change anything. The most important thing is to hear from God. Find out what He wants you to do and do it."

Jesus told us the same thing when He said, "Man doesn't live by bread alone (natural things, i.e., circumstances, bank accounts, human approval, logic), but by every word that comes from God's mouth." Hearing God's voice and following His direction is the most important thing. Once we've heard from the Lord and have His guidance, we can move forward with confidence. It's so simple; we often overlook it. Instead of seeking the Lord and His voice, we spend a lot of time trying to figure things out on our own. Let's make it easy on ourselves and quit leaning so heavily on logic, opinions, news reports and weighing the pros and cons. Instead, let's spend some extra time with the Lord in His Word and in prayer to get His wisdom and listen to His voice.

Read It! Psalm 119

Speak It! "Father, I thank You that You are still speaking to us through Your living Word. I know that when I hear Your voice, I can live by what You say. Help me to spend some extra time with You in Your Word. I ask You to speak to me and give me ears to hear and obey Your voice. In Jesus' Name. Amen."

DAY 20

(God's economy)

"Do not lay up for yourselves treasures on earth..."
Matthew 6:19a

In recent months, many people have had an up-close and personal look at the way "moth, rust and thieves" steal our earthly treasures—retirement accounts, 401Ks, earnings and equity. Earthly treasures are not secure. But, then again, Jesus already told us that almost 2,000 years ago. God has a better way, and those who have followed His principles have discovered His economic and banking plan is better than the world's system.

If we're struggling financially, we need to jump into God's economy. His economy is based on a completely different paradigm—giving. The world says, "Get all you can, and keep all you get," but Jesus said, "Give all you can, and it will be given back to you—and then some." *(Luke 6:38)*

One dimension of God's economic plan is this: when we follow our hearts, seek God's kingdom first, operate in godly wisdom and give our treasures to the Lord—in tithes (10% of our income), offerings (anything over 10%) and alms (gifts to the poor)—He said we would lay up—deposit—treasures for ourselves in heaven.

Many have read this passage and thought it meant we should love heaven more than the earth. Some have even thought it meant as we give to God's kingdom, we should be content in not seeing those treasures again until our "great reward"—heaven. That may be, but there's another important part.

When we seek God's kingdom first and lay up our treasures in heaven through tithes, offerings, alms; we're putting our money where our heart is. We are literally laying up treasures for ourselves in a safe place where no one can steal them. The best part? The government, stock market, banking system, job and housing markets cannot steal them. I don't know how He does it, but He protects and multiplies the financial seeds we sow and supernaturally circulates them back into our lives—here and now. Besides, we won't need them in heaven; we need them now. God has even promised He'll open the windows of heaven and overflow us with the treasures *(Malachi 3:10)*. So, let's get into God's economic wealth plan and give, give, give!

Read It! Matthew 6:19-21

Speak It! "Father, I want to trust in Your economy and lay up my treasures in heaven, not in the world's economic system on earth where moth, rust and thieves break through to steal them. I choose to put my money where my heart is—in the kingdom. Thank You for keeping it safe, multiplying it and giving me full access to it now! You, Lord, open doors of promotion, increase, wealth and success, so I can live a life that honors You. In Jesus' Name. Amen."

DAY 21

(the good life)

"O taste and see that the Lord [our God] is good! Blessed—happy, fortunate, [to be envied]—is the man who trusts and takes refuge in Him."
Psalm 34:8, AMP

The Lord is good all the time!

It's true. We can't let anyone or anything ever talk us out of that. But, be advised; many voices will try to convince us otherwise. Often, the enemy, our own thoughts, circumstances, relationships and life experiences cause us to question God's goodness. When we don't fully understand God's big picture, purposes, timing, kingdom laws and the hows and whys of things we face, we sometimes drift around in the "Yeah, but what about...?" sea of confusion regarding God's goodness.

Settle this issue once and for all. God is good! He's not schizo-God; He's the same yesterday, today and forever *(Hebrews 13:8)*. He is the God who changes not. He is good, and His intentions toward us are always for our good. We may not always understand everything, but we can rest in the fact that the Lord is good. We can have confidence that as we walk in the light of His Word, He will always bring us through any trial, challenge or battle we face into a good land.

The Bible tells us...

- **God is good all the time.** *(Psalm 34:8)*
- **He is a good Father; He gives good gifts.** *(James 1:17)*
- **He satisfies us with good things.** *(Psalm 103:5)*
- **His good hand is upon us.** *(Ezra 8:22)*
- **His plans for us are good and not evil.** *(Jeremiah 29:11)*
- **He wants us to eat the good of the land.** *(Isaiah 1:19)*
- **He goes about doing good things and healing all who are oppressed.** *(Acts 10:38)*
- **He wants us to see good days.** *(Psalm 23:6)*
- **The Lord is good and His mercy endures forever.** *(1 Chronicles 16:34)*

Let's declare God's goodness over ourselves and our lives!

Read It! Exodus 34:6, KJV

Speak It! "Father, I believe You are a good God! There may be some things I don't understand, but I settle this issue right now: You are good all the time! Your intentions toward me are for my good. You love me and have good plans for my life. Help me to walk in Your Word, so I can live in Your goodness to a greater degree. In Jesus' Name. Amen."

DAY 22

(quickened)

"But if the Spirit of him that raised up Jesus from the dead dwell in you, he that raised up Christ from the dead shall also quicken your mortal bodies by his Spirit that dwelleth in you."
Romans 8:11, KJV

Need a supernatural jolt today? Need God's resurrection power to fill every cell, fiber, bone, nerve, tissue, muscle, organ and system of your body? Need your youth to be renewed like the eagle's? Need to be quickened?

The same Spirit that raised Jesus from the dead dwells in us. (We could meditate on that for about a year.) He said He will also quicken our mortal bodies. It's no problem for the Lord to quicken bodies. The word "quicken" generally means: to vitalize or revitalize, to make alive and to give life. If parts of our body need to be vitalized, revitalized or made alive, let's ask the Spirit to do it. He knows the DNA codes for every cell, and He has the power to give life—now and eternally.

We all know that one great day, the Lord will cause our mortal bodies to put on immortality, and death will be swallowed up. What a day of quickening that will be! But, in the meantime, we need a strong, healthy, vitalized, quickened mortal body to do God's will and to fulfill His purposes. Let's pray today for the Spirit's quickening power in our mortal bodies.

Read It! Romans 4:17

Speak It! "Father, I thank You that the very same Spirit that raised Jesus from death lives in me. You have the power to give life to every part of my body. I thank You that You quicken the dead and You call things that be not as though they were. So, today, I agree with You. I call my body quickened. I thank You that the Spirit's quickening power is at work in these parts of my body: _____ . (If you are facing a specific area of weakness, disease or sickness, call out that part of your body.) I thank You, Lord, that You are quickening me from the top of my head to the soles of my feet. I thank You, Holy Spirit, for quickening my mortal body. I thank You for quickening my heart, my brain and my lungs. I thank You for Your quickening power in my circulatory, digestive, respiratory, nervous, muscular, lymphatic, reproductive, endocrine, skeletal, connective tissue and metabolic systems today! (If you have other systems that need His quickening power, ask and thank Him for it.) In Jesus' Name. Amen."

DAY 23

(what not to wear)

"Therefore, as God's chosen people, holy and dearly loved, clothe
yourselves with compassion, kindness, humility, gentleness and patience."
Colossians 3:12, NIV

Ever looked back at old photos and thought, "Are you kidding me?"

If you've watched any of the fashion TV shows, you know those fashionistas
can be brutal! They take one look at someone's style and cut them to shreds.
But, they really do have an eye for style; and, in the end, they make the
dowdiest, mismatched person look amazing!

Consider God the eternal fashion expert. He knows what attitudes and
behaviors look best on us. He's not as harsh as some of the TV show hosts
we've all seen, but He does delight in trashing our selfish, proud, mean-
spiritedness, and impatient outfits. He helps us see ourselves in the mirror of
His Word, so we can toss out any "fashion statements" that reflect moodiness,
discontent, resentment and bitterness.

He knows what not to wear because He paid the highest price to purchase
what to wear...for us. The Lord has some very fine threads for us. He wants
us to put on the designer garment of compassion for others; feeling their pain
enough to be moved to do something about it. He wants us to accessorize
our lives with kindness, humility and patience. He wants us to be high styling
in even-temperedness and a willingness to bear others. Most importantly, the
Lord wants us dressed to the nines by walking in forgiveness and the all-
purpose garment of love.

It's sometimes easier said than done. When we are tired, stressed or living by
unrealistic expectations, we can find ourselves slipping into comfy, old ungodly
attitudes and behaviors. The result is we become short-fused, snippy and
frustrated. (I know.) The fix is: a quick change. We can run into the dressing
room of God's forgiveness and exchange those old duds for the clothing He
has provided. He wants us to put off old clothes and put on the new clothes.

Need some help with your spiritual fashion these days? I encourage you to
clothe yourself in God's attire.

Read It! Colossians 3:12-14, MSG

Speak It! "Father, I thank You for the clothing You have provided for me. Jesus
paid a mighty high price by shedding His blood so that I could clothe myself in
compassion, kindness, humility, quiet strength, discipline, even-temperedness,
contentment, forgiveness and love. I have been wearing some old, ugly attitudes,
and I ask You to forgive me. Help me to put off the old clothes and help me to put
on these new threads every day. In Jesus' Name. Amen."

DAY 24

(bored with prayer?)

"Your kingdom come, Your will be done on earth as it is in heaven."
Matthew 6:10, AMP

Ever wondered how to pray? Why pray? What to pray about? Prayer is a supernatural privilege; and yet, many people are completely bored, frustrated or clueless when it comes to prayer.

Here's some good news: prayer shouldn't be boring. Effective prayer—the kind that gets results—starts in God. We don't have to think up things to pray about. We don't have to come up with a prayer plan; we just need to seek the Lord for His plan in heaven and ask that it be done on earth. Prayer always begins with discovering God's will first and then praying accordingly. When we pray this way, there is nothing boring about it.

Jesus told us to pray that God's kingdom would come, and His will would be done on earth as it is in heaven. What does that mean? One way to look at it is this: God in heaven has a will. His will includes a host of things—from the destiny of nations to His detailed purposes for each individual. God's will includes the most macro things to the most micro things and everything in between. God's will is not a mysterious secret. It's revealed, in large part, in His Word.

When we get into the Word to hear from the Lord and discover what His will in heaven is, we can then pray an effective prayer that gets it done on earth. The Lord has made it quite simple. When we spend time seeking the Lord and reading His Word, we discover His will. When we pray according to His will and ask that His will in heaven be done on earth, He hears us and answers.

The sad thing is, oftentimes, God's will isn't done on earth because we are not asking for HIS will to be done on earth as it is in heaven. Instead, we spend a lot of time asking God to do OUR will. We ask God to bless OUR plans and OUR desires and get frustrated when OUR prayers don't get answered. The best thing to do for our prayer life is to forget about OUR will...and seek the Lord for HIS.

Why not make a big change today and start praying more intentionally in the way Jesus told us to pray? When we have determined something is indeed God's will as revealed in His Word, then we are in a position to pray. We can pray earth-altering prayers just like Jesus said, and we won't be bored no mo!

Read It! James 5:16, NIV

Speak It! "Father, I don't want to pray boring prayers! I ask that Your kingdom come and Your will to be done on earth as it is in heaven. Today, I ask that Your will be done in the micro and macro areas of my life. In Jesus' Name. Amen."

DAY 25

(don't kowtow)

"The police captain went with his officers and arrested them...and brought them in before the Council. 'Didn't we tell you never again to preach about this Jesus?' the High Priest demanded. 'And instead you have filled all Jerusalem with your teaching and intend to bring the blame for this man's death on us!' But Peter and the apostles replied, 'We must obey God rather than men.'"
Acts 5:26-29, TLB

I love a person who is as bold as a lion when it comes to their faith in Jesus. These days, Believers need to stand up and step out! We have some great role models. The disciples filled their town with the Name of Jesus and the Word of God, even after the officials told them to quit preaching about Jesus. Little David went after the big, loud-mouthed Goliath and shut him up for good.

We MUST obey God rather than men. That is the bottom line, and it takes a courageous person to do so. Too many people kowtow to gain the approval of men rather than the praise that comes from God. Or, they base their faith on human thinking and political correctness, rather than on God's values as laid out in His Word. Too many people wimp out when it comes to standing for Christ.

Where are those willing to stand up and step out? Those who are contrary to Christ have no problem standing up, being obnoxious, vicious, loud and intimidating. Yet, Christians remain weak and passive. It's time to stand up!

Where are the modern-day disciples willing to obey God and preach the Word, rather than seek the praise of men? Where are the Christian influencers and leaders willing to stand up for their core Christian values? Where are the courageous Believers willing to fill their cities (schools, workplaces, and communities) with the Name of Jesus and the Word of God? Where are the "Davids" these days?

It's likely that there are more of us than many people realize. Let's allow our voice to be heard. Get busy. Get bold. Get involved and use every bit of technology available to us to communicate the truth of Jesus Christ to a mixed-up world. Let's proclaim the truth. It's time for us to stand up to the politically correct who desperately want to intimidate and scorn Christians. And, it's time to go toe-to-toe with a big-mouthed Goliath and the arrogant Christian-bashers and take a stand for Christ. Let's rise up!

Read It! Matthew 10:32-34, AMP

Speak It! "Father, I'm sorry for being a wimpy, passive Christian. Help me to stand up and step out. Help me to be courageous and gracious in my witness for Jesus as I speak the truth in love. In Jesus' Name. Amen."

DAY 26

(what path to take?)

"Your word is a lamp to my feet and a light to my path."
Psalm 119:105, AMP

How do we know if we're making the right decision? What do we do when facing a crossroads? Today, let's be reminded of this simple truth: God's Word is the lamp we need, and through it He will light our path.

It's really quite amazing! The Lord leads and guides us by His Word—literally. God will always give us direction and confirmation through His Word. We have found over the years that anytime we need to know what path to take, which way to turn or what road to follow, the Lord always gives us a scripture or two that serves as the direction we need.

Trying to decide what to do next? Who to marry? What job to take? Where to live? How to be healed and healthy? When to make a change? What to do with a particular child? How to handle a difficult situation? How to serve the Lord? God always speaks to us through His living Word. No wonder Jesus said, *"Man does not live on bread alone, but on every word that comes from the mouth of God," (Matthew 4:4, NIV).* We can absolutely live by the living Word that God gives us, if we will spend time reading and listening to it.

I can think of numerous times when I needed God's Word to direct my steps. In those important times of decision-making, I spent extra time in the Word seeking the Lord for His direction and wisdom—and it has never failed. At the right time, the Lord would quicken a verse of Scripture to my heart, and I knew I had my answer. At that point, my job was simply to obey His Word and walk it out. It's an exciting and supernatural way to live! I would have to say that my life is chronicled more by Scripture verses that have guided my decisions rather than by dates on the calendar. I trust God's Word more than I trust myself, my circumstances, feelings or great counsel from others. I know God's Word is a safe guide. It's an anchor for our soul. God's Word settles every decision.

If you're facing an important decision, spend extra time in the Word and let Him light your path. If your life has been a series of missteps and self-made disappointments, spend extra time reading your Bible and allow the Lord to lead you into a good place, as He gives you a lamp for your feet.

Read It! Psalm 20:4, NIV

Speak It! "Father, You have made it so simple! Thank You that You still speak to us through Your Word. You are still giving direction and guidance. I will spend extra time in Your Word, so I can hear Your voice and obtain the light I need to make the decisions at the crossroads I face. I pray You give me ears to hear and a heart to receive the lamp of Your Word. In Jesus' Name. Amen."

DAY 27

(you plus a small army)

"And I will ask the Father, and He will give you another Comforter (Counselor, Helper, Intercessor, Advocate, Strengthener, and Standby) that He may remain with you forever..."
John 14:16, AMP

Ever felt like you needed a small army just to function in life? Someone to wrap you in their arms and comfort you while at the same time counsel you, give you some extra help and ramp up your prayer life? Or, just someone to stand up for you and be your defense attorney while imparting inner strength into the core of your being? And, just in case you started to fade, they were there "on standby" to jump into action in any one of these capacities?

Thank God, we have such an army! The Greater One, the Holy Spirit, is...

- **Our Comforter.** The Holy Spirit knows how to pour the warm, healing power and soothing balm into the raw, broken places in our hearts. He knows what we need; and when we're filled with His presence, we experience real comfort.
- **Our Counselor.** When we need direction, insight or therapy in seasons of our life, the Counselor steps in. Since He knows all things—past, present and future—He can truly give us the very best counsel.
- **Our Helper.** Isn't it good to know we are not alone? The Holy Spirit is always there to help us be everything He's called us to be and do everything He's called us to do.
- **Our Intercessor.** When we need a prayer partner, the Holy Spirit initiates prayer and gives us the unction to pray effectively.
- **Our Advocate.** When the world, the flesh and the devil come against us, the Holy Spirit is our Advocate who comes to our defense. He constantly presents us to the Father as the blood-washed, righteousness of God in Christ.
- **Our Strengthener.** The Holy Spirit strengthens and reinforces us in our inner-most being, enabling us to stand strong and prevail.
- **Our Standby.** The Holy Spirit is always on standby to give us that extra boost we need to put us over into victory!

Read It! 1 John 4:4

Speak It! "Father, I thank You that I have the help of a massive army! I am so glad for the Holy Spirit and His work in my life. Holy Spirit, today, I ask You to be my Comforter, Counselor, Helper, Intercessor, Advocate, Strengthener and Standby. In Jesus' Name. Amen."

DAY 28

(on the verge of a major meltdown?)

"Let us therefore come boldly to the throne of grace, that we may obtain
mercy and find grace to help in time of need."
Hebrews 4:16

Thank God for grace! If we've been running at a rapid pace, burning the
candle at both ends and living with very little personal margin lately, let's be
encouraged. We don't have to have a meltdown; we can tap into this empowering dimension of God's grace. Today, let's be bold and sprint to the throne of
grace to obtain grace to help.

When we live a very busy life that seems to be on-the-go more than we'd like,
at times, things can get hectic. We face legitimate demands on our time,
which also pull on our emotional, mental, physical and spiritual quotient. With
business meetings, appointments, family obligations, household chores, duties
and every unexpected thing that comes up on our daily schedule, life is just
plain busy. But, what can we do? Most of it is legit! We all experience seasons
when it feels like there are too many needs, too much on our plate or too
much to do. Right? So, what do we do?

We have two options:

Option A: Have a Major Meltdown
Option B: Get Grace for the Pace

Sometimes Option A doesn't sound too bad. Sure, the thought of having a
meltdown, hissy fit or a cry-a-thon sounds tempting at times, but who really
wants to live like that? Not me.

There's a better way. Let's just run to the throne of God's grace and load up.
God always dispenses grace to those who come and get it. Have you tapped
into His grace lately?

When we access God's grace by faith, He supernaturally downloads His strength
into our very spirit and enables us to do what we thought we couldn't do and
handle what we thought we couldn't handle. He increases our margin and gives
us His ability to do what, to us, seemed humanly impossible. It's His power
strengthening our inner man. When we are weak, He gives us His strength. Go
to God's throne of grace and obtain His grace. It's a wonderful thing!

Read It! 1 Corinthians 15:10

Speak It! "Father, I run to Your throne of grace right now. I need Your grace, Your
ability and Your power to help me do all that is set before me. Let it work
supernaturally in me. I receive it now! In Jesus' Name. Amen."

DAY 29

(laugh a little)

"A cheerful disposition is good for your health;
gloom and doom leave you bone-tired."
Proverbs 17:22, MSG

Been a long week? Tired? Been challenged? Sick? Down in the dumps? Not feeling your best?

Laugh!

That's right! Just give the devil a black eye and laugh! We don't have to submit to the blues today and sign for the "too bad, so sad" package. No, we can stand up and just start laughing. Rejoice! Shout! Do it on purpose. Do it now! A merry heart and a cheerful disposition are good for our health.

Not only that, but medical science has been studying the effects of laughter and humor and their role in the health of our mind and body. Humor therapy is being used for the relief of physical or emotional pain and stress.

It's common knowledge that laughter is known to reduce muscle tension, increase cardio-respiratory function and reduce stress. Recent studies show the benefits of humor and laughter on various immune system outcomes. At the biophysical level, laughter moves lymph fluid around our body simply by the convulsions we experience during the process of laughing. So, it boosts our immune system functions and helps clear out old, dead, waste products from organs and tissues.

Laughter increases the oxygenation of our body at both the cellular and organ level. When we laugh, we intake vast amounts of oxygen. They've discovered that cancer cells are destroyed in the presence of oxygen and many parasites and bacteria don't survive well in the presence of oxygen. Laughing actually boosts circulation and exercises abdominal muscles, as well as the muscles of your face. Maybe it's the next best thing to Botox®? The harder you laugh, the greater the effects.

Have you had a "gut-busting" laugh lately?

Read It! Proverbs 17:22, AMP

Speak It! "Father, I thank You for the ability to laugh. I choose to be merry, glad and happy! I will rejoice, today! In Jesus' Name. Amen." (OK...now start laughing! You can do it!)

DAY 30

(propaganda)

"Watch out for people who try to dazzle you with big words and intellectual double-talk. They want to drag you off into endless arguments that never amount to anything. They spread their ideas through the empty traditions of human beings and the empty superstitions of spirit beings..."
Colossians 2:8, MSG

So, the week before Easter a few years ago, *Newsweek* ran a cover story, "The Decline and Fall of Christian America," conveniently designed in the shape of a cross. Was it supposed to be academic and authoritative? Raise concerns? Tick off Christians? Remind us the blind are leading the blind? Or, confirm what Believers already know—that many in the mainstream media have departed from reporting the news and have resorted to the distribution of propaganda. The problem with today's "fair and balanced" news is that it's totally biased. All the intellectual double-talk and endless arguments—it's all propaganda!

The Church of the living God is alive and well and growing around the world. Religion may be dead—which God has never been into anyway—but true Christianity marches on, full of authentic Believers passionate about their Lord!

Newsflash: Easter happened! Jesus came 2,000 years ago. He chose to die on a cross and shed His spotless blood for the forgiveness of our sins. He wanted to be our substitute in paying the penalty of death that sin demanded, so we wouldn't have to pay by being eternally separated from the Father in a place called hell. After God's justice was served, He raised Jesus from the dead and gave Him the Name above all names! Jesus extends His free gift of forgiveness and eternal life to all who will believe and follow Him. The big news story is this: Jesus Christ is alive!

In their book, *God is Back: How the Global Revival of Faith is Changing the World,* authors John Micklethwait and Adrian Wooldridge take a scholarly, honest and objective look at faith, the rise of evangelicalism and the growth of megachurches around the world. Their conclusions? Polar opposite from the *Newsweek* cover story.

Fellow Believer, let's not buy the propaganda. Christians and the Church Jesus leads are alive and well! And, *that's* news you can believe!

Read It! Matthew 16:18b

Speak It! "Father, I'm so glad Jesus is alive, and Your Church is on the move! I ask You to continue to raise up local, regional, national and global leaders in the Body of Christ in every venue—media, publishing, politics, government, news, film and within Your Church. I thank You that the gates of hell—all the lies and propaganda—will never prevail against it. In Jesus' Name. Amen."

DAY 31

(successful people know three secrets)

"Any enterprise is built by wise planning, becomes strong through common
sense, and profits wonderfully by keeping abreast of the facts."
Proverbs 24:3, TLB

Success is not a mystery. It is not happenstance. It's not arbitrary.

Those who are successful know and do three things:

- **They plan.** Successful people know it takes a plan to build anything. A plan is developed by prayerfully looking ahead—miles down the road—and working backwards creating a step-by-step road map. If we want to build a successful enterprise—a life, marriage, family, job, ministry, department, business or venture—we need to determine the steps it is going to take to get there and design a plan to help us walk it out. We will not magically arrive at our desired destination without some prayerful, intentional, thoughtful, detailed, proactive planning.
- **They have common sense.** Successful people use common sense as they employ financial and human resources to build an enterprise. They avoid extremes and find healthy, balanced and intuitive ways to work. Some people over-spiritualize things by just "letting go and letting God," and often God does not make up the slack for our negligence and lack of common sense. We need to be led by the Spirit as we live by faith and use common sense to build.
- **They stay on top of the facts.** Successful people know how to stay on top of things. They are able to manage all kinds of details. They know they can't "assume" anything, but they must take the initiative to get the best information. To be successful in building and growing something, we must inspect what we expect. We must make decisions, course corrections, implementations and strategic plans according to the best and most current facts.

If success has eluded us, we should give some prayerful attention to these three ingredients. Let's spend some time with the Lord, grab a pad of paper and let the planning, common sense and facts help us get started in building a successful enterprise.

Read It! Joshua 1:8

Speak It! "Father, I pray for Your help! I want to be successful in the endeavors You have called me to. I want to build enterprises that prosper and bear fruit. I ask for Your divine help as I intentionally and proactively plan, use common sense and stay on top of the facts. In Jesus' Name. Amen."

DAY 32

(who's at your table—Judas?)

"After he had said this, Jesus was troubled in spirit and testified, 'I tell you the truth, one of you is going to betray me. ... It is the one to whom I will give this piece of bread when I have dipped it in the dish.' Then, dipping the piece of bread, he gave it to Judas Iscariot, son of Simon."
John 13:21, 26, NIV

So, who's sitting at your table these days? It's been said that everyone has a "Judas" and a "John" at their table. John and Judas were sitting at the same table with Jesus. Judas called himself a follower back in the day and so did John. There was a big difference between the two.

Judas is interesting. He was a betrayer; he let Satan fill his heart and betrayed Jesus with a kiss in the Garden. He pretended to be a disciple of Jesus—which he never was. Probably wore the holy garb, looked real religious and talked a lot about helping the poor. Turns out, he was a thief and skimming out of the money bag. Jesus blessed Judas, provided for his needs, and all Judas could do was criticize Jesus' methods. Judas never really got the message of the Gospel.

In a moment when Jesus needed him most, Judas showed his true colors. He had been bought by others—people who acted religious on the outside; but inside, were full of dead men's bones. And then, there was the kiss—the pretend act of affection that betrayed Jesus into the hands of thugs. Judas was a pious pretender.

Ever had someone pull a "Judas" on you? The sad reality is that Judas loses. In the end, Judas suffered with guilt, shame and remorse to the point he hung himself. It's still true. Betrayers have to live with themselves and answer for their hypocritical behavior.

Are you a Judas? Burned anyone lately? Good at "acting" friendly, but if the truth be known, you're a betrayer at heart? Who's bought you? Have you betrayed innocent people?

If we're being a Judas, we'll suffer with shame and guilt our entire lives, unless we experience real sorrow, repentance and a change of heart. So, let's examine our hearts. If we've been a Judas, let's make things right...today.

Read It! Proverbs 27:6

Speak It! "Father, I repent and I ask You for mercy. I reject Satan's lies of betrayal. Fill my heart with a fresh awareness of Your love for people. Help me spend the rest of my days being a blessing to others, defending them, helping, serving and encouraging them in You. In Jesus' Name. Amen."

DAY 33

(who's at your table—John?)

"Peter turned and saw that the disciple whom Jesus loved was following them. (This was the one who had leaned back against Jesus at the supper and had said, 'Lord, who is going to betray you?')"
John 21:20, NIV

Have you recognized the "beloveds" and the "betrayers" in your world? Just because someone calls themselves our friend or follower doesn't mean they are. Jesus said we'd know people by their fruit *(Luke 6:44).*

John was the beloved, and his fruit proved it. He was a true blue friend to the core—Jesus' dear friend and disciple and the one entrusted with caring for His mother. Loyal friends like "John" are such a gift and what a gem when you have one.

John was completely different from Judas. He really was a disciple and true friend. John understood the core of Jesus' message—love! *"Beloved, let us love one another, for love is of God; and everyone who loves is born of God and knows God. He who does not love does not know God, for God is love," (1 John 4:7-8).* John stayed close to Jesus and practiced what He preached.

Do you have a "John" in your life? A true friend? Someone you would entrust with the care of your own mother or children? Someone who has your back? Someone who prays for you? John was there at the cross, Jesus' lowest moment. John was there at the resurrection, Jesus' highest moment! John was a Christ-follower to the core.

Who's at your table—John or Judas?

Then...the bigger question: which one are you?

Are you a John? A faithful friend? Do you pray for others? Who's leaning on you? Are you a loyal, truthful, honest person and a defender of what is right; unwilling to sell your integrity? There for people in the lows and the highs? Are you a lover of God and others? Good news...you'll be called beloved by Jesus Himself and by many others! And, you'll likely enjoy a life full of supernatural joy and hope!

Read It! Proverbs 17:17

Speak It! "Father, I want to be like a beloved 'John' in the lives of my family and friends. Help me to walk in the God-kind of love towards those in my life to a greater degree. In Jesus' Name. Amen."

DAY 34

(God wants your family to be blessed)

"Don't you see that children are GOD's best gift? The fruit of the womb His generous legacy? Like a warrior's fistful of arrows are the children of a vigorous youth. Oh, how blessed are you parents, with your quivers full of children! Your enemies don't stand a chance against you; you'll sweep them right off your doorstep."
Psalm 127:3-5, MSG

Children are a blessing. That's a good thing to remember when you've had a crazy day with preschoolers, a rough week with hormonal teenagers or a heartbreaking season with a wayward child. Never forget—children are a blessing from the Lord, and He loves them more than we do.

No matter what tactics the enemy tries to throw against our family, remember, Satan is defeated and we, our spouse and our kids belong to the Lord. As we stand strong in our walk with the Lord, He will give us the wisdom and strength we need to keep our family in a good place in God. Not only that, but He will go to work in their hearts doing all kinds of unseen work. God wants our family to be blessed.

As parents, in addition to providing love, nurture, protection, guidance and training in the Word to our kids, the best and most important thing we can do for our kids and families is to pray.

God's will is revealed in His Word. So, if we see a blessing, a promise or a specific instruction given in the Bible for children or families, we can take that Scripture to prayer and ask the Lord to do it for us, our kids and our family. Psalm 112 is a great place to start. We can pray this Psalm right over our kids and family. And, let's pray it by faith—even if, at the moment, it may not look like it's true. Let the **Speak It!** confession show you how to pray for your family.

Read It! Psalm 112, NLT

Speak It! "Father, I thank You that we have a happy, blessed family because we fear You and delight in doing Your will and command. I declare that my children, (name them), will be successful everywhere they go; they will be part of an entire generation of godly people. They will surround themselves with good, godly friends. I thank You that our family is wealthy and known for good deeds. When darkness tries to come around, I am so glad to know that Your light will burst in and dispel the darkness. I thank You that we are a generous family who operate in integrity and everything will go well for us. We don't live in fear; our trust is in You. We know You care for us. Lord, I thank You that we have courage, faith and boldness to stand up for what is right. We are a family of influence to give You honor. No weapon formed against us can prosper and every tongue that rises in judgment against us, You condemn. My family is blessed to be a blessing. I declare it! In Jesus' Name. Amen."

DAY 35

(armed and dangerous)

"The tempter came to him... Jesus answered, 'It is written...'"
Matthew 4:3-4, NIV

This means war! We have an enemy—Satan, the devil...Lucifer—and he still wages a "war of words" against Believers. Satan has one goal: to steal, kill and destroy. He wants to steal the will of God from us—and he uses words to do it!

Satan tried to steal the very purpose for which Jesus was on earth, and he used some pretty flattering, tempting and spiritual-sounding words. Take a minute to read the passage down below in the **Read It!** segment. OK...done now?

Notice, when Jesus faced Satan in the wilderness, He didn't even flinch. He won the war of words by *using* words! Jesus quoted the Word of God every single time Satan came against Him with words.

It's no different today! The Christian life is called a "fight of faith." Like Jesus, we must not flinch but stand strong using the Word of God! In order to be effective, we must know the Word! If we're students of the Word and fill our heart with knowledge of the "it is writtens," we won't be an easy target, and we'll have the weapons we need to stand strong in experiencing God's will.

If we are facing a battle or the enemy is trying to steal, kill or destroy our destiny...our future...our marriage...our health...our kids...our sanity...our job, we can enforce the enemy's total defeat with the Word of God. Let's remind ourselves what we know and put God's Word into practice. Remember this:

- **The enemy doesn't have any weapons; he's been disarmed!** Don't flinch! *(Colossians 2:15, NLT)*

- **The devil's all talk; his only weapon is words.** He roars with reasoning, theories, lies and deception to coax you into missing God's will! *(1 Peter 5:8-9)*

- **You're armed and dangerous!** Using the Name of Jesus and the Word of God, enforce Satan's defeat! Speak God's Word over your life and fulfill your purpose. Go on the offensive and take hold of God's plan for your life by resisting every temptation, thought, reasoning, theory, argument, negative report, flattery or circumstance contrary to God's will. *(2 Corinthians 10:4-5, AMP)*

Read It! Matthew 4:3-11, NIV

Speak It! "Father, I praise You that Jesus completely defeated Satan. I resist the enemy's lies, deception and thoughts by putting Your Words in my mind, heart and mouth. You have disarmed the devil and have armed me with every weapon I need for complete victory. Today, I declare I am armed and dangerous, and I will follow and fulfill the will of God in every area of my life. In Jesus' Name. Amen."

DAY 36

(very cool)

"...count yourselves blessed every time people put you down or throw you out or speak lies about you to discredit me...the truth is too close for comfort and they are uncomfortable."
Matthew 5:11, MSG

Anyone ever tried to tell you that being a Christian is totally NOT cool? Everyone has a definition for "cool." These days the culture has tried to paint Christians as "uncool" because they don't embrace the liberal, immoral, ungodly, party lifestyle and social agenda some people push. Usually, it's the people who think they're the "coolest" who are the most aggressive in minimizing Believers. Perhaps our "culture" has not met any genuinely cool Christians? Then again, I suppose it all depends on our definition of "cool."

It's very cool to...

- **Know Jesus.**
- **Talk with God and be on a first-name basis with the Creator of the universe.**
- **Be forgiven and have eternal life.**
- **Be an on-fire, Jesus-loving, Bible-thumping, joy-filled Believer.**
- **Have a great time with no hangovers.**
- **Know we're going to heaven when we die, 'cuz Jesus said He'd take us there.**
- **Be free from the empty cycle of partying, bad relationships and regret.**
- **Receive new mercy every morning.**
- **Tap into a good Father's blessings of health, wellness and abundant life.**
- **Experience God's help in difficult times and have peace of mind and heart.**
- **Be able to love others, even our enemies, without expecting anything in return.**
- **Pray and know that the Lord actually hears us.**
- **Be loved and accepted and know we are not alone.**
- **Enjoy fulfillment, satisfaction and contentment.**
- **Have a spouse, family and friends we love and who also want God's best for us.**
- **Be full of joy and able to laugh from our heart.**
- **Know what our purpose is and live for something greater than ourselves.**

Read It! Matthew 5:11-12, MSG

Speak It! "Father, I pray for those who don't yet realize how cool it is to know You and to walk with Jesus. I ask You to open their eyes to the absolute 'coolness' that comes with being an on-fire, sold-out, Jesus-loving, Bible-slapping, Spirit-filled Christian. In Jesus' Name. Amen."

DAY 37

(very uncool)

"But if ye will not do so, behold, ye have sinned against the Lord:
and be sure your sin will find you out. "
Numbers 32:23, KJV

What's your definition for cool? Or, uncool? Sometimes, the people who think they are cool are so uncool, they don't even know it. God knows what's uncool. These things are very uncool and every Christian knows it.

Most true-blue Christians think it's totally NOT cool to...

- **Be lost.**
- **Live a self-absorbed life.**
- **Spend our existence adrift, without any eternal purpose.**
- **Be depressed and filled with anxiety and fear.**
- **Live a life of immorality that still ends up in utter emptiness.**
- **Mock the Almighty.**
- **Be bound by addictions and the fear of man.**
- **Have friends just because we're rich and able to supply them with drugs.**
- **Go through the pain of divorce and remarriage a half-dozen times.**
- **Raise kids who don't know the Lord and turn out confused, lost and unhappy.**
- **Be sad, angry and bitter.**
- **Think we are smart, spiritual and all-important—but not know God personally.**
- **Have to compromise our core values to fit in with people we don't even like.**
- **Be separated from the Lord and clueless about Jesus.**
- **End up in hell and wonder why.**

If you are belittled for being a Christian, just smile! Your very cool Christian life has just gotten a little too close for their comfort. Who cares if others don't think you're cool?—God does!

Life is short. Being a Christian is cool...very cool.

Read It! Matthew 5:11-12, MSG (Yeah, that's right! Read it again!)

Speak It! "Father, forgive me for thinking I am so cool that I have become uncool. You are the only One who defines coolness, and I don't want to be bound or trapped by anything that is uncool. I ask You to give me an uncompromising boldness to stand for the things that You think are very cool. In Jesus' Name. Amen."

DAY 38

(power to the peeps)

"Then all the believers were united as they lifted their voices in prayer..."
Acts 4:24, NLT

There's something about praying alone—by ourselves—just us and God. But, there is something completely different and powerful about corporate prayer—praying with a group of like-hearted people.

When we come together to lift our voices and magnify the Lord, He shows up and inhabits the praises of His peeps! *(Psalm 22:3, KJV)*

When we come together to ask Him for His will to be done on earth as it is in Heaven, He sets things in motion. *(Matthew 6:10)*

When we come together and get in agreement in prayer, He hears us and promises it shall be done for us by our Father in heaven. *(Matthew 18:19-20)*

During the construction of our new church building, we held corporate prayer meetings with our people to pray about the things God wants to do in our new church facility. For many, it was a new experience for them. The thrill of being "workers together with God" as we walked through the building, joined our faith and lifted our voices in praise, petition and prayer was just a taste of heaven touching earth.

Today, let's be encouraged to be a people of prayer and—for our benefit and the advancement of His plans and purposes—get involved with the corporate prayer opportunities at our own church. There is nothing like the power of unity and faith that is expressed when people who love Jesus and require His will come together to shout, praise, pray and do kingdom business.

He is a God who hears and answers the faith-filled prayers of His people.

Read It! Romans 15:6, NLT

Speak It! "Father, I thank You for people who pray! What a joy to be united with others through Christ. I thank You that when two or more of us come together in Jesus' Name to ask and agree, You hear, show up, set things in motion to perform Your Word. In Jesus' Name. Amen."

DAY 39

(still standing)

"...and having done all, to stand. Stand therefore..."
Ephesians 6:13-14

Sometimes, the real winners in life are those who just keep standing! Half the battle in life is to simply...stand!

"So, what's the secret to your success?"

"I didn't quit; I just stood."

"How did you make it this far?"

"I stood...and refused to sit down."

"What do you think caused you to be victorious?"

"I kept standing."

When the dust settles, battles end, time elapses, people come and go, the devil quits roaring, fads fade, prayers have been prayed, forgiveness has been extended, mercy has been received, faith has believed, the Word has been confessed, the armor has been deployed...and we've done all we know to do—we just stand! Why? Because the one still standing...wins!

What are you facing these days? The fight of your life? Weariness? Boredom? Persecution? Discouragement? Doubt? Fear? Impossibilities? Remember, once we have sought the Lord, checked our heart and done all we know to do, we only have to do one thing—just stand.

Today, let's keep standing!

Read It! Exodus 14:13

Speak It! "Father, having done all I know to do, I stand! Today, I will stand still and watch You at work. I believe You are accomplishing things for me today. You are bringing me into a place of victory. I praise You that I will SEE Your salvation. In Jesus' Name. Amen."

DAY 40

(God's not a slave driver!)

"He gently leads those that have young."
Isaiah 40:11b, NIV

I still remember the days when our kids were "young-uns." Jeff and I had four kids within a six-year period and were pioneering a church right in the middle of that season. This verse brought me comfort many times.

That season of babies, preschoolers and planting a new church were days of big dreams, daily pressure, stress, lack of sleep, very few funds and tons of "on-the-job training." Sometimes, I found myself feeling overloaded, ill-equipped and completely out of my league! Often, I put too much pressure on myself and felt the weight of a "to-do" list that was never done. Is that your experience these days?

At that time, the Lord consistently reminded me, "I gently lead those that have young." Paraphrased to my heart, "Don't be so hard on yourself. I am not demanding as much from you as you are demanding of yourself. I will lead you gently. I know you have preschoolers. I know the young church is draining at times. Relax. One day at a time. I am with you."

If you are in a "young" season—as a new mom or dad, raising preschoolers, taking care of grandbabies, starting a young business or pioneering a church—just know that the Lord will gently lead you.

Sometimes, we forget this; and we are harder on ourselves than God Himself is. We inadvertently think God is some harsh taskmaster who's driving us to the point of exhaustion and unhealthy productivity—He's not. The Lord knows the season we are in. He understands the challenges of life—leading young ones, raising kids, building businesses and churches. He knows what it's like to deal with pressure, stress, lack of sleep, low funds and big dreams—and He gently leads us.

Read It! Matthew 11:28, NIV

Speak It! "Father, thank You for gently leading me. I am so glad You are not a harsh taskmaster. Help me to rest in Your care in this season. In Jesus' Name. Amen."

DAY 41

(infusion)

"...be strong—strengthened inwardly—in the grace (spiritual blessing)
that is [to be found only] in Christ Jesus."
2 Timothy 2:1, AMP

If we are facing challenges today—unexpected demands, a to-do list that doesn't end, overwhelming responsibilities, the straw-that-wants-to-break-the -camel's-back, spiritual battles, constant output, burdens, cares and deadlines that make our load feel heavy, then we need to take time to appropriate this verse of Scripture.

Let's be strong in His grace! Be strengthened inwardly by God's grace today. Access God's "grace for the pace." I don't know about you, but I have found that the longer I walk with the Lord, the more I realize my daily need for the grace of God—by which I stand. I'll bet you've discovered this, too.

God's grace is a wonderful thing! One dimension of His grace is an internal infusion of His strength. When we access God's grace, He helps us stand strong, and we are supernaturally endued with His power and ability. Grace is a tangible deposit of God's strength. The best news is that He wants to give us more and more grace. Therefore, we can—and should—run to the throne of grace to obtain grace to help us in a time of need *(Hebrews 4:16, KJV)*.

Let's allow God to inject us with an endowment of His grace—His inner strength—and we will have the ability and capacity to accomplish any task or overcome any challenge we face.

Read It! Ephesians 6:10, KJV

Speak It! "Father, I come to Your throne of grace today to obtain grace to help in my time of need. You know all the things I am facing, and I thank You that I can be strengthened inwardly by Your grace. Thank You for Your strength and ability to do all that is set before me. I ask You to load me up with extra grace deposits and spiritual blessings today. I declare, I am strong in the Lord and the power of His grace. In Jesus' Name. Amen."

DAY 42

(searching)

"I meditate within my heart, and my spirit makes diligent search."
Psalm 77:6b

There is nothing better than time to think, ponder and meditate—whether we're facing difficult times or just living everyday life. To quiet our heart and listen to the Lord is the quickest way to peace and internal harmony. To meditate within our heart and allow our spirit to make a diligent search is sort of like sitting at our "God station" turning on our spiritual radar, putting on spiritual headphones and picking up on God's signals.

On a recent family trip, I was able to put this verse into practice. We rented bicycles and cruised around Old Montreal on a hot, sunny, breezy, blue-sky day. I popped in my iPod, pedaled and spent time meditating with my heart on numerous things while my spirit was making a diligent search, endeavoring to hear the voice of the Holy Spirit.

It was my favorite day of our trip primarily because the scenery in front of my eyes, the music in my ears and the miles of trails gave my mind and heart time to simmer down—time to meditate and search! The result? I picked up on some of God's signals. He helped me to see some things in a new light, and He put several creative ideas in my heart. By the end of the 30-mile trip, my legs were rubber, but my mind and heart were at peace, energized and refueled.

How about you? Have you taken any time lately to hook up to God's radar by allowing your heart some time to meditate and your spirit some time to search for God's signals?

Read It! Psalm 77:12, NIV

Speak It! "Father, I ask You to help me tap into Your radar. Today, help my heart to meditate and my spirit to search in such a way that I pick up Your signals. In Jesus' Name. Amen."

DAY 43

(feeling invisible?)

"The LORD has called Me from the womb... He has made My mouth like a
sharp sword; in the shadow of His hand He has hidden Me, and made Me a
polished shaft; in His quiver He has hidden Me."
Isaiah 49:1-2

Ever felt invisible? Forgotten? Overlooked? Sometimes, when the Lord calls us
to serve Him, there can be a season—a very long season—where it feels like
we're hidden, invisible. Those "hidden years" can be discouraging.

Isaiah got discouraged and said, "I've worked for no purpose and spent all that
effort on nothing." Ever felt like that? Wondered if the Lord was taking note of
your labor and service?

When the Lord puts a big vision in our heart, it can feel like it's taking forever
to fulfill it. When we've made choices and sacrifices year after year, decade
after decade, and we don't see that vision coming to fruition, it can feel like
we've been wasting our time—or our life—and the Lord's forgotten all about
us. Let's be encouraged; He hasn't forgotten. Our reward is with the Lord, and
He IS a rewarder of those who diligently seek Him.

It seems that those who the Lord uses in an influential way are often hidden
for years before the "day of their public appearing." Just think about Jesus'
ministry; it was 30 years before His public ministry actually began. The Lord
hid Isaiah for years; but it was during those "hidden years," that He filled his
heart with the sword of the Spirit and loaded His mouth with a penetrating
message. Moses, David, John the Baptist, the Apostle Paul—they all experienced years of anonymity and obscurity before being brought to the forefront.

There are no "overnight, flash-in-the-pan successes" in God's kingdom. Anyone
who wants to be used of God significantly will experience many hidden years on
the backside of a desert. During that time, the Lord polishes, sharpens and
prepares us; so at the right time, He's able to launch us into fruitful service. The
invisible years aren't unproductive years spent dreaming about grandiosity;
they're often busy years of serving, studying, being faithful in another person's
ministry and doing behind-the-scenes work. The Lord never forgets our labor of
love toward Him and His people. Our hidden service has not been in vain, so let's
stay steady and know our time will come. We won't be "invisible" forever, and
we'll be rewarded with an opportunity to fulfill all He has put in our heart.

Read It! Hebrews 11:6, KJV

Speak It! "Father, I believe You and know You're hiding me for Your divine purpose.
You are polishing, sharpening and preparing me. I trust You and know my labor
hasn't been in vain. I know my reward is with You. In Jesus' Name. Amen."

DAY 44

(a lot on your plate?)

"From the end of the earth I will cry to You, when my heart is overwhelmed; lead me to the rock that is higher than I."
Psalm 61:2

Ever felt overwhelmed? Got too much on your plate? Feel overloaded? Too many demands? Deadlines? Pressures? Decisions? Too many people pulling on you? Not enough margin?

I have! Like you, I know the feeling of surviving with one nostril above water. I know what it's like to feel stretched to the gills.

When we get to feeling like that, what do we do? We do just what David did! When our heart is overwhelmed, we should cry out to the Lord and follow Him to a secret place in the Rock!

Remember when Moses asked to see God's glory? Here's what the Lord said, *"Then the LORD said, 'There is a place near me where you may stand on a rock. When my glory passes by, I will put you in a cleft in the rock and cover you with my hand...,'" (Exodus 33:21-22, NIV).*

When we cry out to the Lord, He will take us to a place near Him! Isn't that a reassuring and comforting thought? He'll help us stand on a rock, and He'll cover us! I don't know about you; but when I am feeling overloaded, it is nice to know God has me covered in a place by Him!

In that place near Him, God injects us with "grace for the pace" and gives us an endowment of His ability, His strength and an increased capacity to do what He's called us to do.

If you have a lot on your plate today, cry out to Him!

And then after that, take a break...do something fun and refreshing...go for a motorcycle ride or something—just do something!

Read It! 2 Corinthians 4:6-18

Speak It! "Father, help! I am crying out to You. I have so much on my plate, and it is sometimes overwhelming. I know there is 'grace for the pace'—so, today, I ask You to hide me in that secret place near You. Load me with more and more grace, so that I am infused with Your ability, Your strength and an increased capacity to do all You have called me to do. Thank You for the chance to take a break and do something fun and refreshing! In Jesus' Name. Amen."

DAY 45

(wise up)

"Wisdom is the principal thing; therefore get wisdom."
Proverbs 4:7a

Ready to wise up?

Wisdom is the premier thing...the principle thing...the most important thing, and we should be all about getting it! Wisdom is practical skill and acumen. Wisdom is the ability to apply knowledge.

They say knowledge is power. It's true; people perish for a lack of knowledge, but wisdom turns the power of that knowledge into something even more powerful!

Have you ever met someone who was so intelligent, it boggled your mind? Ever known someone who could quote the entire Bible and parrot every famous preacher? Ever met a professional student? Have you noticed that sometimes people with oodles of knowledge seem to struggle with common sense, intuitive thinking and the practical skills necessary to really find success?

Some people spend so much time accumulating knowledge, they are a walking Bible or encyclopedia with all kinds of degrees; the only problem is they sometimes lack wisdom and the know-how in applying the knowledge they have.

It's no wonder the Bible says wisdom is the principal thing! Ecclesiastes 8:5 says, "...a wise man's mind will know both when and what to do," (AMP).

Proverbs tells us the amazing benefits of getting wisdom: victory, protection, wealth, profit, prosperity, long life, honor, peace, pleasantness, a tree of life, blessings, exaltation, influence, guidance, life, health and more!

Get the idea? We all need more wisdom! Let's get to the getting of it! God has given us great promise regarding our ability to get wisdom. Ask for it!

Read It! James 1:5-8, NIV

Speak It! "Father, I ask You for wisdom today! I need more of Your wisdom, so that I know intuitively what to do and when to do it. I want to know how to apply the knowledge I have in a fruitful and productive way. I know Your Word is loaded with Your wisdom, so I ask You to saturate my heart with Your wisdom as I read and listen to Your Word. I am going to go after wisdom—with all my getting! I thank You in advance for large deposits of Your wisdom into my heart and mind. In Jesus' Name. Amen."

DAY 46

(sweet sleep)

"...when you lie down, your sleep will be sweet."
Proverbs 3:24b, NIV

One of God's great blessings is sleep! Most of us don't get enough of it.

Today, let's be encouraged and exhorted to get some rest! God wants to give His beloved sleep. If we burn the candle at both ends—we need to sleep. If we struggle with insomnia, have difficulty getting into a deep sleep or wake up in the middle of the night unable to go back to sleep, then we need God's help to sleep!

Personally, I've been known to live at a rapid pace and burn the candle at both ends—sometimes, even in the middle! But, I can tell it's time to catch up on sleep when I find myself falling asleep at a movie, in church (shh! don't tell), at a stop light or on a ferry ride—like I did a few years ago.

It's one thing to be a college kid who pulls all-nighters but a whole other thing to be living a responsible life where sleep isn't a luxury—it's a requirement! Our bodies need to sleep in order to recover and rejuvenate, and some studies even tell us sleeping helps us lose weight!

The Bible says, *"He gives His beloved sleep," (Psalm 127:2b)*—so, let's take it! If you need to get into some new patterns of good and refreshing sleep, here are a few verses you can lay hold of:

- **God never sleeps.** *Psalm 121:3-4*
- **God gives us sweet sleep.** *Psalm 4:8; Psalm 127:2; Proverbs 3:24 (NIV)*

Read It! Psalm 3:5

Speak It! "Father, I thank You that You give your beloved sleep, and my sleep will be sweet. I thank You that tonight I will lie down and sleep in peace. Help me get into good and proper habits for getting enough rest so my body and mind can recharge. In Jesus' Name. Amen."

DAY 47

(a performance)

"Then said the Lord to me, You have seen well, for I am alert and active,
watching over My word to perform it."
Jeremiah 1:12, AMP

God is alert...active...watching. He's not asleep on the job. He's not kicked back in His heavenly La-Z-Boy®. The Lord is in the performance business! He is not randomly or arbitrarily at work on the earth; He is purposefully and intentionally at work performing His Word. We can—and should—cooperate with Him.

God loves to perform in our lives, but we need to give Him something to work with—His Word. This is huge! He doesn't promise to perform our whining, begging, wishing, crying or our good deeds, years of devotion or hours we've logged in prayer... He performs His Word. The Lord actively engages with the activities on earth by performing His Word. What does that mean to you and me? It means we need to get into the Word, meditate on His promises, lay hold of His truth, claim His Word by faith and give Him something to perform in our lives.

It starts by digging into the Word to find out what God has promised to us, about us and for us—in Christ! Then, we simply appropriate God's promises by faith. We do this by receiving, believing, acknowledging and confessing His Word in our lives. In this way, we intentionally give back to God His very Word, and He has something to perform. It might sound like this:

"Father, I am so thankful Your Word says, 'You surround me with favor as with a shield.' So, today, I thank You for performing all kinds of favors, opening doors, creating exciting opportunities and doing good things for me.

Father, I am so thankful Your Word says, 'You forgive all my sins and heal all my diseases.' So, today, I thank You for performing a clean heart in me and for making me the righteousness of God in Christ. I thank You that You are doing a great performance of healing, health, recovery and strength in my mortal body each and every day.

Father, I am so thankful Your Word says, 'My God is the strength of my life.' So, today, I thank You for performing a great work of strength in my spirit, mind, emotions and body."

Read It! Psalm 119

Speak It! "Father, I am so thankful that You watch over Your Word to perform it. Today, I thank You for performing Your Word in my life. Specifically and by faith, I receive, believe and appropriate these Scriptures and promises from Your Word _____ . (Let the Lord know the specific Scriptures You are claiming by faith and thank Him for performing His Word on your behalf!) In Jesus' Name. Amen."

57

DAY 48

(get pierced!)

"For the word of God is living and powerful, and sharper than any two-edged sword, piercing even to the division of soul and spirit, and of joints and marrow, and is a discerner of the thoughts and intents of the heart."
Hebrews 4:12

This verse gives new meaning to our "pierced" culture. One of the first and most important revelations—and convictions—I received as a new Christian was the piercing power of God's Word!

So, how about a reminder today?

The Bible is unlike any other book on the planet; it's alive! God actually speaks to our hearts through His Book. It's living and active and able to pierce!

God's Word has the supernatural ability to pierce and divide between our thoughts and God's intentions in our hearts; between what our spirit knows is correct and what our soul desires.

Do you need help discerning God's will? Help in trying to figure out what God is saying to your heart versus what your own thoughts are telling you? Are you facing a decision? A challenge? Need direction? Encouragement? A word from God?

God will talk to you and pierce your heart as you read His Word.

So, today, how about we set aside our USA Today®, Oprah's Book Club recommendation, our favorite fiction novel, Money® magazine and Better Homes and Gardens®—until we have first read our Bible?

Read It! Matthew 4:4

Speak It! "Father, I thank You for Your Word! It's living and active and You are still speaking to my heart today through Your Word. I believe Your Word—the Bible—and I will make a decision to spend time reading it. I want You to pierce between my thoughts and heart and give me the direction and guidance I need from You! In Jesus' Name. Amen."

DAY 49

(living on a prayer)

"The earnest (heartfelt, continued) prayer of a righteous man makes
tremendous power available—dynamic in its working."
James 5:16b, AMP

So, let's think about this for a minute. How would our life be different if God's
tremendous power was available to us? What would our world look like if
God's power was dispensed to us in a customized and dynamic way to meet
our needs? How would the lives of others be impacted if we prayed effective
prayers that got results?

When God's power touches our lives—or the lives of others—it changes everything!

The good news is that God's power is made available—through prayer! God
has given us the tremendous privilege of prayer and the opportunity to pray
in such a way that our earnest, heartfelt, continued prayers make God's
power available. Through spending time with the Lord, we can make "prayer
deposits" for our personal lives, our families, our children, our church, our
jobs, our destiny, our nation and so much more!

When we pray, we can get "ahead of the curve" and put God's power on
deposit for our own lives and on the behalf of others. The result? When we—
or those we pray for—face decisions, crisis or needs, it's easy to make
withdrawals on God's power; because through prayer, that power has been
made available!

Many of us are "behind the curve" in prayer. We are not consistent in our
prayer lives, and we pray crisis or 9-1-1 prayers rather than getting ahead of
the prayer curve and making sure God's power is available for every need! We
can and should change that!

Let's get serious and consistent in our prayer lives by making a decision to
spend some time with the Lord in a secret place and pray earnest, heartfelt
prayers.

Read It! 1 John 5:14-15

Speak It! "Father, I want to pray earnest, heartfelt, continued prayers that make
tremendous power available for my life and on the behalf of others. I ask You for
Your help in establishing a consistent prayer life. In Jesus' Name. Amen."

DAY 50

(kick the devil out of the details)

"Whoever can be trusted with very little can also be trusted with much..."
Luke 16:10a, NIV

Success is all about details. I once worked for an arthroscopic orthopedic surgeon, and I'll never forget the good advice he gave me when he said, "Pay attention to the details." He should know—he was an inventor and a pioneer in arthroscopic surgery and this required great attention to every detail.

The phrase "pay attention to details" was our theme when we spent time with our builder going over every detail of our new church construction project. There were thousands upon thousands of details! We learned that paying attention to details saved us money; while overlooking them, cost us...time and money.

How true this is in life. What details are we responsible for? In our personal life? Relationships? Marriage? Family? Job? Ministry? Are we paying attention to details, making sure we aren't overlooking ones that could cost us or others?

God pays attention to details. He also pays attention to *our* attention to details. He sees how we handle little things like mustard seed faith, words, thoughts, self-discipline, commitments, people—and so much more. Those who can be trusted with a little can be trusted with more; those who are unfaithful in the littlest things won't get the opportunity to take on more.

As leaders and employers, we know that the most valuable people on any staff are those who excel in their ability to pay attention to the details in a timely fashion. Those who watch the details are more likely to be promoted and given more responsibility; they rise and succeed. Unfortunately, those who make excuses and don't pay attention to the details, earn a reputation for being unreliable, untrustworthy and sloppy—reasons to lose a promotion or land a demotion.

Are we faithful in the little things? Some say "the devil is in the details," so why not kick the devil out of our details—all of them! If we want God to promote us in life and want to bless those we serve, let's pay attention to all the little details!

Read It! Luke 6:1-12

Speak It! "Father, help me to be the kind of person who people can trust with little things. I ask You to help me think ahead, think about the big picture and all the small things that make up that big view. Help me pay attention to the details that affect my life, my relationships, my marriage, my family, my job and my ministry. Help me to be faithful in the little things. In Jesus' Name. Amen."

DAY 51

(the one with a strong spirit wins)

"The human spirit can endure a sick body,
but who can bear it if the spirit is crushed?"
Proverbs 18:14, NLT

Are you facing a sickness? Disease? Crisis? One of the most important things to remember when we are facing a physical challenge, a sickness, a bad report or an attack on our body is to keep our spirit strong! When we are strong spiritually—close with the Lord, loaded with His Word and the faith that comes from knowing His promises—it's a lot easier to fight the fight of faith for healing and health. We are more apt to live in peace, joy and confident expectation when our spirit is strong and vibrant.

When facing a physical challenge, it's more important to keep our spirit (our heart) strong in the Lord than it is to keep our body strong. A strong spirit will literally feed, bear, guide, nourish, make provision for and sustain a sick body.

This verse in Proverbs 18:14 is worth looking at in several translations:

- *"The strong spirit of a man will sustain him in bodily pain or trouble, but a weak and broken spirit who can raise up or bear?" (AMP)*
- *"A healthy spirit conquers adversity, but what can you do when the spirit is crushed?" (MSG)*
- *"A man's spirit sustains him in sickness, but a crushed spirit who can bear?" (NIV)*

How do we keep our spirit strong? By feeding our spirit man. When we read, meditate upon and saturate our heart with God's Word, His living and active Word strengthens us, builds faith into the core of our very being.

Read It! Ephesians 3:16-20, AMP (Pray it over yourself.)

Speak It! "Father, may You grant me and out of the rich treasury of Your glory, to be strengthened and reinforced with power in our inner man by the Holy Spirit dwelling our innermost being and personality. May Christ, through our faith, dwell—settle down, abide, make His permanent home—in our hearts! May we be rooted deep in love and founded securely on love, that we may have the power and be strong to apprehend and grasp the experience of that love—what is the breadth and length and height and depth of it; that we may really come to know practically, through experience for ourselves the love of Christ, which far surpasses mere knowledge without experience that we may be filled through all our being unto all the fullness of God may have the richest measure of the divine presence, and become a body wholly filled and flooded with God Himself! In Jesus' Name. Amen."

DAY 52

(bust a move)

"To everything there is a season, a time for every purpose under
heaven...a time to dance..."
Ecclesiastes 3:1, 4

Every now and then, it's time to bust a move!

There is a time to dance!

I'm not talking about provocative dancing, hitting up the bar scene or doing
suggestive fleshly moves—I'm talking about a dance of joy! A dance to
celebrate—to leap, skip or jump. Literally, the word "dance" in Ecclesiastes
means: to stamp, to spring about wildly or for joy.

Some days, some moments—there is just something refreshing and rejuvenating
about getting a groove going. We need to bust a move and sing a song to drive
out discouragement, depression or the blues! Tap our toes and shuffle just
enough to break out of apathy, passivity or exhaustion! Dance for joy to
celebrate the goodness of God.

The Bible has a lot to say about dancing...and rejoicing, celebrating, singing,
shouting and making a melody.

We can bust a move—sing, shout and make a melody by faith because...

- **The lost are found.** *(Luke 15:24-25, NIV)*
- **We are healed.** *(Acts 3:7-8, NIV)*
- **We are filled and drunk in the Spirit.** *(Ephesians 5:18-19, NLT)*
- **Our tears are turned to joy.** *(Psalm 30:11, NIV)*
- **We want to celebrate a happy occasion.** *(Genesis 21:8, NLT)*
- **God gives us victory.** *(1 Samuel 18:6-7, NIV)*
- **We want to praise God.** *(2 Samuel 6:14)*
- **It's time to break free.** *(Psalm 98:4-5, NIV)*

Read It! Psalm 149:3, KJV

Speak It! "Father, I am going to bust a move today! I'm not going to let boredom,
apathy, passivity, depression, discouragement or the blues get me down. I have so
much to celebrate and be thankful for. So, I choose to rejoice, celebrate, shout,
sing and dance my way to victory! In Jesus' Name. Amen."

DAY 53

(don't inherit the wind)

"He who troubles his own house shall inherit the wind..."
Proverbs 11:29a, AMP

One of God's best blessings is our families. Unfortunately, we take them for granted and often hurt them the most. A person "troubles his own house" when he/she chooses...

- **To communicate with their family through manipulation, guilt, silence and fear over communication, mercy, love and care.**
- **Adultery over a commitment to their marriage vows.**
- **Incest and sexual abuse over protection, honor and purity.**
- **Anger and verbal abuse over love and kindness.**
- **Addictions and lust of gambling, drugs, alcohol, pornography, overeating and work-aholic-ism over time and money spent on their spouse and kids.**
- **Selfishness and their own pleasures over giving to their family.**
- **To continually disapprove their spouse or child's best efforts over showing approval and support.**
- **Illegal behavior over doing right by and for their families.**
- **To sow seeds of destruction into their family over seeds of nurturing and growth.**

A person "inherits the wind" when he/she...

- **Cannot leave an inheritance to their children.**
- **Have absolutely no emotional bond or connection to their kids...and vice versa.**
- **Are an empty shell with no real friends.**
- **Are penniless, friendless and known as a person lacking integrity and morals.**
- **Don't receive hugs, kisses or gifts—all part of healthy families.**
- **Consider the bottle, work, a casino or a porn site their "closest friend."**

If these describe us, all is not lost. We just need to repent and go the extra 100 miles to rebuild bridges, communicate, demonstrate humility and acts of love towards them. It might take time—maybe a long time—but we may be able to restore what's been lost. Let's think how we can invest in and bless our family.

Read It! Proverbs 14:1

Speak It! "Father, thank You for my family. I want to be the kind of person that is a blessing to my family. I don't want to inherit the wind; I want to inherit a lifetime of rich, deep, meaningful relationships with each person in my family. Help me take the initiative to invest into the lives and relationships I have with each person in my family. In Jesus' Name. Amen."

DAY 54

(framing your world with words)

"By faith we understand that the worlds were framed by the word of
God, so that the things which are seen were not made of things
which are visible."
Hebrews 11:3

If you've ever been involved with a construction project, you know how crucial the frame is. Once the foundation is poured, it's critical the framing—the beams, posts and studs—goes up plumb. A skewed frame will mess up the whole building. Think about it. What would curtains look like on windows hung on a wall framed at 45 degrees? How would you close a door that was set on a frame missing its header or footer? Can you imagine how funky it would look? A strong, balanced frame is imperative; without it, a building would be a structural disaster.

The same thing is true in our lives. When our lives are built on the foundation of Jesus Christ, the "framing" that goes up on that foundation is critical. We have the ability to frame our world with words—God's words. The Bible says in the same way God framed the world with His words and brought things which were not visible into the visible realm, we too can frame our world—our emotional, mental and physical health; relationships, families, finances, etc.—by speaking God's Word! It's God's principle of faith, the power of God's spoken Word.

How's your world framed? Are windows and doors opening for you? If we want to live the supernatural, victorious Christian life, we have to get our mouth in agreement with God's Word. When we realize what God's Word says about who we are in Christ and what belongs to us, we must then choose to say those things. Over time, they will frame our lives! Let's take a look at some of those:

- **We eat the fruit of our words.** *(Proverbs 18:20-21)*
- **We bring forth things with our words.** *(Matthew 12:34-37)*
- **We can turn our whole body around with our words.** *(James 3:3-5)*
- **We move mountains with our words.** *(Mark 11:23)*

Let's eliminate idle and inoperative words and frame our world by saying what God says about our lives—spirit, soul and body.

Read It! Romans 4:17

Speak It! "Father, help me frame my world with Your Word. I choose to say what You say; and when necessary, I will call things that aren't as though they are. Help me speak words of life, so I may bring forth good things. Help me eliminate negative and idle words. Help me to move whatever mountains I face by speaking Your words to those very mountains! In Jesus' Name. Amen."

DAY 55

(feeling dull?)

"As iron sharpens iron, so a man sharpens the countenance of his friend."
Proverbs 27:17

Ever felt dull? Not sharp? Worn down? Overwhelmed? Depleted? Out of fresh ideas or energy? You need friends, a team of people to help sharpen you.

Sometimes there are so many decisions to make, things coming at us, deadlines to meet and things that must be done, they can wear us out mentally, emotionally, physically—even spiritually. At times, we may feel like it is not humanly possible to know, be, do or fulfill everything that is expected of us. God has actually designed it that way. He wants us to lean on Him, and He's created us to need each other.

If we're feeling tapped out, overloaded, alone or like it's us against the world; we need to look around. God always strategically places people in our lives to help sharpen us. They aren't always easy to find; but if we'll look, they are there. When that dull, helpless feeling creeps up on us or we start to stress out by drawing from our own human ideas, knowledge, wisdom or experience, we need to stop going at it alone and draw on the ideas, knowledge, wisdom and experience God has given to others.

Sometimes, we give people the impression that we are a rock or an island and have it all together. Let's just admit that we aren't, and we don't. Let's allow people in our world to know that we welcome the "sharpening" power they bring to our lives. We are the Body of Christ, and we need each other!

In my own experience, I cannot tell you the relief, refreshing, joy, power, fruit and multiplied strength I have received from the various people God has put in my life. For many years, as my husband and I pioneered a church, we tried to do things "alone." But, when we started developing teams, asking for and receiving the "sharpening" power of others; it was a happy day! We learned that asking for help isn't a sign of weakness; it's a sign of great strength.

Today, let's look at our life and find those precious, intuitive, creative, Jesus-loving people whom we can trust. Who's on our "sharpening" team? Who can we lean on? Call? Bounce an idea off of? Shoot an e-mail to? Have a cup of coffee and brainstorm with? Then...do it!

Read It! Proverbs 11:14

Speak It! "Father, thank You for surrounding my life with wonderful people! I'm not alone! Help me be more open to receiving help and the God-ordained 'sharpening' that comes from others! I also pray that You help me be the kind of person who helps sharpen those around me. In Jesus' Name. Amen."

DAY 56

(insider information)

"However, when He, the Spirit of truth, has come, He will guide you into all truth; for He will not speak on His own authority, but whatever He hears He will speak; and He will tell you things to come."
John 16:13

This is one of my favorite passages in the Bible! I love this promise about the Holy Spirit. We have "insider information" by virtue of the Holy Spirit living on the inside of us. I hope you're encouraged today as you consider two amazing pieces of "insider" info the Holy Spirit gives.

- **He will guide us into all truth.** We have the best Guide in all the world! Ever been on a guided trip? Four-wheeling, rafting, snorkeling or hiking? Isn't it great to have a guide who knows the ropes? A guide who knows all the things you must see *and* all the places to avoid, keeping you safe while taking you on a memorable trip?

  The Holy Spirit is the quintessential Guide. He knows the truth about every turn, bump and curve in the road, and He will guide us all along the way. He knows all the things we must see and all the things we need to avoid. He keeps us safe while guiding us on a truth-loaded, faith-filled adventure. Our job is merely to listen to the Guide and follow His lead.

- **He will tell us things to come.** This may be one of the best promises in the Bible! The God who knows everything about the future lives on the inside of us. Talk about "insider information." Think about it. The only Person who really knows what the future holds is the Holy Spirit. Jesus said the Holy Spirit wouldn't just keep it to Himself, but He would reveal to us the things to come; and you can take that promise to the bank! Rest assured that when you seek the Lord, anything you need to know about your future—the Holy Spirit will show you. He will give you an inclination, a "sense" of what is coming, a knowing and the insider information you need for the circumstances and decisions that affect your life.

Today, let's lean on the Holy Spirit.

Read It! John 16:13, AMP

Speak It! "Father, thank You for the wonderful gift of the Holy Spirit! Holy Spirit, I want to know You better. I want to stay in step and follow You as the Guide of my life. I want to hear Your voice and pick up Your signals as You show me things to come. Thank You for all the 'insider information' I need. In Jesus' Name. Amen."

DAY 57

(what wisdom knows)

"My son, be attentive to my Wisdom [learned by actual and costly experience], and incline your ear to my understanding [of what is becoming and prudent for you]..."
Proverbs 5:1, AMP

What's the difference between knowledge and wisdom? Experience—actual and costly experience!

There's a vast difference between those with knowledge (information, ideas and theories) and those with wisdom (experience and reality). Of course, wisdom is better, and the best case scenario is knowledge...*and* wisdom! But, this takes time to acquire, since wisdom comes with experience.

If you're young—not just in age, but in spiritual maturity, in experience, in a new position or in a new role—you may have acquired some knowledge in the course of your life, but you may still be lacking the experience that gives you wisdom. Be humble enough to recognize that reality and purpose in your heart to go after the wisdom you need in order to best utilize the knowledge you have.

Proverbs tells us to "get wisdom," because it's the principle thing. It comes to us a few ways:

- **From God and His Word.** When we read His Word and listen to His voice, He'll give us wisdom on what to do, when to do it, how to do it, what to say, when to say it and how to say it.

- **From those who have wisdom.** We can accelerate in gaining wisdom by listening to those with experience. If our parents, boss or leaders have more experience than we do in a given endeavor, we should listen to them. The caveat? It takes wisdom to know that we should listen to those with wisdom.

- **From experience.** Some pieces of wisdom come simply by doing something long enough to make mistakes, start over, learn a few lessons and gain the experience, giving us reference points. Ever said, *"Boy, I'll never do that again..."*? That's wisdom speaking from experience! Sure, our experiences help us to eventually connect-the-dots and have a few "ah-ha" moments; but, before you know it, wisdom has arrived.

Read It! Proverbs 20:29, AMP

Speak It! "Father, help me have enough wisdom to know that I need more wisdom. I pray that You add to the knowledge I have with the wisdom that comes from Your Word, from those with wisdom and from experience. I want to be filled with knowledge and wisdom. In Jesus' Name. Amen."

DAY 58

(big words)

"Ah, Lord GOD! Behold, You have made the heavens and the earth by Your
great power and outstretched arm. There is nothing too hard for You."
Jeremiah 32:17

Ready to hear some big words that can absolutely change and revolutionize
your life—your eternity, your mind, your body, your family, your future?
The big life-changing words are: **Whoever. Anything. Whatever. All things.
Always.**

- **Whoever.** Aren't you glad eternal life is open to WHOEVER? Eternal life isn't just
  for a select few; it's for WHOEVER believes on Jesus—regardless of your name,
  age, size, ethnicity, language, religious background or gender. If you are a
  WHOEVER, you qualify for eternal life by believing in Jesus. *(John 3:16)*
- **Anything.** God can handle ANYTHING you are facing. If you will completely trust
  Him, there isn't ANYTHING He can't fix, cure, forgive, heal or bless. Is ANYTHING
  too hard for God? Nope! Not one thing! *(Jeremiah 32:27)*
- **Whatever.** The things we believe in our heart and say with our mouth do come
  to pass. If you think about it, most of us are the product of what we have
  believed in our hearts and said with our mouths over the years. We've all
  experienced the WHATEVER things we have said.

  Now, think how this can work against us. Have you ever heard yourself say, "I
  am so afraid...," or "This just terrifies me...,"—and then notice you were anxious
  or fearful? Exactly. You got WHATEVER you said. We can change the WHATEVER
  by paying attention to what we believe—and what we say.

  This is a law of faith. God created the world with it and His whole kingdom
  operates on it! If we will get our hearts and mouths in agreement with God and
  His Word, we absolutely can have WHATEVER we say. *(Mark 11:23)*
- **All things.** What is possible? All things! What do you need? It's possible!
  Without God, you're on your own; but with God, ALL THINGS are possible!
  (Mark 10:27)
- **Always.** God promises, no matter how dark it may look, how defeated you may
  feel—no matter what—He ALWAYS leads us in triumph in Christ! What does the
  snapshot of you in your current situation look like once you get to victory? Fix
  your eyes on that vision of triumph and do not be moved. He ALWAYS leads us
  to victory! *(2 Corinthians 2:14)*

Read It! Mark 10:27

Speak It! "Father, I thank You for these big words! They're bigger than me, bigger
than my circumstances, bigger than my problem and bigger than my mountain.
Today, I put my complete trust in You and declare: I am a WHOEVER who knows
that there isn't ANYTHING too hard for You. I believe Your Word in my heart and
will say it with my mouth knowing that WHATEVER I say is possible; because with
You, ALL THINGS are possible! I praise You today for ALWAYS leading me into
victory and triumph. In Jesus' Name. Amen."

DAY 59

(a present help)

"God is our refuge and strength, a very present help in trouble."
Psalm 46:1

If you are facing a rough time right now, be encouraged by this verse, today.

- **God is our refuge and strength.** God is a place to which we may flee for safety and strength. He is our shelter; we run into Him and we are safe. The Bible says so in Proverbs 18:10, *"The name of the LORD is a strong tower; the righteous run to it and are safe," (NIV)*. In a time of trouble—need, anxiety, sorrow or danger—we can run into a real place—God. He is our strong tower, and we can hide in Him. In that place, He gives us a strength beyond our own—His. He is the strength of our lives. Think about that. We can hide in God and be filled with His strength.

- **A very present help in time of trouble.** "Trouble" includes all that would give us anxiety or sorrow. When we face trouble, God is already there. He isn't just present; He is *very* present—emphatically present—and He gives us whatever assistance we need. He is present to help us—to strengthen us, to counsel us, to comfort us, to guide us, to rescue us, to heal us and to make a way for us. Think about that, now. We are not alone; He is very present to help us.

Remember, whatever we're facing—we are not alone. Let's run into Him today and get all the help we need.

Read It! Psalm 23

Speak It! "Father, today I am facing a time of trouble, so, I run into You. You are my hiding place. Strengthen me with Your strength. I believe You are very present, and I am not alone. I believe You are here to help me. Thank You for being my very present help today. In Jesus' Name. Amen."

DAY 60

(a long, satisfied life)

"'Because he loves me,' says the LORD, 'I will rescue him; I will protect him, for he acknowledges my name. He will call upon me, and I will answer him; I will be with him in trouble, I will deliver him and honor him. With long life will I satisfy him and show him my salvation.'"
Psalm 91:14-16, NIV

How long should we live? Does the Bible say anything about the length of our days? Actually, the Bible says a lot about the subject. Psalm 91 is a good place to start. I encourage you to read the whole thing.

God wants us to live until we are satisfied—satisfied we have experienced His salvation, satisfied we have fulfilled our purpose and satisfied we have left a godly heritage and legacy. It will take a long life to be satisfied in all of these things. Then, when we are satisfied, we can go be with the Lord. (I have often thought that I'll have to live to be 120 just to be satisfied and fulfill all the things the Lord has put in my heart.)

When we live in the secret place of the Most High—in fellowship with Him, under the Lordship of Jesus Christ—we can count on God's best, including a long, satisfying life. Because we love and obey the Lord, He promises to rescue, protect, answer, honor and remain with us. Jesus said the true sign of loving God was to obey Him. So, you could say that when we walk in obedience to God and His Word, we can count on a long, blessed life and His grace and help to get us through any trials and tribulations along the way.

This is a redundant theme throughout the Bible:

- *"My child, never forget the things I have taught you. Store my commands in your heart, for they will give you a long and satisfying life." (Proverbs 3:1-2, NLT)*
- *"If you are willing and obedient, you shall eat the good of the land." (Isaiah 1:19)*
- *"Children, obey your parents because you belong to the Lord, for this is the right thing to do. If you honor your father and mother, 'you will live a long life, full of blessing.'" (Ephesians 6:1 & 3, NLT)*

Today, be encouraged. God wants to bless you with a long, satisfied life as you live in the secret place of the Most High and set your love on Him!

Read It! Psalm 91

Speak It! "Father, help me live in that secret place, in close fellowship with You. It's my heart's desire to live a life pleasing to You. I thank You for a long and satisfying life where I enjoy the benefits of the great salvation You provided, where I fulfill the purpose for which You created me. In Jesus' Name. Amen."

DAY 61

(God-flavors)

"Let me tell you why you are here. You're here to be salt-seasoning that brings out the God-flavors of this earth. If you lose your saltiness, how will people taste godliness?"
Matthew 5:13a, MSG

Flavors and smells. God wants us to add the seasoning, flavor, taste and aroma of Christ to the world in which we live—to our sphere of influence.

Let's talk about it...

- **Favorite Smells.** What aroma do you enjoy? How about fresh ground coffee? Hot, freshly-popped popcorn? A garden full of fresh flowers in the summer? A sandalwood candle? New leather in a new car? Or, a car full of boys after a long football practice?
- **Favorite Flavors.** What flavors do you love? What foods excite your taste buds? Mint chocolate chip ice cream? Crème brûlée? Peanut butter? Lemon pepper steak? Triple-shot cappuccino? Guacamole? Bananas? Sushi?

Isn't it funny how smells and flavors can take us places? Caramel corn takes me to a Michigan State football game. A burning patchouli candle takes me to Spencer's Gifts in the 70's. The smell of tires reminds me of Sam's Club and being pregnant with our first child.

Where do smells and flavors take you?

There is something wonderful about spiritual aroma and flavor! When we are walking closely with the Lord, there is a fresh aroma that comes from our lives and influences others. Have you ever thought about that? What aroma are we emitting? What flavor are we leaving with people who we know—and those we don't? What flavor is our faith? What do people smell when they're with us?

If we will yield to the Lord, He will express the full flavor and aroma of Christ through us and take others to wonderful places in God!

Why not be intentional today and season everyone and everything around us with the "joy, mercy, kindness, patience and love" flavor and aroma of Christ!

Read It! 2 Corinthians 2:16

Speak It! "Father, I want my life to add the seasoning, flavor, and aroma of Christ to the world in which I live. Help me to live closely to You and let my life express the flavor and sweet aroma of Christ. In Jesus' Name. Amen."

DAY 62

(jump-start your prayer life)

"The earnest (heartfelt, continued) prayer of a righteous man makes
tremendous power available—dynamic in its working."
James 5:16b, AMP

Does your prayer life need a jump-start? Feel a bit apathetic or like you're just going through the motions?

Prayer is not supposed to be drudgery; it's supposed to be a heartfelt, faith-filled conversation with God Almighty. One of the best ways to jump start our prayer life is to get our heart connected to our prayers. When we pray obligatory, dutiful, mental prayers; it's just boring, religious work. When we pray heartfelt, earnest, passion-filled prayers; it's an adventure!

So, here's a simple way to get fired up about prayer again. Let's ask ourselves these questions:

- **What topic or desire is front and center in our heart?** In other words, what is cooking in our heart? What does our heart long for? If God would do anything for us, what does our heart want to see heaven do? Let's identify the things that our heart "feels."
- **What does our heart feel compassion toward?** Is our heart moved with compassion for someone facing surgery? For a lost son or daughter? For kids of divorce? For the salvation of our husband or wife? For a real revival in America? For young girls caught in prostitution or the sex-trade? For those who don't know who they are in Christ? For the men and women in the military? For the homeless? For those addicted to drugs, gambling or porn? For those with AIDS? For those in Hollywood, in government? For those who have lost their jobs? For those in your neighborhood. What things are front and center in our heart? It's easy to pray heartfelt prayers when we identify who and what God has put in our hearts.

Once we identify and locate the things in our heart, let's take some time to see what God has already said and promised us in His Word about those things...and then pray accordingly with earnest, heartfelt and continued prayers for God's will to be done in those things. Then, we will see tremendous power being made available in those areas by God Almighty!

Read It! Psalm 21:2

Speak It! "Father, thank You for jump-starting my prayer life today! I ask You to help me locate the desires You have placed in my heart-of-hearts and help me to pray according to Your Word about these things. I am so glad that prayer is not a boring ritual, but a heartfelt conversation with You! Thank You for the tremendous power that will be made available as I pray! In Jesus' Name. Amen."

DAY 63

(lip lock)

"Don't use foul or abusive language. Let everything you say be good and helpful, so that your words will be an encouragement to those who hear them. And do not bring sorrow to God's Holy Spirit by the way you live."
Ephesians 4:29-30a, NLT

"Sticks and stones will break my bones, but words will never hurt me." That's what they say...but, nothing could be further from the truth! Sticks and stones *will* break your bones, and words *will* break your heart...and others' hearts... and grieve the Holy Spirit. Words are power-packed. They cut to the core or spread honey to the heart; they bless or curse; they build up or tear down. Amazing how that tiny, little tongue of ours can do so much good or...oh, so much damage. What have your words done lately?

Is your mouth giving you fits? Is it out of control? Do you find yourself saying things you regret or wish you could take back? Are your lips being controlled by your anger, flesh, ego, narcissism, strife or jealousies? Do you need serious help locking your lips?

We can teach our mouth how to behave! *"The heart of the wise teaches his mouth, and adds learning to his lips,"* (Proverbs 16:23). Wise people teach their mouths what to say...or not say. The Bible is loaded with wise instructions for our: mouth, lips, tongue, words, speech, speaking, talk, and talking! I wonder if we realize the power in our speech?

- **Words impart.** Can't we just hear the people around us saying, "Tell me something good"? Let's impart grace, strength, courage, hope and victory to those around us. *(Ephesians 4:29)*
- **Words heal.** Let's speak words that have a sweet spirit about them, heartfelt words that bring God's healing power to hearts, minds and bodies. *(Proverbs 16:24, NIV)*
- **Words refresh.** Let our words be full of life and splash those around us with words of encouragement and blessing. *(Proverbs 10:11)*

If our tongue is out of control, there's help for us today!

Read It! Psalm 141:3, NIV

Speak It! "Father, I repent for the damage my mouth has done. I've sinned against You and others with hurtful words and ask You to forgive me. Lord, set a guard over my mouth. I want to be wise; so anytime I start to speak words, help me to pause and teach my mouth what and how to speak. I don't want to grieve the Holy Spirit, and I want my words to impart grace to the hearer, healing to the hurting and refreshing to those who need it. In Jesus' Name. Amen."

DAY 64

(you think you've got it bad?)

"The Mighty Men of the military were Asahel brother of Joab, Elhanan son of Dodo of Bethlehem..."
1 Chronicles 11:26a, MSG

And we think we've got it bad? How would you like to be the son of Dodo? That'll mess you up, won't it? Imagine how harassed Elhanan must have been at school? *"Hey, El-man, what's your dad's name, again? Oh, he's a dodo? (bahaaaa...)"* We should be thankful our dad's name isn't Dodo!

How about a few other things to be thankful for?

"Sanballat and Geshem sent this message: 'Come and meet with us at Kephirim in the valley of Ono,'" (Nehemiah 6:2, MSG). "Oh, no!" is right! How would you like to live in the valley of Ono? That'll give you a constant state of fear and anxiety, won't it? *"Yes, teacher, my address is 777 Main Street, and I live in the valley of...Ono."* The teacher responds, *"What? What's wrong?"* *"Nothing, it's just that I live in the valley of...Ono."* Poor residents were constantly confessing a state of dread!

"At Joppa there was a certain disciple named Tabitha, which is translated Dorcas," (Acts 9:36a). Great, how would you like to be a "Dorcas"? That'll get you nominated for homecoming queen, eh? Her real name was Tabitha. So, why couldn't they just leave it at that? Tabitha is a nice name. But no, they had to announce to the world her real name was Dorcas. Nice.

"Your neck is like an ivory tower. Your eyes are the pools of Heshbon by the gate of Bath Rabbim. Your nose is like the tower of Lebanon looking toward Damascus," (Song of Solomon 7:4, NIV). Wow! How would you like someone to describe your nose as the Tower of Lebanon? Now, that'll give you a complex! "Gee, thanks. It's great to know my nose is so huge it extends into the next country." How do you spell "rhinoplasty"?

So, we think we've got it bad? Someone always has it worse! Let's just be thankful our dad's name isn't Dodo, we don't live in the valley of Ono, our name isn't Dorcas and our nose isn't as large as the Tower of Lebanon!

Read It! 1 Thessalonians 5:18, NLT

Speak It! "Father, today I choose to be thankful for my blessings! When I put things in perspective, I don't have it that bad. Besides, I trust You and know that as I walk in the light of Your Word and seek first Your kingdom, You will continue to meet all my needs and add good things to my life! I thank You and praise You today! In Jesus' Name. Amen."

DAY 65

(scuzz)

"Dear friend, if bad companions tempt you, don't go along with them.
If they say—'Let's go out and raise some hell...' Oh, friend, don't give them
a second look; don't listen to them for a minute. They're racing to a
very bad end..."
Proverbs 1:10-11, 15-16a, MSG

One of my favorite bands in my heathen days was "Bad Company." I didn't know at that time what God had to say about bad company. The Lord tells us to avoid bad companions who don't share His values or motives. Jesus didn't   hesitate in calling people on the carpet with names like: hypocrites, white-washed tombs full of dead men's bones and blind guides. *The Message Bible* makes it even more plain, describing those who don't embrace godly values as: empty heads, know-it-alls, blabbers, chatterboxes, stuck-up, crooks and mean-spirited—not nice titles. Back in my day, we had a few choice, descriptive ways to describe bad companions, too. Remember these titles? Scuzz. Dirt-bags. Scum. Losers. Stoners.

Whatever you want to call "bad companions," the Bible is pretty clear—don't hang out with them! Love 'em? Yes! Pray for 'em? For sure! Reach out to 'em? Most definitely! But...hang out and follow their lead? Absolutely not! The Lord gives very strong warnings about the influence of bad company and our need to separate ourselves from them. It doesn't mean God doesn't love the ungodly or that we shouldn't love them; it just means we shouldn't closely associate with those who don't share His values. (Of course, I'm not throwing stones here since many of us, at one time, walked like a scuzz when we followed our own ways and evil desires until Jesus came into our lives and turned our lives around.)

Sadly, many parents have raised good kids and poured all kinds of love, goodness and esteem into them, only to have all their labor evaporate when a "bad companion" came along and took up residency in their lives.

We shouldn't underestimate the influence of a bad companion. The Bible says that bad company corrupts good behavior—and it's true. Birds of a feather flock together, and often we become like those we hang out with. So, if we're hanging with some bad peeps, it's time to make some big changes, find some new friends! Trust the Lord to help you find "godly clickage" in beneficial relation- ships full of love, laughter, enjoyment and the pursuit of God and His purposes. Then, cultivate those relationships.

Read It! Proverbs 13:20, NIV

Speak It! "Father, I trust You! I will cut off my close associations with those who don't share Your values and are heading away from You. Thank You for filling my life with new, divine friendships. In Jesus' Name. Amen."

DAY 66

(who started the prosperity message?)

"God blessed them: 'Prosper! Reproduce! Fill Earth! Take charge!'"
Genesis 1:28, MSG

These are the very first words God ever said to mankind! Think about it. God had just created Adam and Eve, and He could have said anything. He chose to pronounce a blessing of prosperity, increase, abundance, authority and dominion on mankind—spirit, soul and body.

He could have said, "Love the Lord, your God." Or, "Read your Bible. Pray. Forgive everyone." Or, "Work hard. Save money. Invest in Apple stock."

This was a profound moment in all of eternity. The first blessing, charge and declaration from the Lord God Almighty was: "Prosper! Reproduce! Fill the earth! Take charge!" The *New King James Bible* says it this way: *"Then God blessed them, and God said to them, 'Be fruitful and multiply; fill the earth and subdue it...,'" (Genesis 1:28a).*

Some people are critical of the so-called "prosperity gospel"—as if it were man's invention. While there have been ungodly extremes and eccentric behavior by some Believers; no matter how you slice it, God is the author of the "prosperity message." His desire from the beginning was that we would be blessed to be a blessing!

Today, let's take some time to study God's Word and discover exactly what He had in mind when He declared such a blessing in His first utterance to mankind!

Read It! Deuteronomy 29:9, NLT

Speak It! "Father, I agree with You. I receive Your Word. I will prosper spirit, soul and body and be blessed to be a blessing. I will reproduce the life of Christ in my natural and spiritual children. I will fill the earth with the knowledge of You and Your Word. I will take charge in my life through the authority You have given me in Jesus' Name. Thank You for pronouncing such a blessing in Your first words to humanity! In Jesus' Name. Amen."

DAY 67

(friendship 101)

"Overlook an offense and bond a friendship;
fasten on to a slight and—goodbye, friend!"
Proverbs 17:9, MSG

I've talked to enough people over the years to know that the number one thing that ruins friendships is...being offended. It's a big friendship trap—beware. We've all been offended and been the offender, right?

Ok, so your friend ditched you, and your feelings are hurt—again! She's too busy to return a phone call, and your e-mail is somewhere in her mailbox abyss—no chance of a "reply" anytime soon. You're out to dinner with another couple, and the other guy sarcastically insults your husband in an attempt to look like Captain Funny Boy. You take a few friends for a boat ride and one friend, with the sensitivity of a rock, tells you how much bigger his boat will be—when he can actually afford one. A friend at work says just enough to insinuate that your daughter is about a mile from "Loserville," while boasting about his son's promotion from stockroom to bagger. Your spouse just "toned" you. Your friends want to spend time with you, but they never initiate a get-together; so unless the lower parts of the earth freeze over, you will have to plan the next fun gathering. He promised that he'd be there; but once again at the last minute, "something came up," and he just can't make it this time. You saved up, sacrificed, given and tried to bless someone in a big way, but the weak or non-existent "thank-you" made you regret it.

Get the idea? Offenses come—Jesus said they would. People are people. If we've been offended by a friend or felt slighted, there's only one thing for us to do: get over it! If we've been disappointed and keeping a record of wrongs...only one thing to do: overlook it! We can't let bitterness even think about putting down roots. Otherwise, it's goodbye friend!

If we wanna strengthen our friendship bonds, we must walk in unconditional love! Keyword: unconditional. That means no strings attached. Remember, love doesn't keep a record of wrongs—and hardly notices. I know...seems impossible, doesn't it? Without God's love, it is impossible! So, let's yield to God's love, overlook offenses and walk in love...because next time, it might be us who needs unconditional love from a friend. When it comes to being the perfect friend, we've all blown it; but if we want our friends to overlook our offenses, we need to be quick to overlook theirs.

Read It! 1 Corinthians 13 (the "love" chapter)

Speak It! "Father, thank You for all the relationships You've blessed me with. I make a decision today to release everyone and anyone who has ever offended me. I will offer mercy and unconditional love. In Jesus' Name. Amen."

DAY 68

(how's that working for you?)

"He brought them out of darkness and the shadow of death,
and broke their chains in pieces."
Psalm 107:14

Are things going in the wrong direction in your life? Frustrated? Lost your job? Ran over your cat? Backed into the mailbox? Gone broke? Ticked off your neighbors? Alienated your kids? Flunked your exams? Lost your friends? Going backwards? Bumbling along? Been devastated and heartbroken? Living in anger and depression? Full of anxiety and fear?

This is not God's best for you! Be encouraged; He has something better for you. But, are you willing to take a good, hard look at your life and answer the famous Dr. Phil question: *"How's that working for you?"* If things aren't working so well, maybe it's time for an honest evaluation.

There are a few reasons why things go from bad to worse:

- **We live in a fallen world and have an enemy who seeks to steal, kill and destroy our lives.** It's our job to resist the devil and live by faith in God's Word.

- **We've rebelled against God.** We've been disobedient, glib and stupid. We live in a culture that resists taking responsibility; we always want to blame someone else for our problems—others, the devil, God. Rarely, do we take the blame. The bitter reality is that some of our woes are self-inflicted!

- **We've made dumb choices.** Sometimes, we're miserable, in bondage and burdened down because we made dumb choices and refused to listen to God's wisdom. God is not our problem; He's our answer! God's not against us; He's for us! In a time of trouble, let's not run from God; let's run to Him! He's a good Father, and He wants the best for us! However, He's given us the freedom to make some choices—even if we choose to reject His counsel, and it costs us greatly.

Parents train their kids and offer their counsel; but at some point, parents have to let their kids make their own choices—even if they result in bad consequences. The Lord does the same thing. He trains us with His Word but gives us the freedom to make choices. If we rebel against the Lord and His wisdom, we get to eat the fruit of our own ways and will suffer the consequences.

Thank God for His mercy. When we turn to Him and start making good choices, He will turn our lives around, snap our chains and bring us into a good place.

Read It! Proverbs 1:29-33, NLT

Speak It! "Father, my life is a mess, and I freely admit that a lot of it is my own fault. I have rebelled against You and Your Word. I have done my own thing, and it's not working out so well. So, today, I choose to walk in Your wisdom. I ask You for mercy and help to make the right choices. In Jesus' Name. Amen."

DAY 69

(one thing)

"And Jesus answered and said to her, 'Martha, Martha, you are worried
and troubled about many things. But one thing is needed...'"
Luke 10:41-42

Ever felt like a Martha? Are you a Type A personality? Busy? Compelled to
serve? Feel obligated to coordinate, organize and take care of details? Hello,
Martha! These are actually great qualities—as long as they don't take us away
from the "one thing" that is needed. And, the "one thing" needed is time with
the Lord. Spending time with Jesus—hearing His voice, listening to His Word
and just being with Him.

Perhaps, we all need to be more like Mary. She was able to slow down, sit still
and find contentment sitting at Jesus' feet. This is something that some of us
have to do intentionally. Just like you, we live a busy life, and we have to be
purposeful about spending time with the Lord. We have to find those pockets
of time when we can sit with Him for a while.

This "one thing" is even more needful when we are feeling the most pressure
on our schedule, and when we think we have the least amount of discretion-
ary time. Ironically, once we slow down and listen to the Lord, we come away
from times with Him with a renewed sense of peace, joy and energy—just
what we need to take care of all the duties, demands and "to-do" lists.

Keep in mind, there are always going to be many things clamoring for our
attention and time, but one thing is needed. There are many distractions,
cares and to-do lists, but one thing is needed. Time with Jesus is needed! Let's
be proactive in finding that time every day this week.

Read It! Luke 10:38-42

Speak It! "Father, in the midst of all the busyness, distractions and demands I feel
in my life, help me to set aside time to sit with Jesus—time to read and listen to
His Word, time to sit still and slow down long enough to hear His voice. Help me
remember that although other things might be important, only one thing is
needed. In Jesus' Name. Amen."

DAY 70

(the wanderer)

"Train me in good common sense; I'm thoroughly committed to living your way. Before I learned to answer you, I wandered all over the place, but now I'm in step with your Word. You are good, and the source of good; train me in your goodness."
Psalm 119:66-68, MSG

Sound familiar? Ever wandered all over the place? Tried to figure out how to do life on your own? Been half-hearted toward the Lord or maybe even hypocritical? Felt guilty and thrown God a bone every now and then, so He wouldn't squash you? Ready for a new way of living?

Make this your prayer:

- **Train me in good common sense...** "Lord, it's time for me to grow up some more. Help me to be smart and wise in my choices. Help me to use common sense."
- **I'm thoroughly committed to living Your way...** "Father, I'm in. I will quit living in a half-hearted way toward You. I'm not going to be a lukewarm Christian. You can consider me thoroughly committed to Your ways, even when it's tough and hard."
- **Before I learned to answer You...** "Jesus, I haven't been listening to You very much; I haven't been good at answering or responding to You, either. I'm making a choice to listen to Your voice and Your Word."
- **I wandered all over the place...** "Lord, this describes my life. I've wandered here and there, up and down, confident and then insecure, obedient and then rebellious, strong and then weak, disciplined and then out of control. I'm done with that; I want to follow You. You are a good Leader and Your paths are right."
- **Now I'm in step with Your Word...** "Jesus, I choose to live by your Word—the Bible. Help me to follow Your tracks as I read, obey and do Your Word."
- **You are good, and the source of good; train me in Your goodness...** "Father, You are a good God. You've always been a good Father. You're the source of all good; help me to practice goodness toward others."

In Jesus' Name. Amen.

Read It! Psalm 119 (Yes, the whole chapter!)

Speak It! "Father, thank You for hearing and answering the prayer of my heart. In Jesus' Name. Amen."

DAY 71

(blessed because)

"And all these blessings shall come upon you and overtake you, because..."
Deuteronomy 28:2

I love the magnitude of God's blessings as described in Deuteronomy 28. Notice verse two...all of these blessings will come upon us "because" of something... What is the big "because"?

"And all these blessings shall come upon you and overtake you, because you obey the voice of the LORD your God..." Because you *"obeyed the voice of the LORD your God."* God loves obedience. The Lord prefers obedience over sacrifice, duty, works or obligation. The Lord rewards us when we listen to and obey His voice. He causes blessings to overtake us! God's voice is revealed in His Word; when we obey the Word of the Lord, we position ourselves for His blessings.

Stop and read the Scripture passages in the **Read It!** segment. Now, take a closer look at some of the blessings:

- **Blessed in the city and country—here and there.**
- **Blessed kids—and grandkids.**
- **Blessed job, vocation, occupation—even in a recession.**
- **Blessed when you're shopping—your basket is blessed even on the day after a major holiday.**
- **Blessed in the grocery store and kitchen—your vital needs are met.**
- **Blessed everywhere—to be a blessing.**

Isaiah 1:19 tells us the same thing, *"If you are willing and obedient, you will eat the best from the land..."*

Read It! Deuteronomy 28

Speak It! "Father, thank You for being a good God. You are a giver, a good Father, a 'blesser'! I want to hear and obey Your voice in every area of my life. I thank You for the blessings that have already come into my life and thank You for all the blessings that will continue to overtake my life. I choose to be willing and obedient and I know I will eat the good of the land. In Jesus' Name. Amen."

DAY 72

(who ya working for?)

*"Servants, do what you're told by your earthly masters. And don't just
do the minimum that will get you by. Do your best. Work from the heart
for your real Master, for God..."*
Colossians 3:22, MSG

Who are we working for? Every now and then, we need to remind ourselves
that, ultimately, we are working for the Lord. He really is paying attention, and
He knows how to reward us accordingly.

Perhaps it's time for a little inspection? Today, let's judge ourselves and the
quality of our work before the Lord and, if necessary, make corrections. Let's
use this passage of Scripture as the measuring stick.

Are you...

- **Doing what you've been asked to do, or are you doing your own thing?**
- **Doing personal work on company or ministry time?**
- **Just doing the minimum to get by, or are you really giving your best?**
- **Going above and beyond the call of duty, or are you a slacker who gets away with wasting time?**
- **Working for the Lord from your heart, knowing He'll reward you, or are you going through the motions of a job...just to get a paycheck?**
- **Really serving the Lord, or would you be embarrassed if He showed up to watch you at work today?**
- **Putting on a show for your boss; but behind the scenes, you're lazy, grumbling and unwilling to be a team player?**
- **Moody, sullen and putting out half-baked work?**
- **A joy to work with or receiving constant correction for attitude, work ethic and relationship issues?**

If the shoe fits, you know what they say... We've got to repent and change our
work habits! We might think we're getting away with working below the Lord's
standards; but make no mistake, the Lord keeps records. One day, it will catch
up to us. So, if we need to make things right with the Lord or our employer,
let's do it—today.

Read It! Colossians 3:22-25, MSG

Speak It! "Father, I'm sorry if I haven't worked in a way that truly honors You. You
know the attitudes I've had, the words I've spoken, the quality of work I've put out
and the honesty in which I have served my employer. I repent and ask You to forgive
me. I will make things right, apologize, and go the extra mile. In Jesus' Name. Amen."

DAY 73

(no whiney babies)

"No discipline seems pleasant at the time, but painful. Later on, however, it produces a harvest of righteousness and peace for those who have been trained by it."
Hebrews 12:11, NIV

I have a new appreciation for this truth. When I finally got serious about fitness, I finally decided that a disciplined workout plan was probably a good idea. But, I forgot how painful it would be! When I first began—even though it had only been a short time—I had already began to gain weight, and it was pure muscle. My jeans were tighter, thighs were bigger and my arms were getting more defined. In fact, I was pretty sure I even saw a tricep pop out once or twice! But, I had no idea how much daily pain was involved in working out.

On day one, I looked at the weight bar for the bench press and thought, "How hard can that be?" Yeah, and then when I could barely lift the bar—no weights attached, mind you—and my arms were screaming after six reps, I knew.

So, my trainer—Jeff Jones—showed me the correct way to lift and then ordered me to do six more reps. The bully! He didn't care that my muscles were burning. I was a big whiney baby, but my trainer knew what I was capable of. He knew that this momentary, disciplinary "pain" would be my gain in strength, tone and definition—and he was right. I did get stronger. Soon, I was bench pressing an amazing 5 lb. barbell with a whopping 2.5 lb. weight added to each end of the bar. Now, I am lifting it like a pro—and I think my deltoids are almost visible!

I've discovered if we want to be strong and fit, as Christians, we have to be disciplined and sometimes even corrected by the Lord. At times, He has to push us to see our full potential. We need His discipline because we can be such wimpy, spiritual whiney babies sometimes. The Lord, like any good trainer, knows what we are capable of, and He pushes us to max out! It's not pleasant at the time and can even hurt! He's not abusive and doesn't use evil things to "teach us lessons," but He knows how to expand our capacity and strengthen our core. The Lord knows if we will push through the pain of a disciplined life in the Word, in prayer and in character choices, we'll gain strength in our witness, tone in our walk and definition in our Christ-likeness! People might even see Jesus in us!

Read It! 1 Corinthians 9:25, NLT

Speak It! "Father, I won't be a whiner. I need to be disciplined. I need Your training and power to push through the pain. Expand my capacity, strengthen my core and help me become fit for the Master's use! In Jesus' Name. Amen."

DAY 74

(what makes it worth it?)

"After all, what gives us hope and joy, and what is our proud reward and crown? It is you! Yes, you will bring us much joy as we stand together before our Lord Jesus when he comes back again. For you are our pride and joy."
1 Thessalonians 2:19-20, NLT

It's all about perspective. One day, we'll stand before the Lord, and He will dish out rewards. What will be our reward and crown? It won't be the new boat or custom clubs or a huge selection of shoes or a shopping spree...or even a new motorcycle—as wonderful as those things are. It will be all the people we were able to invest in during our short life on earth.

People are our reward. When we invest our lives into helping people meet Jesus, grow in their faith and experience victory in Christ, this is our proud reward and crown. There is no greater joy than to see people come to Christ and grow in the Lord. There are no words to describe the joy we get from seeing the fruit in people who "get it." Seeing people who were lost, hurt, empty and defeated find Jesus and get a hold of the reality of God's living Word is absolutely thrilling! The apostle, John, understood this and said, *"I have no greater joy than to hear that my children walk in truth,"* (3 John 1:4, KJV). It's true, there is no greater joy than to see our children—natural and spiritual—walking in the truth. That's our reward.

So, who and what is our reward? Who are we investing in? Who is in our sphere of influence? Who do we know who is lost, hurt, empty, disillusioned, defeated, hungry or thirsty? How can we intentionally invest in their lives? Is there a scripture we can share with them? A book or CD you can pass on? A church or class we can invite them to attend? Can we take them to lunch to introduce them to Jesus? Feed them the Word? Can we forward an e-devo? Whatever we do to invest eternal things into the lives of others will bring us great joy in this life...and one day, those very people will be our reward in heaven.

Read It! 2 Corinthians 4:8

Speak It! "Father, help me invest my life and eternal things into others. Those You have entrusted into my sphere of influence are my hope, joy, proud reward and crown. One day, it will be such a joy for all of us to stand before You! In Jesus' Name. Amen."

DAY 75

(face to the wall)

"The earnest (heartfelt, continued) prayer of a righteous man makes tremendous power available—dynamic in its working."
James 5:16b, AMP

Ever prayed the Hezekiah prayer? This is a prayer you want when your back is against the wall, when the doctor hasn't given you good news, when things aren't looking too bright and life is pretty bleak. Be encouraged today if you are facing a tough time.

The Lord told Hezekiah to prepare to die. When the Lord tells you your time is up, most people say, "OK, well, that must be what God wants," but not Hezekiah. He turned his face to the wall and prayed. He didn't pray to the wall; He prayed right into the ears of the Most High.

He didn't pray some milk toast prayer either. He prayed his guts out and got down to business. He presented his request before the Lord, and he pleaded his case. He asked the Lord to remember his life, his walk with the Lord, his heart and his deeds. He wept—not tears of self-pity, but tears of earnest, heartfelt desire.

Here's how the Lord responded. He said, "I've heard your prayer and have seen your tears. Now, I'm going to add 15 years to your life." Now, that's getting an answer to prayer!

Is your back against the wall today? Do you need 15 more years? Are you willing to pray from your heart of hearts to the Lord? Ask Him to remember your life. Remind Him of your relationship with Him and the things that are important to you. Plead your case before God and devote the remainder of your life to the Lord and His purposes. God is no respecter of persons. What He did for Hezekiah, He'll do for you, if you will turn your face to the wall and pray in faith with heartfelt earnestness.

God is for you, and His power is available to you. I hope you are encouraged to turn your face to the wall, today.

Read It! Isaiah 38:1-5

Speak It! "Father, I turn my face to the wall. I am in desperate need of You and Your power in my life. I need Your life-giving, healing, miracle-working power in my life. Remember my life and walk with You. I ask You for mercy where I have blown it. I want You to know that right now, beginning this day, if You will grant me at least 15 more years, I will be completely Yours. I will live for You and will walk in a way that pleases You. I want You to use my life for Your purposes and to tell as many people as I can about Jesus and Your goodness. In Jesus' Name. Amen."

DAY 76

(what happens in Vegas)

*"And you shall remember that the LORD your God led
you all the way these forty years."*
Deuteronomy 8:2a

To celebrate my fiftieth birthday, my husband and I and several good friends spent four days in Vegas. We saw several shows, rode motorcycles, got a fresh dose of compassion and a reminder of how desperately the lost need the Lord. Wow! Vegas is quite a place...

One of the highlights of the trip was a full day of renting Harleys, riding to the red rocks Ring of Fire and Hoover Dam, then riding back to the strip just in time to see the "Donny and Marie" show at the Flamingo. Donny and Marie are fantastic entertainers. Their show was a trip down memory lane, complete with all the songs we grew up with: "Puppy Love," "One Bad Apple," "Go Away, Little Girl," "Paper Roses"—and dozens of retro video clips from the old days...some 40+ years ago! (The highlight for my husband was when Marie came down our aisle and kissed Jeff on the top of his head!) Listening to their music, hearing them reminisce and watching the old TV clips of Donny and Marie was a sentimental journey for everyone in our group. We had some great laughs remembering our own growing up years, hair styles, clothing and all of the things from our era.

While it was great fun to reflect on all the pop culture memories we have, the more important thing that happened to me during my week in Vegas was a chance to reflect on all the ways the Lord has led me all these years. When I think about all the seasons in my own life and the numerous ways Jesus has led, helped, graced, forgiven, strengthened and blessed me, it's overwhelming. He's a good and faithful God. I made it a point this past week to thank the Lord for all the ways He's led me.

How about you? Have you remembered all the ways the Lord has led you, recently? Think about all of the seasons Jesus has walked you through. Have you taken some time to sing, praise and thank Him for His goodness and faithfulness to you? I encourage you to find some time to "remember Him" this week.

Read It! Psalm 31:19, NLT

Speak It! "Father, I remember all the ways You have led me these _____ years! You are a good and faithful God. I want You to know how thankful I am for all You have done in my life. I thank You, Lord! I will sing praises to Your Name! Help me to carve out some time this weekend to get alone with You to 'remember' and reflect on Your work in my life. In Jesus' Name. Amen."

DAY 77

(because we don't know everything)

"Plans fail for lack of counsel, but with many advisers they succeed."
Proverbs 15:22, NIV

There is wisdom in a multitude of godly counselors. God knew that one person couldn't possibly know everything, so He gave us one another. The Lord has gifted people with different talents, bits of wisdom, reference points and experiences. Taking time to learn, glean and tap into the insight and wisdom of others is just a smart thing to do. It takes humility and an appreciation for the gifts and anointing on others to do so. Not only that...it's more fun and fruitful to talk to and work with a variety of people or teams of people to accomplish various plans.

We are thankful that the Lord has put some pretty wonderful people in our path—professionally and personally. Our church board inspects, advises and gives us their counsel for the overall health of the church on an annual basis. Our staff, and the various teams within, give us fresh, godly advice at various levels. Each week, we glean a wealth of wisdom from our executive team, to the pastoral staff, to the creative team and others. Each advisor brings unique pieces of counsel. What a huge blessing it is to obtain counsel! We've also seen the benefits of short-term advisory teams for specific purposes. These teams have helped us think through the details of a number of projects over the years.

In our personal and family life, the Lord has surrounded us with insightful and intuitive friends, peers, consultants and comrades. Our chance of success in life and ministry has been greatly improved by listening to godly counsel.

What about you? Who has the Lord put in your life? What smart, godly, anointed, wise and insightful people has God added to your life? A parent? A pastor or mentor? A wise grandfather? Neighbor? Co-laborer? Consultant? Friend? Be encouraged; you don't have to figure out everything by yourself! No doubt, God has put trusted friends, confidants, comrades and counselors in your sphere; take time to seek out their counsel. Think about ways to tap into the experience and wisdom of those in your sphere. Maybe it's time to take someone out for coffee to pick their brain? Perhaps, it's time to initiate a few catalytic or creative teams to take your organization to the next level. The Lord wants you to succeed and through godly counsel—you can!

Read It! Proverbs 11:14

Speak It! "Father, thank You for the people You have put in my life. Help me to discern the best ways to obtain the godly counsel and advice I need as I move forward with various plans. I pray You fill me with Your wisdom, so I can be a good advisor and counselor for others. In Jesus' Name. Amen."

87

DAY 78

(get a grip...once again!)

"Don't panic. I'm with you. There's no need to fear for I'm your God. I'll give you strength. I'll help you. I'll hold you steady, keep a firm grip on you."
Isaiah 41:10, MSG

Who knew the Bible was so full of the "get a grip" flavor? Must be that the Lord wants us to be at rest and encouraged by getting a grip.

We need to remember...

- **He has a grip on us!** The most important "grip" is His! Think about the fact that He has a firm grip on us! God Almighty has big hands. The Bible says He can measure the universe with the span of His hand. Since that's true, He has no problem keeping a good grip on you and me. When we are confident the Lord has us in His grip, it's easy to rest, be strong and stay steady—not panic and fear.

- **Not to lose our grip on His promises.** Our job is to keep a grip on His promises. What has God promised us in His Word? Perhaps it was a dream or vision for our life, marriage, family, kids, career, ministry, health, wealth? God keeps His Word. Let's not cast away our confidence. If we keep our grip, through faith and patience, we'll inherit those promises. *(Hebrews 10:23, MSG)*

- **To keep a grip on what we were taught.** We have to hang on to what we've been taught by those who have discipled, taught or pastored us and by what we've learned in the Word and through books, CDs and downloads. Our heart is probably more loaded with the Word than we know...so let's keep a grip! *(2 Thessalonians 2:15, MSG)*

- **To keep our grip in hard times.** The strength of our character and faith is revealed in difficult times, so we have to keep a grip on what we know. No matter what challenges we face, we have the faith we need to believe and speak until victory comes—so let's keep a firm grip on our faith! *(1 Peter 5:9, MSG)*

Read It! Hebrews 12:12, NLT

Speak It! "Father, I thank You that You have a firm grip on me, today. I will not panic or fear; I will be strong and courageous and rest in Your grip! Help me to get and keep a grip on Your promises, the things I have been taught and my faith. I know that You are God and You keep Your Word! In Jesus' Name. Amen."

DAY 79

(take courage)

"So take courage! For I believe God. It will be just as he said."
Acts 27:25, NLT

Take courage! What are you facing right now? What has God said to you? What Scriptures has He spoken to your heart? We can take courage in knowing that it will be just as He said. The apostle Paul was in the storm of his life, but when God spoke to him, he believed it and experienced peace in the midst of the storm. In Paul's case, the Lord told him he was about to face a major shipwreck, but he and all the passengers would be saved if they followed certain instructions. In the end, it was just as God said.

Jesus promised us that the Holy Spirit would show us things to come, and we can count on that! When we are able to remove our emotions, our will and our thoughts from the equation...the Holy Spirit can speak to us about what is to come. Perhaps you're wondering, "What if God hasn't said anything to me?" In that case, plant your face in His Word and read the Bible until He does speak to your heart. Pray and seek the Lord for the answers, direction and insights you need from Him. When we call to Him, He promises to answer. Once you hear from God through His Word and by His Spirit, you can prepare, adjust, claim and take His Word to the bank.

God's Word is an anchor for our soul. When the boat is rocking and the waves are slapping against our world, let's take a moment to remember what the Lord has said to us...and find that place of rest in His Word and believe God. It will be just as He said!

Read It! Deuteronomy 31:6, NIV

Speak It! "I believe God! It will be just as He said. I believe His Word. This is what the Lord has said to me: _____ (quote the Scripture passage(s) He's given to you). God's Word is an anchor to my soul. I will rest in God's Word today. In Jesus' Name. Amen."

DAY 80

(under the influence)

"And do not be drunk with wine...but be filled with the Spirit."
Ephesians 5:18

It's no mystery...life is challenging. There are daily stresses, pressures, responsibilities, heartbreaks and challenges. It's no wonder bars are packed on Friday nights for Happy Hour! At the end of the week, everyone says "TGIF!" and they drown their troubles in drinks, hoping a little intoxication will melt away the challenges. The only problem is, being drunk with alcohol is only the counterfeit. God has the real McCoy—getting under the influence of the Spirit. There are some definite things we can learn by comparing and contrasting:

- **The counterfeit.** Have you ever noticed that people who are drunk with alcohol are quite uninhibited? Sure! They're bold, friendly, happy and talkative? Yeah, when people are under the influence, they lose all inhibitions and become quite chatty...and free, often pouring out their hearts, slurring their words, laughing at nothing, dancing in the streets and loving everyone! The problem is that alcohol, drugs and addictive things give people a counterfeit high, and they carry risk of danger, potential for disease and hassle of morning hangovers. God has something better!

- **The real mccoy.** When we live under the influence of the Spirit, we get intoxicated with His real carefree life! Being filled with the Spirit gives us the freedom to be who God has created us to be! When He fills us, we find ourselves with a new sense of liberty and boldness to live for the Lord. We are free to be talkative about Jesus and friendly to others. When we are "drunk with the Spirit," He fills us with joy, laughter, a song in our hearts and the ability to rejoice always. We quit being so serious and sober about everything, and we find it easy to laugh and love people. The bonus: no hangovers, risk of disease or danger.

The book of Acts gives us four evident signs for those who are drunk with the Spirit and live intoxicated with the Spirit:

- **They speak a spiritual language or 'slur' their words.** *(Acts 2:4)*
- **They're uninhibited and speak boldly.** *(Acts 4:31)*
- **Their eyes are opened.** *(Acts 9:17-18)*
- **They're happy, friendly and filled with joy.** *(Acts 13:52)*

Let's experience God's "Happy Hour" and ask God to fill us with His Spirit until we are absolutely under His influence and fully intoxicated!

Read It! Ephesians 5:18-20

Speak It! "Father, I've been born of the Spirit, but now I'm ready to be filled with the Spirit. I'm thirsty for more of You, and I'm ready to drink in all You have for me! I want to live under the influence of Your Spirit. In Jesus' Name. Amen."

DAY 81

(the innovative edge)

"I wisdom dwell with prudence, and find out knowledge
of witty inventions."
Proverbs 8:12, KJV

I love that God is the ultimate innovator. He is the most creative One—the Creator! When we tap into His wisdom, He fills us with the knowledge of creative, innovative, witty inventions.

What does that mean for us today? It means the Lord can give us a witty idea by His knowledge and wisdom that will change our day...our family...our finances...our city—and perhaps, our entire life! Witty inventions include: new plans, insights, ideas, methods, plots, devices and strategies.

The Bible is full of people who tapped into God's witty, creative power. In the Old Testament, there is a story about a creative leader, Uzziah. He led a team of inventors, engineers and fabricators to develop never-before-seen engines and military machinery. It was a witty invention. He was way before his time. God called and filled an artistic craftsman named Bezaleel with the Spirit, and he devised furniture and numerous materials for God's purposes. Others were called to invent, discover, create and design buildings, cities, businesses, utensils, fabrics and even perfumes.

I once worked for a surgeon who knew how to listen to the creative leading of the Spirit. He was used to invent hundreds of medical instruments, and he discovered dozens of surgical procedures in orthopedic and arthroscopic surgery. His medical innovations have helped thousands of people.

So, in what "witty" ways does God want to use us? Everything has NOT already been discovered, created, developed, invented or created. I believe God wants to empower His children to be creative leaders in innovation, discovery, technology, medicine, ministry and more—all for His purposes! Today, let's listen to the Lord and see what creative, innovative ideas He plants in our heart and mind.

Read It! 2 Chronicles 26:14-15

Speak It! "Father, You are the Creator of the ends of the earth—the most creative, innovative Person in all of eternity. Today, I thank You for Your knowledge, wisdom, plans, insights, ideas, methods, plots, devices and strategies. Help me to devise witty inventions—in my home, business and ministry—that will further Your purposes. In Jesus' Name. Amen."

DAY 82

(what makes you stand out?)

"But a generous man devises generous things,
and by generosity he shall stand."
Isaiah 32:8

Wanna stand out in the crowd? Be generous!

I love this verse because it tells us that a generous person is always looking for ways to be generous. They are devising ways to bless others. Generosity makes a person stand out—probably because this trait is so rare these days.

Generous people aren't always rich. In fact, sometimes it's the poorest people who are the most generous. They don't have two nickels to rub together, yet they'll give you one if you need it. Sometimes, the richest among us are the stingiest. Having money doesn't make us stand out; generosity does.

How do we know if we're generous? Simple—we are not governed by our checkbook, bank account, the price of gas or the economy. We are governed by wisdom and faith in God and His Word...and are free to give.

Generous people are tithers—that's where it starts. Generous people help Jesus build His Church, and they make sacrificial gifts to that end. Generous people help the poor and needy. Generous people give a good tip to the waitress, maid, nail tech and hair stylist. Generous people don't "nickel and dime" their friends, but rather they look for ways to pick up the tab, fill up a gas tank or treat others to God's goodness in unexpected way. (Generosity isn't just in dollars and cents, it's in giving of our time, compliments, encouragement, prayer and a host of other things to others.)

It takes faith to be generous. Today, let's be generous people who devise generous things; and, by generosity, we will stand out.

Read It! Proverbs 11:24-25, NLT

Speak It! "Father, I choose to be generous. I rebuke a stingy, selfish, fear-driven attitude in my own heart and mind. You are God, and I believe You have the power to bless and saturate my life with Your generosity. So, today, I am free to be generous toward You, Your Church and those around me. I am actively looking for ways to be generous. Let my life stand out for Your glory! In Jesus' Name. Amen."

DAY 83

(He's got our back)

"Christ is the visible image of the invisible God. He existed before
God made anything at all and is supreme over all creation. Christ is the
one through whom God created everything in heaven and earth. He
made the things we can see and the things we can't see—kings,
kingdoms, rulers, and authorities."
Colossians 1:15-16a, NLT

We are not alone. There is an invisible kingdom that has our back. It's good to
be reminded of this—especially when we feel like it's us against the world!
Just because we can't see the invisible realm, doesn't mean it doesn't exist. It's
very real, very tangible. Now, we see the unseen realm through a glass darkly;
but one day, we shall see the whole invisible realm face-to-face (1 Corinthians
13:12).

There are two very real invisible kingdoms: the kingdom of darkness and the
kingdom of light. Each kingdom has real rulers, laws, servants and citizens. The
kingdom we are in determines who's got our back. If we belong to Jesus
Christ, God the Father has transferred us out of the kingdom of darkness into
the kingdom of His dear Son, then we belong to the kingdom of Light. The
result? All of heaven has our back!

A couple of stories in the Bible are great reminders:

- **We are a majority; God is on our side!** (2 Chronicles 32:7-8, NLT)
- **We have company; angels surround us.** (2 Kings 6:16-17, NLT)

What more can we say? Be bold. As Believers, we have a huge, invisible
advantage. God's got our back!

Read It! 1 Timothy 1:17, NIV

Speak It! "Father, thank You for the reality of the invisible kingdom. We have all
of heaven's power on our side. You are the King eternal, immortal and invisible! I
am so thankful that I am not alone. You have my back! In Jesus' Name. Amen."

DAY 84

(in pursuit)

"Blessed, happy, fortunate, [to be envied] are they who keep His testimonies, and who seek, inquire for and of Him and crave Him with the whole heart."
Psalm 119:2, AMP

Who gets to be blessed, happy, fortunate and envied? Those who seek, inquire for—and of—the Lord and those who crave Him with their whole heart.

- **The Lord loves it when we seek Him.** So much so, that He rewards those who diligently seek Him. I wonder why? Is it because the Lord is not looking for people who are apathetic or who feel obligated to be religious or dutifully Christian; but rather, He's delighted when people seek Him with their own free will?

- **The Lord loves it when we inquire of and for Him.** Probably because it lets Him know that we are truly dependent on His wisdom and help. When we inquire of the Lord, it indicates that we realize our own limitations and the incredible privilege we have to seek wisdom and guidance from the God who knows all things—past, present and future.

- **The Lord loves it when we crave Him.** When our spiritual taste buds won't be satisfied until we taste God and His reality in our lives. There is something about a craving; it's a longing, an intense desire—something we require. Does the Lord reward our craving because, like any good parent, He enjoys being loved by His children, and He loves to satisfy our desires?

One thing we know: God likes to be pursued, and He likes to pursue us with His blessings. So, are we ready to chase God? Seek Him? Inquire of Him...and for Him? Crave Him? Ready to pick up the pace in talking to the Lord? In our prayer and worship life? In listening to the Lord? In reading His Word?

If we will go after God with our whole heart, we will find Him. The result? Our life will be full of Him—His Word, His love, His peace, His joy, His wisdom, His kindness, His compassion...and so much more—and we will be blessed, happy, fortunate and to be envied.

Read It! Deuteronomy 4:29, NLT and Psalm 63:1

Speak It! "Father, I seek You with my whole heart. I want Your presence and reality in my life to a greater degree. Lord, I inquire for You and of You. I want Your wisdom, direction and insights as I make decisions in every area of my life. I crave You. Jesus, I have an intense desire to know You more intimately and more personally. I thank You that You reward those who diligently pursue You with a life that is blessed, happy, fortunate and to be envied. In Jesus' Name. Amen."

DAY 85

(the if...then principle)

"If you fully obey the LORD your God and carefully follow all his commands I give you today, the LORD your God will set you high above all the nations on earth. All these blessings will come upon you and accompany you if you obey the LORD your God."
Deuteronomy 28:1-2, NIV

The big "if." Have you ever noticed that God's blessings are free...but conditional? God is a good God, and He desires to bless His kids—like any good Father! Goodness is fundamental to God's character. While the Lord is good, His promises are not automatic. He is not the "candy man," blindly doling out blessings. He has our best interests in mind; and often, His promises are "conditional."

Sometimes, we get mad at God for our difficulties, because we have the faulty idea that we can be the lord of our own lives and still walk in all of God's goodness. But, it doesn't work that way. We need to fully obey the Lord. We can't "cherry-pick" the Word—sleep around, party all night, cheat on our taxes, lash out at people, be loose with our mouths—and say, "Well, praise God! He's good all the time!" If we're living a life that's not pleasing to the Lord, we may not qualify for the blessings. In the same way an earthly parent won't lavish blessings on a child who's walking in foolishness, disobedience or rebellion...neither does God.

The "if...then" principle is foundational. IF we confess with our mouth the Lord Jesus and believe in our heart that God has raised Him from the dead, THEN we will be saved *(Romans 10:9)*. We cannot be saved, "if" we don't confess and believe in Jesus *(1 John 1:9)*. We don't experience His forgiveness, "if" we won't confess our sins. The Word of God says we won't be counted as a disciple, "if" we don't continue in His Word *(John 8:31)*. Get the idea?

If we've been struggling lately, maybe our breakthrough is as simple as our obeying the big "if!" Today, what big "if's" are standing between us and God's best blessings? Jesus said, *"If you remain in me and my words remain in you, ask whatever you wish, and it will be given you,"* (John 15:7, NIV). He promised, *"If you can believe, all things are possible to him who believes,"* (Mark 9:23).

Read It! Deuteronomy 28

Speak It! "Father, I thank You for Your Word and Your promises. You are a good Father and You give good gifts. I see this 'if...then' principle in Your Word, and I ask You to help me recognize the "ifs" I need to obey fully so that all the 'thens' can flow into my life. Help me to obey Your Word and walk in the light. I know that 'if' I walk in Your Word 'then' I will be truly blessed. In Jesus' Name. Amen."

DAY 86

(inked)

"Your very lives are a letter that anyone can read by just looking at you.
Christ Himself wrote it—not with ink, but with God's living Spirit; not chiseled
into stone, but carved into human lives—and we publish it."
2 Corinthians 3:2b-3, MSG

We were in Sturgis a few years ago with some friends for the infamous motorcycle rally that meets there. It was quite something! The brotherhood among motorcycle lovers is real and tangible. It's a friendly club with lots of Believers.

We noticed the same brotherhood among those with tattoos. On our trip to Sturgis, we saw some tattoos that looked like beautiful works of art, and we saw some others that were real doozies. I remember one girl in particular. When she walked by, I thought something seemed odd. It wasn't until she passed that I realized she had tattooed her entire body! She had spent a lot of time getting marked by ink with images and words that meant something to her. It seems that most people who get tattoos are very intentional about it; each tattoo means something special to them, and they are glad that others see all their ink!

So, how about us? Are we marked by God and showing Christ-like tattoos to the world around us? Have we allowed the Lord to ink us with His Word and Spirit—to truly tattoo our lives in such a way that everyone can see His design carved into our lives?

Do we need the Lord to refresh some tats that have marked our life? Maybe need a new God-tattoo? Does one of our old "marked moments" need to be freshened up? God's Word is loaded with ink! Let's take some time to sit with the Lord and His Word and see if God doesn't absolutely mark our heart, mind and life with some amazing eternal designs!

Read It! Ephesians 1:13, NIV

Speak It! "Father, I want to be marked by You. I thank You that Your 'ink' is the work of the Word and the Holy Spirit carved into my heart. I would like my life to be a giant, Jesus-tattoo known and read of all men. I ask You to ink me with revolutionary tats colored by Your eternal designs. In Jesus' Name. Amen."

DAY 87

(unload the baggage)

"Give all your worries and cares to God, for he cares
about what happens to you."
1 Peter 5:7, NLT

So, you're dragging a giant, loaded piece of luggage through the airport with one arm, carrying your computer bag and purse in the other arm, and you can't wait to get to the ticket counter to unload some baggage! Halfway to your destination, you realize you picked the bag with the missing wheel. No wonder your trapezoid muscles are spazzing!

When you finally make it to the counter, you get to experience this thrill: "Miss Luggage Police" just punched in for her shift, and she demands you to put your bag on the scale. Her tone tells you this one isn't going to be pretty. You grimace when the weight reveals your bag is 53 lbs.—a glorious three pounds over the weight limit. You give her the "paaaleeeze" look, but she's not in the mood for your problems, and she tells you to find a way to lighten your load or pay up. You smile at the 24 passengers behind you, as you unzip your bag (hoping that crazy things don't fall out). Meanwhile, no one says, "Hey, no problem. We understand. We've got all kinds of time." Your goal: try to remove three pounds of clothing that you can stuff in your purse! The clerk wraps your baggage handle with a luggage claim sticker, tags it with an orange "HEAVY" tag, points and says, "Take your bag over there." She must be referring to the giant cyclotron—or security x-ray machine—only 50 yards away! You think, "Sure...no problem!" Smiling, you drag your bag over the toes of a few passengers on your way to the x-ray machine. At last, you unload your baggage into the care of the happy TSA agent...and you are free!

You know that feeling, right? It's wonderful!

Are we dragging a lot of mental or emotional luggage around? Are we full of worry, anxiety, fear or unnecessary burdens? Listen, lying awake at night thinking of all the things on our to-do list won't help anything. (I know!) Tolerating headaches, muscle spasms or an upset stomach isn't going to change anything. It is time to unload our baggage—our cares, anxious thoughts, concerns and worries—and give it to the Lord. We can do that once and for all, *because* He cares for us affectionately and watchfully. That means He won't let anything fall through the cracks. He'll take care of us—He'll take care of you! Are you ready?

Read It! 1 Peter 5:7, AMP

Speak It! "Father, I'm so glad You're not the mean Luggage Police! You take all my cares, fears, burdens, worries and anxieties. Right now, I unload all of my baggage into Your care! Thank You for freedom, peace and joy. In Jesus' Name. Amen."

DAY 88

(E-harmony® by God)

"And the Lord God said, "It is not good that man should be alone;
I will make him a helper comparable to him."
Genesis 2:18

I was 25 years old, single and desperately wanting to be married. (Sound familiar?) To make matters even worse, I had been a bridesmaid in five weddings within the span of two years. By the last wedding, I was ready to meet and marry the man of *my* dreams. But, he was nowhere to be found!

During this time of frustration, the Lord encouraged me with the idea that "He joins together" a man and a woman, and He wouldn't forget me.

Voila! The next year, when I was 26 years old, I met Jeff Jones—the man of my dreams! Now, over 20 years and four kids later, I can say it was well worth the wait! God did some pretty good "joining" for both of us. So much so, we say that this has been the best 18 years of our lives! (No, seriously, every year has been wonderful!)

If you're single—male or female—be encouraged today. It might seem like you've been single for an eternity, but use this time to learn to trust God; not only for your mate, but for your life in general. Just watch... As you do, He will do the "joining" for you.

Read It! Isaiah 34:16

Speak It! "Father, I trust You! Today, I pray for myself *(if you are single)* or for my friend *(the name of your single friend)* and I thank You that You are the One who gives us the desires of our hearts and You fulfill those desires. I ask You, by Your Spirit, to order my steps (or the steps of my friend) and gather me with my God-ordained mate (or my friend with his or her mate). In Jesus' Name. Amen."

DAY 89

(be refreshing)

"...looking forward to being refreshed by your company."
Romans 15:32b, MSG

What refreshes you? Sunshine and blue sky? Snow-covered mountains? White sand and aqua-blue waters? Prayer? A nap? A massage? An ice cream cone? How about good company?

There's something refreshing about being with friends. (Of course, some prayer time and a massage could be close runner-ups!) We weren't created to be Lone Rangers; we need the revitalization that comes from relationships—especially God-knit ones! The Lord created us to laugh, share, comfort and encourage one another. Who refreshes you?

When I am out and about, I like to watch people interact with each other—talking, sharing, debating, persuading, hugging, crying and laughing. I am always amazed that no matter what culture, language or circle we run with, God has wired us to desire and seek the refreshing that comes from the company of others. (Watch people the next time you're in public. The way we interact with one another is fascinating.)

So, here are the big questions: Are we refreshers or drainers? Do people enjoy or dread our company? Do we add to the lives of those we are with, or do we take from them? Is the conversation and focus all about us, or is there a healthy balance of their interests and ours? Do we laugh easily, or are we a serious downer? Which attitude describes us as we walk into a room full of others? Are we the "here I am!"...or the "there you are!" type of person? Are we encouraging, optimistic and fun to be with, or are we a self-absorbed, negative, stick-in-the-mud?

Hopefully, we are great company and superb in recharging others. However, in the event our relationships have been slipping, let's make a new commitment to focus on refreshing others. Hit the relational "reset" button and get busy being good company. Let's be a breath of fresh air to those in our world and the kind of person others look forward to being around!

Let the refreshing begin!

Read It! Acts 3:19

Speak It! "Father, I am so thankful for the great people You have put in my life. They are so fun, encouraging, interesting and refreshing! I ask You to help me be the kind of person who lifts others. I want to be a breath of fresh air to others. Help me to be good company and focused on refreshing those around me with joy, encouragement and laughter. In Jesus' Name, Amen."

DAY 90

(got meat?)

"But he said unto them, 'I have meat to eat that ye know not of. ... My meat
is to do the will of him that sent me, and to finish his work.'"
John 4:32, 34, KJV

Jesus made an interesting statement. He was talking about meat. After a long day, His disciples asked Him if He was hungry. He wasn't. He said that doing the will of God *was* His meat—His food. Jesus found satisfaction, strength, energy and nourishment in doing God's will.

Jesus clarified what God's will was in the very next verse: *"...Lift up your eyes, and look on the fields; for they are white already to harvest,'" (verse 35)*. God's will is reaching the harvest—the lost; and when we pursue His will, it becomes meat for us. This meat energizes and satisfies us like nothing else can. So, if we're hungry for "meat," we should start reaching the lost.

Sometimes, something happens to us as we grow in Christ. We get saved, we start walking with Jesus and we're excited about sharing our faith with others. We seem to know instinctively that our number one job is to tell everyone about Jesus—His mercy, forgiveness, joy and peace. We're compelled to preach this good news, and we stay energized and nourished in doing so.

But then, somewhere along the way, we lose sight of our primary purpose. We read our Bibles, begin growing in faith...and sometimes, get weird. We start to believe that our goal is the accumulation of knowledge, revelation and faith. Sometimes Believers say things like, "I need something meaty," or "I don't want milk; I want meat." By that, they often mean they're looking for a deep, spiritual, meaty truth that will feed their spirit and add one more bit of revelation knowledge to their spiritual bank. These things are important and needful; but they are not our primary focus. We can go to every "meaty" conference for Believers and feed ourselves spiritually until we are fat and sassy and still feel something is lacking—we'll still be hungry for meat.

If we need meat to satisfy our internal hunger, our meat is to do the will of God and go after the ripe harvest.

Read It! Matthew 26:39

Speak It! "Father, I want to be like Jesus. I choose to focus on meat that others don't know about. My meat—satisfaction, strength, energy, nourishment—is to do the will of Him that sent me. In obedience to You, I am lifting my eyes up all over my city, neighborhood, workplace and family and I see a massive harvest of lost people. They are hurting, helpless and ripe for harvest. I purpose to share the Gospel with others; to go after the lost...to finish the work...this is my meat. In Jesus' Name. Amen."

DAY 91

(the white flag)

"Therefore submit to God..."
James 4:7a

So, where are you right now in your life? Do you find yourself in the same position—spiritually, physically, mentally, emotionally, or relationally—than you were last year? Are you worse off? Wouldn't you like to let go of last year's frustrations? Obliterate self-induced pressure? Lower your blood pressure, stomp out stress and release the weight of the world? Throw up the white flag and submit to God.

There is something wonderful about submission! Of course, our human nature rebels against the idea of submitting to anyone or anything—right? After all, we are capable and confident, and we can figure it out—or so we think. The only problem with that way of living is that it's the long way to nowhere! When we submit to and follow the Lord, He leads us into His best. He takes us on scenic routes, shows us some amazing sights, connects us to wonderful people and does supernatural things in and through us.

Submitting to God doesn't mean we become brainless, passive, incompetent, spineless zombies. It simply means we are bright enough to recognize that humbly following the God of the universe is a really smart thing to do. To submit means to take our place in rank—to acknowledge that He's the General; we are the privates. He leads; we follow. He's the Boss, and we subordinate ourselves to His leadership, wisdom, authority, experience and love. It's really a place of great freedom.

A couple of years ago, I made a point to re-submit to God! I intentionally spent some time in prayer to place myself under His Lordship for the upcoming new year—and the rest of my life! I wanted my Father, Jesus and the Holy Spirit to know that I specifically chose to submit my life (spirit, soul and body) to His will, plans and purposes. I asked Him for the wisdom, grace and strength I would need to follow through. There were no fireworks or goose bumps, but there was an immediate sense of freedom, peace, expectancy and joy!

God won't force our submission. He's not a dictator; He's a loving, heavenly Father. He gives us the option and the free will to choose submission to Him. If we've not already done so, let's intentionally submit to God today!

Read It! Romans 8:7, NIV

Speak It! "Father, I submit to You. I throw up the white flag, and I choose to subordinate myself (spirit, soul and body) to You—Father, Jesus and Holy Spirit. I ask You to give me the wisdom, grace and strength I need to follow through! In Jesus' Name. Amen."

DAY 92

(revitalized and reinvigorated)

"And if the Spirit of him who raised Jesus from the dead is living in you, he
who raised Christ from the dead will also give life to your mortal bodies
through his Spirit, who lives in you."
Romans 8:11, NIV

Need God's healing power today? Need a boost of the Holy Spirit's power in
your mortal body? Need a dose of God's revitalization and reinvigoration?

The power of the Holy Spirit gives life to our mortal bodies. Not only in the
future resurrection; but by faith, we can count on His resurrection power to be
at work in our bodies now—each day. Anytime we face any sickness or something coming against our mortal, physical body, we can begin to talk to the
Lord and get the plan for His quickening, revitalizing and reinvigorating power.

A few years ago, I woke up in the middle of the night in excruciating pain. Not
sure what I ate, but it wasn't pretty! I needed God's healing power to flow
through my body. Immediately, I started saying what I knew was true, "I
believe I receive God's healing power." I said that over and over as I laid hands
on my body. Then, I did my best to listen to the Lord for the pathway to
complete the quickening process. In less than an hour, I was pain-free.

Sometimes, He leads us to do simple things: rest, change our diets or exercise.
At other times, He leads us to get the right medication, therapy or surgery.
Then, at other times, His healing power quickens our bodies supernaturally.

When we need a touch from the Lord, it's good to know that no matter what
pathway He leads us to follow; He's still in the healing business.

If you need God's healing power today, spend some time talking to the Lord
and get His plan for receiving the revitalizing and reinvigorating power of God
in your mortal body.

Read It! 1 Peter 2:24

Speak It! "Father, I need Your healing power today. I need the power of the Holy
Spirit to heal, quicken, revitalize and reinvigorate my mortal body. (Lay hands on
any part of your body that is sick or in pain and say this.) Right now, I believe I
receive God's healing power. (Say that a few times and meditate on those words.)
Lord, show me Your pathway to complete the quickening power in my mortal
body. In Jesus' Name. Amen."

DAY 93

(help is on the way!)

"Let us therefore come boldly to the throne of grace,
that we may obtain mercy and find grace to help in time of need."
Hebrews 4:16

Need grace for the pace? Facing a time of need? Ever felt like you had just one nostril above water?

In a particular season of my life, when our four kids were preschoolers and we were pioneering a church, I desperately needed grace to help! I needed "grace for the pace." I latched on to this verse and found out I could hang out at God's throne of grace—and I did just that! It seemed like every day I was running to His throne to obtain more grace—grace that would empower me, strengthen me and infuse me with His ability to do all that was before me. What a pleasant reality to discover that God actually dispensed tangible deposits of grace when I asked.

How about you? Need grace for today's pace? Are you in a time of need when the only thing that will help you is God's grace? When God dispenses grace to us, it's a tangible, spiritual deposit of His strength and ability—*that* is super-natural! God's grace is powerful when we receive it from Him and His throne of Grace. Be encouraged. When life seems overwhelming, His grace will be sufficient for us. Do we need an infusion of God's "grace for the pace," His inner strength and tangible empowerment today?

Read It! 2 Corinthians 12:9, NIV

Speak It! "Father, I come to Your throne of grace today to obtain mercy and find grace. I ask You for a big deposit of grace to help and ask You to fill me with Your strength, ability and help to do all that I need to do today. I receive 'grace for the pace' now. In Jesus' Name. Amen."

DAY 94

(yabadabadoo)

"If you praise him in the private language of tongues, God understands you but no one else does, for you are sharing intimacies just between you and him. I'm grateful to God for the gift of praying in tongues that he gives us for praising him, which leads to wonderful intimacies we enjoy with him."
1 Corinthians 14:2, 18a, MSG

Are we looking for a way to get closer to God? Wanting a deeper sense of His presence or reality in our life? He's given us a wonderful gift for doing so—speaking in the private language of tongues.

Unfortunately, the subject of speaking in tongues has been so misrepresented, many people have no idea what it is, who it's for or what the purpose or benefits of speaking in tongues are. Some people have heard such freakazoid stories about this topic, they have more fear than faith when it comes to experiencing one of God's finest gifts.

Speaking in tongues in our private prayer life is a gift for every Believer who desires more of God. Jesus said when we are thirsty and come to Him, a river of living water will flow out of our innermost being—that includes the private language of tongues. This private language of tongues is just that...a special language where we communicate to the Lord from our heart just between us and Him. It's one of the most intimate ways to spend time with the Lord. When we speak in tongues, we're praising the Lord, thanking Him, loving Him, and praying about things in our future—and so much more!

I've spoken in tongues in my private prayer life now for over 28 years, and I can tell you that it is as normal as breathing air. I can't imagine my life without this wonderful gift any more than I can imagine my life without oxygen! Don't worry—you don't have to say, "Yabadabadoo," go into a "trance," lose control or make up words in your mind. Simply yield to the Lord and allow the Holy Spirit to fill you. The result is, the Lord will give you the ability to speak to Him from your heart-of-hearts in a language only your spirit knows, not your mind.

If you desire a more personal, heartfelt, intimate, deeply personal relationship with the Lord, it's available! Ask the Holy Spirit to fill you to the fullest and yield your heart to the Lord. Speak whatever words or phrases He puts in your heart.

Read It! Acts 2; 1 Corinthians 14:14-15

Speak It! "Father, I thirst for a more personal, free, heartfelt relationship with You. Fill me with Your Holy Spirit right now. Help me yield to You, so I may enjoy this wonderful gift of the private language of tongues. In Jesus' Name. Amen."

DAY 95

(crinnovative)

"Each of you must take responsibility for doing the creative best you can with
your own life."
Galatians 6:5, MSG

I remember reading *A Whack on the Side of the Head* by Roger von Oech in the
80's and *The Pursuit of Wow* by Tom Peters in the 90's and being stirred to my
toes about the limitless, creative, "not-life-as-usual" possibilities. I remember
thinking, "With God, things don't have to be the same old, same old...and in
fact they should not be!"

Back in the 80's, before being creative was cool, I used to teach a little seminar
called, "Be Creative." Funny thing is, what we considered "creative" back then
would be considered extremely boring by today's standards! In recent years, we
have been inspired by some of God's most creative pastors, whose example has
given us "permission" to unleash the creative power of God in our church. The
"not-church-as-usual" approach has been fun, refreshing and fruitful.

God has been anointing people to invent, devise, create and design things
for His purposes for ages. It's always been the Lord's plan to fill architects,
engineers, writers, preachers, musicians, worshippers, builders, craftsmen,
designers, tailors, weavers and all kinds of artists with His creative anointing,
so they could help others know and worship God! As Christians, with the
Creator living on the inside of us, we ought to be the most creative and
innovative people around! (Thus, my new word: crinnovative!)

So, what about you? Ready to crack some creativity? Initiate some innovation?
There is no doubt God wants to do something unique and amazing through
you. What creative, out-of-the-box, off-the-cuff, outside-the-lines and off-the-
beaten-track stuff does the Lord have for your life? Your family? Your kids?
Your business? Your wealth? Your influence? Your ministry? Your church?

Jump-start your creative juices by getting around creative people! Start a
creative team for your biz/department. Read books that inspire innovation.
Go to a concert or play and soak in the creativity. Visit new places—an art
museum, a hip restaurant, Times Square or a coffee shop—and take note of
the colors, lights, design and aesthetics. Then, listen to His voice and discern
how to add more "crinnovation" into your life!

Read It! Exodus 31:2-6

Speak It! "Father, thank You for Your creative, innovative, inventive, artistic
anointing. I will yield to it in every area of my life. In Jesus' Name. Amen."

DAY 96

(still kicking)

"With long life I will satisfy him, and show him My salvation."
Psalm 91:16

How long do you plan to be alive and kicking? How many more years do you have left to serve God? Reach people for Christ? Pour into your kids? Grandkids? Impact this world?

Let's get a vision for long life! Let's not allow the enemy to talk us into being old, weak, tired or weary before our time! If we will take hold of God's Word and His promises for long life and be doers of the Word, we will qualify for God's highest and best.

According to God's Word, we can believe Him for a long life—at least 70 or 80 years strong! Here are a few Scripture passages to meditate on. These give us hope and faith for our future. God's Word promises us...

- **70 or 80 years.** *(Psalm 90:10a, NIV)*
- **Life until we're satisfied.** *(Psalm 91:16)*
- **To prolong our life.** *(Proverbs 3:1-2, NIV)*
- **To live long.** *(Ephesians 6:1-3)*
- **Long life.** *(Proverbs 3:15-16, NIV)*
- **Length to our life.** *(Proverbs 10:27, NIV)*
- **Our years will be many.** *(Proverbs 4:7-10, NIV)*
- **We will enjoy long life.** *(Deuteronomy 6:2, NIV)*
- **Old age.** *(Psalm 92:13-14)*

Footnote: We realize that sometimes, for reasons we don't always understand, some people die before their time. We don't always understand the "whys" of those things, but we can thank God that no matter how we slice it, as a Christian, we win! To depart from this life means we get to be with the Lord! Be encouraged to live a long, fruitful life; knowing that when our time expires, we get to be with Jesus for eternity!

Read It! Proverbs 16:31, NLT

Speak It! "Father, I want to live a long life and honor You. I thank You that You will satisfy me with a long life. I ask You to strengthen me in my spirit, soul and body. Help me to live a life filled with wisdom and obedience to Your Word—so that I may bear all kinds of fruit in old age and remain fresh and flourishing! In Jesus' Name. Amen."

DAY 97

(Teflon®)

"No weapon formed against you shall prosper, and every tongue
which rises against you in judgment you shall condemn."
Isaiah 54:17

I love this verse! No weapon formed against us shall prosper! Every tongue
that rises against us, we shall condemn! We are like Teflon®!

Of course, there will always be adversaries, critics and contrarians, but they
shall not prosper! God is our vindicator. Jesus is our justifier. The Lord is our
defender.

What's our job? What are we to do?

Have no fear! Weapons may come against us—lies, lawyers, editorials, jealousy,
fears, intimidation, anger and hatred—our job is to stay steady, strong and
stand still! God will see to it that those weapons do not prosper! Tongues may
rise against us—people flapping at the jaw in judgment against us—and we
have permission to declare it is wrong! We condemn, refute and dismiss every
accusation.

We are covered in God's Teflon®! Be encouraged and stamp this on your heart
and mind today: *"No weapon formed against you will prosper!"*

Read It! 1 John 4:4, KJV

Speak It! "Father, thank You for Your good Word! I believe it—no weapon formed
against me shall prosper! You have surrounded me with supernatural Teflon®! I
will refute and dismiss every tongue that rises against me in judgment. Jesus
always causes me to triumph in Christ. In Jesus' Name. Amen."

DAY 98

(clutter)

"Keep your heart with all diligence, for out of it spring the issues of life."
Proverbs 4:23

Are you looking for your center? Your core? Your personal headquarters? It's your heart! We contact the physical world through our bodies. We contact the mental world through our minds. We contact God and His spiritual world through our heart. All the issues of life spring out of our heart. Our heart is our personal headquarters for every issue of life—our walk with God, marriage, family and kids, friendships, financial and career decisions—and every choice we make.

The Lord places His wisdom, leading, direction and will in our hearts, and we want to listen and follow those things! Because our heart is so central to all the issues of our life, it's imperative that we guard our heart and keep this "headquarters" clear. There is just one problem: heart clutter!

Just like our newly-organized drawers eventually turn into disorganized, clutter-filled junk drawers; our heart can also get filled with clutter if we don't guard it.

Clutter like...

- **Busyness.** It's hard to hear our hearts and follow the things that God puts there when we are too busy to listen to Him. Remember Martha? *(Luke 10:38)*

- **Voices.** There are many voices these days—the media, advertisers, friends, family, enemies, unforgiveness, hurt...even our own voices—all fiercely vying for our attention. Let's keep our heart tuned into God's voice and His Word.

- **Guilt.** It clutters our heart. When we rebel or disobey God, we feel legitimate guilt. If we'll apply 1 John 1:9 by confessing our sins, then we can receive God's forgiveness and will be free to live from our hearts—with no guilt! Sometimes, the enemy throws illegitimate or false guilt—a sense of unworthiness and shame—on us to discourage, condemn, overwhelm and destroy us. We need to stand on 2 Corinthians 5:21 and declare that through Jesus, we have been made the righteousness of God in Christ...end of story. Amen!

- **Fear.** Another biggie. Through fear of man, fear of losing our security, fear of living by faith, fear of loss—fear of just about anything—we live in anxiety, and the enemy gums up our heart and robs us of the ability to follow our hearts. We have to kick fear out!

Read It! Proverbs 4:23, MSG

Speak It! "Father, I will guard my heart more diligently! I can see that it is my personal headquarters and the very place where You contact me. Help me to keep my heart clutter-free so I can follow Your voice! In Jesus' Name. Amen."

DAY 99

(broken tooth)

"Confidence in an unfaithful man in time of trouble
is like a broken tooth or a foot out of joint."
Proverbs 25:19, AMP

Wanna be a major pain? Be unfaithful. Wanna drive people nuts? Be unreliable.

Ever had a broken tooth or a dislocated joint? I have. It's no fun. It's a pain. It's distracting. It's a big hindrance. Need I go on?

Years ago, we rented motor-scooters in Rome. I figured if Mary Kate and Ashley could do it, so could we! Well, I should have listened to the Holy Spirit; because about an hour after renting the bikes, I crashed into Jeff and my son at an intersection near the Coliseum. Nothing like making a scene—a giant 6' 6" man and 5' 10" lady sprawled out on the streets of Italy! The result? Besides shock, road-rash and complete embarrassment? I broke two toes. The rest of our trip was affected because I couldn't move too fast; crutches were cumbersome and my foot hurt!

An unfaithful person—especially in time of trouble—is just like a broken tooth or a dislocated foot. In other words, a big hindrance! On the other hand, a faithful person is a big blessing!

Faithful people are hard to come by. Would we like to set ourselves apart today? Then, let's be faithful, reliable. Let's be people of our word and do what we say we will do. Fulfill our commitments. Be the kind of people those around us can count on. The Bible says, *"A faithful man will abound with blessings...,"* (Proverbs 28:20a).

Let's not be a pain. Today, let's choose to be faithful, and we will blessed!

Read It! Proverbs 20:6

Speak It! "Father, I repent for being unfaithful and unreliable. I am sorry for the pain I have caused those who have counted on me. I want to be known as a faithful, reliable person. I ask You for Your grace and Your help as I start a new era of my life—I will be faithful to You. I will be faithful to my family, and I will be faithful to those who are counting on me. In Jesus' Name, Amen."

DAY 100

(your generation)

*"...for after David had served his generation according to the will of God,
he died and was buried..."*
Acts 13:36, NLT

This is one of those life-guiding verses for me. I feel a great sense of obligation to my generation. I am a "Baby Boomer." Boomers were born between 1946 and 1964. These days, we are anywhere from 44-64 years old. We grew up with bell-bottom jeans, Led Zeppelin, the Beatles, Coca-Cola®, lava lamps, *Gilligan's Island* and flower power. Our generation—all 76 million of us—is the largest generation ever! We impacted everything: fashion, food, music, schools, transportation, culture—and most notably, technology!

Boomers had kids, a.k.a. the "Baby Bulge" generation, who were born between 1979 and 1994. This generation is 60-million strong and between 15-30 years old. Our kids are the second largest generation ever. They go by a host of taglines: "Generation Y," "Echo Boomers" or the "Millennium Generation," and they are extremely tech savvy! The Boomers and the Baby Bulge generations combined are over 140 million strong! So, what could happen if Believers—parents and kids from the Boomers and the Bulge—got serious about taking the Gospel to their generations? What if we got very proactive in using every tool, including technology, to connect with and serve our generation? We could impact the planet for Jesus Christ!

If you haven't already, why not get started going after your generation? Here are several ways you can use the latest technology:

- **Join Facebook®** (www.facebook.com) to connect with old and new friends. Find ways to serve your generation on Facebook through prayer, preaching, evangelism, sharing resources and networking.
- **Join Twitter®** (www.twitter.com) and follow people who share your interests. It's a great place to communicate in real time and share resources, links, and blogs with your generation.
- Check out these online social communities to connect with other Believers: www.cfaith.com, www.crosswalk.com.

Whatever generation we're a part of, let's do what David did and serve our own generation.

Read It! Exodus 3:15, NIV

Speak It! "Father, there are so many ways to reach my generation. I feel a great sense of obligation to the people in my culture. Help me to share Christ and His Word through utilizing technology for Your purposes! Help me to serve my generation fully according to Your will. In Jesus' Name. Amen."

DAY 101

(do hard things)

"Don't be afraid! Speak out! Don't be silent! For I am with you, and no one will harm you because many people here in this city belong to Me."
Acts 18:9b-10, NLT

Sometimes, God calls us to do hard things—things we don't feel qualified to do, things that make us "fear and tremble," things we have to lean on Him to accomplish. It was 1991. Jeff felt the Lord leading us to start a church to reach Southwest Michigan and beyond. In my heart-of-hearts, I knew it was what the Lord wanted; but in the natural, I had some concerns:

- **Could we do it?** We had just come out of a difficult season. We didn't know anyone in Kalamazoo, MI; Meghan and Annie were preschoolers, and I was pregnant with Luke. How do you raise kids and start a church from scratch?
- **Would people accept a husband/wife pastoral team?** Jeff and I had always worked together as a ministry team—he, the strong business-minded leader and I, the mom who taught and wrote a lot. I was aware that some religious people didn't welcome the idea of women in ministry—much less teaching or leading in a church. Was I ready for the certain criticism?
- **Did the Lord really want us to start a church?** Could we really start a Bible-preaching, charismatic, outreach-flavored, faith church, where traditional conservative churches dominated the landscape? What if people didn't come?

There was a great temptation to run from the whole idea...until one day, out-of-the-blue, while driving around, I heard the Holy Spirit speak this scripture to my heart. Instantly, I believed God's Word, and faith and courage came. The most encouraging phrase was the last one: *"...many people in this city belong to Me."* To me, it meant two things. First, there were people in our city who already belonged to Jesus but had quit church and needed encouragement, relevant Bible teaching and a vision to follow. Secondly, there were people in our city who didn't know Jesus and were lost, discouraged and feeling hopeless.

Years later, we can say the Lord was and is faithful to His Word and Jesus is the God of this city. How about you? Feel called to do hard things? God is faithful. You can do it!

Read It! Joshua 10:25, NIV

Speak It! "Father, You are the God of my city. Help me to overcome my inabilities and fears and do the hard things. I will not be afraid; I will not be silent. You are with me, and You have called me. I believe many people in my city belong to You. Help me to encourage and reach them with the Gospel. In Jesus' Name. Amen."

DAY 102

(light it up)

"The light shines through the darkness,
and the darkness can never extinguish it."
John 1:5, NLT

I love this! It's like a big, "in-your-face" truth. Darkness cannot extinguish the light! No matter how hard it tries, darkness can never overpower light.

I remember a trip to the Mammoth Cave when we were kids. We were deep inside the cave when our tour guide turned off the lights. You couldn't see your hand in front of you. It was the darkest darkness I've ever experienced; you could cut it with a knife. Within moments, he lit a single match, and it lit up the darkness. No matter how hard the darkness tried, it could not extinguish the light from that match.

Light overcomes darkness—always.

Darkness can never overcome light—ever.

What does that mean to you and me? It means that no matter what, you win! Jesus, the Light of the world, lives in us; and no matter how dark the situation may look, darkness cannot put out the light of Christ in us. In fact, just the opposite—light trumps the darkness. Darkness has never—and will never—be able to put out the light of Jesus Christ, the light of Christianity, the light of the Word and the light of Christ-followers around the world.

The light shines through the darkness!

Read It! Matthew 5:14

Speak It! "Father, thank You that Your light always shines through any darkness. May the light of Christ grow brighter and brighter in and through me. Darkness can never extinguish the light! In Jesus' Name. Amen."

DAY 103

(pray it forward)

"But when you pray, go away by yourself, shut the door behind you,
and pray to your Father secretly. Then your Father, Who knows all
secrets, will reward you."
Matthew 6:6, NLT

What's the best and most important piece of advice I can give at any given time? Pray! Pray it forward! In these busy lives we lead, we need "closet time" alone with the Lord—in a closet, a car, a bathtub—some place where we can get alone with the Lord and pray to our Father secretly.

Ever felt "behind" in prayer? I have. It seems like the two things the enemy likes to steal from Christians are: time in the Word and time to pray. The devil knows if he can cut off our communication supply line with heaven, then we're on our own—powerless. When we get too busy to spend time in the Word or in prayer, we start to operate in the energy of the flesh and in our own understanding. We become easy targets for discouragement, fruitless-ness and frustration.

Would you like to spend more time in prayer connected to heaven, praying it forward. If so, pray these things right now:

Father,

I want to be closer to You. You confide in those who spend time with You, and I want to hear Your secrets. (Psalm 25:14) I want to pray prayers that make tremendous power available! I know prayer puts Your power on deposit for anytime I need a withdrawal. (James 5:16) I want to saturate my heart with Your Word, knowing that when I pray according to Your Word, You hear me and will give me the things I have requested. (John 15:7, 1 John 5:14) I want to pray out the future—now. I want to hook up with the Holy Spirit and as I pray with my understanding and in tongues, I know You will help me to pray out Your will for the future. (1 Corinthians 14:2, 13-15) I want to pray so that Your kingdom will come, and Your will is done in my life, in my family, in my church and in all You've called me to do. (Matthew 6:10)

In Jesus' Name. Amen.

Now, let's continue to pray it forward!

Read It! Psalm 91:1

Speak It! "Father, this is my desire: I ask for more grace to make my life dedicated to 'praying it forward.' I know when I pray, according to Your Word, You hear me, and You always answer. In Jesus' Name. Amen."

DAY 104

(who blazed a trail for you?)

"Do you see what this means—all these pioneers who blazed the way, all
these veterans cheering us on? It means we'd better get on with it.
Strip down, start running—and never quit!"
Hebrews 12:1

Who blazed a trail for you? Whose spiritual shoulders are you sitting on?
Sometimes, we forget that the reason we are able to enjoy a strong walk with
God or a place of spiritual maturity is because of the faithful, spiritual pioneers
and veterans who went before us. Today, let's take some time to thank those
whom God has used to give us spiritual freedom and independence.

Who led you to the Lord? Who has taught you the Word? Who has mentored
you? When I think about my own life, there are so many important people
who have helped me spiritually. I have stood on the shoulders of numerous
people and, in various seasons, have been led to thank them in meaningful
ways. I knew it was important to me—and to the Lord—that I give honor and
appreciation to those who have invested into my life and walk with God.

Have you thanked the pioneers and vets in your life lately? I believe that one
of the best things we can do to honor those who have blazed a spiritual trail
for us is to simply live a life that pleases God—with our whole heart! That is:
be an on-fire follower of Jesus, run your race, make an eternal difference and
don't quit! Today, why not pray for and thank the people who gave you big
spiritual shoulders to sit on.

When you're thinking of those who have paved the way for you, don't forget
to remember to honor the pioneers, the military servicemen and women who
have given our country the freedoms we enjoy today.

Read It! Romans 13:7

Speak It! "Father, I thank You for _____ (make mention of the names of
the person[s]) who led me to the Lord, taught me the Word and impacted my life
in an eternal and spiritual way. I appreciate their faithfulness to You and how You
have used them in my life. I pray that You bless them in a significant way today,
and I ask You to show me how to express my gratitude to them in a meaningful
way. Lord, help me to live my life in a way that pleases You and honors their faithfulness. In Jesus' Name. Amen."

DAY 105

(you've got to be kidding)

"Discipline your children while there is hope.
If you don't, you will ruin their lives."
Proverbs 19:18, NLT

Does this verse tell the story or what? How many parents wish they could get a do-over? They loved little Johnny too much to discipline him, and now, big Johnny is ruining his life and theirs with his lack of coping skills, his anger issues, his drug addictions, his inability to keep a job—just one problem after another.

Parents: be advised. Kids need discipline. They want boundaries. Kids want the safety and security that comes with a healthy routine and structure. They want guidelines and consequences when they get outside the boundaries. We can't afford to buy into the psycho-babble of some "modern" parenting gurus; God's Word has the best advice on parenting. How does this play out in real life?

- **Get a plan, work the plan.** Establish a strategy for discipline when our kids are young—very young. Behavior has consequences; they need to learn that early on! Discipline them when they are two, and they'll save us a lot of grief when they are 22.

- **Don't be a wimp; be the parent.** Too many parents are bossed around by their kids. Moms and dads, guess what? We are the "benevolent dictators,"—*you* rule. Kids are pros. We can't be moved by guilt, manipulation, tears, tantrums or tirades! If they learn to submit to our authority now, they'll have a better chance of success as they submit to other authorities in their lives—teachers, coaches, the law, police, etcetera.

- **Establish routine, instill habits.** Kids do better with a little structure. We don't have to be the Gestapo, but we do need to establish some family habits and stick to them. Set a bedtime. Assign chores. Establish computer and Internet guidelines. Go to church regularly. (It's amazing how many parents give their kids "the choice" about attending church. Why? We don't give kids the choice to attend school, do we? No, we don't let our kids call the shots on church or youth group attendance; we make the call.)

When we do the hard work of disciplining them while there is hope, we can enjoy the fruit of our labor for generations to come!

Read It! Psalm 36:8, NIV

Speak It! "Father, thank You for my children. I ask You for Your guidance as I establish and enforce the needed discipline in my home. In Jesus' Name. Amen."

DAY 106

(give a bailout)

"He who is kind to the poor lends to the LORD,
and he will reward him for what he has done."
Proverbs 19:17, NIV

Mark it down! The U.S. government bailout of 2009 will make the history books! With practically everyone getting a bailout these days, why not GIVE a bailout? In particular, Jesus told us to care for the poor, the needy and the less fortunate. Have you considered ways to help the poor?

We've heard a few heartwarming stories of people who are making a concerted effort to extend kindness to the poor. Here are a few to inspire you:

- *A group of friends in Florida decided to forgo their annual gift giving with each other and pooled their resources together to bless a discouraged man and his family. He had just come to Christ and was struggling to start a new business.*

- *One empty nest couple decided to open their nice lake home to a challenged, young couple. Their hope? To help this couple jump start their future by giving them a hand up.*

- *An anonymous business woman decided to adopt a single mom and her daughter over the holidays, and she poured out blessings on them.*

- *More than a dozen churches in our city came together with funds and manpower to help the under-resourced of the world, particularly those affected by the AIDS pandemic in Africa.*

- *Free for Life Ministries founder, Colette Bercu, was watching "48 Hours" when they did an exposé on the travesty of human trafficking, and she decided to do something about it. She started Free for Life to help raise awareness and funds for safe houses that rescue and restore children from labor and sex slavery.*

- *Soles for Souls is an outreach organization founded by Wayne Elsey. When he saw the devastation of the tsunami that hit Southeast Asia, he felt compelled to do something. He started collecting shoes to give to those who needed footwear; and to date, millions of shoes have been given away.*

What could we do to help those less fortunate right now? When we take notice of the poor, God takes it personally. Proverbs 19:17, says, *"If you help the poor, you are lending to the LORD—and He will repay you!"* (NLT).

Read It! Isaiah 1:17, NLT

Speak It! "Father, I will consider the poor. It's a privilege to lend to You and to be used to assist the less fortunate. Lord, show me those You want me to help. In Jesus' Name. Amen."

(still the same)

"Jesus Christ is the same yesterday, today, and forever."
Hebrews 13:8

Great news! Jesus Christ is the same; He hasn't changed. He is the same yesterday, today and forever. What does that mean to us? It means He's alive. He's risen from the dead, and *that* puts Jesus in an entirely different league than any other religious leader on the planet. Jesus couldn't be "the same," if He was dead—but He's not. It also means:

- **He's still doing what He's always done.** If He wasn't, He wouldn't be the same. Jesus, through His Word and by His Spirit, is still revealing the truth about God's kingdom, His purposes and His plans. Jesus is still extending mercy and forgiveness to sinners—prostitutes, adulterers, liars, thieves, murderers—to every person who hasn't been made "perfect."

- **Jesus is still healing.** He wouldn't be the same "today" if He didn't do what He did "yesterday." He is still healing broken hearts, diseased bodies, scarred emotions and every other part of us that is "sick." Jesus is still opening blind eyes, delivering people from demonic bondages and doing miracles for those who believe.

- **He is still giving.** If He was a withholder, He wouldn't be the same; but Jesus is still giving peace, strength, grace, wisdom, favor, food, clothing, good gifts and the power of the Holy Spirit to those who seek Him first and foremost.

What do you need Jesus to do in your life? Jesus said, *"...all things are possible to him who believes,"* (Mark 9:23). Jesus promised He would fill, touch and satisfy those who are thirsty, hungry and desperate for Him. He promised to be found—yesterday, today and forever—by those who believe and seek Him with their whole hearts. (Interestingly, He never promised anything to or for the half-hearted, lukewarm, apathetic, fence-riding, or doubtful person...so let's not be that person!)

Today, let's be ready to seek the Lord and ready to believe. Let's go after Jesus—the One who is the same yesterday, today and forever—with our whole heart!

Read It! Malachi 3:6

Speak It! "Jesus, I do believe that You are the same yesterday, today and forever! I believe You are alive. I believe You are doing today, the very same things You did yesterday. You have not changed; You are the same! Today, I seek You with my whole heart. I am thirsty and hungry for You, Lord. I need Your help in my life in this area: _____, and I ask You to do for me what You have done for others. I trust You. In Your Name, I pray. Amen."

DAY 108

(don't throw gutter balls)

"Do your best in the job you received from the Master. Do your very best."
Colossians 4:17b, MSG

It's okay to do your best. Give God everything you have and allow Him to touch it, multiply it, bless it and maximize it.

For years, I suffered from what I call "gutter ball" syndrome. I was afraid to succeed—for some crazy reason—and I threw "gutter balls" on purpose. Over time, the Lord helped me to gain the confidence I needed, and it was liberating.

Serving the Lord is an interesting thing. On one hand, we need to know that through Christ we can do all things; while at the same time, recognizing that apart from Christ we cannot do anything. A strange, but freeing dichotomy.

If you're feeling unqualified, intimidated and insecure in and of yourself, that's not a bad place to be—just don't stay there. Recognize that apart from Christ, you are unqualified, intimidated and insecure, which is a good place of genuine humility. BUT, through Christ there is confidence, ability and strength to do everything He's called you to do, which is a good place of real faith.

Let this double-edged truth really saturate your heart, and give God your best—no apologies, no gutter balls!

Read It! Ecclesiastes 9:10, NIV

Speak It! "Father, I am not going to throw gutter balls any longer! My trust and confidence are in You! I will give You my best in whatever You have called me to do. Apart from You, I can do nothing—it's true; but through Christ I can do all things! I believe it and today, I will do my best to throw strikes for You. In Jesus' Name. Amen."

DAY 109

(God with us)

"Behold, the virgin shall be with Child, and bear a Son, and they shall
call His name 'Immanuel,' which is translated, 'God with us.'"
Matthew 1:23

When my sisters and I were little girls, we would lay on our beds and talk
about how cool and amazing it was that God became a human being and
walked on the planet He made. The idea that God Almighty became a baby
who grew up and walked on the planet He created just boggled our minds. It's
a thought beyond human understanding.

Have you thought about it lately? God was here...on Planet Earth. Jesus...God
in the flesh. While He was fully the Creator of the universe, He humbled
Himself and became a man so He could save man from himself. God walked
among us. He was here with us. The sad thing is that most people in that day
completely missed His visit.

In all the hustle and bustle of life, the seasons, the holidays, the schedules,
the everyday agendas—let's not miss His visit. Take some time today to
acknowledge, thank and talk to Jesus, our Immanuel. "God with us!"

Read It! John 1:14

Speak It! "Jesus, thank You for stepping out of heaven to visit us. Thank You for
humbling Yourself by becoming a baby and being willing to put on a human body
to visit the planet You created. I praise You for being Immanuel—You are the God
who is still with us. In Jesus' Name. Amen."

DAY 110

(who's drawn to you?)

"Then all the tax collectors and the sinners drew near to Him to hear Him."
Luke 15:1

This verse has always challenged me. Sinners—heathen, non-Christians, unbelievers, godless peeps—were drawn to Jesus to hear Him. What was so winsome and comfortable about Jesus that ungodly people ran to His meetings? We know that Jesus never condoned sin, yet His aroma was so attractive, sinners flocked to hear Him. People didn't run *from* Jesus, they ran *to* Him!

How about us? Is that our desire? Are lost people drawn to us? Or, are they running in the opposite direction? Is the sweet aroma of Christ oozing out of us? Is there something inviting and comfortable about us? Do people want to listen to what we have to say? I find this to be the biggest challenge and most important goal in my life.

Jesus was so full of truth and grace. He was attractive—and He wants us to be just like Him! With God's help, we can continually be conformed to His image, and we'll find sinners drawn to hear us. I am sure this is your desire, just as it is mine. So, let's make this our prayer today and trust the Lord to help us be attractive, winsome Christians who influence our world for Christ.

Read It! Matthew 5:16, NIV

Speak It! "Father, help me to be more like Jesus today! I choose to be a loving, attractive, winsome Christian that others are drawn to. Lord, help the sweet aroma of Christ flow from my words and actions—especially toward those who are ready to know Jesus. In Jesus' Name, Amen."

DAY 111

(everyone needs an Elizabeth)

*"Blessed is she who believed, for there will be a fulfillment
of those things which were told her from the Lord."*
Luke 1:45

Everyone needs an Elizabeth. She was a big encourager. You know the story...
The angel, Gabriel, had given Mary the news that she would supernaturally
conceive a Son—Jesus. A few days after the angel's visit, Mary went to see
someone who she could confide in and celebrate with—her cousin Elizabeth.

Elizabeth must've been one of those people who knew the Lord, probably
a praying person, an encourager, sensitive to the Holy Spirit and full of a sweet
spirit. Why did Mary run to see her? Did she want to tell her the whole
amazing story? Did she need confirmation that she wasn't crazy? Was she
looking for a shoulder to cry on? As soon as Mary came through the door,
Elizabeth perceived God was doing something big in Mary's life. Elizabeth,
being filled with the Spirit, knew Mary needed a big shot of encouragement,
and she immediately spoke a faith-filled blessing over Mary.

Now, stop right here and go to the **Read It!** segment and read the story.

I love the last sentence of Elizabeth's blessing: *"Blessed is she who has believed
that what the Lord has said to her will be accomplished!"* Mary was pregnant
with a promise and took God at His Word. Elizabeth was a faith-filled encourager. She exhorted Mary in her belief that God would fulfill, perform and
accomplish everything He had said. Today, maybe it would sound like this:

> *"Mary, you are blessed girl, and you're not crazy. I have no doubt God is
> doing something supernatural in your life. You are favored by God and have
> been given a special assignment. Mary, God picked you for an amazing role.
> You can do it. I believe in you. You are blessed, so keep believing. Stay strong.
> Don't waver. God is faithful, and He will perform His promises for you."*

Do you have an Elizabeth in your life who's sensitive to the Holy Spirit
and rooting you on? Who's exhorting you to believe God and His Word? Who's
speaking blessings into your life? Or, are YOU an Elizabeth? Are you a "prayer" and perceive the big plans God has for someone in your life? If so, are you
making it a point to speak encouraging blessings to them, cheering them on?

Read It! Luke 1:39-45, NIV

Speak It! "Father, help me to be an 'Elizabeth' for each 'Mary' in my life. Help me
to stay full of Your Spirit so I can perceive when others need encouragement or a
blessing spoken over their lives. I also ask You to send an 'Elizabeth' to me in those
times when I need someone to cheer me on in the faith. In Jesus' Name. Amen."

DAY 112

(your family rocks)

"I will bless those who bless you, and I will curse him who curses you; and in you all the families of the earth shall be blessed."
Genesis 12:3

God wants your family to be blessed. He wants your family to rock this world. God is very into families. He is a Father—the Father of the family of God. It's always been His plan to bless families. God gave Abraham, the father of our faith, many wonderful promises—one, being the promise to bless families. This promise has been passed down through the generations, and it's still available today to those who have Jesus Lord of their lives and are "in Christ." Take a minute and read the **Read It!** segment right now. Okay, good!

Over the years, I've stood on several verses of Scripture—claiming them and doing my best to obey them, so God's blessing would be poured out on our family—and, it's worked. Although our family is far from perfect, we've been blessed and have seen God's amazing grace in our immediate and extended family. These specific verses have meant a lot to me, and perhaps they will encourage you as you believe for God's best in your family:

- *"...as for me and my family, we will serve the LORD."* (Joshua 24:15, NLT)
- *"Praise the LORD! Happy are those who fear the LORD. Yes, happy are those who delight in doing what he commands. Their children will be successful everywhere; an entire generation of godly people will be blessed. They themselves will be wealthy, and their good deeds will never be forgotten."* (Psalm 112:1-3, NLT)
- *"The righteous man leads a blameless life; blessed are his children after him."* (Proverbs 20:7, NIV)
- *"She watches over the affairs of her household and does not eat the bread of idleness. Her children arise and call her blessed; her husband also, and he praises her:...a woman who fears the LORD is to be praised..."* (Proverbs 31:27-28, 30b, NIV)

We are in Christ; and as we walk in obedience to God's Word, we can declare that our families are blessed!

Read It! Galatians 3:16, 26-29

Speak It! "Father, I declare my family is blessed—no matter what it looks like at the moment! We are in Christ and are heirs according to the promises. As for me and my house, we will serve the Lord. I thank You that Your amazing grace is changing, shaping and molding all of us. By faith, I declare that in Christ, my family is blessed to be a blessing! In Jesus' Name. Amen."

DAY 113

(God cares)

"...the Father of compassion and the God of all comfort, who comforts us in all our troubles, so that we can comfort those in any trouble with the comfort we ourselves have received from God."
2 Corinthians 1:3b-4, NIV

Just maybe you need to be reminded today that God cares. He really cares about you. Perhaps you've lost a loved one in the past year, and you are going through all of the "firsts." First birthday, first anniversary, first holiday season, first time going to an all-church function—all these firsts, and without them. It can be the toughest year of your life. Or, maybe you're single and feeling lonely. It's possible you're heartbroken about something. Maybe you're going through a rough season, a dry patch—spiritually. Maybe you can't remember the last time you laughed hard—or even at all? God understands the deepest places in your heart today. The psalmist said, *"Deep calls to deep..."*—the deep places in God call to the deep places in our hearts. Yes, God cares.

He is the *"Father of compassion"* and *"the God of all comfort"* (2 Corinthians 1:3, NIV). Do you need a little compassion? Need God's comfort? Sometimes, we feel so much discouragement or pain, we wonder if anyone could possibly care or understand. But, God does. If there is any compassion or comfort to be found, He is the Author, Supplier, Father and God of it. He will comfort you in *all* your troubles. No matter what you are going through, call out to the Lord. He's a compassionate Father and the God Who will give you all the comfort you need—for all your troubles.

Don't worry. It will happen. Your pain and heartache will be replaced with God's soothing comfort and joy. You'll laugh again. Your heart will be healed. Your soul will be restored. After you have been comforted, you'll be able to comfort others with what you have received from the Lord. After a while, something good will come out of the troubles you've experienced. When you've been through something others are going through and have experienced the reality of God's compassion, you are in a unique position to really comfort others.

Today, if you need a special touch from your Heavenly Father, ask Him to pour out His compassion and comfort on you.

Read It! Psalm 119:50, NIV

Speak It! "Father, I believe You care about me. You are the Father of compassion and the God of all comfort. You comfort me in *all* my troubles. I need Your compassion and comfort today, so I ask You to touch my heart and mind in a special way. I know You will heal my broken heart; I will laugh again, and I'll comfort others with the comfort You give to me. In Jesus' Name. Amen."

DAY 114

(get the life!)

"I came that they may have and enjoy life,
and have it in abundance (to the full, till it overflows)."
John 10:10, AMP

You know, sometimes we just need to be reminded why Jesus came to Planet Earth. And, why did He? Very simple. So you and I could have LIFE. He defined the type of life He wants us to have: a life in abundance...to the full, till it overflows!

Don't ever forget this basic truth. Jesus is good, and His highest and best is that we have and a full, abundant LIFE. If we are ever going to be a blessing to others, we must tap into this LIFE.

God's definition of this type of life can be seen in creation. If you've ever seen a fruit tree full of apples, peaches or cherries, then you know that during its peak season, it's full and overflowing with fruit. Some fruit ends up being picked and eaten; other fruit falls to the ground, is stepped on and rots. That's God's idea of abundance and overflow. We look at the unused, overflowing fruit and think, "What a waste!" But, God looks at the overflow of apples, peaches or cherries that never get used, and He calls it abundance! God is not stingy, and He is not the God of the "get by." During this season of economic ups and downs and the high price of gas, it's a great time to refresh your faith in the God of more than enough and His laws of abundant LIFE.

If our lives are not defined by "abundance" in various areas—love, peace, joy, contentment, wisdom, compassion, boldness, resources, wealth, strength, health—or other spheres of our lives, we can begin to believe God today. Let's talk to the Lord about His strategy, His plan and any adjustments we need to make to enter into all that He has for us.

While the life of abundance is progressive—and we are all at various seasons in our experience of that LIFE—let's be encouraged today as we move forward. Remember, it's God's will that we are "blessed to be a blessing," and it starts with experiencing His abundant LIFE...to the full, till it overflows!

Read It! Matthew 7:11

Speak It! "Jesus, I believe it. I believe You want me to experience the abundant LIFE...to the full, till it overflows! Today, I agree with Your Word. I want to be blessed to be a blessing! I ask You to help me understand and walk in Your strategies and laws of abundance and make any necessary adjustments. I declare today that by Your grace, I will experience LIFE—in abundance...to the full, till it overflows—in various areas of my life! I am blessed to be a blessing to others. In Jesus' Name, Amen."

124

DAY 115

(others)

"Don't think only about your own affairs,
but be interested in others, too, and what they are doing."
Philippians 2:4, NLT

In his final address to the officers of the Salvation Army, founder, William Booth, stood before his audience and said, "Others," and sat down. What a speech! The Salvation Army is all about...OTHERS!

What a great reminder to us. Being interested in others is a lost art these days. We all get so consumed with our affairs, busyness, details, schedules and checklists, that we forget it's really not about us. I don't know how it works; but somehow when we put others first, God has a way of putting us first on His list.

Who in our world needs our attention? Who needs a visit? A phone call? A note? A lunch date with us? Or, maybe even just a coffee or a short e-mail of encouragement.

One major way to focus on others is to show an interest in what they are doing. What challenges are they facing? What project are they working on? What joy or accomplishment have they achieved? Have we taken time to let them know we have noticed? Are we praying? Are we rejoicing with them?

Being interested in others will make us a member in a very small club. The key to being an interesting person is to be interested—interested in others. The secret to being interested is to learn how to ask questions...about them.

Read It! Luke 10:27, NLT

Speak It! "Father, it's not about me! It's about others. Help me to focus on others and not be so self-conscious. Help me to ask questions and seek You. I ask for Your help, Lord, so I can become genuinely interested in others. In Jesus' Name. Amen."

DAY 116

(give the gift of honor)

"'Honor your father and mother'—which is the first commandment
with a promise—that it may go well with you and that you may
enjoy long life on the earth."
Ephesians 6:2-3, NIV

What can we give our parents for any special day? Birthday? Christmas?
Father's Day? Mother's Day? How about...honor? It will totally bless them, and
the Lord will honor you. Two things are guaranteed to those who honor their
parents: one, things will go well with them; and, two, they will enjoy a long life
on the earth. Sounds like a very good deal, doesn't it?

We have to consider creative ways to honor our parents. If we've been
blessed with good parents, how can you honor them? Is there something
they've desired that we can provide? Perhaps, you've not had perfect parents?
How can you show them honor anyway? Focus on the good things and find a
way to bless them. Most of our parents don't need more "stuff."

So, what do they want? Here are a few things:

- **Thanks.** Some parents want acknowledgment and thanks, so try writing them a
  note to thank them for being your mom or dad?
- **Success.** Most parents want their kids to succeed, stay off drugs and be nice to
  others. How about letting your folks know that, in honor of them, you are
  making a commitment to do those very things from here on out?
- **Time.** Many parents want "time." They want time with their kids and/or grandkids. How can we honor our parents with our time? Can we give up something
  to spend some time with them or treat them to a dream trip?

*Special Note: If our parents are not living, we should continue to honor their
memory, and the Lord, in turn, will honor us.*

What are we willing to do to honor our parents? Unfortunately, this generation
doesn't know a lot about honor. We live in a culture that seems to disrespect
most things—including parents. So, why not set the standard in our families
and show our kids how to honor others as we make a decision to focus on
honoring our parents. If we want things to go well with us and want to live
long on the earth, we need to honor our mother and father.

Read It! Proverbs 19:6, NLT

Speak It! "Father, thank You for my mom and dad. Help me to honor them in a
way that honors You. In Jesus' Name. Amen."

DAY 117

(pleasure)

"Let the LORD be magnified, Who has pleasure
in the prosperity of His servant."
Psalm 35:27

A friend of mine made a great statement. She said her goal in life was to give God pleasure. I pondered her statement, and this verse came to mind. God gets pleasure when we prosper. Ever thought about it that way? If we want to give God pleasure, we need to do well and prosper in every way; so others can see what a great God we serve. It's a wonderful reflection on the Lord when His children succeed, prosper, are blessed, well-adjusted and full of love, joy, peace, generosity and humility.

Sadly, many Christians think the opposite is true. They think God's most pleased when they're poor, struggling, defeated, living on "barely-get-along-street." They can't imagine God wanting their lives to be blessed and prosperous. They see God, the Father, as an abusive, manipulative, twisted Father. Nothing could be further from the truth! What would you think of a father who took pleasure when his child failed, struggled or couldn't make ends meet? Worse, what would you think about that father if he actually "caused" them to fail or struggle, just to teach them a lesson or humble them?

The Bible says God is good all the time, and He's a giver of good gifts. He takes pleasure in the prosperity of His servants. If you're serving the Lord, it means...

- **When the stock market's going south or the banks collapse, you can shout for joy and know that God has a plan for your victory!**
- **When the doctor gives you a bad report, you are courageous because you know the God who heals, gives wisdom and orders your steps.**
- **When your relationships are being tested, you keep walking in love no matter the outcome, because God's love never fails.**

The Holy Spirit knows the things to come. He'll give insight on what to do, how to live in peace, how to tap into joy, how to walk in divine health and how to connect with others. He'll help you know when to make investments, where to buy and sell property, when to pursue a witty idea or opportunity. Why? He takes great delight in your prosperity. Wanna give God pleasure? Do well and prosper!

Read It! Proverbs 10:22

Speak It! "Father, I believe it! You take pleasure in my prosperity. You are a good God and You're good all the time. I want to live my life in such a way as to give You pleasure. Help me to walk in faith and in Your wisdom and do so... In Jesus' Name. Amen."

127

DAY 118

(women with issues)

"And a certain woman, which had an issue..."
Mark 5:25, KJV

Got issues? Most people do. "Issues" are God's specialty!

Jesus touched a certain lady who had a serious issue—a messy, long-standing, limiting, embarrassing bleeding disease—and she was healed. Have you been struggling with any issues? First, read her story in the **Read It!** segment, and let's take a look at what happened to this woman that changed her life!

Now that you've read her story... How did this woman overcome a 12-year, stump-the-doctors, messy, major issue?

- **She heard...**about Jesus. The Bible says, *"faith comes by hearing...," (Romans 10:17).* She'd heard so many things about Jesus, her faith grew and she was expectant! She didn't allow herself to wallow in self-pity. She wasn't passive; she was full of faith and proactively seeking Jesus for healing!

- **She said...**words within herself. She believed in her heart that Jesus could—and would—heal her. She said in her heart, "When I touch His garment, I will be healed," putting her faith in action! The Bible describes this principle of faith, *"...we also believe; and therefore we speak," (2 Corinthians 4:13).*

- **She felt...**she was healed. Can you imagine how amazing that must have been for her? To have touched Jesus and felt God's healing power flow into her body?

Jesus commended her faith and said, *"Daughter, thy faith hath made thee whole; go in peace, and be whole of thy plague."* Notice that He didn't say, "Daughter, as God in the flesh it was My faith that has made you whole..." In this case, it wasn't God's sovereignty that healed her; Jesus said it was *her* faith that touched Him and drew out His healing power that made her whole. She heard...faith came. She said...faith was released. She felt...faith resolved her issue!

Need faith to overcome your issue? Spend time "hearing" God's Word on your issue, and faith will come! Faith comes by hearing. What are you saying? Get your mouth in agreement with God's Word and declare your outcome by faith. Stay strong. Through faith and patience, God's power will flow into your life, and His wisdom and guidance will heal your issue.

Read It! Mark 5:25-34, KJV

Speak It! "Jesus, I believe You are my Healer. Help me to hear Your Word more clearly and more purposefully. Help me to speak words that are more congruent with Your will, Your Word and what I believe in my heart. Today, I believe I receive God's help and healing power to overcome my issues. In Jesus' Name. Amen."

DAY 119

(edit your life)

"GOD rewrote the text of my life when I opened
the book of my heart to His eyes."
Psalm 18:24, MSG

Ever wanted a do-over? Rewrite chapters of your life? Hit "control-z" on seasons you've been through? Or, wondered if God had a plot for your life? Who hasn't?

Good news. We can, and He does! Perhaps, we've had seasons where we tried to write chapters of our lives on our own—without the Lord—and ended up with a dark thriller. It's not over for us. We can start over, get a second chance. The Lord has so many more chapters to write in our lives! When we walk with the Lord, He writes and rewrites the text of our lives into a combination of God-filled mystery, romance, sci-fi and drama! Good things are ahead for us.

If we want the remaining chapters of our lives to be full of God's perfect, pleasing and good will, Romans 12:1-2 tells us how. The editing process starts with offering ourselves to God and being surrendered to Him and His purposes. Then, the big transformation—the editing, rewriting—comes by renewing our minds. When we renew our minds with God's thoughts, we will be transformed day by day. We don't have to strive or strain to transform, edit or rewrite our own lives. In fact, *we* can't transform anything; we just allow the Lord to transform us. "Renewing of minds" means we reprogram and renovate our minds with the truth of God's Word.

When the Lord tells us we can be transformed—edited, rewritten—He's literally talking about a complete metamorphosis of our personality and life. We can get a do-over! It's true! A year from now we can be different people; we can be changed!

In real life, that means we make a choice to give our attention to His Word, day and night. We intentionally study the Bible to learn and understand more about God and how He operates. We make time to discover the laws by which His kingdom works and how to cooperate with them. We purposefully read the Bible to get to know the character and Person of our Father, Jesus and the Holy Spirit. When we do that, God does the work of editing, rewriting and transforming us! Simple? Yes. Profound? Yes. Supernatural? Absolutely!

Read It! Romans 12:1-2, NIV

Speak It! "Father, I open my heart and surrender to You. I need a do-over and some serious 'editing' in areas of my life. Help me renew my mind in Your Word and rewrite the text of my life. In Jesus' Name. Amen."

DAY 120

(the spirit of generosity)

"The generous prosper and are satisfied; those who refresh others
will themselves be refreshed."
Proverbs 11:25, NLT

So, how do you get ahead in these uncertain economic times? What's the best route to take to beat the recession?

Be generous! I know. It sounds a bit unconventional and definitely goes against all logic, mathematics and rules of self-preservation. It's God's way, nonetheless.

If we want to be prosperous, satisfied and refreshed, then we should be generous and refresh others. Give our words generously. Give our caring heart generously. Give our wealth generously—even if it's something small.

Need a couple of ideas? Try one of these:

- Buy a co-worker or friend their favorite candy bar—unexpectedly.
- Insist on giving a tired and worn-out mom an hour of free babysitting.
- Buy a drink at your favorite fast food place or coffee shop and take it to a friend or co-worker.
- Post something positive on someone's Facebook® wall about who they are and how they make a difference.
- Pay for someone's lunch—even if you don't know them.
- See someone at the grocery check stand fumbling trying to scrape change together? Just hand the clerk the money and tell them to have a great day!
- Gift a friend or relative with a subscription to their favorite magazine—a good, godly one, of course!
- Sponsor a child for a school or youth trip, event.

The list could go on and on. Bottom line? Let's refresh the people around us with kindness. Who gets to taste prosperity? The generous. Who gets to be refreshed? Those who refresh others.

Read It! Luke 6:38, NIV

Speak It! "Father, I am going to do things Your way. I am not going to be caught up in the fear and anxiety of this world's economy. I trust You for wisdom to be a good financial manager, and I thank You for Your promises to the generous. I receive it! In Jesus' Name. Amen."

DAY 121

(the visit)

"...because you did not recognize the time of God's coming to you."
Luke 19:44, NIV

I marvel at the thought that God visited the planet He made. Think about it. God Almighty—the Most High God—took on a body and came to those He created. God visited man! There was just one problem... Many didn't want Him!

Jesus, the Creator of the ends of the earth, came to His own, and they didn't receive Him! Unbelievable, right? Yes, Jesus—"Emmanuel, God with us"—was born as a baby in a manger, a stall. Jesus was God in the flesh, living in the Middle East, working as a carpenter, kickin' the dirt He'd used to make Adam—and people were clueless as to His real identity! The King of kings and Lord of lords walked among men performing miracles, healing the sick, walking on water; and yet, many people completely missed or rejected His visit! Signs were everywhere, but they didn't get it! They didn't recognize God coming to them and missed the day of their visitation! Maybe they were too analytical, philosophical, religious or just too proud? Can you believe it?

Sadly, for some, it's the same today. God-signs are all over the place, and people still miss it! Creation reveals our infinite Creator. Volumes have been written about Jesus. Bibles are easily accessible for the majority of the people on earth. Millions of Christians give eye-witness accounts of the Jesus who has saved, healed, mended, blessed and changed their lives. Many tell stories of God's mercy, protection and miraculous help in their time of trouble. The Internet gives people instant access to any bit of Jesus-knowledge they desire. Churches offer every style of worship service known to man in an effort to reach out to people. Global headlines confirm—and current events fulfill—predictions God gave us in His Word thousands of years ago. Yet, in spite of all of these things—whether it's apathy, laziness, indifference, philosophy, religion or hardness of heart—some still have not received or recognized God's visit to man through Jesus Christ. Sadly, the consequences are eternal.

Have we recognized God's presence and visitation in our own lives? Heard His still, small voice, His direction? Felt His heart? His compassion? His purpose? Let's not miss out on the time of God coming to us but recognize and respond to His visits.

Read It! John 1:11-12, MSG

Speak It! "Father, I don't want to be like those who totally missed Your visit. I receive You. Jesus, I invite You into my life to be the Lord of my life. Thank You for Your patience and for forgiving all my sins. I pray that You help me to know You in a real and fresh way. In Jesus' Name. Amen."

DAY 122

(what are angels doing these days?)

"The angel of the LORD encamps all around those who fear Him,
and delivers them."
Psalm 34:7

Angels are realities in this unseen world. God's invisible kingdom is all around us and is very real. God, the Father; Jesus, the Son; the Holy Spirit and legions of angels—they're all tangible realities in the unseen world,

A big bonus is that God has specifically assigned angels to protect those who fear Him! Angels are spirit-beings. We see their activity throughout the entire Bible. God's Word is loaded with info on angels: who they are, what they do, where they show up and why God created them. Angels are definitely on assignment. They appear, declare, protect, enforce, fight, visit, serve—and so much more!

- **Angels protect us.** God has commanded His angels to protect us *(Psalm 91:11, NLT)*. What a comfort! No matter where you go, you are surrounded by angels. I like to envision God's big, honkin' angels encircling me and my family front-to-back, side-to-side and top-to-bottom. This brings me great peace—whether we are riding motorcycles, walking, driving, skiing, shopping or sleeping.

- **Angels are here to serve those who receive salvation.** God has sent His angels to serve those who are saved *(Hebrews 1:14, MSG)*. How cool is that? The Lord has given angels a mission: to serve those who are heirs of salvation. They help us carry out God's will in our lives!

- **Angels respond to God's Word.** God's Word is living and active and angels move into action by the sound of God's Word *(Psalm 103:20, NIV)*. When God speaks, angels jump! When we agree with God and speak His Word, angels obey His Word.

Today, we can be encouraged! We are never alone. Not only do we have the indwelling presence of the Holy Spirit and Jesus' promise that He would never leave or forsake us, but we have the added benefit of God's army of angels performing God's Word—protecting and caring for you. Wow!

Read It! Psalm 34:7, NIV

Speak It! "Father, I thank You for the reality of the invisible world. Today, I thank You that the angel of the Lord encircles me and (say the names of other Believers you know) front-to-back, side-to-side and top-to-bottom—and protects us wherever we go. Thank You that Your angels are ministering spirits sent to minister and care for me as I have need. I thank You that Your Word is living and active and angels go into action as soon as they hear Your Word. I believe angels are obeying God's Word today, and they are on assignment to care for me today! In Jesus' Name. Amen."

DAY 123

(what is on the front burner?)

"At the center of all this, Christ rules the church. The church, you see,
is not peripheral to the world; the world is peripheral to the church.
The church is Christ's body, in which he speaks and acts,
by which he fills everything with his presence."
Ephesians 1:22-23, MSG

I arrived early—a small miracle—and was sitting in the school cafeteria await-ing the opening scene of our daughter's elementary program...many years ago. I decided to kill some time by reading the little *Message Bible* in my purse. I happened to read the above passage, and it hit me in a fresh way. This passage lit a fire in my heart, and I have become a champion for the local Church.

I'm passionate about the Church and have dedicated myself to helping Jesus build His Church. The Church is one of God's greatest expressions of Himself! The Church—that is, the global Body of Christ around the world and specific local churches that make up that global group—is on the front burner of God's heart. It's His number one priority! He said, "...*I will build My church; and the gates of hell shall not prevail against it," (Matthew 16:18, KJV)*.

Jesus is seated in heaven as the Head of the Church, and we are His Body on Planet Earth! Through His Body, He speaks, acts and fills everything with His presence. Wherever the Church is strong—faith-filled, outreach-minded, flow-ing with God's structure and changing lives—Jesus shines and that community, city or country is blessed!

Unfortunately, many people, including Believers, don't fully understand the God-ordained power of the Church and the potential impact of a corporate group of Believers. The devil hates the Church and our culture would like us to believe that the Church is some unimportant, peripheral organization. God has a different view. The Church is NOT peripheral to the world; the world is peripheral to the Church! The Church is definitely on God's front burner. So, the big question is this: today, what are we doing in, for and with His Church?

Read It! Romans 12:6-8, NLT

Speak It! "Jesus, I purpose to hook my heart up with the thing that is on Your front burner—Your Church. I want to be busy with Your priorities...going about Your business! (If you already have a church home, say this... Lord, show me how I can help build Your Church. I want to be counted faithful in using my time and talents to honor You by helping Your Church.) (If you don't have a church home, say this... Lord, Your Word says You place us in the Body as it pleases You. Forgive me for being a rebel. I ask You to show me what Church You want me placed and planted in.) In Jesus' Name. Amen."

DAY 124

(willing to be willing)

"For God is working in you, giving you the desire
to obey Him and the power to do what pleases Him."
Philippians 2:13, NLT

Sometimes people know what God wants them to do, but have a REALLY hard time doing it. What do we do? Take a look at a few scenarios:

- They're living with their boyfriend/girlfriend. Sure, culture approves; but deep in their heart, they feel unsettled and ashamed about it. They know God has told them to move out and trust Him but are REALLY struggling to do it.

- They've been cheating on their taxes for years, and their own heart condemns them for it, but so far they haven't been caught. They want to do what's right, but it's been REALLY hard to take that step.

- They've been the victim of some type of abuse—verbal, physical, sexual—and they hate the person who caused them such pain. They know God wants them to forgive, so they can be truly free; but it's been REALLY hard to let it go.

- They've been running their own life, calling the shots. They've given God the token, *"Hey, what's up? Thanks for blessing me..."* acknowledgment, but they know the Lord is calling them to a real place of surrender and sacrifice for His purposes. They want to serve the Lord with all they've got, but they REALLY struggle giving up "lordship" of their life or their desires.

- They've been the brunt of someone's angry outburst. People have said words that have cut like a knife and hurt them deeply, and they're tired of apologies and promises to do better. They've forgiven them, but are REALLY struggling getting past the feelings of resentment and hurt.

These, and many others, can be a real challenge. We know what we ought to do, and often we want to do right; but we REALLY have a difficult time obtaining the desire "to do" it. The answer is to be willing to let Jesus work "in" us "to will and to do." That means He'll work the "want to" and the power "to do" into the fabric of our lives—as long as we stay willing!

Let's be proactively willing to let the Lord work in us and not hit the brakes. Let's not run from God but run to Him. Let's not hold onto resentment, rebellion, hurt or control. In time, the Lord will change our desires to be congruent with His desires, and He will give us the power to actually do what pleases Him.

Read It! Romans 7:15-25, NLT

Speak It! "Father, I am willing to be willing for You to work in me. I know the things I need to do. Help me to have the desire to obey You and the power to do what is pleasing to You. I don't just want to desire Your will; I want to do Your will. I know, when I am living in a way that is pleasing to You, life is good. Thank You for working in me 'to will' and 'to do' Your good pleasure. In Jesus' Name. Amen."

DAY 125

(the greed monster)

"Then he said to them, "Watch out! Be on your guard against all kinds of greed; a man's life does not consist in the abundance of his possessions."
Luke 12:15, NIV

Has our culture reached a new low? Was the Black Friday tragedy of 2008 at a Wal-Mart® store a grizzly manifestation of the greed monster? Was the $400 flat screen TV or the $4 Hannah Montana p.j.s really worth the price of a man's life? The most stunning part of the incident was that after the store authorities announced his death and their need to close the store, shoppers began shouting, complaining and continued to shop! Unbelievable!

As Christians, how do we defeat the greed monster? First, go to the **Read It!** segment and see what Jesus had to say about it.

- **"Watch out."** Pay attention; be on the offensive. Look for good deals, but also recognize the greedy at-all-costs mindset—and run from it!
- **"...be on your guard..."** Don't just be offensive; be defensive. Things aren't bad, in and of themselves; but when we crave, idolize and are willing to go to any unethical or immoral lengths to have them, we may have been bitten by the greed monster. A friend of ours told us he defeats the greed monster by what he calls the "24-hour shopping test." If he's about to make an impulse purchase, he chooses to wait 24 hours before doing so. He's been amazed at how many things he thought he just couldn't live without. Yet, 24 hours later, he didn't even want them.
- **"...all kinds of greed..."** There's nothing wrong with having "things"—but there's a lot wrong when "things" have you.
- **"...a man's life does not consist of the abundance of his possessions."** We've been sold a lie that if we have all the stuff—the most stuff, the stuff with the right labels, the latest and the hottest, new stuff—we would have a great life. We've been sold on the idea that it's okay to be owned by a job, to sacrifice our family, overlook our health and treat our bodies in an abusive way—all for our materialistic, greedy desires. Jesus tells us the opposite. He says our life doesn't amount to the abundance of our possessions but in our relationship with God through Jesus *(John 17:3, MSG).*

Possessions can never fill the God-shaped hole in us—only Jesus can. The irony is that when our life is all about knowing the Lord, He adds all kinds of possessions to our lives.

Read It! Ephesians 5:3, NLT

Speak It! "Father, I know my life's not defined by 'things' or 'stuff.' Help me to guard against all kinds of greed. Real life is knowing You and having a genuine relationship with You. You always find ways to bless me with all kinds of possessions. In Jesus' Name. Amen."

DAY 126

(GPS)

"For as many as are led by the Spirit of God, these are sons of God."
Romans 8:14

Need some life-navigation insight? Navigating uncertainty, challenges and decisions? Need help in positioning? Positioning your business or product in the marketplace? Positioning your kids for success? Positioning your life for God's best? Positioning yourself to be used by God?

One of the blessings of being a Christian is the supernatural GPS system God implants on the inside of us! "God's Positioning System" (GPS) is the dynamic way He leads His people. If we're a child of God, the Holy Spirit wants to lead us; and if we listen and follow Him, He'll lead us to be at the right place, at the right time, with the right people, doing the right things, for the right reasons!

You don't need a TomTom®. You already have a superior navigation system—the Holy Spirit! The Lord's transmitting signals from His heavenly throne of grace directly to the "receiver"—the Holy Spirit—in our hearts!

First, read the **Read It!** segment to see what Jesus said about this nav system:

- **What does this mean?** It means that because we are His children, He wants to lead, protect and help us; guiding us into safe places, divine connections, open doors and supernatural opportunities. He wants to be the leader of our lives.

- **How does He lead us?** Primarily through His Word and by His Spirit. The Holy Spirit, indwelling our spirit, transmits God's signals to our hearts. We often recognize His leading through peace or a lack of peace, a "knowing," a "hunch," a directive; a still, small voice or an authoritative command. The Holy Spirit is always looking for ways to transmit God's direction to us. It's our job to keep the channel open and clear and to be attentive.

- **Why is this important?** The Lord wants to position us for all He intended and protect us. He'll give us a "knowing" or a sense of peace about where to go and not go, what roads to use, when to depart, who to associate with, who to avoid and so much more! The Lord wants to lead us into goodness, blessing and abundance. He'll give us a "hunch" or directive on how to succeed, innovate and work smart; how to invest, when to sell, what to buy and how to identify God-ordained opportunities. He'll lead us to encourage others and will give us a dose of His compassion for others, so we will pray for them and know what keys to use to unlock a person's heart, so they can come to Christ.

Let's be attentive to God's Word and follow our internal GPS.

Read It! John 16:13-15, AMP

Speak It! "Father, thank You for positioning me for success. I am so glad I have a supernatural GPS inside of my heart. Help me listen to the Holy Spirit's signals and follow Your leading. In Jesus' Name. Amen."

DAY 127

(what are you looking at?)

"All the land that you see I will give to you."
Genesis 13:15a, NIV

What do you see? The Bible is loaded with the faith principle of "seeing." It's a basic we constantly need to "get a grip" on. Think about how many times God told Abraham to "see" the stars and the sand in order to get a vision for his future. How many times did Jesus tell His followers to "look" at the harvest fields in order to get a vision for the Gospel? The power of vision can absolutely influence the fulfillment of our purpose and destiny. The Bible tells us where there is no vision—where nothing is seen—the people perish. The Lord needs us to see what He sees for us, so He can give it to us!

Do you see yourself the way God does—in the light of His Word? Do you see your future as bright as the Lord does? Do you see your marriage, kids, job or calling the way God sees them? If you can see it, He will give it to you—eventually. If you can't see it, you can't have it.

I remember a time when I didn't see myself in the same way God did. When we built our first church building, it was a very challenging and draining season. One day, I noticed I hadn't laughed in months. Jeff and I were overloaded with four little kids, a demanding teaching schedule and the pressures of leadership and a growing church. I realized I needed to get a new vision. I knew God's will for my life was to have joy—in marriage, as a mom and in pastoring a growing church with Jeff. If I could see it by faith, I knew I could have it.

So, I did something crazy in order to "see" myself laughing again! At that time, the only husband/wife ministry team we knew—who both husband and wife taught the Word—were Aquila and Priscilla (from Acts 18) and Kenneth and Gloria Copeland (from Ft. Worth, TX). Since I couldn't find a photo of Aquila and Priscilla, I found a photo of Kenneth and Gloria Copeland teaching side-by-side. I cut their heads out of the photo and pasted a laughing version of my head and Jeff's head onto the photo of their bodies! (It was quite strange looking, but I carried that photo in my Bible for years and stared at it often.) Once I "saw" Jeff and me laughing, teaching the Word and enjoying ministry via this photo—and believed it and expected it—I started to experience it.

How about you? What are you "seeing" these days?

Read It! Proverbs 29:19, KJV

Speak It! "Father, help me to see what You see! Remind me of what Your Word has declared as Your will for my life and help me find creative ways to 'see' those things. I choose to 'see' all the land You want to give me. In Jesus' Name, Amen."

DAY 128

(help, I need somebody)

"And the Holy Spirit helps us in our distress..."
Romans 8:26, NLT

Need help? Are you facing a challenge? A weakness? An inability to produce results? Listen, you are not alone. You have a Helper! The Holy Spirit is your Helper. What are you facing? What frustration? What impossible situation? What mountain is staring at you? You have a Helper! The Holy Spirit will help you move towards God's will for your life. He will!

(Now, take just a minute to read the **Read It!** segment.)

Specifically, when you face a bit of distress, and you don't even know what or how to pray, the Holy Spirit will help you pray according to God's perfect will for your life. He will help you to pray in such a way that you will be able to know with certainty that everything will work together for the good.

So, how does this play out? Simple. Just ask the Holy Spirit to help you and then...begin to pray—and keep praying! Pray it out. Don't pray some mealy-mouthed, professional, vanilla, religious-sounding prayer; pray from your guts! Pray from your heart-of-hearts and allow the Holy Spirit to help you! Pray earnest, heartfelt, continued prayers. Pray *"with groanings which cannot be uttered," (Romans 8:26, KJV).* The Holy Spirit will help you pray out His perfect plan. He knows God's will, and He will help you to pray in such a way that all things will work together for good *(Romans 8:28).*

Read It! Jude 1:20, NIV

Speak It! "Holy Spirit, thank You for being my Helper! I need Your help today. I don't know how to pray about the challenges I face, but You do. I ask You to help me pray from my heart-of-hearts with 'groanings that cannot be uttered.' I have great confidence that with Your help, at the end of my prayers, all things will work together for good. In Jesus' Name. Amen."

DAY 129

(God is not a liar!)

"God is not a man, that he should lie, nor a son of man, that he should change his mind. Does he speak and then not act? Does he promise and not fulfill?"
Numbers 23:19, NIV

I can take God at His Word. He won't lie. He can't lie. He won't change His mind.

What has the Lord promised you?

In moments when the enemy has worked overtime trying to convince me that God wouldn't keep His Word, I have reminded myself of what God's Word has said to me. Then, I have memorized, meditated and muttered this Scripture passage within my own heart: "God is not a man. He doesn't lie. He won't change His mind. He fulfills His promises to me!"

Be encouraged. God is still God—the Creator of the ends of the earth, the Most High, the Lord God Almighty! Sometimes, right before the fulfillment of something amazing, the devil works overtime trying to steal our faith, dreams, vision and destiny. Usually, his first strategy is to steal the Word and try to convince us that God won't keep His promises. The enemy is the liar, not God.

Is the enemy working on your mind? Is he trying to convince you to waiver in your faith? Rise up and resist him right now! Deny him the pleasure. Will not the Judge of all the earth do right? He will! Today, remind yourself of God's promises and have renewed confidence in Him and His Word.

Read It! Deuteronomy 32:4, KJV and Psalm 31:5

Speak It! "Father, Your Word is true. I declare it: God won't lie to me. God can't lie to me. God's Word is more true than how I feel. My God is not a man that He should lie. He doesn't change His mind. If He said it, then He will do it. I am fully persuaded that He is able to keep His promises. I believe it. In Jesus' Name. Amen."

DAY 130

(your clan)

"...A solitary person, completely alone—no children, no family, no friends—yet working obsessively late into the night, compulsively greedy for more and more, never bothering to ask, 'Why am I working like a dog, never having any fun? And who cares?'"
Ecclesiastes 4:7-8, MSG

Solitaire might be a good game to play, but it's no way to live. Being a workaholic loner is no fun at all. Deep inside, people want to know other people, be known by other people and belong. They long for relationships. Whether it's with God Himself, family, friends, gangs, tribes, clans, groups, clubs, communities, in-laws or out-laws—everyone wants to feel like they belong to something or someone. It's in our human nature that desires to belong, and God intended it to be that way—vertically and horizontally.

- **The vertical relationship.** This is the most important one. Having a personal relationship with the Lord is the ultimate. Jesus is the "round peg for the round hole" in our hearts, and no one and nothing else can fill that spot.
- **The horizontal relationships.** These are huge, too. We may have a fantastic relationship with the Lord; but without heartfelt relationships with others, we feel empty. God created us to interact with one another; He's big on clans!

Faith Popcorn, a futurist, culture and marketing mind, describes "clanning" as a future trend in society, defining it as: *"Belonging to a group that represents common feelings, causes or ideals; validating one's own belief system."* Our need for clanning is more obvious and vital today than ever. Busy lives, economic uncertainty and transit families leave people longing to find "their peeps"—their clan! They're looking for others who share their core values, beliefs and personal style—causes, lingo, tastes, preferences, etc. People are looking for "clickage" with a clan, and when they find it—bingo! They'll jump in with both feet!

How about you? Have you found your peeps? Are you playing too much solitaire or becoming a workaholic? Are you looking for people whom you have personal "clickage"? There are lots of places to connect with others within your family, workplace or neighborhood—none better, of course, than your local church which is loaded with people who share your core values and are prospects for personal "clickage." Your peeps are out there...find your clan!

Read It! Ecclesiastes 4:7-12, MSG

Speak It! "Father, I'm so thankful I have a strong vertical relationship with You! Help me find my clan and the personal 'clickage' I desire. Help me take the initiative to reach out to those around me. In Jesus' Name. Amen."

DAY 131

(invest now)

"'Behold, the days are coming,' says the Lord GOD,
'That I will send a famine on the land, not a famine of bread,
nor a thirst for water, but of hearing the words of the LORD.'"
Amos 8:11

Remember Joseph from the Old Testament? In a dream, the Lord told him about the coming 7 years of plenty, followed by 7 years of famine. The Lord also gave him a strategy for saving the crops of grain in storehouses during the years of plenty, so he'd be in a position of influence to help others during the years of famine. It all happened just as the Lord had said. Joseph invested wisely; and when the famine hit, everyone ran to Joseph for food.

In the same way, God tells us that one day there will be a famine. It won't be a famine of bread or water, but a famine where people are starved for God's Word. People will crave hearing the Word of the Lord. Those who have been wise during the years of "plenty" will invest the Word of God into their hearts, and they'll be in a position of influence to help others during a time of "famine."

Over decades, we've had years of plenty, where the Word is concerned. We've had the Word of God available to us on every front—Bibles in every color, TV preachers, CD/DVD teaching series, the Internet, conferences and numerous other means to load up on God's Word. The wise are taking advantage of these opportunities to listen, study and learn the Word, allowing the Word to dwell in them richly. They're investing heavily the Word of God in their hearts. They're diligent in seeking the Lord, listening to the messages they hear in church and praying for a spirit of wisdom and revelation in the knowledge of the Lord.

Today, a famine of the Word may be on the horizon. Anti-Christ influencers are working to take the Word off the air waves. Liberal groups are suing Bible printers for passages that make them "uncomfortable." Some emerging churches have even taken God's Word entirely out of their services in an effort to "connect" with their audience. Slowly, our culture is eliminating the Word.

So, what do we do? Invest our time in the Word and be more intentional. Let's listen, study, meditate on the Word and allow it to dwell in us richly.

Read It! Revelation 1:3

Speak It! "Father, help me to fill my heart with Your Word. Give me wisdom to take advantage of the 'plenty,' so that in a time of 'famine,' I am able to help others. In Jesus' Name. Amen."

DAY 132

(what makes God happy?)

"But without faith it is impossible to please Him..."
Hebrews 11:6

There is one major way to please God. Faith! The Bible says without faith it is impossible to please God *(Hebrews 11:6)*. In other words, God is pleased by our faith. If we want to live a life pleasing to the Lord, we have to be faith-people! We are going to have to live by faith.

What does it mean to have faith, be a faith-person? Why does faith please God? Is God some mean, hard-to-please ogre that just won't be satisfied, unless we all have faith? Of course not! God is a good Father who has given us thousands of promises in His Word, and faith-people believe them, which pleases the Lord. Like any good Father, He is pleased to see His children living the faith-adventure and walking in obedience, benefits and supernatural blessings!

Faith defined is: taking God at His Word. Faith believes what God said in His Word and considers it as a fact even before it is revealed to the senses. I believe one reason faith pleases God is because God Himself is a faith God, and His kingdom operates by faith. He knows the only way we will experience all of His promises and blessings is through activating and walking by faith. In other words, the primary way we appropriate the blessings of God is through faith, and God is happy, pleased, and satisfied when we experience His goodness!

In our Christian walk, everything we have, we do as an act of faith. By faith, we...

- Are saved.
- Have God's wisdom.
- Move mountains.
- Are healed.
- Prosper.
- Overcome fear.

- Forgive.
- Love.
- Obey.
- Serve.
- Witness.
- Live.

Faith-people look at the whole counsel of God's Word and rightly divide it; then, they pray and believe they receive it—and God is pleased!

Read It! Mark 11:23-24

Speak It! "Father, I believe Your Word. I want to live a life pleasing to You, and I can see You are pleased when I appropriate Your promises by faith and walk in Your will, Your goodness and Your blessings. Help me to be led by the Spirit to identify and believe the promises in Your Word. In Jesus' Name. Amen."

DAY 133

(the real deal)

"But you know yourselves that Timothy's the real thing."
Philippians 2:22, MSG

What a compliment...to be called the "real thing"!

These days, people are looking for people with the real deal—a follower of Jesus who *really* follows Jesus and His ways!

Who wants to be a phony, hypocritical, pretend Christian? I remember, some 30 years ago when I became a Christian. I actually debated about my decision for nine months before I decided to fully surrender and invite Jesus into my life. The reason for the delay? I knew that once I made a decision to follow Jesus, I wanted to BE a Christian; I didn't want to profess something and then not live a lifestyle that reflected that belief. So, I took some time to count the cost.

Andi led me to the Lord, and she was definitely the "real deal." I saw in her life a real, genuine relationship with Jesus Christ, a real faith in God's Word and real choices that reflected her walk with God. Seeing those things in her life, I decided I wanted the same thing. I haven't been a perfect Christian, but my heart's desire and goal has been authenticity—to allow people to see the "real" me. And, hopefully, when they see the "real" me, they'll also see the "real" Him—the God of all truth.

1 Samuel 3:20, tells us that everyone in Israel, from Dan in the north to Beersheba in the south, recognized that Samuel was the real thing. Today, the real question is: does everyone in our family know we're legit? Do the people in our school, our church or our work know we are the genuine article? The real deal? Are we a credit to Christianity or a liability?

Remember, everywhere we go, people are watching our life—our words, our actions, our deeds, our decisions—to see if we're the real deal. The big question for us to answer is: are we?

Read It! 2 Corinthians 13:5, NLT

Speak It! "Father, I don't want to be a plastic, carnal Christian! I ask You to forgive me for discrediting You in any way. I want to be the real thing, not religious or churchy or fake; I want to be an authentic follower of Jesus. I ask You to help me live in such a way that You are seen, honored and recognized. In Jesus' Name. Amen."

DAY 134

(flack)

"Now, Lord, consider their threats and enable Your servants to
speak Your word with great boldness."
Acts 4:29, NIV

Been taking any flack for being a Christian? Representing Christ? Standing for
His Word? Not cow-towing to political correctness? Be encouraged to keep
speaking the Word with great boldness!

Perhaps you heard about the elderly lady in Palm Springs, CA who carried a
Styrofoam® cross in a peaceful demonstration at City Hall and was attacked by
militant protesters. The police officers encouraged her to press charges.

Maybe you read about the militant activists who recently disrupted and
attacked peaceful church-goers at Mount Hope Church in Lansing, MI, which
just so happens to be our old home church.

So, how should Christians respond to flack, persecution and threats? How can
Believers be proactive in exercising their rights to freedom of religion and free
speech? Sometimes, legal action is necessary; but for most of us, this little
primer might be helpful:

- **Love 'Em!** People don't know what they don't know, and they need a revelation
  of God's love. (Matthew 5:43-33, NLT)
- **Be Happy!** You are storing up some big rewards...heaven applauds! (Matthew
  5:10-12, MSG)
- **Fear Not!** You know in Whom you have believed...don't flinch! (Philippians 1:28,
  AMP)
- **Look Up!** Your future is bright, but for those who reject God's love and mercy,
  it's sad. (Philippians 3:18-20, NLT)
- **Be Bold!** Just like the apostle Paul some persecutors can be won to Christ...keep
  preaching! (Acts 4:29-31, NIV)

Read It! Deuteronomy 31:6, NIV

Speak It! "Father, I pray for those who are enemies of the cross. I ask You to open
the eyes of their hearts and remove the blinders. Help them to see Jesus as He is
and know Your love, forgiveness and mercy. Lord, I pray for those who live by and
preach the cross. I pray You enable me and all Your followers to speak Your Word
with great boldness. I ask You to confirm Your Word with signs following. In Jesus'
Name. Amen."

DAY 135

(feel like you're goin' through hell?)

"For thou wilt not leave my soul in hell..."
Psalm 16:10, KJV

Going through a rough time? There is light at the end of the tunnel...hang on!

Up until that time, it was the hardest season of our ministry and married life, and it seemed like we were hit on every front, and it felt like "hell on earth." We were parents of four preschoolers, pioneering a church that didn't seem to be growing, living in a microscopic house, surviving sleep deprivation and dealing with the pressures of life and a ministry on a serious shoestring budget! It sure didn't feel like "the blessings" were falling in our lives at that time; it felt more like we had been forgotten, overlooked and sentenced to outer darkness! As it turned out, it was a season of sheer faith, obedience and endurance.

Somehow, this verse of scripture comforted my soul. Pitiful, isn't it?

Sometimes, we just need to know that deliverance is on the horizon. I know it's tough sometimes. There are rough seasons where life can feel like all of hell is against us. We all face those times but be encouraged. The Lord promised He will never leave us or forsake us!

If hell has launched an all-out attack against you, be strong and full of hope today and know that the Lord is working to deliver you from "hell!"

Read It! Psalm 3:3

Speak It! "Father thank You for Your promise of deliverance. I will keep my eyes on You, and I know that You will bring me through this season of 'hell' to the other side! I trust in You and Your Word. In Jesus' Name. Amen."

DAY 136

(almost too good to be true)

"Therefore I say to you, whatever things you ask when you pray, believe that you receive them, and you will have them."
Mark 11:24

Mark 11:24 is the classic "faith" verse. Each one of Jesus' words seems to be loaded with life-giving revelation. It's a verse that's almost too good to be true! Need a God-intervention? Need the Lord to do what only He can do? Need a miracle? Jesus is offering us a huge gift! Let's break Mark 11:24 down...

- *"Therefore, I say to you..."* Keep in mind, these are words from Jesus, not man's idea or words of some "extreme faith preacher."

- *"...whatever things..."* Whatever! What do you desire? What things do you need or want from God? What desires has He put in your heart? The *King James Version* of Mark 11:24 says, *"What things soever ye desire..."* Have you taken time to identify the things you desire?

- *"...you ask when you pray..."* Have you prayed and asked God for the things you desire? James 4:2 tells us we have not because we ask not. Let's not forget to ask! Take time to ask God for the specific things you desire.

- *"...believe..."* Once you ask, believe that God heard you, and that He will answer! *(1 John 5:14-15)*

- *"...that you receive them..."* What are we supposed to believe? We must believe that we receive "them things" we asked God for. When do we believe we receive them? When we pray. By faith, we believe that we RECEIVE them the minute we pray. If you have received something, what does that mean? You have it! By faith, we pray and ask God for whatever things we desire—in accordance with His Word. We know He hears us and we believe that we receive those very things—right now! We must receive it by faith in the invisible realm before we ever see it with our eyes in the visible realm. That's faith! The result is...

- *"...and you will have them."* When we receive "whatever things" by faith now; we will obtain "whatever things" in a tangible form later. When will we have the things we desire? After we pray, ask and believe we receive them. If we never believe we receive them, we will never have them! We don't "hope" or "wonder" or "beg" that we'll get these things one day; we "believe" and we "receive" them now—when we pray—and we'll have them later...in God's timing!

Mark 11:24...it's not too good to be true. It is true. I encourage you to take Him up on it!

Read It! 1 John 5:14-15

Speak It! "Father, thank You for Your Word. If Jesus said it, I believe it. Thank You for helping me identify the desires and 'whatever things' You put in my heart. I ask You to help me appropriate Your Word by faith through praying, asking, believing, receiving and obtaining. In Jesus' Name. Amen."

DAY 137

(bad devil)

"...no doubt you know that God anointed Jesus of Nazareth with the Holy Spirit and with power. Then Jesus went around doing good and healing all who were oppressed by the devil, for God was with Him."
Acts 10:38, NLT

Just a reminder: God is good—all the time.

And, the devil is bad—all the time. The devil is in the business of stealing, killing and destroying *(John 10:10)*. He goes about as a roaring lion seeking whom he may devour *(1 Peter 5:8)*, deceive and depress. He's a liar and the father of lies *(John 8:44)*; a thief, murderer and accuser. He's dishing out the spirit of fear, infirmity, bondage and oppression. He's our enemy, adversary and foe; and he's been defeated and disarmed!

God is good all the time. Jesus is in the business of setting people free from all the oppression of the devil. He went around forgiving sins, speaking the truth, blessing kids, healing the sick, calming storms, performing miracles for those in need and giving abundant life to those who believed in the power of His Name. Jesus was anointed to do good everywhere He went. It's great that Jesus did these things when He was on earth...but, it's even better to know that Jesus is *still* doing these things! He's the same yesterday, TODAY and forever *(Hebrews 13:8)*. He's our Savior, our Lord and our Redeemer!

Be encouraged today. God is good. He's always been good. He's never had a day when He wanted anything but good for you. He gives good gifts *(James 1:17)*. No matter what you are facing, remember His intentions toward you are always for good. Don't ever let anyone talk you out of knowing the very nature and character of God: goodness!

Remember how God revealed Himself to Moses? *"Then Moses said, 'Now show me your glory.' And the LORD said, 'I will cause all my goodness to pass in front of you...,'" (Exodus 33:18-19, NIV)*.

Remember what Jesus said? *"If you, then, though you are evil, know how to give good gifts to your children, how much more will your Father in heaven give good gifts to those who ask him!" (Matthew 7:11, NIV)*.

Read It! Psalm 34:8, AMP

Speak It! "Lord, I believe You are a good God. I am so glad that Jesus still goes about doing good and healing all who are oppressed of the devil. I receive Your goodness today. I ask You to 'show me Your glory' by causing all Your goodness to pass in front of me. Help me to taste and see that You are good. I thank You that goodness and mercy shall follow me all the days of my life. In Jesus' Name. Amen."

DAY 138

(what a fool believes)

"A fool gives full vent to his anger, but a wise man keeps
himself under control."
Proverbs 29:11, NIV

Ever gotten a nasty, angry, mean-spirited phone call, letter or e-mail from someone? What's your first knee-jerk reaction? Does your flesh sound something like this: *"Well, who do they think they are? I'll let them know a thing or two. They dished it out; I hope they can take it! They sent 'a pup to party with the big dogs' and now I'm gonna let them have it. They don't know who they're messing with...,"* blah, blah, blah!

Then, when you simmer down and listen to your heart, do you come to your senses and keep yourself under control? Remember, let's not answer a fool by becoming a fool. Fools have a need to run off at the mouth; they rant, rave and pick fights. But, wise people keep themselves under control.

It's one thing when a wise person gives constructive criticism worth heeding; but when a fool starts dishing out advice, a wise person doesn't answer. Wise people don't even waste time coming up with a response.

Anybody been messing with you lately? Some fool trying to get in your head?

Just remember what Proverbs says: *"It's a mark of good character to avert quarrels, but fools love to pick fights,"* (Proverbs 20:3, MSG).

Don't be "fooled" any longer!

Read It!   Proverbs 26:4, NIV

Speak It!   "Father, I will not become a fool by answering a fool according to his folly. I choose to walk in wisdom and good character no matter who's bugging me, dissing me, picking on me or criticizing me. I'm a wise person; and with Your help, I will let a fool's rant roll off my shoulder like water off a duck's back! In Jesus' Name. Amen."

DAY 139

(God's diaries)

"Then those who feared the LORD spoke to one another, and the LORD
listened and heard them; so a book of remembrance was written before
Him for those who fear the LORD and who meditate on His name."
Malachi 3:16

I can't wait to see the big library in heaven! I love that God is so into books. The
Bible describes the variety of books in God's Library: a Book of Remembrance, a
Book of Tears, books describing The Days of Our Lives—and I'm not talking
about the scripts to the TV soap opera either—the Book of Works...and the most
important book, The Book of Life, a.k.a. The Lamb's Book of Life.

All the books intrigue me, but the Book of Remembrance is particularly interesting because it's the book that records all of our conversations about the Lord!
God is taking minutes of our meetings. It's like He's keeping a diary! Isn't that
amazing? Think about all the chats you've had with people about Jesus, His
Word and life in God. Think about those with whom you've shared Christ, those
you've encouraged in the faith, those you've prayed with...and on and on. God is
writing a memory book including all those conversations!

The Message Bible and the *New Living Translation* of the Bible describe this
book...

> "Then those whose lives honored GOD got together and talked it over. GOD saw
> what they were doing and listened in. A book was opened in God's presence
> and minutes were taken of the meeting, with the names of the GOD-fearers
> written down, all the names of those who honored GOD's name." (Malachi
> 3:16, MSG)

> "Then those who feared and loved the Lord spoke often of him to each other.
> And he had a Book of Remembrance drawn up in which he recorded the names
> of those who feared him and loved to think about him." (Malachi 3:16, TLB)

Be encouraged this week. God is listening and taking good notes as you talk
about the Lord with family, friends and strangers in cafés, cars, planes, parks,
malls, meetings and over meals!

Read It! Revelation 20:11-15 (You want to make sure your name is in THIS book!)

Speak It! "Father, what a cool thought to know that You are writing a Book of
Remembrance that includes all the conversations I've had about You with others. I
can't wait to see Your big library when I get to heaven. I am so glad I'll have eternity
to read the volumes You have written about Your people over the ages. Today, may
the words of my mouth and the meditations of my heart be acceptable in Your sight,
O Lord. In Jesus' Name. Amen."

DAY 140

(God laughs!)

"He who sits in the heavens laughs..."
Psalm 2:4

God laughs...think about that. Really, take some time to ponder the thought! Ever just watched people? Your kids? Yourself? Yes, the Lord has plenty of "laughter fodder." God laughs at many things. He laughs at the heathen who think they're smarter than He is. I am sure God gives us teenagers simply so He can sit in heaven and laugh.

He is not the harsh, sober, stoic, mean judge that so many people have made Him out to be. The Bible says in God's presence there is "fullness of joy." When we hang out with the Lord, we find Him to be a fun, refreshing, happy, smiling, joy-filled, positive Person with an easy laugh. I know that rocks some of our stereotypical ideas about God. There are many dimensions to the wonders of His person and joy and laughter are a part of God's very nature and character.

Most of us need a fresh dose of knowing our Father as One who laughs! Ever thought about what makes God laugh? What makes you laugh? Been too serious lately? There's nothing like a good, "gut-busting" laugh. Spend time in God's presence to refuel on the "fullness of joy" and be on the lookout for "laughable" things today. Remember the joy of the Lord is your strength!

Read It! Hebrews 1:9

Speak It! "Father, if You sit in heaven and laugh; then, today, I will sit in my car or truck and laugh. I will sit at work and laugh; I will sit at home and laugh. Help me to spend more time in Your presence where there is no lack for joy. Help me to see things with a new set of eyes so I can relax and laugh. In Jesus' Name. Amen."

DAY 141

(a big trap)

"The fear of man brings a snare,
but whoever trusts in the LORD shall be safe."
Proverbs 29:25

The fear of man is a big trap. Trusting the Lord is the place of safety. It's not always easy to avoid being a man-pleaser. Most of us prefer the approval of others, and our ego feeds on their good words. The problem: it's a trap. When we listen to flattery, it clouds our judgment; we begin to believe our own press. When we care about the approval and praises of others more than God's approval and His praises, it's a snare.

Human nature is sometimes fickle, and people end up loving to hate those they love. Sad, but true. Consider this scenario:

At first, when someone's personal stock and potential is moving up in value, the crowds cheer, "Hosanna...," and sing praises! The bright and shining star gets a hero's welcome everywhere they go—kudos, approval ratings and great headlines full of high hopes and great promise. But, it's a big set up, and here's why...

At some point, the hero will make a mistake, let people down, not live up to everyone's expectations and prove that he or she is not perfect. At that point, the crowds will start cheering, "Crucify him/her!" The balloon has popped. The bar was set so high, no human being could reach it, and now the crowds critique and disapprove. Last month, they were singing "Hosanna..."; but today, they're saying, "Crucify..."

Most people in leadership, the public eye or the limelight have discovered these truths—sometimes the hard way. When we are unmoved by the "hosannas" and the "crucifies," we are truly free to live for an Audience of One, and we can rest in the safest place in all the world! Trusting the Lord, rather than the approval of men, gives us freedom to truly be the person God created us to be.

Now, a little caveat... There is nothing wrong with being well-liked and gracious with people. In fact, it's a blessing! The problem is when gaining the approval of others is more important to us than God's approval. When we love the praises of men more than the praises of God, it's a snare. However, when our ways please the Lord, the Bible says He gives us favor with God and man *(Proverbs 3:4)*—and even our enemies *(Proverbs 16:7)*.

Read It! Proverbs 3:4

Speak It! "Father, help me live for Your pleasure. Lord, strengthen me in my inner man, so I'm not moved by the crowd. Help me to be the person You've created me to be and live a life worthy of and pleasing to You. In Jesus' Name. Amen."

DAY 142

(hit your knees)

"...If My people who are called by My name will humble themselves, and pray and seek My face, and turn from their wicked ways, then I will hear from heaven, and will forgive their sin and heal their land."
2 Chronicles 7:14

America needs healing in every way—spiritually, politically, financially and relationally. Does God have a remedy? Yes, He does! Hit our knees and pray.

- **Humility.** To be humble doesn't mean to berate ourselves or to think of ourselves as unworthy worms. Rather, to be humble simply means to place ourselves under the Lordship of Jesus and to submit to His Word. That eliminates the temptation to yield to ego, arrogance and a "told-you-so" haughtiness. True humility is to see ourselves the way God does and to submit to the authority of God's Word. God won't force us to be humble; we get the choice to go low. If the truth be known...if it wasn't for the Lord, we would know nothing, have nothing, be nothing and do nothing of any significance. In that light...it's easy to be humble!

- **Prayer.** James 5:16, promises that when we pray earnest, heartfelt prayers, they make tremendous power available to us. Let's pray for our country, our leaders and for Americans. Let's pray that our hearts will be receptive to the things God values and the truth of His Word, that the eyes of our hearts will be opened to see the things God wants us to see. Pray that we will be filled with the knowledge of God's will for this country. When we pray, it's our opportunity to ask! God said we have not because we ask not *(James 4:2)*. So, let's ask...for mercy, grace, wisdom, help, favor and all that He's already promised in His Word.

- **Seeking.** Seeking God is a lost art among many. To seek the Lord is to pursue God, to go after Him and His plans and purposes with vim and vigor. To crave God is to desire and require His thoughts, His will and His direction. Seeking God is the expression of a heartfelt desire to know Him, to walk with Him and to have His heart. The level of our seeking can be determined by our hunger and thirst for the Lord and His ways. Are you hungry and thirsty for God? Cry out to the Lord from the depths of our soul and seek to know and find Him afresh!

- **Turning.** We have to weigh things and turn from the things that are not pleasing to Him. We have to be willing to admit, repent and forsake, turning away from wickedness, ungodliness and sin. I know these aren't popular words, but they are things we really need to evaluate—and let go of, so we can lay hold of the things God has in store for us?

God's promised to hear from heaven and heal our land, if we will demonstrate humility, prayer, seeking and turning. Put this verse into practice, today!

Read It! James 4:2, KJV

Speak It! "Father, I humble myself before You and Your Word. Lord, help our nation. Open the eyes of our hearts, so we can see one another the way You see us. Fill our leaders with Your knowledge, wisdom and discernment. I ask You to hear from heaven and heal our land. In Jesus' Name. Amen."

DAY 143

(insider trading)

"Friendship with the LORD is reserved for those who fear Him.
With them He shares the secrets of His covenant."
Psalm 25:14, NLT

It's really not fair.

Our friendship with the Lord gives us a major advantage—insider information!
It's true. The Lord reveals secrets to His friends. How does He do it? Two ways:

- **He gives us "inside information"**—inside the Bible. God's Word is loaded with
  wisdom, the scoop, pathways, maps and all the information we need to live a
  life of victory and adventure in Christ! Most of us have barely scratched the
  surface of all that is available to us in Christ, as revealed in the Word. We've
  relegated the Bible to a list of do's and don'ts, rather than what it really is—a
  treasure map, a mystery novel, loaded with revelation and insider information!

- **He gave us an "inside trader"**—inside of us! The minute we receive and
  confess Jesus as our Lord, the Holy Spirit moves in! He lives in us, and He knows
  everything. Jesus said a big part of the Holy Spirit's job is to reveal, announce,
  declare, transmit and tell us everything we need to know! When we meet with
  God in the "secret place of the Most High"—in prayer and spending time with
  Him—He reveals all kinds of things to us. He'll tell us things to come, things to
  anticipate, things to cut-off-at-the-pass, things to prepare for, things to avoid,
  things to do, things about our kids, health, purpose and so much more!

You don't need to be in the dark or the "last one to know" about anything that
concerns you. Spend some time with the Lord—in the Word and in the secret
place of the Most High—and enjoy the benefit of insider information!

Read It! Daniel 2:22, 28a

Speak It! "Father, I thank You for the major advantage You give to Your children.
Thank You for inside information on everything I need to know. I ask You to give
me ears to hear, eyes to see and a heart to receive all You want to reveal to me in
Your Word and by Your Spirit. In Jesus' Name. Amen."

DAY 144

(blueprints)

"What is faith? It is the confident assurance that what we hope for is going to happen. It is the evidence of things we cannot yet see."
Hebrews 11:1, NLT

Faith gives substance to the blueprint of hope! Have you ever noticed that it's impossible to build a house without a blueprint? Once you have the blueprint, you have the potential for a house. The blueprint is NOT the house; it's the "hope" of a house. You cannot sit down at the kitchen table or watch TV on your blueprint; it only lets you see the hope of where the kitchen table and the TV could go. Hope is a blueprint. It's the dream of what could be. Hope is a vision. Hope is future tense.

So, what gives substance to the blueprint? What makes the blueprint a reality? A builder! Faith is the builder. Faith gives substance to the hope. Faith brings hope into reality. Faith is now. Many times, we are just "hoping and praying" God will show up and do something for us. Hoping for something is the blueprint, but we have to go *beyond* "hope" to "faith," if we ever want to see the actual manifestation of our blueprint. If we want "hope" to turn into a reality in our lives, we need to start building that blueprint with faith!

Two things are necessary if we want faith to start working on the blueprints of hope. First, believe God's Word; and second, say what the Word says. Faith believes and says, "God is good, and He's on my side. My God will meet all of my needs according to His riches in glory. His favor surrounds me like a shield. He is for me. He's faithful. God blesses me in the city and in the country." Every time faith believes and speaks God's Word, it's like the builder putting up 2 x 4's and drywall. Faith gives substance to the things we hope for; it is the evidence of the things we don't see yet—the things on the blueprint.

In the same way a massive blueprint and a giant building don't go up overnight, building the blueprints of hope by faith takes patience and persistence. Faith and patience work together to give substance to the blueprints of hope!

What are the blueprints God has for your life? What is His hope for you? Today, start building those prints by faith. What does God's Word say about your hope? Believe it and speak it!

Read It! Jeremiah 29:11

Speak It! "Father, help me see more clearly the blueprint of hope You have for my life—Your vision and dream for my future. Help me start building that blueprint of hope through faith! I believe that through patience and persistence, my faith will give substance to the things hoped for. In Jesus' Name. Amen."

DAY 145

(don't drink the Kool-aid®)

"First off, you need to know that in the last days, mockers are going to have a heyday. Reducing everything to the level of their puny feelings..."
2 Peter 3:3, MSG

I love that the Bible doesn't candy-coat things or mince words! God makes it plain. In these days, there will be mockers, scoffers, pundits, spin doctors, seducers, new-age talk-show hosts, sacrilegious sit-coms, partisan news anchors and outright liars. Unfortunately, the credit crisis, global uncertainty, personal agendas, anti-American world leaders and the polarized political climate have just amplified the noise of the mockers.

It would be funny, if it wasn't so sad. The good news is that none of this is taking God by surprise. In fact, He's already given us His input. Listen to His advice for Believers:

"How well God must like you—you don't hang out at Sin Saloon, you don't slink along Dead-End Road, you don't go to Smart-Mouth College. Instead you thrill to GOD's Word; you chew on Scripture day and night. You're a tree replanted in Eden, bearing fresh fruit every month, never dropping a leaf, always in blossom... GOD charts the road you take. The road they take is Skid Row." (Psalm 1:1-3, 6, MSG)

So, what's our job in the midst of all this? Don't drink the Kool-Aid®!

The mockers may not go away anytime soon...then again, God already knew that... *"Unscrupulous con men will continue to exploit the faith. They're as deceived as the people they lead astray. As long as they are out there, things can only get worse. But don't let it faze you. Stick with what you learned and believed, sure of the integrity of your teachers—why, you took in the sacred Scriptures with your mother's milk! There's nothing like the written Word of God for showing you the way to salvation through faith in Christ Jesus. Every part of Scripture is God-breathed and useful one way or another—showing us truth, exposing our rebellion, correcting our mistakes, training us to live God's way. Through the Word we are put together and shaped up for the tasks God has for us." (2 Timothy 3:13-17, MSG)*

Be bold, stay steady and strong in the Lord and His Word!

Read It! Ephesians 5:11-16, MSG

Speak It! "Father, thank You for truth. Your Word is truth. Jesus is the Truth! I am so glad I don't have to resort to mocking, scorning, deception, degrading and arguing with others. Help me make the most of every chance I get to share the truth! I choose You, and I choose Your Word. In Jesus' Name. Amen."

DAY 146

(get the word out)

"Oh, magnify the LORD with me, and let us exalt His name together."
Psalm 34:3

Are you ready? I am! It's time to bust loose and proclaim the Name! This is no time for us to shrink back. No time to live in fear. No time to be intimidated. No time to back down. No time to quit. This is the time to join with other Jesus -loving peeps and proclaim the reality of His goodness to a hurting, scared, confused and angry world. Now is the time to exalt the Name of Jesus without apology! If the world ever needed to know Him, now is the time!

I love how *The Message Bible* words it, *"Join me in spreading the news; together let's get the word out."*

What word? The word that...

- **Jesus is alive.** *(Luke 24:5-6)* When we pray, He actually hears us, and He has promised to answer the prayers of those who believe!

- **Jesus is the same today as He was yesterday.** *(Hebrews 13:8)* He's still forgiving sins, teaching, mending the broken-hearted, healing bodies, doing miracles and changing lives.

- **Jesus is the Name above every name.** *(Philippians 2:9)* He's got the power to help us overcome everything that can be named; e.g., abuse, cancer, A.D.D., addictions, recession, depression, jealousy, resentment, fear and every other thing with a name.

- **Jesus does good and heals all that are oppressed.** *(Acts 10:38)* His intentions toward us are always only for good. He's not the "bad" guy; He's a good God who gives good gifts—like freedom from oppression, deliverance from any bondage, breakthroughs of all kinds, healing for every illness, joy and peace in the midst of every storm.

- **Jesus is building His Church, and the gates of hell will not prevail against it.** *(Matthew 16:18)* No matter what the world or media tells you, Jesus and His Church are alive and well on Planet Earth. There is a vast army of Christians, united by the Spirit, intently working with Jesus to build His global Church and local churches around the world.

Do you believe it? Today, let's ask the Lord to reveal Himself and the power of His Name to us. Then, let's tell everybody how good Jesus really is!

Read It! Philippians 2:9

Speak It! "Father, thank You for Jesus! Jesus, I believe You are alive, and You have the Name above all names! You are a good God who is still doing good things for Your children. Help me to know the power of Your Name more in my own life and help me get the word out to others! In Jesus' Name. Amen."

DAY 147

(two)

"Two are better than one, because they have a good
return for their work..."
Ecclesiastes 4:9, NIV

Barbra Streisand sang it, *"People who need people are the luckiest people...,"*
but God already knew that. After all, He was the one who said, *"It is not good
for man to be alone."* He knew that *"two are better than one."*

Most married couples will agree that two are better than one. My husband
and I both know we are stronger and more fruitful simply because we have
each other. We make each other better in every way, which is God's plan for
married couples. We ought to be better together, than we could be alone. If
your marriage is struggling, remember two isn't worse than one...it's better!

What does this passage mean for the single person? If you're single, it means
God doesn't want you to be alone—or at a disadvantage. He has a friend for
you, and it may be that spouse you've been dreaming of, or a God-knit friend.
If you're single and in need of that other person, ask the Lord to supply your
need—since it *was* His idea in the first place!

Relationships are God's specialty. He knows how to bring people together;
assembling friendships, marriages, families, teams and churches to accomplish
amazing things together! But, sometimes we forget that we need each other.
God never intended for us to do the Christian life alone or be the "totally-
together, rock of Gibraltar and pillar of society" all by ourselves. It's okay to
lean on others and ask for help, prayer or a good word. If that's what God
intended for us, He would've said, *"One is better...,"*—but He didn't! Why?
Because two can get more work done, regardless of what they're doing. They
can help each other stand up when they've fallen down or are feeling weary in
well doing. They can agree in prayer and lend each other a shoulder when
needed and can defend themselves—whether they're facing the weight of the
world, criticism or persecution for their faith. Two can stand together in faith
and defeat anything the enemy throws their way.

Better yet...three! A three-fold cord is a great picture of Jesus living smack
dab in the middle of our relationships. Invite Him to be the center of your
marriage, family and every other relationship you have. Let's take stock of the
wonderful people God has put into our lives and encourage one another,
remembering that two are better than one—and three is the best!

Read It! Ecclesiastes 4:9-12, NIV

Speak It! "Father, thank You for the people You've put in my life. I ask You to
continue to add God-knit friends to my life. I believe two are better than one, but
three is even better—so I invite You to be in the center of every relationship I
have. In Jesus' Name. Amen."

DAY 148

(come to the light)

"The people who sat in darkness have seen a great light, and upon those who sat in the region and shadow of death Light has dawned."
Matthew 4:16

I love this visual. For thousands of years, mankind sat in darkness. Then, in one day, a great Light was turned on!

From the time Adam sinned in the Garden, mankind had experienced darkness and death—a separation from God. So, for hundreds of years, while God was working a plan to send His one and only Son, He was willing to put a bandage on the problem. Through the Old Testament annual sacrifice of a spotless lamb and the shedding of innocent blood, sin covered sin; and God was able to lead His people—He was their light and salvation. All the while, the Father was working on the ultimate and eternal plan of sending His Son, the Lamb of God, who would shed His innocent blood once and for all for the complete and final payment for sin and the legal impartation of life and light back into all of humanity.

A great Light dawned on that first Christmas morning. As always, God has given each person the right and dignity of choosing to come to the Light. For those who choose Jesus, He turns their darkness into light and gives them eternal life. For those who reject Jesus, things stay pretty dark for a really long time—eternity. Here's the summary:

"For God so loved the world that He gave His one and only Son, that whoever believes in Him shall not perish but have eternal life. For God did not send His Son into the world to condemn the world, but to save the world through Him. Whoever believes in Him is not condemned, but whoever does not believe stands condemned already because he has not believed in the name of God's one and only Son. This is the verdict: Light has come into the world, but men loved darkness instead of light because their deeds were evil. Everyone who does evil hates the light, and will not come into the light for fear that his deeds will be exposed. But whoever lives by the truth comes into the light, so that it may be seen plainly that what he has done has been done through God." (John 3:16-21, NIV)

Today, come to the Light!

Read It! John 8:12

Speak It! "Father, I choose to come to the Light—Jesus. I invite Him to be the Lord of my life—my light and salvation. Thank You for turning the lights on for me. Thank You for life—eternally! In Jesus' Name. Amen."

DAY 149

(stay in the game)

"I consider my life worth nothing to me, if only I may finish
the race and complete the task the Lord Jesus has given me..."
Acts 20:24, NIV

What's the difference between a starter and a finisher? A lot!

Sometimes, I think about what it will be like to finish my race on earth and stand before the Lord. It's hard to imagine what it will be like. I think I will cry. Then, I think I will stare at Jesus to see what He really looks like, and then I will probably look for Eve...to tell her I forgive her. (*smile*) Then, I will...who knows...dance, laugh, sing, explore heaven, check out my mansion, have a cappuccino with Abraham and the apostle Paul. It's gonna be great!

The finish line will be wonderful. But, for now, I just want to run my race and complete the assignments He's given to me! How about you? What is it that keeps us in the game and strong to the end? You know people just like I do, who were strong starters when they began their Christian life and relationship with Jesus. But, today...where are they? Many who have started...quit. Many who started strong...got weary. Many who began...will not finish.

I think the thing that keeps us in the game and filled with joy is the connection we have with the Lord. If running the race is a religious duty, we'll drop out. If it's obligatory, we'll get tired. But, if we have a real, dynamic, present-tense personal relationship with the Lord, and we know...that we know...that we know Him, then He gives us the "go juice" we need to find endurance, stamina, joy and strength to complete our God-given purpose!

Need a booster shot for your race today? You started strong; and through a renewed personal connection with the Lord, you can finish strong! Remember this...

- **Jesus is the Alpha and the Omega...for you!**
- **Jesus is the Author and the Finisher...of your faith.**
- **Jesus is the Beginner and the Completer...of the good work He started in you!**

Read It! Hebrews 12:1

Speak It! "Father, I plan to run my race and finish my course with joy! I want to fulfill the purpose that You intended for my life. Thank You for Your help in getting me started. Today, I ask You for some extra 'go-juice' in my personal relationship with You, so I stay in the game and finish strong. In Jesus' Name. Amen."

DAY 150

(all about who you know)

"...the people who know their God shall prove themselves strong
and shall stand firm and do exploits [for God]."
Daniel 11:32, AMP

Life is all about who you know. The people who know God will be strong,
stand firm and do exploits! I want to be in that group. How about you? Do you
know God? Really know Him? Not just know *about* Him... Do you *know* Him?

There is a huge difference between knowing "about" someone and really
"knowing" someone. The difference is called: a relationship! For example, I
might know a lot "about" John McCain or Sarah Palin or Barak Obama, but I
don't know any of them personally. I watched the debates, saw the news
stories and read the articles; I'm loaded with information "about" them, but I
don't have a close, personal relationship with any of them.

God wants us to know Him—not just listen to others talk "about" Him, hear
what Hollywood says "about" Him or read great, religious best-sellers written
"about" Him. He wants us to know Him in a very personal way.

If you find yourself facing some fear, anxiety, instability and uncertainty, now
is the time to know God—really know Him! Let me encourage you. Here's
what I've come to know about my God and you can, too:

He's good—always. He's faithful and true to His Word. He's fair, merci-
ful, and just. He's generous, a giver...of nice things. He extends a lot of
grace and is patient. He's fun and makes me laugh. He likes my singing.
He heals me and empowers me daily. He's changed and transformed me
so much, I hardly recognize myself. He strengthens me and gives me
courage. He delivered me from all my fears and sets me free from too
many things to mention. He's truthful. He's encouraging. He's been my
Comforter when things were tough. He's my closest Friend. He's easy to
talk to, and His voice is still and quiet. Yet, He speaks in a language I
understand when I read His Word. His presence is tangible and full of
joy. He's always there, never leaves. He's as real to me—and perhaps
more real—than anyone I know.

Those who know God will be strong and do exploits! It's all about Who we
know. I pray we all know Him better in the coming days.

Read It! 1 Timothy 1:12b, NLT

Speak It! "God, I want to know You. I don't want to just know 'about' You; I want to
know You personally. I want to walk with You, talk with You. I want You in every
area of my life. Help me to know You better. In Jesus' Name. Amen."

DAY 151

(the lid)

"According to your faith let it be to you."
Matthew 9:29

Ever bumped into the "Law of the Lid"? It says we can only go as high as the lid above us. John Maxwell describes the "Law of the Lid" in leadership as: when following, working or serving under someone whose vision, leadership skill or capacity is smaller than our own, we keep hitting a lid. For instance, if on a scale of one to 10, our vision, leadership skill or capacity is an 8, but our boss is a only a four, the Law of the Lid makes it difficult for us to go any further.

The "Law of the Lid in Faith" is another way this law plays out. Sometimes, the lid we bump into isn't another person; it's our own faith. Often, the number one limitation we face is simply our ability to believe. What do we believe? What hinders our faith? What causes us to doubt? What should we believe?

Jesus had many things to say about the supernatural, mountain-moving power of our faith. He wants us to believe Him and His words and set the faith lid at "nothing is impossible" and "all things are possible." Consider these:

- **Do you believe God surrounds you with favor, or do you believe nothing ever goes your way?** (Mark 9:23)
- **Do you believe you can overcome any challenge you face, or do you believe you are down for the count?** (Mark 10:27)
- **Do you believe God is on your side and moving mountains for you, or do you believe He's forgotten about you?** (Luke 18:27)
- **Do you believe that your faith plays a role in your lot in life, or do you believe the "que sera, sera—whatever will be, will be" mantra?** (Matthew 15:28)
- **Do you believe you can have great faith that produces great results, or do you believe God only selects a few people to have great faith?** (Matthew 15:28)

If you're not satisfied with what has "been unto you," then kick your faith into a higher gear! What impossibilities need to change for you? What possibilities await you? What has God promised you in His Word? According to your faith, let it be unto you. If you need a faith booster, I encourage you to spend more time reading God's Word, because He said that's the only way to get the type of faith He's pleased with—"faith comes by hearing and hearing by the Word," (Romans 10:17).

Read It! Romans 1:17, KJV

Speak It! "Father, thank You for the ability to believe and for setting the lid at 'all things are possible' and 'nothing is impossible.' I place my faith in You and Your Word. According to my faith, be it unto me. In Jesus' Name. Amen."

DAY 152

(catch your breath)

"True to Your word, You let me catch my breath..."
Psalm 23:3, MSG

Been pedaling as fast as you can? Running hard? Burning the candle at both ends? Need a breather?

(Just take a minute and read the **Read It!** segment.)

The Lord is your Shepherd, and He'll help you catch your breath! How?

- *"He makes me lie down in green pastures..."* Isn't that a pleasant thought? Sometimes, the Lord requires us to take a break. He makes us lie down, chill and rest. "Green pastures" are a picture of an abundant supply of all we need. No worries. No stress. No lack. A place of comfort where we can recharge.
- *"He leads us beside still waters."* Another pleasantry! When we listen to the Lord and yield to Him, He leads us to stillness. Quiet. Peace. The turbines wind down. Mental noise simmers. Busyness slows. We can stop and smell the roses.

How does the Lord do this? Sometimes, the green pastures and still waters are literal places; other times, they are emotional, spiritual or mental places. Either way, He helps us catch our breath.

The Lord is your Shepherd. Today, may you hear His voice as He makes you lie down and leads you to still waters.

Read It! Psalm 23 (the whole chapter)

Speak It! "Thank You, Lord, that You are my Shepherd. Help me to hear Your voice and follow You to the place of green pastures and still waters. I need a breather—physically, emotionally, mentally and spiritually, and I thank You for making me lie down to rest and recharge. Help me follow You to the place of peace, quiet and refreshing. In Jesus' Name. Amen."

DAY 153

(God is not mad at you)

"For He made Him who knew no sin to be sin for us,
that we might become the righteousness of God in Him."
2 Corinthians 5:21

This verse sounds so religious and theological, doesn't it? Sometimes, we get tripped up by certain words in the Bible and don't realize their full impact. When I finally understood this scripture, it revolutionized my life! Today, let's be encouraged by a fresh reminder.

Guilt and condemnation are some of the enemy's biggest tricks. He's often successful at using these things to make us feel like unworthy worms; and as a result, we feel estranged from God and think He's mad at us. A lot of us struggle being so "sin-conscious." We can't always put our finger on it, but we live under a cloud of the "blecks." The truth is, if it weren't for Jesus Christ—in God's sight—we would all be sin-laden, guilt-ridden, shame-filled, dirty dogs. BUT...here's the big but!

BUT...God demonstrated His love toward us; when we were still sinners, Christ died for us (Romans 5:8, NIV). Jesus took our sins away. He never sinned, but He became sin, so we could be made as righteous as God Himself. This means God is not mad at us! He's not holding our sin against us. He's already forgiven us, pronounced us "not guilty" and declared us to be His righteousness! He did this—not because we are perfect, but because He is perfect.

God wants us to comprehend this reality and live as free as if we had never sinned! Most of us have a hard time believing it. We've gotten so used to being "sin-conscious," that we somehow resist the idea of being "righteousness-conscious." Think about that? Today, since we are in Christ, what would it be like to consider ourselves as righteous as God, free from shame, condemnation and any sense of inferiority? It's almost too good to be true—but it is!

If we truly believe God's Word and this particular verse, then we should choose to live in the "righteousness-conscious" reality—free!

Read It! Romans 3:23-24, KJV

Speak It! "Father, thank You that You are not mad at me—and never have been. You loved me so much, You sent Your Son to give me the chance to be righteous before You! I am so glad that my right-standing with You is not based on my good works or failures, but is entirely based on Jesus' work on the cross. What a gift—to be made the righteousness of God in Christ! I declare it today. Jesus, thank You for taking all my sin, so I could be free from guilt, condemnation and inferiority. I am the righteousness of God in Christ! In Jesus' Name. Amen."

DAY 154

(friendship famine?)

"Let each of you look out not only for his own interests,
but also for the interests of others."
Philippians 2:4, NKJV

You've heard of a food famine, but how about a friendship famine? Well, I believe it's important that we sow friendship seeds in every season of our lives.

I remember a time in my life where I was so focused on Jeff and the kids that I didn't sow very many friendship seeds into others. The result was, I experienced a "friendship famine" for a while. Once the light bulb went off, and I realized my dilemma, I intentionally began to pray and show interest in others. I sowed friendship seeds into the lives of those I cared about, and the result has been a wonderful friendship harvest.

We all get busy and consumed with our own affairs, circumstances, desires, pressures, needs and interests, and we forget about OTHERS. What are their concerns? Needs? Daily challenges? Interests? We can't go A.W.O.L. in relationships. Let's not be "absent without official leave" in friendships—sow friendship seeds.

How do you sow friendship seeds? Years ago, I read a great book called, *The Friendship Factor,* by Alan Loy McGinnis. He tells the story of a college girl who felt socially inept. She asked him, as a counselor, how she could be more interesting at parties and in social settings. He answered her with a little phrase that has stuck with me throughout the years: "The key to being interesting is to be interested."

If our relationships need a booster shot and a fresh spark, we can sow these seeds: be interested in others and ask questions! We shouldn't worry about being interesting or clever or funny. If we just ask questions of others and show interest in their interests, people will line up to be our friend, and we'll experience a great harvest of wonderful friends.

Read It! Galatians 6:7, NIV

Speak It! "Father, help me to be better at sowing friendship seeds into the lives of others. Help me to be better at asking questions and showing interest in their concerns, rather than being so focused on my own interests. Thank You for the friends You send into my life. In Jesus' Name. Amen."

164

DAY 155

(score)

"When you win, we plan to raise the roof and lead the
parade with our banners. May all your wishes come true!"
Psalm 20:5, MSG

One day, I took my son, Eric, to see the Detroit Pistons play an exhibition game against the San Antonio Spurs. It was a fun date night and a great reminder of the importance of scoring points! The Pistons had a different strategy that night—not sure what it was, but...the Spurs won by 22 points. It was apparent to everyone the Spurs had won—the scoreboard told the story; they had scored the most points.

Sometimes, we need a good reminder about the importance of scoring points in everyday life. What does the scoreboard tell us? What does a win look like? How do we keep score? In Luke chapter 19, Jesus told us how to score points and measure wins: when we seek the lost and make disciples, we score! When lost, irreligious, unbelieving, seekers come to Christ, plug into His church, grow in the Word and become great at leading others to the Lord—it's a win!

So, the big question is: are we scoring points on heaven's scoreboard?

Think of it this way...

How strange would the Pistons have looked if they showed up to the giant arena in a fancy bus, wore cool uniforms, went through a warm-up routine, dribbled the ball all over the court, but never shot a basket? They would have lost for sure and missed the real reason for being there. The same is true in our own lives. If we just showed up at a nice church each weekend, wore some stylin' clothes, went through our weekly work routine, mingled with friends, but never preached the Gospel or made any disciples; we would have missed our whole reason for being alive.

In these days, while there is still some time left on the game clock, let's get busy shooting and putting some points on the board! In seasons of fear and uncertainty, let's seek and save the lost and make disciples of all nations.

Today, let's score big!

Read It! Matthew 28:19-20

Speak It! "Father, help me to score points that matter! You can count on me, Lord. I am a member of Your team and will do my part to shoot baskets and rack up points for eternity. Help me to seek and save the lost and help me to make disciples. In Jesus' Name. Amen."

DAY 156

(good medicine)

"A merry heart does good, like a medicine..."
Proverbs 17:22

God. Just who is God, anyway? The old-time preachers call Him, "Gaaaawwwd!" To those who don't know Him, He's just a swear word. But, I want to introduce you to a side of God we don't often consider: God laughs. Yes, that's what the Bible says. Yet, many can't even imagine a God who laughs; the only God they know is the serious, stern, severe, kill-joy who's ready to bop you when you mess up.

I don't pretend to know everything about God, but I do know this: God is not sad or down in the dumps. How can He be when in His presence is fullness of joy? When you get around God, you can't help but laugh. How have we missed this? The Bible tells us God sings and rejoices over His kids. The angels in heaven have parties when people turn to the Lord. And, while on earth, Jesus was loaded with more joy than anyone else. To top it off, we're told to serve the Lord with gladness and to rejoice always. Apparently, God is into joy.

Sadly, I think the reason more people aren't attracted to God is because of us Christians. We often look like we've been baptized in pickle juice, rather than radiating joy and laughter. Some of us are trying so hard to impress others with our brilliant intellect, stoic spirituality, status and success that we have become incredibly boring. Some of us feel guilty about being glad in a world gone mad! But in uncertain times, lauaghter is good medicine.

Big question: do we cry more than we laugh? We're supposed to be conformed to His image, right? Then, we need to laugh, lighten up, smile, giggle—feel the joy. Today's scripture tells us *"a merry heart does good, like a medicine."* God intended for us to go through life...medicated. So, c'mon get happy!

- **Laugh anyway.** We need to just laugh when we'd rather not. We need to imitate God and laugh...by choice...a lot—even at ourselves! If it's been a while, you might be surprised at how refreshing it is just to laugh.
- **Talk right.** We have to tell our mouth what to do if we want to live a happy life. The Bible's clear on this! *(1 Peter 3:10)*
- **Thank God.** C'mon, let's do this! Let's be thankful for our life, breath, family, health and blessings, and the joy will come.

Read It! Psalm 2:4; Psalm 16:11

Speak It! "Father, thank You for reminding me how to take Your medicine...and laugh! In the midst of life's uncertainties, You have given me so many reasons to be joyful and thankful. As I spend more time in Your presence, I will be refreshed; and others will see Your goodness in my life. In Jesus' Name. Amen."

DAY 157

(the umbrella)

*"I was young and now I am old, yet I have never seen
the righteous forsaken or their children begging bread."*
Psalm 37:25, NIV

What a time to be living under the umbrella of God's economy, rather than the world's financial system! As Christians, living under the Lordship of Jesus and cooperating with God's economic laws, we can be greatly encouraged in the midst of financial turmoil and Wall Street's Black Friday—not begging for bread.

Why? Because God's promised to meet all our needs through His riches in Christ, we have the assurance of Malachi 3 as our umbrella.

If we've laid up treasures in heaven by giving our financial tithes—10% of our income—to the local church and offerings—anything above our 10%—to the work of God, then we can take comfort in knowing we are under His umbrella, and He's promised to meet our needs. The Lord promises to open the windows of heaven upon us and rebuke the devourer for our sake. What does it mean to be under God's umbrella? It means the Lord will...

- **Provide opportunities, favor, increase and advantages.**
- **Give us wisdom on how to steward our wealth, manage our debt/credit and increase our assets and cash reserves.**
- **Give us insight on how and where to invest for increase and profit in this opportune time and protect our investments and give us wisdom on how to recoup any losses.**
- **Give us the knowledge of witty inventions.**
- **Supernaturally provide for our needs, if necessary.**

As Believers, this is no time to be in fear, panic or turmoil. Rather, this is the time to be full of faith, courage and wisdom as we trust the Lord and operate according to His economic laws.

Read It! Malachi 3:10-13

Speak It! "Father, I trust You, and I'm living under the umbrella of Your economy. Thank you for Your promise to meet all of my needs according to Your riches in glory. Thank You for opening the windows of heaven for me and pouring out blessings on me and for rebuking the devourer for my sake. Now, I'm not dominated by the world's economic system; instead, I'm fully vested in Your economy. *(In the event, you haven't followed or obeyed the Lord by operating according to His economic laws, say this:)* Father, I repent and ask You to forgive me. I've trusted in my money more than I've trusted in You. Today, I make a decision to 'prove You' and get in alignment with Your economic laws. As I begin to tithe and give offerings, I ask You for Your mercy, grace and wisdom in my finances. In Jesus' Name. Amen."

DAY 158

(you passed)

> "Most assuredly, I say to you, he who hears My word
> and believes in Him who sent Me has everlasting life, and shall
> not come into judgment, but has passed from death into life."
> John 5:24

I love this reality! Jesus plainly tells us that if we hear His Word and believe in Him, we have passed from death to life. That is, whosoever believes on Jesus will have everlasting life *(John 3:16)*. Do you know what this means?

Now, go to the **Read It!** segment and check out *The Amplified Bible* translation! Isn't that awesome? We will not come into judgment, because Jesus took the judgment we deserved. We have already passed from death into life. Do you see that? *"...Passed from death into life..."* This is a past *and* present tense reality, not just a future reality. We have already received eternal life through Jesus Christ! What does that mean?

If I were to ask most Christians, "When will you experience eternal life?" They would say, "After we die," but that's NOT correct! We have eternal life now! The minute we accepted Jesus Christ as our Lord and Savior, we received eternal life and passed from death to life.

Eternal life is not just a quantity of timelessness in which to live; it's a quality of life. Eternal life, everlasting life is the God-kind of life; Jesus also called it "abundant life." We are present-tense possessors of eternal life right now! It means that we'll never die. We've already taken a pass on death! Sure, our body will die; but the real us—the person who lives in our body—will never taste death...ever! Now, that is something to shout about! We are free to live in God's goodness, mercy, blessings, righteousness, kindness, power, favor, grace—and everything else eternal life includes.

Let's meditate on this amazing truth: through Jesus Christ we have already passed from death to life. We are blessed with the quantity and quality of this amazing thing called "eternal life." Let's make this our declaration of faith today.

Read It! John 5:24, AMP

Speak It! "Father, thank You for giving me eternal life now! Thank You that I—the real me, the spirit me—will never die, but I have already passed from death to life. I will not come under judgment, because You took the judgment I deserved and You gave me the eternal life I didn't deserve. Thank You so much. I will talk today as a person who truly understands that. In Jesus' Name. Amen."

DAY 159

(go small or go home)

"Samuel said, 'Although you were once small in your own eyes,
did you not become the head of the tribes of Israel?
The LORD anointed you king over Israel.'"
1 Samuel 15:17, NIV

The secret to our success in life: stay small in our own eyes. Go small, or go home. When we stay little in our own estimation and avoid "getting a big head" after having a few successes, God can actually anoint, use and promote us.

However, when pride enters into our lives, we are heading for a fall, a loss, a demotion and a slow boat to God's destiny for our lives. The Lord cannot endorse or promote pride. In fact, the Bible says God resists the proud *(James 4:6)*. How's that for hitting the big emergency brake in our lives? When God resists us...we have big problems! The only solution? Go small!

So, why is pride such a universal problem? Unfortunately, when God gives us a bit of success, we can be tempted to start believing that we are "all that," and this creates serious issues. It's a temptation we all face. If we pay attention to the red flags, we can take action and go small.

If we notice these warning signs, we need to find a way to become little in our own eyes—immediately!

- **Warning Signs!** Showing an attitude of superiority. Speaking in condescending tones. Patronizing others. Being discontent and unwilling to serve in little things. Having a territorial attitude. Needing to toot our own horn. Becoming angry when corrected. Feeling that we are "above" certain tasks. Disregarding the "little people." Needing to always be right. Being unable to admit mistakes. Blaming others for our inadequacies. Displaying an arrogant attitude, rude behavior or ungrateful expectations. Needing to "one up" others.

Maybe we're struggling and wondering why things are not going so well for us. We know God has gifted and anointed us, but doors are not opening up. Could it be a pride problem?

Read It! 1 Peter 5:5-6

Speak It! "Father, I want to stay small in my own eyes. I know the best place to be is in a place of humility. Show me areas of my life where pride has crept in and help me choose to go small. I know You resist the proud but give grace to the humble, so I humble myself under Your Hand. Today, help me serve You and live this out in a way that honors Jesus. In Jesus' Name. Amen."

DAY 160

(a big thank you)

"Let every detail in your lives—words, actions, whatever—be done
in the name of the Master, Jesus, thanking God the Father
every step of the way."
Colossians 3:17, MSG

Did you know we can give God something He doesn't already have? It's true.
We can give God thanks! How about giving the Lord a big "thank You," today...
for everything! Thank Him for every detail of your life.

Just think. How do we feel when others thank us? It's nice when others notice,
appreciate and thank us for our efforts, kindness, sacrifice, encouragement,
smiles, help, support, prayers and friendship, right? When people are thankful,
what does it move us to do? It inspires us to continue blessing and doing good,
doesn't it? I wonder if God feels the same way?

Today, let's notice, appreciate and thank the Lord for His goodness, faithfulness, kindness, mercy, grace, patience, favor, forgiveness, blessings, health,
family, friends and sooooooo much more.

Get started and be specific.

Read It! 1 Chronicles 16:8, NLT

Speak It! "Father, I thank You. Jesus, I thank You. Holy Spirit, I thank You. Lord, I
thank You for everything! You have blessed my life in so many ways. I am thankful
for: (Tell the Lord all the specific things you are thankful for.) In Jesus' Name.
Amen."

DAY 161

(bucket list)

"Tell those who are rich not to be proud and not to trust in their money, which will soon be gone, but their pride and trust should be in the living God who always richly gives us all we need for our enjoyment."
1 Timothy 6:17, TLB

Have you made a "bucket list"—a list of things you want to do before you kick-the-bucket? (If you haven't seen *The Bucket List,* it's a good, thought-provoking movie to rent.)

I believe there are two sides to the "coin of life" God wants us to see before we kick-the-bucket. If you'll read the **Read It!** segment, it describes the two sides of the "coin of life" and gives us food-for-thought for our bucket list.

- **Heads: Effectiveness!** God wants us to invest our lives. What will our lives amount to? Who will we have helped and influenced for eternity? Let's make sure we've already made a decision to invest our temporary life—time, energy, money, gifts, talents—into eternal things. Let's live a purposeful life with "no regrets" to glorify the Lord and be rich in good deeds, generous and willing to share Christ and our abundance with others. Assuming that is the case, let's look at the other side of the life coin...

- **Tails: Enjoyment!** God wants to bless our lives and give us all things to enjoy. Sometimes, we have a hard time accepting the fact that the Lord wants us to enjoy a blessed life—but He does! When we live for "heads," He blesses us with "tails." When we seek first His kingdom and His priorities, He gives us richly all kinds of things for our enjoyment—family, friends, nature, stuff—and so much more *(Matthew 6:33).* So, the idea is to live for 'heads' and enjoy "tails!"

Years ago, we went to a funeral for a man named George (not his real name). The sad part wasn't that George died but how he lived. George only lived for "tails;" he never lived for "heads."' His life was all about his enjoyment and nothing else. When people reflected on his life at the funeral, here's what they said: *"Well, George loved the Elks club. He was one heck of an Elk. The other thing I remember is how he loved sports... What a guy. We'll sure miss him."* We were slightly stunned. That's it? George kicked the bucket, and all that his closest family and friends could say was that he was an Elk and loved sports? Wow! The moral of the story in our temporary lives? Get it right! Lets make our bucket list now. Let's live for "heads," and we'll enjoy "tails."

Read It! 1 Timothy 6:17-19, TLB

Speak It! "Father, at my funeral, I want Jesus be honored as people eulogize my life. Help me create a bucket list that reflects that desire in me. Help me maximize my temporal life with effectiveness for Your eternal purposes. Thank You that when I live for Your purposes, You give me rich blessings to enjoy! Thank You that when I live for 'heads,' You overload me with 'tails.' In Jesus' Name. Amen."

DAY 162

(God is for you)

*"What then shall we say to these things?
If God is for us, who can be against us?"*
Romans 8:31

OK, get this. You and God are a majority! If God is for you, who can be against you? Name one person who can successfully be against you. Come on... What's their name? That's what I thought you said—no one! Nobody can successfully come against you!

Be encouraged. Come what may, you win! If you're feeling the weight of the world on you and against you, cheer up—God is for you. If the devil has been eating your lunch, just lick your lips and smile—God is for you. If you lost a few rounds, wipe the blood from your nose and laugh—God is for you. There is only one outcome: you win!

Listen...

- **No weapon formed against you will prosper.** *(Isaiah 54:17a)*
- **Every tongue that rises against you in judgment, you shall put down.** *(Isaiah 54:17b)*
- **No plague shall come near your dwelling.** *(Psalm 91:10)*
- **He always leads you in triumph.** *(2 Corinthians 2:14)*
- **You are more than a conqueror through Christ.** *(Romans 8:37)*

What a position of victory we have in Christ!

(Now, quickly, go read the **Read It!** segment.)

If God already gave His best and finest gift—His own Son—to free us from the eternal penalty of sin and death that was against us, how will He not freely give us all the other things we need?

God is for you! Who can be against you? Today, shout for victory!

Read It! Romans 8:31-33

Speak It! "Father, I shout the victory today! I am a victor in Jesus' Name! God is on my side. My God is for me; so who can be against me? I choose to cheer up, to smile, to laugh because it's true—You and I are a majority and we win! Thank You for giving up Your Son for me and for freely giving me all I need. God is for me, and I have the victory in Jesus' Name. Amen."

DAY 163

(run, Forrest, run)

"The name of the LORD is a strong tower;
the righteous run to it and are safe."
Proverbs 18:10

Need a safe place? A place of refuge? Strength? The Name of the Lord is a strong tower, so run to it!

What a comforting verse of Scripture. Though the enemy may roar, the storms may blow, the waves may rage, the winds may howl and the earth may shake, the Name of Jesus is a safe place. His Name is the name above every name. Jesus is the Name at which everything else bows.

If fear, anxiety, distress, depression or other things are trying to harass you— run! Run, Billy Bob, run! Run, Suzy Q, run! He will lift you up, high above it all!

The Amplified Bible gives us a more "amplified" understanding of this verse:

"The name of the Lord is a strong tower; the [consistently] righteous man [upright and in right standing with God] runs into it and is safe, high [above evil] and strong."

Be encouraged today!

Read It! Psalm 46:1

Speak It! "Father, I run to You today. I run right into the Name of Jesus, my strong tower! I am safe, free from the enemy, storms, fear, anxieties and distress. Jesus is the Name above all Names, and I thank You for lifting me up to a safe and strong place, high above evil. In Jesus' Name. Amen."

DAY 164

(multitudes)

"But when He saw the multitudes, He was moved with compassion for them... Then He said to His disciples, 'The harvest truly is plentiful, but the laborers are few. Therefore pray the Lord of the harvest to send out laborers into His harvest.'"
Matthew 9:36-37

We were walking around Times Square in NYC recently, and I was struck—once again—by the multitudes. People everywhere. Sometimes, I look at people and try to imagine who they are and what their lives might be like. Are they lonely? Happy? Empty? Lost? It doesn't matter whether we're in Mexico City, Bangkok, Rome, Montreal, Orlando or Kalamazoo...people are everywhere. Real people who live real lives, and face real challenges, who need a real God. They will spend a real eternity in a real place—heaven or hell.

When I look at the multitudes, I always end up thinking, "Wow, look at all of these people! God, You know all of them. You know their thoughts...the number of hairs on their heads, and You love every one of them. How many of these people know You? How many are saved and on their way to heaven?" It's an overwhelming, mind-boggling thought.

Multitudes. Multitudes. Sometimes we can get so busy, taxed or focused on our own lives that instead of feeling compassion or any genuine care for the multitudes, we find ourselves flat-lined, desensitized and detached from humanity. When that happens, real people become strangers, empty shells, nuisances, problems, tools, inconveniences or simply a means to an end.

In those times, we need to pray. We need to ask Jesus to rekindle His heart in us for the people He loves. We need to feel what He feels when He looks on the multitudes and sees the harvest. We need Him to expand the capacity of our hearts so we are moved with compassion for people and are willing to be laborers in His harvest of souls.

If you've been feeling a little glazed-over, emotionally detached and desensitized to the "multitudes" around you—at work, in the airport, at school, in the mall, downtown, at the stadium...or any other place where you encounter people—watch and pray.

Read It! Joel 3:14

Speak It! "Father, my life has been so busy and preoccupied. I need a fresh wave of Your love and compassion to fill my heart. Help me to be moved with compassion when I see the multitudes and 'see' them with Your eyes. Help me listen to Your heart. Lord, I ask you to send laborers for the harvest. In Jesus' Name. Amen."

DAY 165

(man up)

"Watch ye, stand fast in the faith, quit you like men, be strong..."
1 Corinthians 16:13, KJV

This passage has always intrigued me. It's a very proactive and surprising statement. It's like the Lord gives us a motivational kick in the rear, tells us to pay attention, put up our dukes and man up!

The phrase, *"quit you like men"* has always caught my attention—such a "King James" way to say, "Be strong and man up!" As a kid, I played the "harp" in a Jack and the Beanstalk drama. I still remember a line from that play: "Be a man, Jack!"—or Mike...or Tim...or Linda...or Jennifer! They say testosterone is one of the hormones that make men "manly," giving them added strength. It sounds like God wants all of us—men and women—to tap into His spiritual "testosterone" and be spiritually strong and courageous.

(Quick note: Girls, in the natural, let's be feminine and godly and sweet; but spiritually, let's put the devil on the run as we *"quit you like men"*—or man up!)

This is no time to be a wimpy Christian. A milk-toast Believer. A spineless Christ-follower. No, let's, *"Watch ye, stand fast in the faith, quit you like men, be strong..."*

Today, stand up straighter. Hold your head higher. Put up your dukes. Take action. Man up and tell weakness, intimidation, fear, failure, anger, depression, grief, self-pity and anything else that is coming against you to take a hike, in Jesus' Name.

Read It! Ephesians 6:10, KJV

Speak It! "Father, I will watch. I will stand firm in the faith. I will be a 'man' of courage. I will be strong in the Lord and the power of His might. No more wimpy Christianity for me. Count me in! I will 'man up' for Your purposes. In Jesus' Name. Amen."

DAY 166

(secret weapons)

"But the fruit of the Spirit is love, joy, peace, patience, kindness, goodness,
faithfulness, gentleness and self-control. Against such things there is no law."
Galatians 5:22-23, NIV

There is no law against love, joy, peace, patience, goodness, faithfulness,
gentleness and self-control. These are our secret weapons!

When the world around us is angry, intimidating, hateful, unhappy, mad,
stressed, discontent, mean, bad, suspicious and accusatory, critical, doubt-
filled, rough, harsh and out-of-control, we have a secret weapon.

People can't figure out how we can be...

- **Loving and kind toward those who seek to hurt, discredit and annoy us.**
- **Full of joy and peace when gas prices are up and Wall Street is down.**
- **Patient and faithful when people around us act like whack-jobs.**
- **Good and gentle toward our critics who want to see our demise.**
- **Full of self-control when facing a crisis, an injustice or frustration.**

There is no law against love, joy and peace—and all the fruit of God's Spirit.
May we be "armed and dangerous" today!

Read It! Matthew 5

Speak It! "Father, thank You that Your love has been poured out in my heart, and
all the fruit of the Spirit is within me. Help me yield to these secret weapons so
others are touched by You when they see and experience the love, joy, peace,
patience, goodness, faithfulness, gentleness and self-control in my life. Thank You
that there is no law against these things! Help me to be 'armed and dangerous'
today. In Jesus' Name. Amen."

DAY 167

(liars are fryers)

"But there were false prophets, too, in those days, just as there will be false teachers among you. They will cleverly tell their lies about God, turning against even their Master who bought them; but theirs will be a swift and terrible end... God condemned them long ago and their destruction is on the way."
2 Peter 2:1-3, TLB

"Liars are fryers." "Honesty is the best policy." We told our kids these things because God hates lies, and He loves truth—and so should we! But, how do we know for sure if something is true? From the Lord? Approved by God? The litmus test for godliness and true Christianity is whether what is being said, touted, preached or proclaimed is congruent with God's character and His Word. God will never endorse or put His stamp of approval on anything that contradicts His own Word—not a person, a book, a movie, a song, a TV personality, a preacher or anyone and anything that espouses something in opposition to Jesus Christ or the truth, integrity, character and morality of God's Word. This is Christianity 101.

We must be wise and not fall hook, line and sinker for everything that appears to be "spiritual" or has the word "God" in it. The enemy has one tool: deception. Through the cross and the resurrection, Jesus defeated and disarmed the devil. Satan doesn't have any real power; the only thing he has is deception. Therefore, he uses everything and everyone he can to promote blatant lies. Lies about God. Lies about Jesus...about Christians...about the Bible...about people. Lies about life and living—and everything in between. The worst part is, many of the lies are told using spiritual vocabulary. We must not be naïve. Just because we hear or see phrases like, "your inner self," "conversations with God," "I died and went to the light," doesn't mean it's legit.

Take a minute and go to the **Read It!** segment. Jesus predicted it long ago. Today more than ever, we need to be smart and intuitive to the various types of deceptions. We are bombarded 24/7 by the constant worldly influences and liberal persuasions of an "anti-Christ" media and popular culture, but only attend church, pray or read our Bibles a few times a week. The odds are stacked against us. To be a solid, Jesus-exalting, Bible-believing, integrity-living, victory-enjoying Christian, it's going to take some grit, determination and intentionality! Let's not be easily duped, naïve, or gullible, going after religious fads; let's be strong in the Lord and in His Word!

Read It! 2 Timothy 3:1-8, MSG

Speak It! "Father, I choose You. I choose Jesus and Your Truth. Thank You for empowering me to stand strong—even in the face of the blatant lies. Greater is He that is in me than he who is in the world. In Jesus' Name. Amen."

DAY 168

(got your number?)

"So teach us to number our days, that we may gain a heart of wisdom."
Psalm 90:12

Ever numbered your days? Literally? It goes like this...

If you were able to decide, how old would you like to be when you die?

Of course, no one knows when they will die and go be with the Lord, other than we do know the Bible promises us if we will set our love on Him and walk in the light of His Word, He will satisfy us with long life.

How old are you now?

Subtract your current age from the age you'd like to be when you die. That's the number of your days.

What was your number? Have you lived half your life yet? Have you lived 25% or 75% or somewhere in between? How many days do you have left to know God, serve the Lord and leave a legacy?

Life is ticking at a rapid rate of speed. We blink...our life passes by. We live busy, messy, fun, complex lives day-after-day. We are literally living our life time—now, in real time. There are no do-overs. We get one shot at this thing called life. We get to invest it in eternal things or temporal things.

How are we investing our time? Today, let's take some time to analyze our time and be intentional about how we spend and invest the rest of our lives. Let's number our days and make sure Earth knew we were here before we leave. Let's make our lives count for eternity!

Read It! 2 Timothy 4:7, KJV

Speak It! "Father, help me to number my days. Help me to maximize my life for Your purposes. I choose to spend my life investing in eternal things. Show me how to do it more effectively. In Jesus' Name. Amen."

DAY 169

(workaholics)

"For what profit is it to a man if he gains the whole world, and loses his own soul? Or what will a man give in exchange for his soul?"
Matthew 16:26, KJV

Does the one with the most toys win? What price is a soul worth? These days, people spend so much of their time, energy, mind, strength and life seeking things. Seeking to outdo their neighbors. Seeking to impress people they don't even care about, don't even know. Seeking to gain the world. And, for what purpose?

Know any workaholics? They've gained the world and have the "stuff" to prove it. The only bummer—the cost! Gaining the world will cost us—maybe our health, our joy and peace, our integrity and reputation, our marriage, our family, the relationship with our kids and others—and who knows what else. If a workaholic has no place for a relationship with Jesus in their life, it will cost them their soul. Eternity is a long time. But, eternity without God is a *really* long time.

Jesus talked about the workaholic. Take a minute and go read the parable in the **Read It!** segment and see what He had to say about it.

There is a better way—God's way. When we live life the way God intended and do things His way, we end up gaining a lot—including eternal life! The caveat? At first, it's going to cost us everything we've got—like our whole life. He who loves his life has to lose it...to gain it *(Luke 17:33)*. When we give up our life—as we know it, we gain His life. When we quit doing it our way, we win. When we give up our baloney sandwich, we gain His banqueting feast. And, when we make our relationship with Jesus and doing things His way a priority, He blesses our lives and makes us rich in every way, without the need for sorrow, remorse, regret or apology. *"The blessing of the LORD makes one rich, and He adds no sorrow with it." (Proverbs 10:22)*

Read It! Luke 12:16-21, NIV

Speak It! "Father, I repent! I have spent way too much of my life focused on the wrong things. The world has owned me, and it's cost me a lot. I ask You for Your mercy and grace to help me get on the right track. I don't want to be a workaholic. I don't want to lose my health, marriage, kids, integrity or relationships, and I definitely don't want to lose my soul. Lord, I quit! Today, I quit doing things my way, and I choose to do things Your way. I give up my life to gain Yours. Jesus, I ask You to be the Lord of my life. Help me to follow You for the rest of my days. I would rather have Your blessings in my life than all the toys in the world. In Jesus' Name. Amen."

DAY 170

(bored as a gourd)

"Revive me, O LORD, according to Your word."
Psalm 119:107

Bored these days? It's time to eat and drink...the Word. God's Word has the power to revive us.

We need a revival of the Word in America! We don't need a revival of religion or denominationalism. We don't need the dead, "letter-of-the-law" message of condemnation and legalism. We don't need the Bible to be relegated to some piece of historical literature. We need a revival of the living Word.

The Bible is alive! We need a fresh meal and a refreshing drink. God's Word is living and active and has the supernatural power to revive us *(Hebrews 4:12, NIV)*. God's Word will effectually work within the person, family, community or nation who believes and does what it says. We need a fresh revelation of the Word of the Lord. We need a revival of the living, "spirit-of-the-law" and the life-changing message of redemption through Jesus Christ!

If our eyes have been glazed over and we're bored as a gourd with Christianity-as-usual, then let's get serious about eating and drinking. Today, let's grab our Bible, find a quiet place and then pray a heartfelt prayer, asking the Lord to revive us according to His Word.

Read It! Psalm 19:7-11

Speak It! "Father, revive me according to Your Word. I ask You to create in me such a hunger and thirst for You and Your Word that nothing else will satisfy. In Jesus' Name. Amen."

DAY 171

(keep it simple)

"But I fear, lest somehow, as the serpent deceived Eve by his craftiness, so your minds may be corrupted from the simplicity that is in Christ."
2 Corinthians 11:3

I am so glad the Lord is not complex. He keeps it simple, and He's leveled the playing field for all of us. There is simplicity in Christ. Sometimes, we're tempted to think that unless we understand all the Greek, Hebrew, theological arguments, historical context and every hermeneutical law of Biblical interpretation, we cannot possibly understand the deep things of God!

Relax. Jesus did not intend to be confusing; He's made it simple. God meets us right where we are at. The religious people of His day, the doctors of the Law—the Pharisees and Sadducees—tried to muddy the waters and make God austere, formal, religious and mystifying. Jesus ruined their whole paradigm.

If you're a brainiac, the Lord will connect with you in an intelligent way that makes sense to you. If you're not the sharpest pencil in the drawer, have no fear! Jesus is a person, not a subject. He's personal, not a research project.

The beauty of the Lord is that He makes the most wisdom-laden realities... simple! Take redemption, for example. When you study God's eternal plan for man, it's absolutely amazing. His foreknowledge, His attention to detail, His patience, His prophetic words, the literal and symbolic types and shadows, the biological and miraculous Incarnation and Jesus as the Son of God and Son of man... It's beyond man's mind—yet, simple. If you don't fully understand all the mechanics of your great salvation, no worries; you can still enjoy the experience of all that redemption means. You can have a personal, life-filled relationship with the Lord God Almighty. Jesus is our Redeemer. We know Him, and that's enough. There is simplicity in Christ.

Think about it this way. We don't need to know all the mechanics of our car in order to enjoy the simplicity of putting our key in the ignition and driving it. The same way, we don't have to impress anyone with deep theological speaking. We can just take pleasure in the reality of our personal relationship with the Lord and all the wonders of His Person—in all its simplicity! Today, let's relax and not make the whole Christian thing too complex and confusing. Let's keep it simple!

Read It! 1 Corinthians 1:27, KJV

Speak It! "Father, I am so glad You've made it simple. Jesus, today, I am not going to worry about all the things I don't know or understand. I am going to focus on enjoying the simplicity of just knowing You as my Lord and very best friend. In Jesus' Name. Amen."

DAY 172

(the "in crowd")

"Therefore, if anyone is in Christ, he is a new creation;
old things have passed away; behold, all things have become new."
2 Corinthians 5:17

There is one little word that can change our world, if we let it. The word is: "in." If we will renew our minds to the truth of this little word, our whole world can change—literally! Everyone wants to be "in"—a part of the "in crowd"—these days. Well, God has given the true meaning to being "in." Is Jesus the Lord of your life? If so...get "in" on this.

As Believers, we are "in" Christ, and the ramifications are enormous! Being in Christ, we have a completely new identity. In Christ, we are seen by God in the same way He sees Jesus. In Christ, we are more than conquerors. In Christ, we have been made as righteous as God Himself.

As far as God is concerned, we are not unworthy, unrighteous or unholy Believers; rather, we are the recipient of God's immeasurable mercy and grace and we've been placed "in" Christ. He's made us worthy, righteous, and holy. Yes, that's right! Let's look at a few verses that tell us what's true for us "in" Christ:

- **Jesus made us each a new person.** *(2 Corinthians 5:17)*
- **Jesus is not condemning us.** *(Romans 8:1)*
- **Jesus sees us just as righteous as He is.** *(2 Corinthians 5:21)*
- **Jesus has accepted us.** *(Ephesians 2:13)*
- **Jesus picked us to be holy.** *(Ephesians 1:4)*
- **Jesus has made us complete.** *(Colossians 2:9-10)*
- **Jesus has forgiven our sins!** *(Ephesians 1:7, NIV)*
- **Jesus marked us.** *(Ephesians 1:13, NIV)*
- **Jesus wants us to come to Him with freedom and confidence.** *(Ephesians 3:12, NIV)*

Let's agree with God and who He's made us "in" Christ, instead of living by our failures, feelings, circumstances or experiences. Let's declare that we're "in"!

Read It! 2 Corinthians 5:21

Speak It! "Father, thank You that I am 'in' Christ, and that You see me 24/7 'in Him.' I declare by faith that I see myself the way You do. I am 'in' Christ! In Christ, I am a new person. There is no condemnation, for I am righteous in Christ. In Christ, I am accepted, holy and complete. In Christ, I am marked for You and approach You with complete freedom and confidence! I receive Your mercy and grace. In Jesus' Name. Amen."

DAY 173

(wanted: true worshipers)

"Yet a time is coming and has now come when the true worshipers
will worship the Father in spirit and truth, for they are the kind of
worshipers the Father seeks. God is spirit, and His worshipers must
worship in spirit and in truth."
John 4:23-24, NIV

God is looking for a specific type of person. His search engine is always scroll-
ing, crawling, looking and seeking. How would you like to be found by the
Lord? The Father is seeking "true worshipers."

A true worshiper worships the way God commands—in spirit and in truth.
God isn't looking for people who dictate their own definition of worship
or spirituality or religion; He is looking for those who have embraced His
definition. What does a "true worshiper" look like?

- **Worshiping in spirit.** This person loves, praises and obeys the Lord from their
  heart—or spirit. "Worshiping in spirit" means that we love, seek and obey the
  Lord with our whole heart, mind, soul and strength. It's when the "deep" in us
  calls to the "deep" in God and vice versa. This person loves and obeys God from
  their heart-of-hearts, their guts and the depths of their being.

- **Worshiping in truth.** This person worships God according to His truth—not the
  truth they invent or the truth which comes from men. Jesus told us that He is the
  truth, and His Word is the truth. When the foundation for our worship is the truth
  of God's Word, we are worshiping in truth. When the object of our worship is
  Jesus, we are worshiping in truth. God is seeking people like this, but they are
  hard to come by. To worship in "spirit and in truth" requires a choice.

- **It's a sacrifice.** We sacrifice our own opinion, feelings and will. We don't always
  feel goose bumps when we praise the Lord. In fact, sometimes the goose bumps
  are a million miles away, and we are in the throes of our greatest personal pain.
  True worshipers offer Him a sacrifice of praise anyway. *(Hebrews 13:15, AMP)*

- **It's a choice.** We don't always "feel" like worshiping God, but we choose to do so
  anyway. Sometimes, I marvel at the people that just stand still with a bored, blank
  stare on their face during worship. More importantly, I wonder what the Lord
  thinks about that? It's a choice of our will to worship God—to love, to sing, to
  shout, to pray, to praise and to obey the Lord. True worshipers *will* to worship!
  (Psalm 34:1-3)

Today, be sure God's search engine finds you!

Read It! Hebrews 13:15

Speak It! "Father, I want to be a true worshiper and worship You in spirit and in
truth. I offer You a sacrifice of praise and worship and choose to seek, love, praise,
exalt and obey You. When You're seeking true worshipers...find me! In Jesus' Name.
Amen."

DAY 174

(plumb line)

"The entirety of Your word is truth..."
Psalm 119:160

What's the standard these days? Is it all relative? Is "whatever works for you" the measuring stick? Is there a plumb line for life? Who's right...on anything? The smartest person in the room? The one with the most money? The loudest and most arrogant? Are there any "rights" and "wrongs"? Whose opinion counts?

At some point, we have to establish what we believe about truth. We also have to remind ourselves of the truth when constantly barraged by the waves of humanism and relativism. What is the truth? Who is the truth? Where is the truth?

I remember crossing that bridge during the summer of 1979. I came to two definitive conclusions. First, Jesus was who He said He was: *"the way, the truth and the life,"*—not "a" way, but "the" way *(John 14:6)*. Second, the Bible, God's Word, is truth. It didn't just "contain" truth; it *was* the "truth." On these two things, I could build my life. I made a choice to invite Jesus to be the Lord of my life and to bank the rest of my life on God's Word. I've never regretted it and have found security, peace, stability and freedom in aligning my life with Jesus and His Word. I don't know it all, but I know what I know based on God's absolute truth.

What does the truth of God's Word mean for us? When opportunities, trials, challenges, temptations, questions or crossroads come before us, we're able to seek God's Word for truth-filled answers. We don't have to ask ourselves, "What do I think?" or "What does my party say?" or "What does my church believe?" or "What do my family or friends think?" We can ask the Lord and see what His Word says on the subject; then, do our best to align ourselves with it.

It's good to keep this in the forefront of our hearts and minds when opinions and tempers start flying regarding any topic—purpose, politics, elections, banking, finance, morality, sexuality, ethics, war, drinking, drugs, rock-and-roll, religion, heaven, hell or eternity—we have a plumb line...the Word. We don't have to argue, shift our opinion based on what's popular, or be dependent on any person's wisdom, insight or the some Internet poll. God's truth doesn't change to meet the culture; the culture needs to adjust to God's truth. Truth is absolute, not relative. Truth is. Everything else adjusts. The truth will set us free!

Read It! John 8:32

Speak It! "Father, You are the truth and God's Word is truth. Help me make all the adjustments to live a life built on the truth of Your Word. In Jesus' Name. Amen."

184

DAY 175

(make a difference)

"And of some have compassion, making a difference..."
Jude 22, KJV

Having compassion on people makes a difference. In these busy lives we all live, perhaps today we can take some time to see people through the lens of compassion. Sometimes, when I am in an airport or a restaurant or driving through a busy city with lots of pedestrians, I look at people and try to imagine what their lives might be like. If someone looks overly concerned or serious, I wonder what's weighing on their minds. If they look scared, I wonder why?

Often, God's compassion fills my heart for them. Sometimes, I pray. Sometimes, I initiate a conversation. Sometimes, I do nothing. I'd like to be better at doing something. When we have compassion on others, it makes a difference.

Can you think of a time when someone had compassion on you? Maybe you deserved an unpleasant consequence for your behavior, but someone gave you a break. Maybe you were late, missed a deadline, or forgot an important event and someone cut you some slack. Maybe you experienced disappointment, loss, heartache or discouragement and someone reached out to you with compassion and kind words. Maybe you failed, messed up and blew it and someone, moved with compassion, lifted you up in prayer. Wasn't that nice?

Doesn't it feel great when people extend compassion towards us?

Let's do the same for others. Today, as we go about our business—whether we are grocery shopping, eating out, attending a school function, working at the office, cleaning house, rebuilding a motor or traveling across country— let's be on the hunt to extend God's compassion to others...and make a difference!

Read It! Matthew 15:32, KJV

Speak It! "Father, help me recognize those in my world who need a dose of Your compassion. Today, help me to make a difference. In Jesus' Name. Amen."

DAY 176

(pray for the sick)

"And when Jesus went out He saw a great multitude; and He was moved
with compassion for them, and healed their sick."
Matthew 14:14

Recently, I was talking to a young lady. She told me how she and a friend were
being moved with God's compassion, and they felt led to go up to the local
hospital to see who God might want them to pray for. These two girls—whom
we'll call M & M—arrived at the hospital and saw a family from their church
whom they knew were in the fight of faith to overcome cancer. M & M sat
with this family for a bit and then asked if they could pray with them. Each
member of that family was so blessed and in high spirits when the girls left.

Then M & M went to a waiting room where they saw a 13 year-old girl waiting
for her brother who was in one of the hospital rooms. They asked the girl if
they could pray for her brother, and she said, "Yes." The next thing you know,
M & M were in his hospital room, praying for God's love and healing power to
touch him.

When they left his room, M & M ran into a girl they had both known in high
school and found out her sister was in the hospital, also. Soon, M & M were in
the hospital room and praying with the dad and the two sisters.

On the way out of the hospital, they ran into a homeless man and prayed with
him. They left the hospital after a few hours and thought, "Wow! Look what
the Lord can do when we follow compassion."

How about you and I? Have we noticed others? Have we prayed for the sick
lately? The discouraged? The weary? When I heard the story of these two
girls, I was challenged to my core. I have no doubt that those two girls, moved
by compassion, were the hands of Jesus in the hospital that day.

Lord, help us all find and follow Your compassion for others.

Read It! 1 Peter 3:8

Speak It! "Father, help me tune into Your heart long enough to locate Your compassion. Help me to be moved in such a way that I follow compassion and pray for the sick, discouraged, weary and oppressed. In Jesus' Name. Amen."

DAY 177

(sweet sleep)

"It's useless to rise early and go to bed late, and work your worried fingers to the bone. Don't you know He enjoys giving rest to those He loves?"
Psalm 127:2, MSG

Got a lot on your mind? Having trouble getting a good night's sleep? Claim this verse.

A while ago, I noticed I wasn't getting a good night's sleep. It seemed like there were so many things on my mind, and I'd wake up in the middle of the night and instantly have a million things on my mind; or I would wake up in the morning having had a bad dream. I started to dread going to bed. This went on for a few weeks, and it dawned on me that God had a better plan: He gives His beloved sleep. I claimed it.

The result?

Great sleep! In fact, I slept so well that I didn't even wake up during a recent thunderstorm which apparently shook houses, knocked down trees and took out traffic signals. When the people at work were talking about the massive storm, I asked, "What storm?" I never heard it!

He gives His beloved sleep.

If you've been fighting some late night "sleep battles," here are a few verses of Scripture to meditate upon and lay hold of by faith.

"I will lie down and sleep in peace, for you alone, O LORD, make me dwell in safety." (Psalm 4:8, NIV)

"Do not be afraid of the terrors of the night..." (Psalm 91:5, NLT)

Read It! Psalm 127:2

Speak It! "Father, thank You that You give sleep to Your beloved. I lay hold of this promise, and I thank You for Your peace, rest and sweet sleep tonight. In Jesus' Name. Amen."

DAY 178

(addicted)

"For sin shall not be your master..."
Romans 6:14, NIV

Ever had to deal with a habit or addiction? Ever felt powerless to overcome? Ever wondered what to do? Here are some helpful things to know and do.

- **Know what God says about your issue and call it what He calls it.** If you have a habit, addiction, lust or desire of the flesh that causes you to be condemned in your own heart, then call it what God calls it: sin. I know, no one likes the "S" word; but, sometimes, when we call these things our "little problem," our "issue" or "something I'm struggling with," we make excuses and pet it, rather than kill it. So, are you willing to call your habit, addiction, lust or fleshly desire a sin?

- **Meditate, read, reread, marinate, saturate and soak yourself in God's Word.** Find scriptures that speak to your situation and meditate on them day and night. As you soak in the Word, it will begin to cause overcoming faith to rise up in you, and you will begin to see yourself the way God sees you.

- **Don't let sin reign?** It's as if we have a choice! Well...we do! We can choose not to offer parts of our body to sin, and only offer ourselves—and our bodies—to God. He's simply telling us, "Don't put yourself in a position to sin." *(Romans 6:11-14, NIV)*

- **What actual benefit did we receive from the things we are now ashamed of?** When you really think about it, what actual benefit did you get? A momentary high? A little bit of pleasure? Was that worth the guilt? Shame? Condemnation? Broken fellowship with the Lord? Was the price more expensive than the benefit gained? Did you lose your self-respect? Family or friends? Job? Reputation? Was it worth it? *(Romans 6:21, NIV)*

So, the big question is: how do we overcome an addiction? The Bible says it starts with our mind, our thoughts. When we set our minds on what's right and allow our minds to be controlled by the things that please God, through Christ and the help of the Holy Spirit, we have the power to control our thoughts. We can't spend hours thinking about how we can quit; instead, we need to fix our mind on things that please God. It might be a huge battle at first, but the longer you make your mind focus on things that are right, true, lovely, good and pleasing to God, the more quickly the addiction, lust or desire to sin will lose its grip. *(Philippians 4:8)*

Read It! Romans 8:5-9, NIV

Speak It! "Father, I call my issue, addiction, habit or lust what You call it: sin. Today, I repent and turn 180 degrees from that sin. I ask You to help me set my mind on the right things that please You. I will not offer my body to sin; I offer myself to You. Sin will not be my master; Jesus Christ is my Master. Thank You for Your help to be completely free from this sin. In Jesus' Name. Amen."

DAY 179

(work it)

"Work from the heart for your real Master, for God..."
Colossians 3:23, MSG

OK, here's our booster shot for the day: work it!

Yes, that's right! Let's be the best employee at our place of work and give new meaning to the phrase: "work ethic." Let's make it obvious to our co-workers that we live by a different standard. Let the quality and quantity of our work be excellent and superior and work from the heart for our real Master—God.

The rest of the passage in Colossians says this, *"Servants, do what you're told by your earthly masters. And don't just do the minimum that will get you by. Do your best. Work from the heart for your real Master, for God, confident that you'll get paid in full when you come into your inheritance. Keep in mind always that the ultimate Master you're serving is Christ. The sullen servant who does shoddy work will be held responsible. Being Christian doesn't cover up bad work,"* (Colossians 3:22-25, MSG).

No slacking today! The Lord doesn't want us to use the title "Christian" as an excuse for bad work. That would be a pretty pathetic testimony wouldn't it? Your boss says, "Hey, Elvis, why are you getting to work late every day? Why do you take twice as long to get the same amount of work done as everyone else? Why do you take a long lunch and leave three minutes early?" You respond, "Um...well, I'm a Christian, and I was praying...and...I just like to praise God...and the Lord knows my heart... Wanna come to church this Sunday?" What response do you think you'll hear? How about, "You're fired!"

If we are going to call ourselves Christians and let everyone know that Jesus is the Lord of our lives, then let's represent Him well on the job. Work hard! Not complain. Not diss the boss. Not take an extra ten minutes on our lunch hour. Let's go the extra mile, not steal paper, paperclips, pens and sticky pads. Let's be so excellent and efficient that Jesus is seen in us! Let's make our boss want to hire ten other Christians just like us! And, if our boss or supervisor never notices all our extra effort, no worries—God's watching. He'll reward us.

Today, at home, at school or at work...let's do our best! Let's work from the heart for our real Master.

Read It! Proverbs 12:24, NIV

Speak It! "Father, I want to represent the Name of Christ well. I want to work hard, with excellence and diligence as a God-pleaser. I won't just work hard when the boss is watching; I will work hard when You are the only one watching. May my work and words honor You today! In Jesus' Name. Amen."

DAY 180

(shuuuuuuut up)

*"When words are many, sin is not absent,
but he who holds his tongue is wise."*
Proverbs 10:19, NIV

Now, here's a verse that will step on our toes! *"When words are many, sin is not absent"*? What's that all about? What kind of words?

Many words that are:

- **Empty and void of substance.**
- **Full of anger, bitterness and resentment.**
- **Full of pride, ego and "it's all about me."**
- **Arrogant rants, selfish tantrums, opinionated outbursts.**
- **Insensitive, hurtful, critical, damaging.**
- **Out of place, inappropriate, lacking in judgment.**

How do we avoid talking too much? By being slow to speak...and quick to listen. James had it right when he said, *"Everyone should be quick to listen, slow to speak and slow to become angry,"* (James 1:19b, NIV).

Do we find people are running from us? Not answering our calls? Avoiding contact?

Could it be a "words" problem?

Read It! Proverbs 10:19, MSG

Speak It! "Father, help me. I need to shut up! I need to be slow to speak and quick to listen. I pray You give me discretion, discernment and good judgment to know when to speak and when to listen. In Jesus' Name. Amen."

DAY 181

(big honkin' angels)

"A thousand may fall at your side, ten thousand
at your right hand, but it will not come near you."
Psalm 91:7, NIV

In the post 9/11 era, some of the most common fears we face have to do with safety issues. The enemy works hard to keep us in fear about things—big and small—but God wants us to operate by faith. Regardless what it is, God wants us to be free and live by faith in big and small things!

Recently, I overcame a small fear. I was fearful of driving a motorcycle. I had been a very content passenger on the back of my husband's motorcycle for many years. I never considered getting my motorcycle endorsement or becoming a biker. Until...this past summer, when my husband encouraged me to take a class and get my license. I resisted! The reason? Well, as a kid, I rode dirt and mini-bikes. So, when we took a trip to Italy, I figured if Mary Kate and Ashley could ride motor scooters in Rome, so could we! (Well, I should've listened to the Holy Spirit and the "inner-check" I had in my heart on that one.) We rented the scooters, and I crashed...right into my husband and son...right in front of the Coliseum, breaking two toes and damaging the scooter. After that little episode, I was fearful about driving motor scooters, motorcycles or any other motorized two-wheeler!

When my husband encouraged me to get my motorcycle license, the Lord began to speak to my heart, encouraging me to overcome my fear with faith. At first, I shrugged it off. After a few months of hearing the Lord speak this to my heart, I opened up to the "possibility"...and lo and behold, faith (in God, His wisdom and protection) began filling my heart and removing the fear. As I meditated on Psalm 91, I found faith in my heart instead of fear and believed I could trust the Lord to protect me. I found great comfort in knowing the Lord will command big honkin' angels to protect me front-to-back, side-to-side and top-to-bottom! I enrolled in a motorcycle safety class with my fearless instructors and passed! Today, I have my motorcycle endorsement. I'm an official biker chick!

What about you? Is some fear trying to intimidate you? Is it standing in the way of your progress and freedom? I encourage you to read and meditate on Psalm 91 until your faith replaces your fear! Then, step out and do something intentional by faith!

Read It! Psalm 91

Speak It! "Father, thank You for speaking to me as I read and meditate on Psalm 91. I trust You to protect me, my spouse and my kids with Your big angels—front-to-back, side-to-side and top-to-bottom. A 1,000 may fall at my left and 10,0000 at my right hand, but it shall NOT come nigh me. In Jesus' Name. Amen."

DAY 182

(a river runs through you)

"'...He who believes in Me, as the Scripture has said, out of his heart will flow rivers of living water.'"
John 7:38

A river runs through you...it's true! What is this river? It's powerful. Refreshing. Fast. Slow. Shallow. Deep. Tranquil. Exciting. Going Places. Taking you places.

Yes, we have a river running through us; Jesus said so. When we are filled with the Spirit, we receive rivers of living water. *(John 7:37-38, MSG)* So, what does this mean in real life? It means once we believe in and receive Jesus and are filled with His Spirit, a river is downloaded to our innermost being. It's important we allow that river to really run through us—to refresh us and splash on others.

There are many ways to let this river flow. Let's look at two specific ways to yield to the Spirit and His river: pray and sing. (For those who already know and do this...here's a bit of encouragement. For those who are new to this type of thing...here's a bit of instruction.)

- **Pray.** Pray from our heart, not our head. Pretend no one is listening but God. Don't try to impress anyone with our prayers. We don't have to sound professional or holy—just heartfelt. There is a huge prayer river inside of us, and we all need to spend more time letting that river flow. There's no telling what God can and will do if we will give Him more time in prayer. Praying His Word. Praying for others. Declaring and decreeing His Word. Let the river of prayer flow like never before! Pray in English. Pray in tongues. Pray!

- **Sing.** Sing it out! We don't have to sound amazing. In fact, most of us don't. God loves our joyful noise anyway! There is a song in our hearts. Singing from the river inside of us is fun. There is a melody that flows like a river in the heart of every Christian. We just need to let that river gush out through singing and making a melody to the Lord. How? Easy. Start singing any words that are pleasant to your spirit in English and in your spiritual language. It starts with a phrase...and more words will follow—that's the river beginning to rumble.

So, today, let's get started praying and singing from our heart and let that river really run through us!

Read It! Ephesians 5:18

Speak It! "Jesus, I am thirsty, and I come to You and drink! You said 'out of my innermost being rivers of living water' would flow. I believe You! I ask You for grace to help me tap into that river in a new and fresh way. Holy Spirit, help me to yield to You in prayer and singing, so this river of living water comes out and refreshes me and splashes on everyone around me! In Jesus' Name. Amen."

DAY 183

(a word for the weary)

"And do not be drunk with wine, in which is dissipation; but be filled with the Spirit, speaking to one another in psalms and hymns and spiritual songs, singing and making melody in your heart to the Lord."
Ephesians 5:18-19

God has a word for the weary. I was driving to Chicago a few years ago, enjoying some time with the Lord, when I began singing psalms, hymns and spiritual songs in my car...just having a big time. When I started listening to the words, here's the song the Lord gave me then...and it certainly is a timeless truth.

God Has a Word for the Weary

God has a word for the weary; God has a word for the weak
God has a word for the weary and His word is simply: SPEAK!
Don't be silent, don't be silent
Don't doubt, don't pout
Don't be silent—don't you doubt and don't you pout
But let the weak speak...let the weak speak,
Let the weak say, "I am strong."
God is not wrong.
Let the weak and the weary, let them not become bleary.
But let them speak and sing the Word.
Sing the Word, sing the Word...declare what you know
And you'll find God is with you from your heart as you go.
Sing it out, sing it out—sing it loud, sing it strong.
You may not even know what to say, but that's okay
The words will come, just speak and sing it now.
God has a word for the weary and God has a word for the weak
And this is His word are you listening?
His word to you is SPEAK!

So, if you've been weary, start speaking and singing from your heart! Take a few moments how to speak the Word.

Read It! Psalm 107:2

Speak It! "Father, I want to take some time to sing and speak the Word. I thank You for refreshing and strengthening me. In Jesus' Name. Amen."

DAY 184

(the search is on)

"For the eyes of the LORD range throughout the earth
to strengthen those whose hearts are fully committed to Him."
2 Chronicles 16:9, NIV

God's eyes are searching to and fro! Think about that. The Almighty God is on a search! His eyes roam throughout the whole earth and He's looking for a specific kind of person.

Who is He looking for? He's looking for *"those whose hearts are fully committed to Him."* Are you one of those people? Will God's eyes land on you today?

It's an interesting thing to visualize...the idea that God's eyes are scanning the entire planet. His eyes begin to roam, and He searches...in China, Australia, India, Russia, Iraq, Israel, Kenya, Ivory Coast, Cayman Islands, Italy, Ireland, New York City, Kentucky, Iceland, Wyoming, San Diego, Mexico City, Michigan, Brazil, Columbia, Tokyo, Bangkok, Fiji, Alaska—every other square inch of the earth.

When He finds someone fully committed to Him, I wonder if a heavenly buzzer goes off and a big announcement is made: *"Bingo...we have a winner! Ladies and gentlemen, we have found a fully-devoted follower of Jesus Christ...a true, blue, on-fire, real McCoy, genuine, authentic Christian. We have done a thorough search, and this is no pretend, hypocritical, fake-dog, lip-service, Sunday-only type of Christian. This person is legit. Angels, what do we have for our winner?"*

So, what does the winner get? Strength! That is, God's supernatural show of strength! He gives us a fresh impartation of mental, emotional, physical and spiritual strength. A fresh anointing. A fresh infusion of energy, endurance and grit! He shows up and shows off in our lives in such a way that it's obvious—to us and anyone observing—that God is the strength of our lives.

With the increased pace at home, work, school, church—and in all the challenges that face busy kids, teens, moms, dads, singles and families—we need God to seriously show Himself strong on our behalf. Let's make a fresh commitment to the Lord, today.

Read It! Psalm 32:8

Speak It! "Father, as You search the whole earth, I pray Your eyes find me! Today, I want You to know that I renew my choice to be fully committed to You. Jesus, You are the Lord of my life, and I dedicate myself to be all about Your purposes and priorities. I ask You to fill me with Your strength, today—spirit, soul and body. In Jesus' Name. Amen."

DAY 185

(how deep do you wanna go?)

"Launch out into the deep and let down your nets for a catch."
Luke 5:4b

A few years ago, I was sitting in the bleachers at my daughter's basketball game, and the Lord asked me this question right in the middle of the game. He asked, "How deep do you want to go?" I knew what He meant.

I knew God was asking me if I wanted to go "deeper" in Him. Of course, I did! I love rich, meaty, "deep" times in my personal walk with God, in corporate worship services, in prayer and in meetings where the Holy Spirit is flowing. Personally, I love all of that, but somehow I knew that wasn't what the Lord was talking about.

When He asked me how deep I wanted to go, I was immediately reminded of this passage of Scripture in Luke 5:4b, where Jesus told his disciples, "...'Now go out where it is deeper and let down your nets, and you will catch many fish,'" (NLT). The Message Bible says, "...'Push out into deep water and let your nets out for a catch.'" I sensed the Lord giving me a completely new and different definition for being "deep" in God. His definition of going "deeper" had something to do with catching fish—reaching people who are lost without Christ. Then, it occurred to me: the deeper we go, the more it leads us to let down our nets in order to win people to Christ! The deep things lead us to evangelism! Fishing for men...reaching seekers...going after lost people!

Think about a simple example of what it means to be "deep." Ever lost a child in the grocery store or the mall? Instantly, the parent's deep love for their lost child causes them to look for them with a passion that is unmatched! The purpose for going "deeper" with the Lord isn't to accumulate more revelation knowledge or to parse the Greek and Hebrew; it's to get His heart of compassion—to love Him and others deeply—and reach out to lost people with passion!

Reaching the lost—fishing for men—is about as deep as it gets. If we're not winning people to Christ and loading our nets with seekers, we may not be as "deep" as we think. Deep equals: soul-winning! Let's seek to be deep Christians and launch out into the deep in our neighborhood, workplace and family and win souls!

Read It! Proverbs 11:30, AMP

Speak It! "Father, I want to go deeper with You! I will launch out into the world around me to share Jesus with those I know and meet. You love people deeply, and You don't want any child of Yours to be lost. I want to be deeply moved to reach the lost. Help me to be a 'deep Christian' by being a fisher of men. In Jesus' Name. Amen."

DAY 186

(traditions, traditions)

"Thus you nullify the word of God by your tradition that you have handed down. And you do many things like that."
Mark 7:13, NIV

Jesus didn't mince any words. He had a way of speaking the truth in love that penetrated the heart of the issue. Have you ever noticed that? Jesus was blunt. He was hard on those who chose tradition over Him.

As human beings, we have a way of "worshiping" things—even our traditions. Jesus wanted these religious leaders to know that God was most interested in their hearts...as reflected in their lives. He rebuked them for empty lips, vain worship, man's teachings and traditions of men. Have you noticed that Jesus was not a fan of tradition or religion? The reason was simple: religious tradition was robbing people of a legitimate relationship with the Lord. Religious leaders were sacrificing God's Word for the sake of tradition.

What does that mean to us? It means if we find ourselves worshiping our religious traditions (rituals, liturgy, programs, style) at the expense of a heart-felt, personal relationship with the Lord, we need to ditch the tradition. If we find ourselves holding to traditions (rote prayer, obligatory exercises, vain repetitions) that keep us from truly walking with Jesus Christ and His Word, we need to ditch the tradition. If we find ourselves trusting in symbolic traditions (religious bling, "good luck" charms, religious tattoos or icons) more than actually living by and obeying God's Word, we need to ditch the tradition.

Jesus isn't looking for empty traditions; He's looking for a genuine, personal relationship with Him. He's looking for people who will follow His Word.

Perhaps religious traditions have prevented you from experiencing all that God has for you. Are you willing to exchange those traditions for a personal relationship with Jesus? Are you ready to ditch some traditions and just take God at His Word?

Read It! Mark 7

Speak It! "Father, I am sorry for worshiping my religious traditions more than You. I don't want empty lips, vain worship, man's teaching or the traditions of men to rob me of the authentic relationship You want to have with me. I make a decision to choose You and Your Word over any religious tradition. Jesus, I invite You to be the Lord of my life, and I submit to Your Word. In Jesus' Name. Amen."

DAY 187

(peace rules)

"...let the peace of God rule in your hearts..."
Colossians 3:15

Is your heart troubled? Anxious? Agitated?

Let peace rule today. Jesus told us we could.

Jesus said, *"Peace I leave with you, My peace I give to you; not as the world gives do I give to you. Let not your heart be troubled, neither let it be afraid,"* (John 14:27).

Unfortunately, for many people, living in strife, anxiety, agitation and fear is a way of life. Peace is the oddity. Jesus wants to turn that around in their life...in your life...in my life.

The ability to live in peace can be a way of life. In fact, we can get so used to living in peace that it's an oddity to experience anxiety, a troubled heart, strife or fear.

Sometimes, we have to "force" ourselves to surrender to peace. We have to choose to "let peace rule;" because, at times, our minds are filled with fear, overload, frustration and any number of "peace robbers."

Peace only comes from keeping our minds on the Lord and His Word. If you need Jesus' peace to rule your heart today, set your mind on Him. Don't allow any thought that is contrary to His character and His Word to have any place in your mind. The result? God's perfect peace will rule!

Read It! Isaiah 26:3

Speak It! "Father, thank You for perfect peace. I choose to surrender all of my anxious, fear-filled, agitating thoughts to You right now. I fix my mind on Jesus. You are good, You can be trusted, and You are bigger than anything I am facing. Peace...rule my heart! In Jesus' Name. Amen."

DAY 188

(whose opinion matters?)

"The fear of human opinion disables; trusting in GOD protects you from that."
Proverbs 29:25, MSG

It's true. The fear of human opinion disables. When we are overly concerned about what others think, whether we meet with their approval or disapproval, our judgment becomes blurred; and we veer from our core values. When we find ourselves saying or doing—or not saying or doing—things merely to please people, we become men-pleasers rather than God-pleasers.

We need to seek God's approval and accept the fact that we'll never have a 100% approval rating from others—and be okay with that. John, who addressed this topic when he spoke about some religious leaders of his day, said it best, *"for they loved praise from men more than praise from God," (John 12:43, NIV).*

Human opinion can be fickle, so go for praise that comes from God! Everyone will have an opinion about you; and the more the Lord uses you, the more opinions there will be! But, don't be disabled by the opinions of others; trust the Lord and accept these truths:

- **Some people like you; some people don't.**
- **Some people admire and respect you; some people despise and hate you.**
- **Some people agree with you; some people like to argue with you.**
- **Some people encourage you; some people criticize and tear you down.**
- **Some people rejoice with you; some people rain on your parade.**
- **Some people are thrilled with the changes in your life; some people dismiss it.**
- **Some people love to see you break out of stereotypical paradigms; some people get mad.**
- **Some people approve of your spouse, kids, hair, clothes, hobbies, style; some people dislike the whole package.**
- **Some people see your potential; some people are threatened by it.**
- **Some people are happy when you're blessed and successful; some people are jealous.**

Let's go for the praise that comes from God! If the opinions of others are disabling you, make a change today. Living for an Audience of One is the secret to being truly free. When you're confident that your decisions, actions and words are pleasing to the Lord, then move forward—full steam ahead!

Read It! Proverbs 3:4

Speak It! "Father, help me not to be more concerned with others' opinions than Yours. Help me live in a way that pleases You. In Jesus' Name. Amen."

DAY 189

(crave God)

"Seek, inquire of and for the Lord, and crave Him and His strength
(His might and inflexibility to temptation); seek and require His face and
His presence [continually] evermore."
Psalm 105:4, AMP

Crave Him...those two words say it all!

Notice the other keywords in this verse: seek, inquire, crave and require. They all describe a certain intensity. A proactive behavior. These are not passive words. This is not "Que Sara, Sara" Christianity.

This is going after God with both barrels blazing! I have found it interesting over the years to notice that God does not obligate Himself to be found by anyone who is not seeking Him with their whole heart. He's not obligated Himself to cater to the apathetic, whimsical, lukewarm Believer. In fact, in the book of Revelation, He tells us that lukewarm Believers make Him want to vomit. (Pretty graphic, isn't it?)

However, God *has* obligated Himself to be found by those who seek Him; those who inquire, crave and require Him.

Where are we at today? Do we require God as a necessity? Are we craving Him to the point that we get up early, stay up late, take our lunch break and moments throughout the day to read, pray, worship and talk with Him? Do we inquire of the Lord, checking in with Him on a regular basis? Do we seek the Lord with our whole heart?

If we're not there, we can stir it up. Let's do that today!

Read It! Isaiah 55:6, NIV

Speak It! "Father, I seek You. I want You. I require You. Jesus, I seek You. I inquire of You, and I crave Your presence in my life. Holy Spirit, I seek You. I need You. I require You as a necessity in my life. God, I am so glad that when my heart reaches out to You, You answer and fill each and every seeking, inquiring, craving and requiring. In Jesus' Name. Amen."

DAY 190

(don't be a grenade)

"A soft answer turns away wrath, but a harsh word stirs up anger."
Proverbs 15:1

Do people have to walk on egg shells around us? Are we wound so tight, people think we could blow at any minute? There is nothing fun about being around an angry person—a.k.a. a grenade. If we find ourselves being rude to the waitress, kicking the cat, slamming doors and growling at people around us, that means it's time for us to lighten up! Life is way too short to fling shrapnel everywhere we go.

For a season, grenades might feel mighty and empowered as they intimidate people. They might have everyone living in fear and trembling; but in the long term, they will experience a very lonely future. Eventually, they'll lose any genuine relationships they have with family and friends.

If we are being a grenade, we'd better hope we wake up before we blow everyone in our life a hundred miles away from us. We need to talk to the Lord about the root cause of our angry disposition and seek God's wisdom—perhaps, even seek out spiritual guidance from a trusted, mature Believer, so we can move on.

If we live or work with a grenade, we can't allow ourselves to be contaminated by their anger. It's their issue, not ours. Some people are always looking for a fight—don't give it to them! We are not required to be friends with an angry person. Proverbs 22:24-25 actually says, *"Don't hang out with angry people; don't keep company with hotheads. Bad temper is contagious—don't get infected."* 'Nuff said.

If we have to deal with anger issues, God has a starting point. The solution is a soft answer. A soft answer turns away wrath. Whether we are the initiator or the recipient, when we are on the verge of perpetuating anger, we need to stop and soften our response. We will be amazed at how quickly anger is diffused.

A gentle response defuses anger, but a sharp tongue kindles a temper-fire.

Read It! Proverbs 37:8, NIV

Speak It! "Father, I surrender myself to You. Help me to overcome anger with a soft answer. Help me to resist the temptation to fight with sharp words. In Jesus' Name. Amen."

DAY 191

(had a bad day?)

"Rejoice in the Lord always. Again I will say, rejoice!"
Philippians 4:4

Had a bad day, lately? Things not going your way?

Rejoice always! That's what we need to do on those days. The apostle, Paul, had some really bad days when he wrote the book of Philippians from a prison cell; and yet, 10 times in his short letter, he talks about rejoicing anyway!

At the end of his letter he says, *"Rejoice always!"* Then, in case, we didn't hear him the first time, he says it again, *"Rejoice!"* And, I repeat, rejoice! Be glad, celebrate, revel and be full of joy!

What does it mean to rejoice? It means: be glad. Celebrate your life in Him. Revel, be full of joy—no matter what circumstance we face, there is power in rejoicing.

But, you say, "I don't want to." I know...rejoice anyway! But, you say, "I don't feel like it." I know...rejoice anyway! But, you say, "I don't have anything to be happy about." I know...rejoice anyway! But, you say, "I am tired of rejoicing." I know...rejoice anyway.

So, are you going to do it? Gonna rejoice? I know it's hard some days. Here's some help to prime the pump...start with this, say: "Fine, I rejoice." Say it again...with a little attitude. One more time, say it again. Now, laugh out loud. Do it—really—do it. If necessary, start with your worst fake laugh, then a real laugh will come. Do it again. One more time. (Ah, ha! Is that a smile we see?) C'mon, this is just priming the pump. The joy of the Lord is starting to make a dent in your bad day. Get the idea? Just keep rejoicing, by faith! Always.

OK, if you've had a really, really bad day, you might have to go overboard with the rejoicing thing. Do this: start shouting, "I had a really bad day, and I'm not gonna take it anymore! I laugh in the face of a bad day. I shout for joy! I choose to rejoice! I will be stinkin' glad, and I will celebrate, and I will revel, and I will be filled with joy...no matter what this day says! Yeah, you heard me! I rejoice! I rejoice! I rejoice...and again, I say, I rejoice!"

There...now, don't you feel better?

Read It! 1 Thessalonians 5:16

Speak It! "Father, one more time, I choose to rejoice. I choose to be glad, to celebrate, to revel in Your goodness and to be filled with joy. I rejoice in the Lord...always! In Jesus' Name. Amen."

DAY 192

(follow the hand)

"The hand of our God is upon all them for good that seek Him..."
Ezra 8:22, KJV

I love this truth. God's hand is upon us when we seek Him. The good hand of the Lord gives us favor, blessings, strength and goodness.

Years ago, my husband and I took a ballroom dancing class. It was a lot of fun. One thing we learned in class was that the man always leads the dance with his hand. The woman responds to both the obvious and ever-so-subtle movements of her partner's hand. Ever wondered how those *Dancing with the Stars* people make it look so easy? It's all about following the leader's hand.

In our class, it was my job to follow Jeff's hand in the dance...to respond. I was not the leader—and he reminded me of that numerous times, after I stepped on his feet! As the leader, he knew the next dance step he had in mind. He knew when he wanted me to fling me out, spin me around, move me closer to him or sway with the music. I had no idea what he would do next; the only way I could follow him was to pay attention to the pull, push or pressure of his hand moving me in the direction he wanted me to go. It took a while to get it, but eventually I realized my job was simple: don't lead; relax and follow his hand.

In the same way, we are to follow the hand of the Lord. The good hand of the Lord is a picture of God's power, favor and leading. When we quit leading our own lives and relax and follow His hand, He leads the dance and guides us into a faith-filled adventure!

Today, let's quit leading, relax and just follow the Lord's hand.

Read It! Psalm 25:9, NASB-U

Speak It! "Father, I am looking forward to learning some new 'dance steps' with You! Help me recognize and follow Your hand. Thank You for leading me into favor, goodness and blessings; for flinging me into the world as you desire and for spinning my life around as You see fit. I look forward to a fresh, faith-filled adventure as I follow the good hand of the Lord. In Jesus' Name. Amen."

DAY 193

(the mirror never lies)

"Those who hear and don't act are like those who
glance in the mirror, walk away, and two minutes later
have no idea who they are, what they look like."
James 1:22-25, MSG

Looked in the mirror lately? What's the purpose of a mirror? The mirror tells us the truth. There's no built in Photoshop® or air brush hidden inside the mirror—just the true reflection of what it sees. The mirror tells us what we look like. Unfortunately, the mirror never lies! When we look into a mirror, we always notice what's wrong, don't we? Our hair isn't behaving, our "muffin top" has grown, a few wrinkles have surfaced. Sometimes, the mirror is a bitter pill—and the 10x magnified mirror is even scarier.

In raising four kids—two girls, two boys—we've noticed that girls aren't the only ones who live in front of the mirror. In fact, I am beginning to believe our teenage boys spend more time looking at themselves in the mirror than our daughters! Posing, flexing... They keep looking for their abs... (Yeah, me too!)

God's Word is a mirror. It's a reflection of what we look like in God's eyes! The mirror never lies; it reflects the truth. The mirror of God's Word tells us exactly what we look like...in Christ. The Bible is God's mirror, and He shows us what we look like from His view. He reflects the reality of who we are in Christ. Most of us have not stared at that mirror long enough! We need to, though. He wants to show us what's right and point out our spiritual muscles...our spiritual abs.

We often see ourselves as sinners, failures and unworthy worms, but that's not how God sees us in Christ! If we aren't intentional, we'll quickly forget how God sees us and fall back into patterns of condemnation, guilt and inferiority. The mirror of God's Word shows us we are more than conquerors through Christ *(Romans 8:37)*, and we are overcomers by faith. We see that we can do all things through Christ who strengthens us *(Philippians 4:13)*. When we believe the mirror, instead of how we see ourselves or how we feel, we find real freedom, joy, strength and God's power to move forward into all that He has for us.

That means on days when we don't feel like overcomers, we trust the mirror and declare all it says about us! What is the mirror of God's Word reflecting for our lives today? Let's study the mirror and not forget what we look like! Let's believe what it says, trust it and be doers of what we see!

Read It! James 1:22-25, MSG

Speak It! "Father, thank You for the mirror of Your Word. Thank You for showing me who I really am because I am in Christ. Help me to live by the image You show me in the mirror. In Jesus' Name. Amen."

DAY 194

(floundering or flourishing?)

"Those who are planted in the house of the LORD shall flourish
in the courts of our God. They shall still bear fruit in old age;
they shall be fresh and flourishing."
Psalm 92:13-14

The Lord wants us to flourish and bring forth fruit all of our days! We've watched it over the years...those who were planted in God's priorities—namely, His Church—flourish; those who weren't, sometimes floundered.

The big keyword is: planted. It seems to be important to the Lord that we are planted in a local church where Jesus is exalted, the Word is taught, the Holy Spirit is present and a spirit of faith and love prevail. In that house, Jesus does amazing things—namely, causing His people to flourish! To be planted in the house of the Lord, by definition, requires a strong root system of humility, submission, commitment, loyalty, trust and forgiveness. To stay planted requires a willingness to serve, overcome offenses and exercise endurance.

Being planted in the house of the Lord is for OUR benefit. In the same way that the ark was Noah's vehicle for divine protection, the Church is our vehicle for divine flourishing! Jesus loves the Church and has obligated Himself to care for it in the same way a husband cares for his wife. Those who are planted in His Church flourish; they are washed by the Word, cherished, enriched, nourished, strengthened, blessed and loved by Him!

Today, are you flourishing or floundering? Are you planted with unmovable roots in a local church? If so, you can expect to flourish for a long time—even in your old age!

Read It! Psalm 1:3, NIV

Speak It! "Jesus, I choose to be planted in the house of the Lord. Help my roots go deep in You and Your purposes. I believe You love Your Church, which includes me and all those who make up the Church, like a husband loves his wife. I am so thankful that You love, cherish, nourish and wash me with Your Word. I will bloom where I am planted and declare that I will be fruitful, fresh and flourishing until I am old and gray. In Jesus' Name. Amen."

DAY 195

(raise your price)

"An excellent wife, who can find? For her worth is far above jewels."
Proverbs 31:10, NASB-U

So, what are you worth? The experts tell us most people have a low self-esteem and sense of self-worth. That means...most people don't really understand how truly valuable they are. Often, it's women who struggle with this topic, but men are not exempt.

It's easy to spot someone who doesn't value themselves, because they usually don't value others very much either. They often let others mistreat, abuse and demean them. If you've found yourself listening to external voices or internal thoughts telling you: "you're ugly," "you're stupid," "no one likes you," "no one cares about you," "you're a wasted excuse for a human being,"—and on and on—it's not true!

God values you. You've been created in His image. He thinks you're worth something. You are fearfully and wonderfully made. It's true. No matter who rejects you and regardless what anyone else says, God thinks you are a beautiful somebody!

Don't sell yourself short. Raise your price! Recognize your value as far above jewels. Don't give yourself away for free and don't allow others to treat you as though you had no value. Set the bar of your value where God sets it.

Read It! Psalm 139:14

Speak It! "Father, I choose to agree with Your Word, whether I feel like it or not and whether anyone treats me as valuable or not. You see me worth more than precious jewels. I am fearfully and wonderfully made, and You purchased me at a great price. I am valuable. My price is far above rubies. Today, I believe it! In Jesus' Name. Amen."

DAY 196

(bennies)

"Bless the LORD, O my soul, and forget not all His benefits:
Who forgives all your iniquities, Who heals all your diseases..."
Psalm 102:2-3

Ever read the fine print in God's benefits package? You should! Most people are up to speed on their employment benefits—the major medical, dental, optical, retirement plans. We ought to know all the details of the benefits God has put into His redemption plan!

- **Benefit #1.** He forgives all our sins. Aren't you glad for that? I am. When Jesus is the Lord of our lives, we qualify for this benefit! Major forgiveness! There isn't one sin He won't forgive. He forgives all our sins—the little ones and the biggies. Praise God!

- **Benefit #2.** He heals all our diseases. What a bonus! Jesus is the same yesterday, today and forever, and He's still in the healing business. If part A of this verse: *"He forgives all our sins,"* is true; then part B of this verse: *"He heals all our diseases,"* has to be true!

Forgiveness and healing have been called the "Redemptive Twins." If you study Jesus' ministry, you'll see that forgiveness and healing have always been God's will. In fact, back in the day, people had an easier time believing Jesus could heal than He could forgive sins. Today, it's just the opposite. People believe Jesus forgives sins, but they have a hard time believing He will heal a disease.

Jesus made an very interesting comment in verses 23 and 24 of the **Read It!** segment. Take a minute to go and read it, first. Isn't it strange Jesus had to say that in the first place, especially after they witnessed the miracle with their own eyes? But, Jesus let us know that it's just as easy for Him to forgive sins as it is for Him to heal a body! Both are included in His benefits package!

I encourage you to talk to the Lord and study His Word on the subject of His will and wisdom when it comes to forgiveness and healing. Perhaps you're facing an injury, sickness, disease or some illness. Be encouraged to know that the Lord uses a variety of pathways to bring health and healing to our bodies—whether it is through supernatural measures, doctors, medicine, therapy, surgery or simply diet and exercise. In the event you're facing a situation where the doctors have done all they can do, thank God as you seek Him and appropriate your redemptive benefits. Jesus is still in the healing biz!

Read It! Luke 5:1-26

Speak It! "Father, thank You for such a great salvation—one that includes the 'Redemptive Twins': forgiveness of sins and healing. I ask You to forgive me from all my sins and heal my body. Thank You for Your forgiveness and healing in my life right now. In Jesus' Name. Amen."

DAY 197

(a major shift and open doors)

"About midnight Paul and Silas were praying and singing hymns to God, and
the other prisoners were listening to them. Suddenly there was such a violent
earthquake that the foundations of the prison were shaken. At once all the
prison doors flew open, and everybody's chains came loose."
Acts 16:25-27, NIV

Do you need a big change? Need supernatural doors to open up for you? Need
some chains to fall from your life? Need something to happen "suddenly"?
Start praying! Keep singing!

Paul and Silas were in their midnight hour—the time when things looked the
bleakest. After a day of accusations and being stripped, beaten, flogged, placed
in the innermost prison cell and chained in stocks, most of us would be severely
depressed, scared and defeated—not Paul and Silas. They got their groove on!
They busted out with prayer and singing songs to God so loud the other prisoners heard them.

Can you imagine the scenario? It's almost as if they said, "What do we have to
lose? Things can't get any worse down here, so let's just let everyone within
earshot know that there is a glorious God in heaven. If they kill us...oh well,
we'll get to be with Jesus that much sooner." And off they went singing and
praying, "Oh, we worship You God of heaven and earth. We praise Your
glorious Name. We pray for our enemies...open their eyes, Lord...," and then
suddenly...

Suddenly there was a big shake-up! A shift. A change. Foundations were
rocked. Doors flew open. Everyone's chains fell off.

What a picture! God is into "suddenlies." He can change your life, circumstances,
location, relationships, situation and future in a millisecond! If you're facing a
midnight hour and you need a change—a major shift, open doors and freedom
from chains that try to bind you—get your praise on in a big, loud way!

Read It! Acts 2:2, KJV

Speak It! "Father, I shout Your praise! You are the Most High God, the Creator of
the ends of the earth. Jesus, I worship You as the Lord of Lords, my Redeemer,
Savior, Healer and King. Holy Spirit, I praise You as my Helper, Strengthener,
Counselor, Comforter and Guide. I worship You, Lord God Almighty. In Jesus'
Name. Amen."

DAY 198

(a fearless life)

"I sought the LORD, and He heard me, and delivered me from all my fears."
Psalm 34:4

Need freedom from nerves? Anxiety? Panic? Fear? Good news... God wants you to be free!

We live in a society where more and more people are dealing with anxiety issues. Fear of the future, terrorists, safety, cost of living, sickness, disease, death—and a host of other things—keep people locked in debilitating little personal prisons. There are phobias for just about everything.

Fear is a tactic of the enemy. If fear has tried to dominate your life, direct your decisions or paralyze your progress, be encouraged! God has promised to deliver us from ALL our fears! Jesus said, "Fear not!" more than 300 times; so it's obviously God's will for us to live a fearless life!

What fears have been harassing you? Fear of failure? People? Success? Public speaking? Flying? Spiders? Loss? Commitment? Many people live life based on their fears. They let fear dictate what they will do and not do, where they go and not go and how they will get there or not get there. God has something better for you...a life lived by faith!

God leads us by faith, not by fear. He is not the author of fear. He never motivates us through the type of fear that brings anxiety. If fear has been trying to control your life, you can be free! Meditate on this verse and seek the Lord. As you spend time reading the Bible and talking to Him about His power to deliver you from fear, He will give you divine peace, faith, strategies and confidence to overcome every fear! When we seek Him, He promises to hear us and He promises to deliver us from ALL our fears!

Read It! Philippians 1:28, AMP

Speak It! "Father, I seek You and Your power and wisdom! I am so glad that You hear me. Today, I declare that You deliver me from ALL my fears. I am not going to live a life dictated by fear; I am going to live by faith. Jesus is the Lord of my life, not fear! In Jesus' Name. Amen."

DAY 199

(guilt-ridden)

"If we confess our sins, He is faithful and just to forgive us
our sins and to cleanse us from all unrighteousness."
1 John 1:9

This is a simple reminder... He is faithful and just to forgive our sins. We know it in our heads; but often, we forget this in our hearts and live guilt-ridden lives. Listen, God is not interested in holding things against us. He's on our side. He's not mad at us. In fact, quite the opposite. Remember these Scriptures? *"For God so loved the world...," (John 3:16); "...while we were yet sinners, Christ died for us," (Romans 5:8b); "...If God is for us, who can be against us?" (Romans 8:31b).*

If Jesus loved us enough to die for us when we were heathen sinners, how much more does He love us when we are Believers who makes mistakes? When we blow it, we don't run from the Lord—we run straight to Him!

Guilt and condemnation are some of the enemy's main tools for defeating Christians. If he can keep us feeling inferior and guilty, he robs us of the confidence and victory the Lord wants us to walk in through Christ. Don't fall for the devil's trap. If you've messed up, then confess your sins to the Lord and choose obedience the next time. He is faithful and just to forgive you.

Notice the other major thing this verse tells us: He cleanses us from all unrighteousness. Not only does the Lord forgive us and forgive us and forgive us, but He cleanses us. He makes us squeaky clean in His sight; not because we're perfect, but because He is perfect. He didn't stop there either. Jesus went beyond cleansing us from unrighteousness; He made us as righteous as He is, because we are "in Christ"! Jesus never sinned, but He took on our sin so we could become His righteousness *(2 Corinthians 5:21)*. This is the good news of the Gospel. We can't take any credit for it; we just receive His forgiveness and His cleansing by faith, and then we walk in the righteousness of God He has made us to be in Christ.

Today, we can get a fresh grip of freedom from the guilt, condemnation and shame that sin brings by confessing our sins to Him. Then, we will walk in the victory and liberty that comes through knowing we have been cleansed and made righteous in Christ.

Read It! 2 Corinthians 5:21

Speak It! "Father, thank You for Your mercy! I confess my sins to You today and thank You for forgiving me and cleansing me from all unrighteousness. I'll not let guilt and condemnation dominate me, because You paid too high a price to set me free and make me the 'righteousness of God in Christ.' Lord, as I move forward, help me live my life in a way that pleases You. In Jesus' Name. Amen."

DAY 200

(God is not Scrooge)

"For the LORD God is a sun and shield; the LORD will give grace and glory; no good thing will He withhold from those who walk uprightly."
Psalm 84:11

God is not Scrooge! He is not a stingy, grump! He is not a withholder. God is a giver. He always has been. He won't withhold any good thing from those who walk uprightly and from those who walk in truth, sincerity and integrity. Don't ever forget it. Don't ever doubt it.

Sometimes the devil seems to work overtime trying to convince us that God is just like Scrooge. He plants thoughts that sound like this: "God doesn't like you. You're not worthy. You don't deserve any blessings." "God is overlooking you." "You just don't measure up. You're no good." "Sure, God could help you, but why would He? It's time you suffered a little, learn how to do without and barely get by." "What? You think Jesus promised you an abundant life? Who do you think you are?" "You ungrateful thing, God's withholding from you." Sound familiar?

Perhaps you've been discouraged or grown impatient? Maybe you've been in a season of waiting on the Lord and His promises, and you've been tempted to move into doubt, unbelief, anxiety and depression? Don't go there. Stay strong. Stay patient. Stay in faith. God's Word is true; and through faith and patience, you will inherit all that God has promised you. God is not Scrooge!

Today, make a fresh commitment to walk uprightly before the Lord and remind yourself of this basic truth about God; that He is good and He is not withholding anything that would be good for you. Here's a little more ammo... He's a giver *(John 3:16)*. He gives good gifts *(Matthew 7:11)*. He goes about doing good and healing all that are oppressed of the devil *(Acts 10:38)*. He desires that you prosper and are in good health as your soul prospers *(3 John 2)*. He doesn't withhold any good thing from those who walk uprightly *(Psalm 84:11)*. If it's good for you...God is not withholding it. Declare it!

Read It! James 1:17

Speak It! "Father, I declare it: You are good! You're not Scrooge; You're a giver. You always give good gifts. If it's a good thing, then You are not withholding it from me. Today, You are making a way to get good things to me. You have already blessed me with every spiritual blessing that overflows into every area of my life. I believe You are doing good things for my family. You are opening doors for me, granting me favor and connecting me with the right people. You've given me a sound mind and freedom from fear. You're filling me with the power of Your strength, healing, grace, and You are empowering me to be a witness for Christ. No matter how I feel, how long it takes or what the enemy says, I know You are not withholding any good thing from me as I walk uprightly. In Jesus' Name. Amen."

DAY 201

(you're in the army now!)

"Endure hardship with us like a good soldier of Christ Jesus. No one serving as a soldier gets involved in civilian affairs—he wants to please his commanding officer."
2 Timothy 2:3-4, NIV

Did you know you're enlisted? The day you invited Jesus to be the Lord of your life, you joined the Lord's army. God has an important assignment for you, a special op for you to fulfill. Unfortunately, a lot of the Lord's soldiers have gone AWOL ("absent without leave"). Many Believers still think they're in charge of their lives and calling the shots; but if Jesus is the Lord of our lives, He's the Commander-in-Chief, and we are under His command. What does it mean to be in the Lord's army? It means we...

- **Join "boot camp."** We lay aside our rights to anything, everything. We've been bought with a price, and we learn new disciplines for a life of service.
- **Comply with a new "dress code."** We put off the rags of selfishness, pride, strife, anger and put on the uniform of love, patience, kindness, humility.
- **Don't whine.** When the Commander or any of His delegated officers ask us to do anything—100 push-ups in prayer, sharpen our skills, serve other soldiers or any other task, menial or great—we serve with a salute and a great attitude.
- **Are trained to be armed and dangerous.** We're engaged in a spiritual battle with eternal consequences and learn how to use our weapons—the Word, the Name of Jesus, the blood of Jesus and more—to fight for freedom on behalf of others.
- **Understand rank and file.** We understand the Lord sets people in rank as it pleases Him; calling some to be generals, officers, privates and foot soldiers.
- **Realize the military is more than the perks.** While we are thankful for the benefits that come with being the Lord's soldier—joy, peace, freedom, health, abundance, provision, life, blessings—we know the real reason we are in the army is to serve our great God and His cause.
- **Make sacrifices.** We make a commitment to do what the Lord wants us to do, say what He wants us to say and go where He wants us to go—even if it means sacrificing our comfort, time, money, preferences and very life, if needed.
- **Are at war.** We know the eternal stakes, our enemy and the rewards of victory; so we gladly stay alert, ready, proactive and focused on the things that matter most. We won't accept anything less than victory!

If we've been a faithful soldier, one day we'll hear the Lord say, "Well done!"

Read It! Matthew 25:23

Speak It! "Father, I renew my commitment to Your army. I freely lay down my life to serve You and others. Jesus, You are my Commander-in-Chief, and I salute You! In Jesus' Name. Amen."

DAY 202

(too good to be true)

"Therefore I say unto you, What things soever ye desire, when ye pray, believe that ye receive them, and ye shall have them."
Mark 11:24, KJV

What a classic faith passage! Jesus said so much in such a short statement. I've talked to Christians who think this verse is too good to be true! Did Jesus really mean what He said? Of course He did! What does He mean? Several things here:

- **His promise is contingent on us remaining vitally connected to Him.** The way we remain in Him is to spend time with Him in His Word. When we do this, our desires line up with His desires for us. When our desires are in line with His Word, it's easy for Jesus to make such an amazing promise.

  He can say with great confidence that we can ask for whatever we desire... whatever we wish, and He would give it to us; because He knows our desires will be congruent with His desires for us. So, don't pray or ask God for "things" until you've spent time with Him in His Word identifying His will and His desire for you. Once you're saturated with His desires, it's easy to pray, believe and receive.

- **One major keyword in this passage is: "receive."** Once we identify the things we and the Lord desire for our lives (as discussed above), then we are to pray and ask God for those things. After we pray in faith believing that we receive them. That means...we believe we receive them now—as in present tense... as in, "I have it now!"

  Sometimes, we get it backwards. We want to have them first...and then we'll believe we receive them. Problem: faith doesn't work that way. We "receive"—present tense—by faith after we pray; then we "shall have"—future tense.

Sounds simple enough, right? Faith pleases God, and it's the very thing Believers are called to live by. I encourage you to stir up your faith once again and spend time thinking, meditating and soaking in the principles of faith. Marinate yourself in God's Word until His desires become your desires. Read faith-building books and listen to podcasts from those who preach a strong faith message. Jesus meant what He said; it's not too good to be true! Take some time to talk to the Lord about these things and ask Him to help you "get it," so you can experience His goodness is a fresh way.

Read It! John 15:7, NIV

Speak It! "Father, I want to please You with my faith. I believe Your Word, and I ask You to help me "get this" in my heart. Help me saturate my heart in Your Word, so my desires line up with Your desires for me. When I pray, I will believe I receive. I will take You at Your Word. I'm so thankful that You're a good God. I know if I abide in You and Your Word abides in me; I can ask whatever I wish, and it will be given to me. Thank You Lord for helping me to grow in faith! In Jesus' Name. Amen."

DAY 203

(two basics)

"...To Him Who ever loves us and has once [for all] loosed
and freed us from our sins by His own blood..."
Revelation 1:4, AMP

The bottom line on all the hassles of this life, the junk we go through, the challenges, mistakes, tribulations, failures, trials, hard work, messing up, effort, patience and endurance we experience is this: He loves us. He forgives us.

Two basics. When I read this verse in the *Amplified Bible,* I was struck by what it revealed:

- **Basic #1: Jesus loves.** *"...to Him Who ever loves us..."* Have you pondered that lately? He ever loves us. He loves us. Jesus loves us. Jesus ever loves us. He can't stop loving us, because He is love. I have to be honest; I often have a hard time grasping that. I know it's true, but the daily experience of this reality is something we all need more of! God's love—the deep love of Jesus. Wow, He ever loves us.

- **Basic #2: Jesus forgives.** *"freed us from our sins..."* Simple truth, but what a doozy! Jesus, through His shed blood, has freed and loosed us from all of our sins. All of them. Have you sinned lately? We probably all have. But, whether our sins have been giant, blatant, massive and ridiculous or little, itty-bitty ones; Jesus has freed us from every sin...and the penalty that went with them! We have been made as righteous as God Himself because of what Jesus did in shedding His blood. Ponder that for eternity!

Let's get a fresh revelation of His amazing love and His forgiveness today. Let's meditate on the fact that He will never not love us; and because of His great love, He shed His blood on the cross for our forgiveness—to wipe our slate clean.

Read It! Ephesians 3:14-20

Speak It! "Father, these things are so basic; and yet, so true. I pray for a fresh revelation of Your love in my life. Help me to know the length, depth, breadth and height of it. May I come to know practically, through experience for myself, Your great love. I thank You for Your mercy and forgiveness. Jesus, thank You for shedding Your blood so I could be free from every sin. My slate is clean, and I have been made the righteousness of God in Christ. Today is a good day because God loves me and my sins are washed away. In Jesus' Name. Amen."

DAY 204

(the b team)

"Isn't it obvious that God deliberately chose men and women that
the culture overlooks and exploits and abuses, chose these 'nobodies'
to expose the hollow pretensions of the 'somebodies'?"
1 Corinthians 1:27-28, MSG

Have you ever been on the B Team? Picked last for kickball? Stuck on the JV?
Never got nominated for homecoming anything? Didn't get asked to the
prom? Always the "first alternate"? Assistant to the assistant? Eleventh man
off the bench? Invisible? Feeling like a nobody?

Rejoice and just wait! God delights in picking "nobodies" to do great things!

Reread this whole passage:

*"This 'foolish' plan of God is far wiser than the wisest of human plans,
and God's weakness is far stronger than the greatest of human strength.
Remember, dear brothers and sisters, that few of you were wise in the
world's eyes, or powerful, or wealthy when God called you. Instead, God
deliberately chose things the world considers foolish in order to shame
those who think they are wise. And He chose those who are powerless to
shame those who are powerful. God chose things despised by the world,
things counted as nothing at all, and used them to bring to nothing what
the world considers important, so that no one can ever boast in the
presence of God." (1 Corinthians 1:25-29, NLT)*

If you read the Bible, you'll notice the Lord often looks for the "weakest links,"
so He can display His greatest glory through them! Don't ever rule yourself
out, when God has ruled you in! Just keep your eyes on Jesus, live for an
Audience of One, obey His Word, be led by the Spirit and watch what God will
do in and through you.

The world will marvel. You will be blessed. Jesus will get the glory.

Read It! Acts 4:13, KJV

Speak It! "Father, I am so glad You pick 'nobodies' to be 'somebodies.' I choose to
keep my eyes on Jesus, to live for an Audience of One, to obey Your Word and be
led by Your Spirit. I thank You in advance that the world will marvel, I will be
blessed, and Jesus will be glorified in and through my life. In Jesus' Name. Amen."

DAY 205

(your labor day is coming)

"...'Joseph, son of David, do not be afraid to take to you Mary your wife, for that which is conceived in her is of the Holy Spirit. And she will bring forth'..."
Matthew 1:20-21

Have you ever been expecting a baby? The whole process is miraculous—definitely one of the wonders of the world. How does God knit an eternal person inside of a womb? Labor and delivery...just as amazing. At just the right time, your "labor day" hits, the next thing you know, you—or, if you're a man, your wife—have delivered what you believe to be the most beautiful child ever known to man! (Then, you blink...18 years go by, and you're moving them to college, sanitizing their dorm, kissing them goodbye and crying big salty tears!)

There are many parallels to being pregnant with a promise from God! It's a miraculous process how God knits something supernatural in our lives and conceived a dream inside us. Have you been carrying a "baby"—or "babies"—in your heart for a long time? Are you "great with child" and beginning to wonder if you'll ever give birth? Be patient. Your labor day is coming!

Unlike natural-born babies, the gestation period for some "babies" conceived in our hearts usually isn't an exact 9 nine months. Sometimes, it can take decades for that baby to develop inside of us. God wants us to enjoy the journey, while we prepare for the arrival of His promises, dreams and visions in our lives. One thing's for sure: if we don't interrupt the pregnancy, we'll deliver! We don't always understand God's timing, and the way our lives intersect with His divine purposes; but we do know that when the Holy Spirit conceives a dream or vision inside of us, we will bring it forth! It may be now...it may be 10 years from now. God doesn't bring us to the moment of birth and not delivery!

You can't fake labor and delivery—but who'd want to? When it's time for a natural baby to be born, a woman's body automatically shifts gears and goes into action. When that baby is ready to come out, there is a great urge to push; and mom, the midwife and/or doctor find a way to make it happen! The same is true for spiritual babies. When the time is right, God's grace will be on you to change gears, and there will be a great urge to pray, take action or push; God will set things in motion, and He'll help you find a way to give birth. If you've been pregnant for a long time...be encouraged. Your labor day will come!

Read It! Isaiah 66:9, NIV

Speak It! "Father, I'm pregnant with Your promise and dreams for my life. Help me to prepare and supplement for their arrival. My labor day will come and this 'baby' will be born right on time. (If you'd like to be pregnant with God's promise, say this:) Father, I'd like to be pregnant with a promise. I ask You to conceive Your Word and dreams in my heart by the power of Your Holy Spirit. In Jesus' Name. Amen."

DAY 206

(things to come)

"However, when He, the Spirit of truth, has come, He will guide you
into all truth; for He will not speak on His own authority, but whatever
He hears He will speak; and He will tell you things to come."
John 16:13

When you think of all the advantages God gives to Believers, it's almost not fair
for the rest of the world. Salvation, eternal life, forgiveness, mercy, favor, grace,
strength, wisdom, knowledge, power and...oh, yeah,...the God of the Universe
living on the inside of them! *(1 John 4:4, KJV)* Just some slight advantages.

One major edge Believers get is a personal relationship with the Holy Spirit.
The Holy Spirit—the third Person of the Godhead—is the One who lives in us
when we come to faith in Christ. Our bodies become the temple of the Holy
Spirit and we are never, ever alone *(1 Corinthians 6:19)*. God is always with
us—on the inside!

Jesus promised us that the Holy Spirit would do something very unique and
very special for every Believer. Jesus said the Holy Spirit would "tell us things
to come." This is a wonderful promise and I encourage you to take Him up on
it. It doesn't mean the Holy Spirit will tell you everything about the future of
everything. He may not tell you who will be elected President or what the
price of gas will be in 10 years; but you can count on Him to tell you things to
come in your particular life. Often, the Holy Spirit will give us a "heads up" on
things to come; He will give us a "sense" or a "glimpse" or a "knowing" about
something coming up. Sometimes, He'll give us a dream. We can't always
put our finger on it, but somehow we "know" things to come. The Holy Spirit
doesn't always give us a detailed map of the future, but just enough information for us to take the steps of faith that are required. Sometimes He tells us
things so that we can pray or prepare.

In our lives, we've come to expect the Holy Spirit to show us things to come in
our family, church and general life. We're not expecting to be taken "completely
by surprise" on anything, because Jesus promised that the Holy Spirit would tell
us things to come. We've faced some challenges in the past few years, but when
we reflect on things, we can see the Holy Spirit has given us a "knowing" about
things to come and the grace and faith to push forward with Him!

Today, listen to the Spirit and discern if He is showing you things to come.

Read It! John 14:26

Speak It! "Holy Spirit, thank You for showing me things to come. I trust that You
will tell me anything I need to know, so I can pray or prepare. I'm so glad that You
are the Greater One, and You live in me. In Jesus' Name. Amen."

DAY 207

(the wood)

"For lack of wood the fire goes out, and where there is
no whisperer, contention ceases."
Proverbs 26:20, AMP

Ever sat around a big, blazing bonfire? There's nothing like sitting around a campfire, roasting marshmallows and telling stories. When the fire starts to die down, you just throw another log on top, and the fire gets rejuvenated. At the end of the night, when it's time for bed; if you quit putting logs on the fire, it goes out.

Gossip and strife are like the bonfire, while words and whispers are like the wood. A big, blazing bonfire of gossip can set a person or a whole family, office, church, school or company on fire; and words can keep that fire going for a long time.

Have you ever noticed how we can get a whole group fired up with words? One person says this, another person whispers that and more and more logs are added to the fire... Ultimately, there's a raging fire, and people get burnt.

Have you ever noticed that we can even stir ourselves up into an angry fire by talking? When we are frustrated or hurt, we can start talking and work ourselves up into a frenzy...simply, because we keep throwing logs onto the fire.

If we want strife, gossip, anger or contentious fires to go out, we have to quit putting logs on them. As Believers, we have a responsibility to guard our words. If we just flap-at-the-jaw, complain, whine, gossip, criticize or share our negative opinions, thoughts, hurts or offenses with others, we just add wood to the fire.

The next time you're tempted to stir up the fire within your own heart or among your family, friends, peers or coworkers, just remember: "...where there is no wood, the fire goes out."

Read It! Proverbs 18:8, 21

Speak It! "Father, I am sorry for throwing logs onto gossip and strife bonfires by speaking words I shouldn't have spoken. I have worked myself into a fired-up frenzy, and I have started fires among others with my words. Help me to remember and obey the simple truth: 'where there is no wood the fire goes out.' In Jesus' Name. Amen."

DAY 208

(sound bites)

"Peter asked Jesus, 'What about him, Lord?' Jesus replied, 'If I want him to remain alive until I return, what is that to you? You follow me.' So the rumor spread among the community of Believers that that disciple wouldn't die. But that isn't what Jesus said at all. He only said, 'If I want him to remain alive until I return, what is that to you?'"
John 21:21-23, NLT

Don't believe everything you hear. Whether it's political frenzy, election sound-bites, liberal and anti-Christian agendas in the media—don't accept everything hook, line and sinker! Ever "heard it through the grapevine,"—only to discover the grapevine was polluted?

Maybe you've been the target of defamatory comments. If you've ever been misquoted and taken out of context, you're in good company. Jesus was, too! He dealt with the plague of misinformation. On numerous occasions the authorities thought they had it right about the things Jesus had said, but they were often wrong.

Sad to say, you can't trust most of the headlines, editorials or reporting that's done in the name of fairness. There always seems to be a bias in this culture of sound bites, video clips, organizational motives and political spin. Unfortunately, there are many who can't tolerate the "good news," so they resort to mocking, scorning and sarcasm. Misinformation, rumor and the grapevine does damage. The bummer is that good people get hurt; bad people get notoriety and the average citizen never gets the truth. Sometimes, a completely innocent person is the brunt of terrible grapevine lies—like Jesus! A Christian named Stephen was also the object of blatant lies *(Acts 6:13-14)*, and it cost him his life. Then, sometimes a completely guilty person is the object of rumors. Some of the Lord's favorite people really messed up: Moses, David, Peter and Paul. Can you imagine what the news headlines about them might have been back in the day? But, the Lord extended great mercy and continued to use them mightily. Even today, in the Christian world, there is a grapevine.

Don't start a rumor and don't believe the grapevine. Sometimes, even Believers hear one juicy tidbit, and the suspicions, accusations or dissing begins. Don't do it. Love believes the best. No matter what you hear, it's not the whole truth. Remember this: whoever digs a pit for others will fall into it himself. Retribution belongs to the Lord. The summary: believe the best about everyone.

Read It! Proverbs 26:27, NLT

Speak It! "Father, I will believe the best about others, and I will do unto others as I would like them to do to me. In Jesus' Name. Amen."

DAY 209

(with persecutions)

"Peter said to Him, 'We have left everything to follow You!' 'I tell you the truth,' Jesus replied, 'no one who has left home or brothers or sisters or mother or father or children or fields for Me and the gospel will fail to receive a hundred times as much in this present age (homes, brothers, sisters, mothers, children and fields—and with them, persecutions) and in the age to come, eternal life.'"
Mark 10:28-30, NIV

Following Jesus and serving God is the best life on Earth! Jesus promised many blessings to those who would give up all to faithfully follow Him. But, there's one other thing, here, Jesus promised. Along with a 100-fold blessing, there will be persecutions. Did you read that? Yes, Jesus promised blessings—with persecutions! Sure, we'll be persecuted by people because the Name of Jesus and the cross of Christ is an offense and stumbling block to those who won't believe. But, let's look at persecution from another angle. Often, we're persecuted not only for our faith—but also for our blessings. Isn't it ironic? Jesus promised to bless us when we leave all to follow Him, and He let us know that not everyone will be thrilled with our blessed life. Some people will find a way to criticize, mock, envy, diss and question the very blessings Jesus gives us. If you want to be blessed, you'd better be prepared to be persecuted.

People are funny. When you live like everyone else—just barely getting along, half-depressed, feeling empty, unchurched, without direction and purpose and struggling to survive—everybody likes you. In fact, if they think they're doing just a little better than you are, they love you! But, when you start to serve God, live by faith and climb out of the "average Joe club"—you start to prosper, your marriage gets better, you laugh more than you cry, your kids obey, you hook up with an on-fire church, you have enough money to bless others, you find purpose and life is looking up—you're booted out of the average club. All of a sudden, the same people who were singing your praises are now so jealous of you, they could spit! In fact, they are convinced you don't deserve the blessings, and there must be more to the story. You must be doing something wrong or illegal...or both; you must know someone in high places (fact is...you do); you must have a Sugar Daddy (fact is...you do!); you must be crazy, selfish, egotistical, spoiled...and on it goes.

Let's always find ourselves on the side of "being blessed" or "rejoicing with those who rejoice" and never side with the persecutors.

Read It! 2 Timothy 3:12

Speak It! "Jesus, I choose to leave all and follow You! Thank You for blessing my life, for giving me grace to endure any persecution that comes. Help me to never side with the persecutors, but rejoice with those who rejoice. In Jesus' Name. Amen."

DAY 210

(liar, liar)

"...there is no truth in him. When he lies, he speaks
his native language, for he is a liar and the father of lies."
John 8:44-45, NIV

Newsflash: Satan is a liar. There is no truth in him. He is the father of lies and cannot tell the truth—even if he wanted to. He's a deceiver, and his primary weapons are lies. Be advised. Satan's goal is to steal, kill and destroy. He has no love-loss for God or any human being. He couldn't care less about you; he simply wants to take you out through deception.

If you've found yourself having unusual doubts, questioning basic things you believe and standing against unbelief like never before, you are in a spiritual battle—a real battle. The devil doesn't want anyone established in the truth and he works day and night to steal the Word, to deceive and lie. He knows the power of God's Word more than most Believers, and that's why he wars against our minds to steal our faith in God and His Word.

Listen, any thought that comes to your mind and is contrary to the Word of God is a flat-out lie. It was sent from the father of lies to harass and torment you. Satan's goal is confusion, double-mindedness, doubt and unbelief. The last thing he wants is for you to be strong in the Lord and His Word—and a threat to him and his kingdom. He works to intimidate, confuse, defeat, discourage, harass and torment Believers through lies.

His lies go something like this... "What if God doesn't exist? What if the Bible isn't true? What if God doesn't fulfill His promises? What if you are too stupid to hear from God? What if you are wasting your time serving God? What if you're too old to fulfill God's plan? What if you're too young to be taken seriously? What if you don't make it? What if it's all a hoax? What if you didn't live for the Lord? What if you weren't a goody-two-shoes? What if you're missing out on a big time by not partying, gambling or sleeping around? What if God doesn't protect you? What if God doesn't love you? What if..."

And, on it goes... Once you identify Satan's lies, take authority over him in Jesus' Name and get in his business. Make a choice to believe God and deliberately choose to speak the Word. Let him know you're not falling for his lies. Jesus said His Word is truth, and you can have great confidence in the Lord and His Word.

Read It! Revelation 21:8

Speak It! "Satan, I am not falling for your lies. I take authority over you and every lying spirit that has been whispering in my ear. I bind you in Jesus' Name, and I loose the power of God and His Word in my life. My God is not a man and He cannot lie, and His Word is truth—and I believe it! In Jesus' Name. Amen."

DAY 211

(don't judge a book by its cover)

"The LORD does not look at the things man looks at. Man looks at the
outward appearance, but the LORD looks at the heart."
1 Samuel 16:7, NIV

It's great... God looks at the heart. But, it's still true; man looks on the outward appearance. So, let's not be over-spiritual and neglect the outward appearance. Believe me, it's no sign of spirituality. But, for the benefit of humanity, we ought to do the best we can with what we have. So, if a curling iron, mascara and blush, fitted shirt or a polished pair of shoes, a clean shave, and some cologne help the cause...go for it! But, at the same time, don't judge a book by its cover.

Some of God's finest people may not be considered "beautiful" by man's estimation. We probably all know people who face great physical handicaps and limitations. Consequently, they have been mistreated, teased, ignored, dismissed and overlooked on many occasions in their lives. They could be bitter and insecure; however, I've been both amazed and humbled time and again as I've watched them deal with life with a sweet spirit—always loving and serving others, often smiling in the midst of great pain. I have no doubt the Lord is pleased with them...because He looks on the heart.

I doubt Jesus would've ever made People® magazine's "Prettiest People" issue? Isaiah says, *"...There was nothing beautiful or majestic about His appearance, nothing to attract us to Him," (Isaiah 53:2, NLT)*. It doesn't sound like Jesus was a "head turner," and maybe that's one reason He was dismissed and overlooked by so many when He was in their midst. The masses were looking for a knight in shining armor...a handsome, powerful king to lead them. Jesus was the lowly son of a carpenter and exercised humility in everything He did. No wonder he wasn't accepted. He didn't match the picture they had in their minds of what their king would look like. But, Jesus was the beloved Son of His Father; and because of His humility, He has been exalted to the highest place of honor and given a Name above every name!

Today, be encouraged in your own life. It's not about the outward appearance; it's about the heart. Sure, do the best you can with your looks, but keep your focus on your inner beauty first. Let's not judge a book by its cover, but take time to notice those around us who may be overlooked and dismissed. God looks on the heart...let's endeavor to do the same.

Read It! Isaiah 53:2

Speak It! "Father, thank You for looking upon my heart. Others may judge me by my looks, size, color, height and appearance, but You look at the real me—my heart. Today, help me to look at people through Your eyes. In Jesus' Name. Amen."

DAY 212

(take a flying leap)

"Jesus was matter-of-fact: 'Embrace this God-life. Really embrace it, and nothing will be too much for you. This mountain, for instance: Just say, "Go jump in the lake"—no shuffling or shilly-shallying—and it's as good as done.'"
Mark 11:22-23, MSG

Faith is a leap. It's not a blind leap, but it is a leap. Faith is taking God at His Word. It's letting go of the trapeze bar and trusting the Lord will catch you. It's getting out of the boat and believing God will enable you to walk on water. It's jumping out of the natural realm of the five physical senses into the realm of the spiritual reality of God's Word.

Have you taken a flying leap lately? Have you jumped out on God's Word? When we take God at His Word, He has authorized us to speak words of faith! Not only can we take a leap of faith, we can tell "things" to take a flying leap. Have you told the mountains in your life to go "jump in the lake"? Jesus said we could! When we embrace the God-life and all that goes with it, He empowers us with His authority and nothing is impossible!

Today, just make a decision to take a flying leap of faith—on the authority of His Word—and tell those mountains in your life to jump in the lake, too!

Read It! Mark 9:23

Speak It! "Father, I believe You! I embrace Your God-life and I choose to live the 'faith leaping' kind of life. Thank You for authorizing me to tell the mountains in my life to jump into the lake. With You, nothing is impossible. In Jesus' Name. Amen."

DAY 213

(mavins)

"Go, sell the oil and pay your debt; and you and your sons live on the rest."
2 Kings 4:8

Mavin: "Someone who is dazzlingly skilled in any field—ace, adept, champion, sensation, virtuoso, genius, hotshot, star, superstar, whiz, megastar."

Yeah, where's the next Bill Gates ace? Who's the up-and-coming Mark Zuckerberg hotshot? Where are the Stephen Spielberg, Sarah Palin or Oprah-like sensations? How about the political, entertainment and sports champions of tomorrow? Where are the next Christian mavins? Who are the next brilliant Christian business minds? Influencers? Wealth producers? Pastors and leaders?

The Bible tells the story of a godly, widowed, single mom with two sons who was in a crisis. In debt up to her eyeballs and about to lose her kids to the creditors, she decided to seek the Lord's help. He answered her in a big way. In short order, she became a very successful and prosperous, entrepreneurial CEO mavin! (Take a minute and go read it for yourself in the **Read It!** segment.)

Four things brought this woman from desolation to success:

- **She knew what she wanted.** Survival for her and her kids! Before we can release the mavin in us, we need to have a desire in our heart.
- **She used what she had.** A jar of oil. Even though it doesn't sound like much, it was all God needed to perform a miracle! Everyone of us have something—a talent, gift, or experience—just waiting to be used by God.
- **She got creative.** One witty idea from the Lord, used in obedience to His direction, gave her a garage full of supernatural inventory! And that was just the beginning. She got busy marketing, advertising and selling that oil! Her need for survival was now producing a great income for her and her boys.
- **She had motivation.** This woman simply wanted to pay her debts and get her children back! Whether it's financial freedom or a spiritual debt to preach the Gospel to as many people as possible, our mavins need motivation to manifest.

God is doesn't play favorites. If He pulled an entrepreneurial mavin out of a widowed, single mom in crisis, He will do it for anyone who is willing to believe Him! It's time to turn that idea into a successful business. When we know what we want, use what we have, get creative, are driven to succeed, and follow God's plan, the mavin's are coming out!

Read It! 2 Kings 4:1-7

Speak It! "Father, help me tap into Your entrepreneurial wisdom. I want to be a 'mavin' for Your kingdom! In Jesus' Name. Amen."

DAY 214

(the other side)

"Let us cross over to the other side."
Mark 4:35

If your boat is rocking, the waves are blowing, the wind is howling, and your boat looks like it will sink, have no fear. If you have God's Word on your situation, no matter what storm brews, you will get to the other side!

Remember the story of Jesus calming the seas in a storm? Go to the **Read It!** segment and read that passage. In Mark 4:35, Jesus said, *"Let us cross over to the other side..."* Seven verses later, Mark 5:1 says, *"Then they came to the other side..."* That's because God always fulfills His Word! If Jesus said it, we can take it to the bank. But, we may experience a few things between the *"Let us cross..."* and the *"Then they came..."* finale. We may face things like circumstantial storms, emotional waves, people-driven winds that try to rob us of our faith in God and His Word. Keep believing God's Word; don't be moved by the storm.

Has God given you a promise and spoken His Word to your heart? His Word is your anchor in the midst of any storm. You will make it to the other side.

Twenty years ago, we moved to Kalamazoo, Michigan, to start a church. We didn't know anyone in town, except my cousin and her family who lived about 20 miles away. One day, I was driving our black Chrysler minivan with our two toddler daughters in tow down a street called Westnedge Avenue when the Lord spoke this "let us go" scripture to my heart: *"Do not be afraid, but speak, and do not keep silent; for I am with you, and no one will attack you to hurt you; for I have many people in this city," (Acts 18:9-11).* I had no idea, then, how God-breathed this scripture would be over the years as storms came; it has been an anchor for our life and ministry. When the storm of "I don't believe in women preachers..." rains down, the Lord reminds me to speak and not keep silent. When the waves of criticism and hurtful words bang against our minds, the Lord reminds us He is our refuge and strong tower. When winds of discouragement blow, He reminds us He has many people in the city; and we are not alone. We have kept our faith in His Word, He has brought us to "the other side" in victory after victory.

What "let us go" scripture has the Lord spoken to you? Stand on it. You can trust the Lord. In due season, He will take you to "the other side" of victory!

Read It! Mark 4:35-5:1

Speak It! "Father, I'm so thankful for Your Word. When You speak a 'let us go' word to my heart, no matter what storm I face; I believe You will bring me victoriously to 'the other side.' In Jesus' Name. Amen."

DAY 215

(faith boost)

"And the apostles said to the Lord, 'Increase our faith!' And the Lord said,
'If you had faith like a mustard seed, you would say to this mulberry tree,
"Be uprooted and be planted in the sea"; and it would obey you.'"
Luke 17:5-7, NASB

The apostles were desperate for more faith, and what does Jesus do? He tells them to talk to a tree. What's the connection?

Our faith is more in our mouth than we realize! Notice the phrases: *"...if you had faith...you would say..."* Our faith goes into action when we speak. Faith is a heart-voice-activated thing—from the abundance of the heart our mouth speaks—so our faith is very much connected with what we say *(Matthew 12:34, KJV)*. If we want our faith to increase, Jesus told us to use the faith we have by speaking.

When the disciples asked Jesus to increase their faith, He DIDN'T say, "Well, boys, your faith doesn't make any difference. Just be passive and leave everything to Me." He DIDN'T just say, "Well, you just need to hear more of the Word because faith comes by hearing and hearing by the Word." He DID say to use the little bit of faith you have and start talking! Hook the faith in your heart up to the words of your mouth; talk to the "trees" and watch what happens!

It's no different today. Do you need to increase your faith in a given area of your life? If you had faith, you would *say*. What things are you saying? Your words, which come from the abundance of your heart, reveal your faith. What do you hear yourself saying? What do you need to say?

Today, if you need more faith, use the little bit you have...and say!

Read It! Mark 11:23

Speak It! "Jesus, I am so glad You didn't make the realm of faith complex, confusing, theological or theoretical! You have given me the ability to use the little bit of faith I have to get results. There is simplicity in Christ. Today, I will intentionally use the faith I have by speaking words—specifically Your Word—to the various 'trees' in my life. Thank You that Your power goes to work as I release my faith in You and Your Word. In Jesus' Name. Amen."

DAY 216

(what moves you?)

"But when He saw the multitudes, He was moved with compassion for them, because they were weary and scattered, like sheep having no shepherd."
Matthew 9:36-37

Do the multitudes bug you or move you? When was the last time you were moved with compassion for the lost? At times, I am guilty of being distracted with my own life, and I need to be reminded that Jesus came for the express purpose of helping others—seeking and saving the lost! Sometimes, we get so busy in our own worlds, that we lose sight of the bigger picture. Worse, we become cold, detached and indifferent to the pain, hurt, suffering, emptiness and despair that defines life for many people.

If we need to be stirred up in compassion, let's take some time to "see" the multitudes. The next time we're around a crowd—at the mall, airport, amusement park, local restaurant, wedding reception or driving in traffic, let's take some time to stop and stare! Look at people. Make eye contact. Smile. Ponder what their lives might be like. Ask and allow the Lord to give you His heart of compassion for people.

Without the Lord's compassion, we become selfish zombies—like everyone else—just moving through life. God forbid! Today, we need the Lord to stir us up with His compassion, and we need to be moved by it!

Read It! Matthew 14:14, KJV

Speak It! "Father, I want to be moved with compassion for people. I have gotten cold and indifferent and I ask You to forgive me. Help me to see people the way You do. In Jesus' Name. Amen."

226

DAY 217

(first love)

"I know all the things you do. I have seen your hard work and your patient endurance. I know you don't tolerate evil people. You have examined the claims of those who say they are apostles but are not. You have discovered they are liars. You have patiently suffered for me without quitting. But I have this complaint against you. You don't love me or each other as you did at first! Look how far you have fallen from your first love! Turn back to me again and work as you did at first."
Revelation 2:2-5, NLT

This is the ever-present challenge for those in ministry. For those who work hard to serve the Lord; those who refuse to quit and those who live by God's Word... we must keep the light of our first love burning brightly.

If we are not careful, we can get so engaged serving the Lord, that we forget to love the Lord. We can find ourselves loving the ministry, the people and the fruit we see—but not loving the Lord. We are so busy, we have no time left to spend with the Lord in prayer and devotion to Him. I know...I've been there.

What are we to do? Return and do the "first works."

What was it like when you first came to know the Lord? What "works" did you do then? Return to that place. I remember when I first became a Christian, I would stay up late reading my Bible, praying and writing in my journal. I would listen to Christian albums over and over and over. I went on "dates" with the Lord and enjoyed His company, pouring out my heart to Him. When I need to return to my first love, I do those things again more intentionally.

In various seasons of my life, I have pictured my walk with the Lord like a dining room table. At the dining table of my heart, there is one seat reserved for Jesus alone. As my first love, He gets to sit at the head seat of the table of my heart. As much as I love my husband, my kids and the people the Lord has put in my life, I don't want anyone else or anything else to take His place in my heart.

How about you? Who or what is sitting at the head seat of the table of your heart? Does your first love need to be relit? How long has it been since you've told Jesus how much you love Him? Think about the days when you first knew the Lord and return and do those works once again!

Read It! Matthew 22:37-38

Speak It! "Jesus, I love You. You are my Lord, Savior, Healer, Redeemer, Light and First Love! You have been so good to me. I don't want to be so busy with my life or serving You that I leave my first love. I want You to know that You will always have the head seat at the table of my heart. In Jesus' Name. Amen."

DAY 218

(God commands his blessing)

"Behold, how good and how pleasant it is for brethren to dwell together in unity!...For there the LORD commanded the blessing—life forevermore."
Psalm 133:1, 3b

How would you like to be in the place where God commands His blessing? He has commanded His blessing in the place of unity! How good and pleasant to be in a marriage, a family, a company, a neighborhood or church free from strife and discord; to be in a place where there is unity, harmony and agreement. The Lord is particularly interested in seeing unity among the "brethren"—Believers and churches.

God hates discord! He commands His blessing where there is unity. Unfortunately, some people enjoy being disagreeable, contrary, argumentative and critical. We live in a culture that thrives on controversy, accusation, competition, jealousy and envy; and all of these things breed division and disunity. God cannot command His blessing "there."

In the church world, political arena, media and the arts, we need more peacemakers, unifiers and lovers who won't compromise on God's values.

Being in unity doesn't mean we need to become "vanilla" or "spineless" in our core values, beliefs or doctrine; it means we choose to walk in love and avoid strife. The Bible says love believes the best *(1 Corinthians 13:7)*, so let's choose love, unity, and peace in and through Jesus.

Today, are you in strife, division, disunity or competition with anyone? Do you need to make any "unity" adjustments, so the Lord can command His blessing upon your life?

Read It! Ephesians 4:3, NIV

Speak It! "Father, I want to walk in a way that is congruent with Your Word. I want Your commanded blessing in my life. I ask You to forgive me for _____ (list any situations where you have not walked in love and harmony), and I will do what is necessary to make it right. I choose to love others, especially the 'brethren,' and I will walk in agreement and unity. In Jesus' Name. Amen."

DAY 219

(eat well and live)

"Your words were found, and I ate them, and Your word was to me the joy
and rejoicing of my heart; for I am called by Your name..."
Jeremiah 15:16

Living on the go? Eating strange meals at weird hours? Visiting the fast food joint a little too often? We all have seasons that seem to get us out of our desired routines and healthy habits.

The other night I was working late and eating the "dinner of champions"—a piece of cheese, a box of raisins, a V-8 and a giant cappuccino. It seemed perfectly healthy to me; I had the vegetable, fruit and dairy food groups covered!

My little snack-like dinner reminded me of how things can be spiritually at times. We get so busy doing things—even worthy things—that we forget to eat the Word. We snack on a verse here and a verse there, but we get busy and end up treating God's Word like a fast-food operation. I know I have been guilty. On crazy days, we pull up to "the Lord's drive-up window" and ask Him to super-size a verse for us...and off we go to our busy lives. Thankfully, God is merciful and gracious; and, at times, He does accommodate us in this way. But, we all know for the long-haul, this is no way to eat.

We need a healthy, regular diet of God's Word...loaded with all the spiritual vitamins, nutrients and energy we can get for life and godliness. Today, I hope we are all encouraged and reminded to set aside the time we need to spend with the Lord—eating His Word.

Read It! Psalm 119:103

Speak It! "Father, I thank You that Your Word is my bread, honey and milk and contains all the nutritional value I need to operate in life. Help me to manage my time in such a way that I sit down with You to eat regular, healthy meals from Your Word! In Jesus' Name. Amen."

DAY 220

(there is a season)

"To everything there is a season, a time for every purpose under heaven..."
Ecclesiastes 3:1

The peak fall season here in Michigan is always an absolutely spectacular show of colors and beautiful foliage. For those of us who live in the northern part of the country—while all our southern or tropical friends are enjoying sunshine, blue skies and warm breezes year round—we get the blessing of having four distinct and beautiful seasons!

When seasons change, many things change. The atmosphere. Humidity arrives or dry air kicks in. Our clothing changes, as we peel off layers or pile on layers. The attitudes of people change; people hunker down, go on diets or have a pep in their step—depending upon the season. The temperature changes; it gets really hot, really mild or freezing cold.

There is no question when fall season hits. The air is crisp, and everyone pulls out their favorite sweatshirts! When winter arrives and the snow starts to fall, people pull out the gloves, boots, snow skis and snow scrapers. By the time spring comes along, people are desperate to pack away snow shovels and winter coats and are ready to see blue skies, budding trees and life again! Summer might be most people's favorite season—shorts, tank tops, flip flops, bikes, boats and sunshine give everyone great joy and enjoyment.

The same is often true when our spiritual seasons change. God is always working out His purposes. When the Lord's purpose has us preparing for or entering a new spiritual season, we can sense atmospheric changes, our "clothing" changes, our attitude changes and the spiritual temperature changes. We find our desires, activity and expectations are affected in positive ways.

Seasons in God are wonderful! Let's make sure that when seasons change, we are prepared for each one. Let's make the necessary adjustments in each season, so we will be effective for the kingdom of God and fulfill His plans and His purposes for that time.

Read It! Ecclesiastes 3:11, AMP

Speak It! "Father, I thank You for every season—fall, winter, spring and summer. I know You will provide a time and season for every purpose under heaven. Today, I trust You to help me recognize and cooperate with Your purposes for each one of Your divine seasons. In Jesus' Name. Amen."

DAY 221

(some things are black and white)

"Jesus said to him, 'I am the way, the truth, and the life.
No one comes to the Father except through Me.'"
John 14:6

In this age of political correctness, tolerance, double-talk, rationalization, relativism, "if it feels good" mentality and personal expediency; it's important to be reminded that some things are still ABSOLUTE—some things ARE black and white! It takes people of courage to stand up for what is right, true and correct, regardless of the heat they may take. That doesn't mean they have to be rude, condescending, obnoxious, arrogant and mean-spirited—which seems to be the modus operandi of many—but it does mean we have to have some backbone, guts and boldness in unapologetically standing up for the absolute truth!

Many things are black and white—everything in life is not relative. Absolutes exist. For example: try playing golf or basketball without black and white rules. Try driving to work without absolute traffic rules. It doesn't work. Many people are trying to live life without following God's absolutes, and the result is a life of emptiness, confusion, hurt, dissatisfaction and disillusionment.

Let's embrace this eternal absolute, black and white truth: Jesus is God. Jesus is the only way to the Father.

- *"Jesus said to him, 'I am the way, the truth, and the life. No one comes to the Father except through Me.'"* (John 14:6)
- *"For there is one God and one mediator between God and men, the man Christ Jesus, who gave himself as a ransom for all men..."* (1 Timothy 2:5-6, NIV)
- *"Who is the liar? It is the man who denies that Jesus is the Christ. Such a man is the antichrist—he denies the Father and the Son. No one who denies the Son has the Father; whoever acknowledges the Son has the Father also."* (1 John 2:22-23, NIV)
- *"Salvation is found in no one else, for there is no other name under heaven given to men by which we must be saved."* (Acts 4:12, NIV)

It's amazing what happens when we align our lives with God's absolutes. He finds a way to harmonize our entire lives. Some things really ARE black and white! Be courageous today as you live by God's absolutes.

Read It! Acts 4:12 and 1 Timothy 2:5-6

Speak It! "Father, we've made it so confusing, complex and relative, but You make it so simple. I choose to agree with You, to live by Your absolutes. Thank You that when I align my life with Your truth—there is great freedom and harmony! In Jesus' Name. Amen."

DAY 222

(little things)

"'Well done!' the king exclaimed, 'You are a trustworthy servant. You have been faithful with the little I entrusted to you, so you will be governor of ten cities as your reward.'"
Luke 19:17, NLT

Man looks at the big things. God looks at the little things. Why? Because little things matter! Small things like words, deeds and details are the things God promotes into "big" blessings. If we want all of God's best, maybe it's time to take a moment and do a "little" evaluation. (We must be brutally honest with ourselves and God!) Ready?

- Do we finish what we start and follow through on promises made?
- Do we work with excellence in every detail?
- When tempted to be a fault-finder, do we zip our lip?
- Are we giving an honest day's work for our wages?
- How well are we taking care of our family?
- Do we steal, lie, or cheat, even on seemingly unimportant issues?
- When someone is down, do we provide encouragement, even if we need it ourselves?
- Do we forgive when we don't want to and show mercy to those who don't "deserve" it?
- Are we teaching our kids to love God?
- Is tithing and generous giving a regular part of our lives?
- Instead of griping and complaining, are we always thankful?

There is no "get-rich-quick" route to "big" blessings! The way to the "big" is through the "little." Promotion comes through small things. Staying focused and doing seemingly insignificant things well is the way to promotion. Of course, the opposite is just as true. Wake up and take notice! Having to go back and take the "little" evaluation over and over and over again is not a good sign! When we pass the "little" things test, and are faithful with what God has given us, then greater things are coming. The simple truth is: paying attention to little things is huge!

Read It! 1 Timothy 1:12

Speak It! "Father, I make a decision to focus on doing the 'little things' well. I want to be counted faithful in the small things, and I know You'll promote me to big things in due season. Help me to pass this test with excellence. In Jesus' Name. Amen."

DAY 223

(everyone is a critic)

"You shall hide them in the secret place of Your presence from the plots of man; you shall keep them secretly in a pavilion from the strife of tongues."
Psalm 31:20

People will always have an opinion about you. Some people will feel the need to tell you their opinion. The cowards rant, rave and don't sign their letters. The average critic foams at the mouth and tells you all the reasons they are so smart and you are so dumb. People who love you will speak the truth...in love.

Anyone been criticizing you lately? We get our share, just like you. Why is it that 50 people can tell you they love your company, product, sermon, song, family or kids; but one person can cut you like a knife with one vicious comment? So, how do we respond—short of transforming into King Kong and slapping them upside the head?

For the constructive critics—those who love you: evaluate. If there is any morsel of truth in their criticism, then adjust accordingly.

For the negative critics—usually those who are jealous and envious of your growth and success: follow Rick Warren's advice. He says:

"When you're small, they'll dismiss you; when you're growing, they'll criticize you; and when you're large, they'll resent you. So ignore 'them' and get on with whatever God has told you to do!"

Fortunately, God doesn't allow us to hear most critics. He hides us in His presence from the strife of tongues. Today, the bottom line is whether people are being critical of your business, church, faith, family, hair or home is this: "...ignore 'them' and get on with whatever God has told you to do!"

Read It! Proverbs 25:12, NLT

Speak It! "Father, I want to live a life that is pleasing to You and You alone. Help me listen to the constructive advice from people who love me and thank You for hiding me from the strife of tongues by those who don't. I plan to ignore the negative critics and get on with all that You have called me to do. In Jesus' Name. Amen."

DAY 224

(stand up and step out)

"Christ has set us free to live a free life. So take your stand!"
Galatians 5:1

OK, it's time to bust out and be free, be a Christian anomaly! An anomaly is a deviation from the norm; a person who is unusual, different and not easily classified. That means...not Christianity as usual. Not a carbon copy. Not cookie-cutter.

Is your Christian life like that? Or, is your life pretty predictable? Normal? Boring? Are you willing to stand up and step out?

I don't recommend being rude, stupid or doing things that displease the Lord; but maybe today you need to break free from your comfort zone? From the fear of man. From boredom. What does "free to be an anomaly" look like for you? Time is ticking...get going!

I'm thinkin' it's time to take a stand. Color outside the lines. Go against the grain. Do something out of the box. Shout. Run around your desk. Laugh until you snort. Forget proper English, punctuation and grammatical rules. Don't worry about nuthin'. I know...it's misspelled. So, whatcha gonna do?

Wanna do something significant with your life? Quit running from God? Preach the Gospel? Help disaster-stricken people? Wanna do something fun and different? Learn how to play the drums? Raft down the Colorado River? Hike around Europe? Wanna love people? Hug your kids until their eyes roll back into their head? Kiss your spouse ten times? Pay for the car behind you at Starbucks? Wanna do something you thought it was too late to do? Go back to college or Bible school? Become a lawyer? Make a film? Write a book? Wanna go to another level? Share your faith? Pray in tongues? Laugh at your enemies? Roll your windows down, sing praises loud and off key?

So...do it! Quit worrying about perfection...rock on...live...be free!

Christ has set us free to live a free life...today. Be an anomaly!

Read It! Proverbs 28:1

Speak It! "Father, today, I choose to live a free life! Free to serve You and to be myself. I want to be an anomaly! Help me to break free from fear and pride to experience a greater degree of freedom in Christ! I declare, I am free in Jesus' Name...and the only opinion that counts is Yours! In Jesus' Name. Amen."

DAY 225

(godly sarcasm)

"You are my witnesses. Is there any God besides me?
No, there is no other Rock; I know not one."
Isaiah 44:8

I think this passage is rather funny. It's like God looked around the universe and said, "Is there any other God besides me?" Then, in a micro-millisecond He answers, "Nope! There's no other. I don't know of one!" The whole context of this passage in Isaiah is in connection to the idol gods people had created. I love the sarcasm...

All those who make no-god idols don't amount to a thing, and what they work so hard at making is...nothing. Their little puppet-gods see nothing and know nothing; they're total embarrassments! Who would bother making gods that can't do anything, that can't "god"? Watch all the no-god worshipers hide their faces in shame. Watch the no-god makers slink off humiliated when their idols fail them. Get them out here in the open. Make them face God-reality.

Pretty stupid, wouldn't you say? Don't they have eyes in their heads? Are their brains working at all? Doesn't it occur to them to say, "Half of this tree I used for firewood: I baked bread, roasted meat, and enjoyed a good meal. And now I've used the rest to make an abominable no-god. Here I am praying to a stick of wood!" This lover of emptiness, of nothing, is so out of touch with reality, so far gone, that he can't even look at what he's doing, can't even look at the no-god stick of wood in his hand and say, "This is crazy."

It's not a whole lot different these days. People worship the "created" rather than the "Creator." Today, "get a [fresh] grip" on the basics and be His witness. There is no other God! *"For there is one God and one Mediator between God and men, the Man Christ Jesus," (1 Timothy 2:5).* No apologies!

Read It! Isaiah 44:9-11, 18-20

Speak It! "Father, I don't care what the world preaches, what the media espouses, what is politically correct or what the surveys show, I believe in You—the Lord God Almighty and Jesus Christ, Your Son. Is there any other God? I agree with You; I don't know of any! In Jesus' Name. Amen."

DAY 226

(imagine)

"And the LORD said to Abram, after Lot had separated from him: 'Lift your eyes now and look from the place where you are—northward, southward, eastward, and westward; for all the land which you see I give to you and your descendants forever... Arise, walk in the land through its length and its width, for I give it to you.'"
Genesis 13:14-15, 17

At this moment, if you were to lift up your eyes and look from the place where you are—northward, southward, eastward, westward...one month, three months, 6 months, 12 months from now—what do you see? Go ahead. Let your imagination—in alignment with God's Word—run free for a while. What do you see?

Do you see your relationship with the Lord getting stronger? Do you see yourself becoming more Christ-like? Do you see the fruit of love, joy, peace, patience, kindness, gentleness and self-control growing in your life? Do you see your prayer and worship life taking on a fresh intensity?

Do you see your relationships with specific people getting better? Your marriage growing closer? Your kids on fire for the Lord? Your family bonding and having fun together? Do you see yourself succeeding on your job? See yourself leading others to Christ? See yourself free from oppression and addictions? See yourself healed, healthy and whole? See yourself being generous? See yourself free from fear? Worry? Anger? Insecurity? Have you thought about it? What do you SEE?

This is important because all the "land" you can SEE, God can potentially give to you. If you can't SEE it, it's likely you'll never have it. By faith, we have to imagine—or SEE—God's Word fulfilled in our lives—before it is actually fulfilled. By faith—we look forward and we SEE the Lord at work changing us, our relationships, our families and our entire lives. By faith, we can arise and walk through the width and breadth of the land God has promised us in His Word.

Today, take some time to sit with the Lord and imagine the plans and purposes He has for you in multiple areas of your life. With the help of the Holy Spirit, "arise and walk through the land,"—all the land you can SEE—and in due season, He can give to you!

Read It! 1 Kings 18:44, NLT

Speak It! "Father, help me to SEE all the 'land' that You see for my life. Holy Spirit help me to 'arise and walk through the land' by faith. I trust Your plans and purposes Lord—in the right time—You will give me all the land that I can see. In Jesus' Name. Amen."

(your season of purpose)

"And we know that all things work together for good to them that love God, to them who are the called according to his purpose."
Romans 8:28, KJV

So, what spiritual season are you in? You can be encouraged today. No matter what season you are experiencing, there is a season for every purpose under heaven. What an encouraging truth! In other words, if heaven has a purpose— and if it's a purpose God needs us to be a part of—then it will indeed have its right season. We don't need to waste our time worrying or focusing on things that aren't His purpose. If we know that there is a time for every purpose heaven wants for us, then we can rest. We can know that His purposes will be fulfilled in and through us in the right season! Did you follow all that?

Back in 1982, I remember a season in my early Christian life when God gave me a poem about seasons. It continues to encourage me even now, many years later. Be encouraged as you read it and consider the season you are in.

The Rosebush

The rosebush is the queen of flowers in the summer when she blooms;
But when the leaves are changing colors, it's her turn to be pruned.
The bush that once was marveled at and praised for all her splendor;
Is cut right down to the ground—a stub with no one to tend her.
She doesn't like the way she looks—so short, so bare, so dead;
She wonders if she'll bloom again...the way the Handbook said.
Through rain and winds and blizzards of snow, her bark is still the same;
She really feels like a failure now and begins to take the blame.
But as the snow begins to melt, and the Son shines on her branches
She feels the growth well up within, and she does a few rose dances.
When the pruning season comes to a close,
All the work that went on in that stub reveals itself in a rose.
Fuller, more beautiful, more fruitful she grows;
But what it took to get her there only she and her Maker knows.
The rosebush is the queen of flowers, in the summer when she grows.

Remember, God is working a great purpose in and through you as you continue to follow Him and walk in the light of His Word. He is working all things together for your good. Declare this to be your season of purpose!

Read It! Ecclesiastes 3:1

Speak It! "Father, I thank You that You are Lord of the seasons. I thank You that whatever season I am in, you are working all things for my good to accomplish Your plans and purposes in my life. Help me to be patient with the process and, in the end, let me flourish as beautifully as a rose. In Jesus' Name. Amen."

DAY 228

(something from nothing)

"By faith we understand that the worlds were framed by the word of God, so that the things which are seen were not made of things which are visible."
Hebrews 11:3

God framed the world with His words. There was nothing, and then... "God said...,"...and there was something. Think about that! The Holy Spirit was hovering over the face of the earth; and as soon as God spoke—bam—matter came into existence. God's Word still frames things today. In fact, God's Word can frame our world, if we'll allow it to do so.

Watching the construction of our church building project was fascinating. The contractors set the steel and framed the entire building. Then, another crew of workers began framing the rooms. After they were finished, specialists came in and framed all the windows and doors. What we came to realize is that everything relies upon the frame. If it is skewed or put up in a haphazard way, then doors will jam and not close properly, and light fixtures hang in awkward ways. A bad frame job could even cause problems with decor and hanging pictures.

The same thing is true with the way we frame our world. When God's Word frames our lives, everything else falls into place. For example, God's Word tells us we can do all things through Christ who strengthens us *(Philippians 4:13)*. When we begin to say, "I can do all things through Christ who strengthens me...today!" our world is being framed. We may actually feel weak and incapable, but we are not to walk by feelings; we are to walk by faith. And when we do, the proper framework is being established!

Even when the things we see look contrary to what the Word says, this is when God says to *"call things that are not as though they were," (Romans 4:17, NIV).* (Notice, He doesn't tell us to "call things that are as though they are not"—that would be denial and ignorance.)

I don't know how it works, but I do know that when the Holy Spirit is hovering over our lives, and we choose to say what God says in faith and consistency—bam—He begins to create something from nothing. He begins framing our world.

Read It! Proverbs 12:14

Speak It! "Father, I will say what You say. I will agree with Your Word and trust You to frame my world. I thank You in advance that the things which will be seen in my life are not made of things which are visible. In Jesus' Name. Amen."

DAY 229

(distinguished?)

"The act of faith is what distinguished our ancestors,
set them above the crowd."
Hebrews 11:2, MSG

Looking for an advantage in life? What makes us the head and not the tail? Above and not beneath? What makes a person stand out above the crowd these days?

Faith. Faith that takes God at His Word.

It's so easy to live by our circumstances, feelings, sight and our five physical senses. So, where are the people of faith?

Faith propels us into the realm of "Wow!" Faith takes us to the arena of "this is the Lord's doing, and it is marvelous in our eyes." Faith lifts us up above average, normal and ordinary and puts us above the crowd. Faith redirects our motion and puts us into a supernatural orbit.

Faith soaks in the Word. Faith knows what it knows. Once faith has come, it is not moved by circumstances or feelings. When weak, it knows that faith comes by hearing and hearing the Word. Faith is not passive. Faith acts like God meant what He said. Faith says, "No," when everyone else says, "Yes," and faith says, "Yes," when everyone else says, "No." Faith speaks. Faith acts. Faith rests. Faith obeys. Faith works by love. Faith is patient. Faith distinguishes those who have it.

Where is your faith today? What Word are you standing on? May your acts of faith distinguish you!

Read It! Genesis 12:1-3, AMP

Speak It! "Father, I want to be distinguished by You. I want to live by Faith. I ask You to help me fill my heart with Your Word. Help me to live a life of Faith...a life that takes me beyond normal, ordinary and average. May You be seen and recognized in my life. In Jesus' Name. Amen."

DAY 230

(what do you know?)

"My people are destroyed for lack of knowledge..."
Hosea 4:6

When we celebrated our 10th year anniversary as a church in 2001, our congregation sent our family on a 7-day cruise. What a huge blessing that was! It didn't take long for our kids to discover all the amenities that were included in the price of their ticket. Our youngest son, Eric, found the ice cream machine immediately—that knowledge gave him great pleasure on the cruise! The rest of us discovered that cruising means you are at an all-you-can-eat 24/7 buffet—we definitely didn't lack knowledge about that!

The result? We totally enjoyed our cruise, made great memories, gained weight and had lots of fun! What a shame it would've been for our church family to have sacrificed their hard-earned money to purchase such a great gift for us, but we never bothered to discover all that was included in the ticket.

Sadly, many Christians have no idea the magnitude of all that Jesus purchased for us on the cross by shedding His blood. They live on crumbs their entire life on the earth, unaware that Jesus has purchased their complete redemption! Sure, we will face adversity, tribulations and persecutions in this life; but we can triumph in Christ since our salvation includes: forgiveness from sin, freedom from hell, eternal life, a home in heaven; healing for our spirit, soul and body; wellness, safety, abundance, prosperity, purpose, destiny; the power and fruit of the Spirit—love, joy and peace—and so much more! We need to recognize all that Jesus has included in salvation.

The enemy uses one major tool to destroy, discourage, and keep God's people from experiencing all that belongs to them in Christ—ignorance! We've heard for years that "what you don't know won't hurt you," but nothing could be further from the truth! What we don't know can hurt us! In fact, it can kill us! We shouldn't be surprised. Jesus warned us that we have an enemy—Satan— and his primary goal is to "steal the Word" from our hearts. He knows if Believers discovered all that belonged to them in Christ, they would reign in life through Christ.

Let's not insult Jesus and His completed work on the cross by not recognizing all His blood paid for. But, let's dive into the Word of God and discover all He has purchased for us and appropriate God's Word by faith.

Read It! Luke 11:52

Speak It! "Father, thank You for purchasing such a great salvation for me. Help me not to be lazy, but diligent in studying Your Word. Help me to obtain the knowledge of all that You have purchased for me in redemption. In Jesus' Name. Amen."

DAY 231

(how sweet it is)

"Hope deferred makes the heart sick, but when the desire is fulfilled,
it is a tree of life."
Proverbs 13:12, AMP

We've all been there, haven't we? Our hopes are crushed. Something we longed for is postponed...again. We exercise "faith and patience" for what seems like an eternity, only to discover there's another delay. Maybe the delay is that dream job or launching into ministry or finding the mate of our dreams or giving birth to a child...and our hearts have been sick because of deferred hope. Maybe our prayers haven't been answered as quickly as we had hoped, or maybe the Lord has answered them—but not in the way we envisioned— and we have to trust the Lord's wisdom instead of our own. Sometimes, for a season, our hope is deferred, and it can be very discouraging.

On the other hand, there are those times when the desire is fulfilled, and it truly is a tree of life! The fruit from that tree brings joy, peace, favor, increase, unity, healing and blessing. There's something satisfying about the end of patience, a battle won, a mission accomplished, a finish line reached, a "ta-da" moment and the fulfillment of a desire. A desire satisfied is sweet to the soul *(Proverbs 13:18)*.

So, can we do anything to bridge the gap? Can we speed up the time frame from "hope deferred" to the "desire accomplished"? Ultimately, we must trust the Lord and walk in the light of His Word, no matter what happens. But, with that in mind, we can be proactive in our faith to minimize the "hope deferred" moments and maximize the "desire accomplished" realities. We do this by continuing to walk in the light of the Word, obeying God, standing in faith and resting in the Lord.

Read It! Psalm 37:4

Speak It! "Father, I trust You. If I am in a season where it feels like my hope has been deferred, I still trust You. I know my ways are not Your ways. My timing is not Your timing. My plans are not Your plans. I will continue to delight myself in You, and I know that You will give me the desires of my heart—my 'deferred hope' will turn into a 'desire fulfilled' one day. In the meantime, I thank You for the many other 'desires fulfilled' in my life. You have been good to me and I praise You for Your faithfulness. 'Whom have I in heaven but You? There is none on earth that I desire besides You!' In Jesus' Name. Amen."

DAY 232

(it's all good)

"I would have lost heart, unless I had believed that I would see the goodness
of the LORD in the land of the living."
Psalm 27:13

Life can be tough. Things can take their toll. People can be mean. Stuff can
happen. BUT...don't lose heart! If you've been broken-hearted, discouraged,
weary and in need of some hope, be encouraged. You can see the goodness of
the Lord in the land of the living.

Will you believe it? God is good and He wants you to experience His goodness
while you're alive.

The Bible says, *"Hope deferred makes the heart sick...," (Proverbs 13:12).*
Sometimes, when we face a long season of waiting, tribulation, patience and
fighting the fight of faith, we can feel heart sick due to deferred hope. Don't
lose heart. Good things are on the horizon for you, if you will believe.

I encourage you to reread Psalm 27:13 and think about each word. Then,
believe God, trust in His mercy and kindness and let the Holy Spirit blow some
fresh wind into your sails as you anticipate the good life He has for you. The
Lord knows the plans He has for you, and they are plans for your good
(Jeremiah 29:11).

Think about it. What would the good life look for you? How would God's
goodness change your outlook, your relationships, your marriage, your family,
your kids, your job, your finances and your influence and purpose? Today,
believe that indeed YOU will see the goodness of the Lord in the land of the
living!

Read It! Psalm 34:8

Speak It! "Father, I believe. I would have lost heart and thrown in the towel,
but today I choose to believe. I believe that I will see Your goodness while I am
alive on planet earth. I thank You for moving heaven and earth, opening and
closing doors and making a way where there is no way so that I can see Your
goodness. In Jesus' Name. Amen."

242

DAY 233

(get ripped)

"Spend your time and energy in training yourself for spiritual fitness. Physical exercise has some value, but spiritual exercise is much more important, for it promises a reward in both this life and the next."
1 Timothy 4:7-9, NLT

Ever looked at a fitness magazine...and then ate a candy bar? Got a treadmill and weight set in the basement? Yeah, great towel rack! The older I get, the more impressed I am by people who are physically fit. However, I am MOST impressed with people who discipline their lives to be *spiritually* fit! Champions—physical or spiritual—don't develop overnight; it takes a lot of commitment, sacrifice and discipline to excel.

Those Godly six-packs don't come overnight. We must be commitment to get ripped—spiritually. So, today, let me be that spiritual trainer that kicks us into gear. So, listen up, Cupcake! It's time to get serious about spiritual health, fitness and strength training! ... Oh, this could be brutal, but let's get started!

- **Prayer.** Oh, yeah, baby, let's start with the tough one! Drop to those knees and give me 10! Ten minutes of non-stop prayer. Hey, don't roll those eyes. I might just add another 10 minutes to it!

- **Bible reading.** C'mon, Princess, put down the tabloid magazine. Say, "Goodbye," to the sport's channel, Buckaroo! It's time to feed that skinny rack of spiritual bones. Read the whole book of Colossians right now...in 30 minutes. Move it! Then, Psalm 119...twice! Are we sweatin' yet?

- **Cardio.** Everybody's favorite, right? Well, we can't have a meltdown every six minutes. Doing kingdom business requires a little backbone. So, dry those big salties and stop grumbling. Put on 40 minutes of hard-core worship music and start thanking and praising the Lord. Sing your heart out, honey! Get that heart rate up!

- **Push through the pain!** We're not gonna call the "waaahmbulance" are we? No way! Push through that pain! Let the weak say, "I am strong." Say it! "I am strong. I will not be defeated. I will not quit!" Stir up your pretty self. People who are dying and going to hell are depending on you. Push, push, push!

Being a Christian isn't for wimps. While the Lord is not a harsh, drill sergeant, He is in the business of raising up spiritual champions. So, stay with it! It won't be long before all the sacrifice and discipline will be revealed in one toned, fit, ripped Christian—ready for the Master's use.

Read It! 2 Timothy 2:3

Speak It! "Father, I have been such a spiritual wimp. Help me to get with the program and become spiritually strong, fit, alert and ready for Your use! In Jesus' Name. Amen."

DAY 234

(get some satisfaction)

"For He satisfies the longing soul, and fills the hungry soul with goodness."
Psalm 107:9

Can't get no satisfaction? And you try and you try and you try...but you can't get no satisfaction? No worries. I have good news! The Lord can and will satisfy your soul. It's true. A complete satisfaction really does exist, and the Lord is the only One who can dispense it.

There isn't a drug on earth that can give it to you. There isn't a human person on earth who can satisfy you. There isn't a nirvana anywhere that can do it. Music, sports, money, fame, sex, sleep, food, exotic vacations, adrenaline or even a good cause—nothing can satisfy us. God, alone, authors satisfaction.

How does He satisfy us? It starts with a longing. Literally, an appetite. Do you have an appetite for God? We all know what it's like to have an appetite for a good steak or burger. A strong appetite leads to hunger. Hunger leads to a craving. A craving leads to a requirement and necessity. God promises to fill and satisfy those who have an appetite for Him—those who crave, require and desire Him as their necessity.

Interestingly, God has never obligated Himself to those who are half-hearted or lukewarm. Have you noticed that? He promises to satisfy the "longing" soul. He promises to fill those who hunger and thirst. He obligates Himself to be found by those who seek Him with their whole heart, but He never guarantees much of anything to those who are indifferent to Him. For those who are apathetic, passive, indifferent, half-hearted or lukewarm toward the Lord—they can't get no satisfaction.

So, do you want God? Do you want to experience His goodness? Are you ready to be filled? Stir up your longing—your appetite, hunger, craving, requirement and necessity for Him. Spend some time talking to the Lord. Tell the Lord how much you hunger for Him. Let Him know you crave the reality of His presence in your life. Tell him you require His goodness.

He guaranteed He would satisfy the longing soul.

Read It! Matthew 5:6, NIV

Speak It! "Father, I thank You for Your promise to satisfy my longing soul! I have an appetite for You. I am hungry for You. I crave Your reality in my life. I require You God. I won't be satisfied with anything less than You. I require and desire You in my life—not as an option, but as my necessity. Fill me Lord. Satisfy my longing soul. In Jesus' Name. Amen."

DAY 235

(body parts)

"The body is a unit, though it is made up of many parts; and though all its
parts are many, they form one body. So it is with Christ."
1 Corinthians 12:12-13, NIV

Have you ever noticed how important each part of your body is? Ever had a
toothache? A broken toe? A splinter in your finger? They are little parts of the
body; but when they hurt, we are reminded of how important they are.

In the same way, every part of the Body of Christ is important—each one who
has received and confessed Jesus as Lord. Jesus is the Head, and we are His
Body. Each member is valuable and provides something unique, needful and
important to the whole Body. But, if we aren't careful, we can begin to think
that our part is the most important, the most needed. Or, we can do the
opposite and minimize our role to the point that we're dysfunctional. The
reality is that every follower of Jesus Christ is an important, vital and needed
part of His Body.

Unfortunately, the Body of Christ sometimes suffers from an "auto-immune
disorder" and begins to attack, criticize and destroy itself. When one denomina-
tion thinks they're more important than another, we have a serious disorder.
Regardless whether we agree on every doctrinal detail or the denominational
tags we wear, we all need each other and can all learn something from one
another. There is so much work to be done around the world; the last thing
the Body needs are schisms, divisions and sects; criticizing, labeling, dividing,
down-grading or dissing other members of the Body. It only ruins our effectiveness and our impact—and our Head, Jesus, doesn't appreciate it.

As unique members of the Body, let's hold fast to the Word and our particular,
distinctive roles; while at the same time, appreciating the valuable roles of
other Body parts. Every part of the Body of Christ is supplying something to
the whole. Let's do our part to work together to accomplish His purposes.

Read It! 1 Corinthians 12:14-27, NLT

Speak It! "Father, forgive me for being proud and critical toward others in the
Body of Christ. I don't want to contribute to a spiritual 'auto-immune disorder' in
the Body of Christ. Help me to be the part You've called me to be and help me to
appreciate all the other separate and necessary parts of Your Body. In Jesus'
Name. Amen."

DAY 236

(help, I need somebody!)

"And God hath set some in the church, first apostles, secondarily prophets, thirdly teachers, after that miracles, then gifts of healings, helps, governments, diversities of tongues."
1 Corinthians 12:28, KJV

One of the most important and yet overlooked role in the Church is called: helps! Look at today's scripture and what do you see tucked right in there with the apostles, prophets, and teachers? "Helps," which literally means "to provide relief."

The helps ministry is huge! Those who are called and gifted to help are a great source of power and strength in a local church. When those called to help take their place, things get done. If you think about it, most areas of ministry fall under the "helps" category. Areas like: prayer, worship, IT, graphics, web design, audio, video, lighting, finances, administration, clerical, secretarial, food service, construction, cleaning, maintenance, ushers, greeters, traffic, organization, hospitality, teaching kids or teen classes, small groups and providing spiritual guidance and care—they're all called to the ministry of helps.

Now, you can see why the heart-cry of every pastor is: "Help, I need somebody!"

Those in the helps ministry are the answer to that cry. They provide the needed relief for those called to serve as leaders in the Body of Christ. This was so evident to us when we were approaching our first service in our new building. Day after day and night after night, a small army—and sometimes a big army—would arrive at the church to do whatever needed to be done. They provide a great sense of relief. Because of their efforts, we did hit our deadlines and launched our first service right on schedule. Only eternity will tell what their help has meant.

Never underestimate or ill-esteem the power of the ministry of helps. Without them, things would not get done. Don't ever forget what a major blessing they are to the Body of Christ.

Read It! Romans 12:4-6

Speak It! "Father, I thank You for those you have called to the important ministry of 'helps.' I pray you encourage, strengthen, empower, reward and bless every person who has been faithful to serve You, to support their leaders, and who have 'helped' get Kingdom business done. In Jesus' Name. Amen."

DAY 237

(obligated to the peeps)

"For I have a great sense of obligation to people in our culture..."
Romans 1:14, NLT

If there is something you can be sure will be constantly changing, it's our culture. Don't believe me? Just go to work today with that 80's mullet (or poodle hair if you're a female), bell-bottom pants, and tie-dyed shirt! You'll know very quickly that our culture has seriously changed since 1985!

Culture is always changing, more rapidly now more than anytime in history. The trouble is, some Christians—particularly churches—don't want to keep up! They're happy just to have church just like it was 20, 30, or 40 years ago. I've heard people say, "If it worked to get me saved 30 years ago, it will work now." Of course, they champion their cause by quoting, "God is the same, yesterday, today, and forever."

True, God is the same; but people and cultures are changing—and will be forever.

A few years ago, the thought of having a "great sense of obligation to the people in our culture" really came alive to us. We knew the Word was unchangeable, but the mindset of people in our community was changing. At that time, we began making some dramatic changes at our church in the "methods" we used for preaching the uncompromised "message" of faith in Jesus. Our job: to impact our sphere of influence with the Gospel of Jesus. In order to do that, we had to become culturally relevant.

So,...we changed. Updated our décor to a modern Starbucks®-like feel; started to wear jeans instead of dresses and three-piece suits (thank you, Jesus!); changed our style of music and incorporated more media. The results? Over 100 people left the church in six months. But, we gained over 700 in the following four months! That's a pretty good trade off!

Now, over 3,500 people a weekend attend our services, and the life-changing power of Jesus is touching lives on a weekly basis. We are so glad we made the shift, so glad we followed our "great sense of obligation." That responsibility—to reach our culture—belongs to every Believer. Let's get busy taking this unchanging message to the world who needs it...in a way they can understand it.

Read It! 1 Corinthians 9:19-23

Speak It! "Father, help me to look at the people in my culture through Your eyes. Help me become all things to all men so that I might win them to Christ. Help me to connect with the culture in my sphere of influence in relevant ways! In Jesus' Name. Amen."

DAY 238

(secrets)

"The secret things belong to the LORD our God,
but the things revealed belong to us and to our children forever..."
Deuteronomy 29:29, NIV

Things happen. We don't always understand why. Sometimes we don't know why someone who is half-backslidden seems to be walking in the blessings, while an on-fire, sold-out Christian dies of a sickness before their time. We don't always understand why one person's prayers seemed to go unanswered, while the person who didn't even pray received a miracle. We don't understand why a sweet young person dies and a mean-spirited old geezer lives to be 104.

What are we to think, believe, or do when we don't understand the "whys" of life? Start with the basics... God is good all the time. He is always for us. He's not a "schizo-God" who blesses one day and curses the next day. He is love. So, when things happen that we don't understand, what do we do? Get bitter? Turn our back on God? No. We need to understand the two basic categories of life: secret things and revealed things.

- **Secret things.** God knows everything; but thankfully, He often keeps some things a secret. Perhaps the reason is because He's not a gossip. He doesn't reveal the "whys" of everyone's business to any old Joe. Secret things do belong to the Lord.
- **Revealed things.** Sometimes, God does reveals the "why" when things happen. When He does, then it's our turn to walk in the truth we learned, by faith. For example, He's revealed His character, His will and the laws of His kingdom to everyone through His Word. Revealed things belong to us.

While we might not understand why something happened or didn't happen, here's what we do know: God's Word is truer than circumstances or experiences. If God could have, He would have. When we don't understand, we know He does. Even if it looks bad, we know that God is still good. Just because God knows everything about us, doesn't mean He tells us everything.

Today, be encouraged that no matter what comes, goes, happens or doesn't happen, at the end of the day...we still win! Jesus is still Lord, and we'll have all of eternity to discuss the "whys."

Read It! Hebrews 13:8

Speak It! "Father, I trust You. There are some things I don't understand, but I do trust You. I give you all my questions today. If You choose to keep something a secret, I respect that. Today, I'll move forward in faith, and walk in what You have revealed to me: Your character, Your Word, and Your will. In the end...I win. Your Word is still true. In Jesus' Name. Amen."

DAY 239

(whatcha thinkin' about?)

"For those who live according to the flesh set their minds on the things of the flesh, but those who live according to the Spirit, the things of the Spirit. For to be carnally minded is death, but to be spiritually minded is life and peace."
Romans 8:5-6

Need life and peace these days? God offers it—the real thing. Our job? We simply set our minds on things of the Spirit. It has nothing to do with our circumstances or how we feel; it simply means we get proactive in thinking about, meditating on and focusing on spiritual things—God, His Word and His Spirit. To be spiritually-minded doesn't mean we become a hyper-spiritual whack-job; it just means we think, ponder, meditate, fill our thoughts and set our minds on the Lord and His things, and we make no room for carnal things.

Setting our minds on the Spirit includes the fruit of the Spirit—love, joy, peace, patience, kindness, gentleness, faithfulness and self-control. It includes the gifts of the Spirit—the supernatural, miraculous, present-tense power of God demonstrated in a variety of ways. So, dig into the Word and decide what scriptures or spiritual truths you are going to set your mind on.

It's true. What we think upon is what gets lodged in our hearts. Whatever fills our hearts in abundance is what we will say; and what we say is, eventually, what we have (Matthew 12:34). So, if we want to have "life and peace," we need to start by setting our minds on the Spirit and on His things. After a short time of setting our minds on these things, they will fill our hearts. Once these things fill our hearts, out of the abundance of our hearts, we will speak. And the Bible tells us that eventually, we'll eat the fruit of what we have said; the result will be "life and peace." This is how God's Word really works in our lives.

The polar-opposite is true, as well. When we set our minds on carnal things—worldly things, envy, strife, divisions, ungodly, unholy, impure things and things that contradict God's Word—those things will fill our hearts; and, in that instance, we'll have what we say, too. Ultimately, it will lead to death: a lack of life and vitality. That, my friend, is what we call a bummer life.

The Lord has something better for us. God wants us to live a life loaded with "life and peace," so let's set our minds on the things of the Spirit!

Read It! Philippians 4:8-9, NLT

Speak It! "Father, thank You for offering a life that's loaded with 'life and peace.' I choose to set my mind on You, Your Word and the realities of the Spirit-filled life. I know Your Word will go to work in my heart, in my mouth and in my reality. I thank You in advance for a fresh infusion of 'life and peace.' In Jesus' Name. Amen."

DAY 240

(He's still the One!)

"Salvation comes no other way; no other name has been
or will be given to us by which we can be saved, only this one."
Acts 4:12, MSG

Andre Crouch used to sing the song and the words went like this: "Jesus is the answer for the world today, above Him there's no other, Jesus is the way."

It's still true. Salvation comes no other way. Jesus is the answer for every ill, every war, every hurt, every pain, every sin, every injustice, every broken heart and every empty, lost person on Planet Earth!

I know it's not politically correct these days, but it's true nonetheless. Jesus is still the way, the truth, the life and the only way to the Father. As Christians, we need to keep a constant "grip" on this basic reality. Jesus didn't say He was "a" way; He said He is "the" way—He is in His own league! Jesus wasn't just a great teacher, prophet or religious leader...He was God in the flesh. This gives His life more weight than any other person in all of history. His veins carried the only sinless, spotless, eternal blood that would be shed for the forgiveness of all sin and salvation. No other Name has been given by which we can be saved.

Have you received salvation? If so, have you thanked Him lately? Have you given Jesus the appreciation, praise, honor and acknowledgment He deserves for the salvation He's given you? Let's do so, today.

Do you need salvation? Do you know for sure where you'll go when you die? Is your life marked by a genuine relationship with God? If not, you can make a change today. It's as simple as praying this prayer from your heart and surrendering your life to Christ.

Read It! John 14:6

Speak It! "Father, I come to You today, and I want to thank You for sending Your Son, Jesus Christ, to this world. Jesus, I thank You for coming to earth as a baby, for showing us the Father, for going to the cross, for shedding Your sinless, spotless, eternal blood, so I could experience salvation and eternal life. Thank You! Thank You! Thank You! Jesus, today, I invite You into my life. I surrender to You. I ask You to forgive me of all of my sins and be the Lord of my life. In Jesus' Name. Amen."

DAY 241

(true love)

"Those who obey my commandments are the ones who love me. And because they love me, my Father will love them, and I will love them. And I will reveal myself to each one of them."
John 14:21, NLT

What's the sign of true love for the Lord? Heartfelt worship? Hands raised in worship? Extended prayer? Fasting? Giving to the poor? Telling the Lord we love Him? No. These things are great, but they are not the signs of true love. True love for the Lord is revealed in a very simple way: obedience.

If we love Him, we will obey Him. Jesus said the people who obey His Word are the ones who love Him. He promised the true lovers of God something quite amazing. He said that He and the Father would love those who obey Him and He would reveal Himself to them.

Think about that. When we love the Lord by obeying the things He asks of us; He promised to love us in a very tangible way by revealing more of Himself to us! How would you like the reality of the Father's love and the manifested, revealed presence of the Lord to show up in your life in a real way?

The Lord said, *"To obey is better than sacrifice...," (1 Samuel 15:22, NIV)*. God is more interested in our obedience than all the things we could sacrifice. He'd rather have us obey His voice than walk on hot coals, crawl up wooden stairs on our bare knees, fast for 40 days or give all our money to the needy. He doesn't want us to sacrifice things to gain His favor or show Him our devotion; He'd rather have us listen to His voice and obey the things He tells us to do.

The opposite of obedience is rebellion and stubbornness. God takes a rebellious spirit seriously and equates it to the sin of witchcraft and worshiping idols *(1 Samuel 15:23, NLT)*. When we set our will to compete with His will, its displeases the Lord.

Obedience is a sign of true love and complete trust. Do you love the Lord? What's the last thing He told you to do or not do? Have you obeyed Him? If so, you can expect Jesus to love you and reveal Himself to you in a greater way. If not, make a decision today to turn from rebellion and stubbornness and obey the Lord.

Read It! 1 Samuel 15:22

Speak It! "Father, I do love You, and I want to demonstrate my love for You by obeying Your commands. Help me to be a doer of Your Word. I know that as I obey Your Word, You will love me and reveal Yourself to me in a greater way. In Jesus' Name. Amen."

DAY 242

(the resistance)

"Therefore submit to God. Resist the devil and he will flee from you."
James 4:7

Has the devil been bothering you? Resist him! Put him on the run. Make him flee! When the enemy comes knocking on your door—resist him. When he tries to throw thoughts of fear, discouragement, anger, temptation or other things your way—resist him.

The devil is persistent. He usually starts his efforts with a thought—called a "fiery dart." He watches to see what we will do. If we give him any attention, he continues to throw thoughts our way and flings one fiery dart after another with the hopes that he can penetrate our shield of faith—and ultimately steal, kill and destroy areas of our lives...or our very lives themselves!

For example, a thought comes to you: "God isn't real; why do you even believe in Him?" or "God won't protect you; you should live in fear...," or "Why don't you just give that person a piece of your mind...," or "It's too hard to live by faith, so why try?" or "God's not going to heal you!"...and on it goes.

But, if we want to have victory in this life, we cannot allow those thoughts to continue. If we listen to them and mull them over in our head, rather than resisting them, the devil will get the upper hand; and those thoughts will turn to imaginations, arguments, reasonings and, ultimately, strongholds that hinder us—not to mention torment us daily.

So, let's cut him off at the pass—resist him! One of the best ways to resist the devil is with silence. Let's not even acknowledge the thoughts he throws our way. Let's not even give them a voice. Let's not say what he says, only say what God says. When the enemy throws a thought our way, let's not give it any attention and just quote the Word of God on the topic.

When we do this by faith using the Word of God, we will quench every fiery dart the enemy sends our way! So, let's stay submitted to God and resist the devil—and he has no choice but to flee from us!

Read It! Ephesians 6:16, NLT

Speak It! "Father, I submit to You and Your Word. I resist the devil every time he throws a thought or a fiery dart my way. I know that when I resist him with Your Word, he must flee! In Jesus' Name. Amen."

DAY 243

(big gossips)

"Listening to gossip is like eating cheap candy;
do you want junk like that in your belly?"
Proverbs 26:22, MSG

It's hard to turn on the TV, news, see the AOL® or Google® headlines or check out at the grocery store without hearing, seeing or reading gossip. What has happened to our society? It's vulture-mania out there.

As soon as anyone has any bit of success, failure, sadness, happiness, blessings or reaping what they sowed, the gossips are right there to spread the news. And, they always spin it just enough to make the news suspicious, question-able or negative.

Why? What is it about human nature that loves to build up idols, only to wait for their first weakness or failure...so they can be ripped to shreds? They glory in the destruction of marriages and family. They salivate over human demise. And, even if someone accomplishes something great, they're always eager to demean, criticize distort and destroy.

Jesus knew human nature; that's why He said things like, *"Whoever is without sin among you throw the first stone." "Hypocrites!" "Do unto others as you would have them do unto you." "Love one another as I have loved you..."* In fact, the Bible talks a lot about how to treat people in love. Here are just a few:

- **Love doesn't delight in evil but rejoices with the truth.** *(1 Corinthians 13:6)*
- **Love covers a multitude of sins.** *(1 Peter 4:8, NLT)*
- **The greatest thing is love.** *(1 Corinthians 13:13)*

What would happen if we decided to ignore the gossip we hear and see all around us and started believing the best about people? Started covering their mistakes—their sins—with prayer. Started rejoicing with the truth, instead of the tabloid and media untruths? Why don't we resist the temptation to believe everything we hear? Why don't we consider the source before embracing the toxin? Why don't we judge a person by their tested character instead of by the off-the-cuff, agenda-ridden gossip someone spreads? Perpetuating, feeding on and believing gossip is a completely unchristian thing to do. Listening to gossip is just what the writer of Proverbs said: *"It's like eating cheap candy."* Let's not do it.

Read It! Proverbs 20:19, NLT

Speak It! "Father, I choose to believe the best about people and judge them by the merits of their character and track record, not by gossip. In Jesus' Name. Amen."

DAY 244

(power to the people)

"The earnest (heartfelt, continued) prayer of a righteous man
makes tremendous power available [dynamic in its working]..."
James 5:16, AMP

I love the reality of this verse! Prayer makes tremendous power available to us in our marriages, families, ministries, work and every area of our lives. Through prayer, we can make "deposits" into our future. What type of deposits have you been making?

I have found a great sense of peace in certain seasons of life. When I knew that prayer deposits had been made, it was easy to have faith for "withdrawals" from heaven's powerhouse. Prayer makes tremendous power available. That means, without prayer, this tremendous power may not be available. God's mercy is always available, but many times we need "tremendous power"—and this comes through prayer.

Prayer was never intended to be boring, ineffective or dutiful. When it comes to prayer, we should be "feelin' it!" So, if you need a prayer booster shot, pray earnestly, continually and in a heartfelt manner. When you pray, remind yourself that you are putting God's power on "deposit." You are making tremendous power available; and in a time of need, the Lord will send that dynamic power to do its work!

Read It! Romans 8:26-28

Speak It! "Father, today I ask You to help me put this scripture into practice. I don't want my prayer life to be boring, predictable or full of vain repetition. Help me to pray earnestly, continually and in a heartfelt manner for the things You have put on my heart. Thank You that my prayers make tremendous power available! In Jesus' Name. Amen."

DAY 245

(don't be snooty)

"Haughtiness comes before disaster, but humility before honor."
Proverbs 18:12, AMP

Humility versus Haughtiness.

There is something refreshing about being around people with a humble spirit and something strained, tense and unsettling about being around those who are haughty. So, what's the difference?

To be "haughty" is to be proud, arrogant, exalted, raised up in your own mind. It's the person who's closed-off and won't take the initiative to reach out to others, but rather insists on others reaching out to them. It's the person who speaks in condescending or patronizing tones to others. You know...the ego-driven one. It's the one who walks into the room with body language that exudes the "Here I am!" persona and screams, "Hey, everyone, look at me!" To be haughty is to be snooty, snobbish, vain, aloof or exclusive.

To be "humble" is to be gentle, meek and respectful to others. It's the person who's open and willing to go low. It's the person who's not paying attention to the pecking order, but is eager to greet and interact with all kinds of people. It's the person who's others-driven. The one who walks into a room with body language that exudes the, "There you are!" persona and celebrates others. To be humble is to put people first and to be courteously respectful of others.

No doubt, we all know people in both categories; but the bigger question is...the more important question is: which one are we?

Let's not be snooty!

Read It! James 4:6, AMP

Speak It! "Father, help me to not think more highly of myself that I ought. Haughtiness, pride, ego and being snooty is ugly. Help me to run in the opposite direction. I choose to humble myself before You and I ask You to help me have a humble spirit as I relate to others. In Jesus' Name. Amen."

DAY 246

(beautiful feet?)

"'Everyone who calls on the name of the Lord will be saved.' How, then, can they call on the one they have not believed in? And how can they believe in the one of whom they have not heard? And how can they hear without someone preaching to them? And how can they preach unless they are sent? As it is written, 'How beautiful are the feet of those who bring good news!'"
Romans 10:13-15, NIV

This passage changed my life and destiny. I wanted to be a dentist; but one day, when I was minding my own business as a biology major in college, God interrupted my plans with this passage of Scripture. Once I read these words, I knew I couldn't be a dentist.

How could I? If people couldn't hear about Jesus unless I preached; if they couldn't believe without hearing; if they couldn't call on Him without believing in Him and if they couldn't be saved unless they called on the Name of the Lord...I couldn't be a dentist, I had to be a preacher! In my case, preaching and teaching the Word has been God's full-time calling and destiny for my life, and I can't imagine doing anything else.

What about you? Who needs to hear the Gospel from you so they can hear, believe and call on the name of the Lord, so they can be saved? Today, get those beautiful feet of yours moving!

Read It! Isaiah 52:7

Speak It! "Father, forgive me for neglecting my responsibility to preach Jesus to those around me. Lord, help me bring the good news to others in a way that they can hear, believe and call on Jesus to be saved. Help me to move my feet in the direction of those who need a 'preacher' today. In Jesus' Name. Amen."

DAY 247

(don't just sit there)

"Be strong and of good courage, and do it..."
1 Chronicles 28:20, KJV

This is your pep talk. Don't just sit there; do something! Certainly, there is a time to wait on the Lord to renew your strength and to get direction, but then it's time to get busy about the Master's business.

Too many people waste their lives away doing nothing, thinking the ball is in God's court; when, often, the ball is in our court. As the old saying goes, "God can't move a parked car..." Sometimes, we need to start heading in a direction and get the wheels moving then keep our spiritual radar on to see which way the Lord wants us to go.

C'mon...how long are you going to stay in that dead-end job? How long are you going to date the person you know you'll never marry? How many times are you gonna rehash all the unfair misdeeds that have been done to you? How many more people are you going to blame for your lot in life? Why not shake off all that negative, irresponsible, apathetic way of thinking and get moving!

Today really is the first day of the rest of your life. You can't change the past. Forget your past and press toward God's plan for you and your future in Christ. You can reinvent yourself and have a personal "grand opening" to introduce the new and improved you to the world! If you're really serious about reinventing yourself, you're going to have to change your...

- **Thinking and your words.** Start thinking like a Christian. Start seeing yourself as a person who walks with God and is surrounded by His favor. Start seeing your-self as the person God has called you to be and talk like them. Do it!
- **Friends.** Our youth pastor tells our kids, "Show me your friends, and I'll show you your future." Look around... Is that what you want? If they are visionless, lazy, critical and going nowhere, that is exactly where you will end up. It won't be easy to transition from one group of friends to another, so you better get started. Do it!
- **Habits and your actions.** As the old saying goes, "If you do the same things you've always done; you'll have the same results you've always had." You can't continue with bad habits, making bad decisions and expect your life will improve. You really have to change some things.

Chart yourself a new course and do it!

Read It! Philippians 4:13

Speak It! "Father, I'm tired of going nowhere, wasting my life away. Help me surrender my life completely to the Lordship of Jesus. In Jesus' Name. Amen."

DAY 248

(get loaded!)

*"Blessed be the Lord, who daily loads us with benefits,
the God of our salvation!"*
Psalm 68:19

I love this verse! When I was a new Christian walking in the light of His Word, the Lord helped me to get a hold of this simple revelation: God is good, and He desires to load His children with benefits!

You have to understand, I was raised by a single mom, and we learned how to get by with the bare essentials. We grew up shopping on the clearance rack and buying everything on sale. I thought you were rich if you bought Del Monte® fruit cocktail, rather than the generic brand. The idea of being blessed with abundance and a load of benefits was amazing news!

Once I saw this simple truth, I began to say this verse out loud every day and I trusted God to load me with His benefits! At night before bed, I would check my daily load and thank God for every benefit He had given me. I took inventory, from the smallest things—a parking space, a discount at TJ Maxx®, a nap, happy kids—to the largest things—a new baby, a good deal on a house, our 10-year anniversary, someone inviting Jesus into their lives or a cruise to the Caribbean.

God is good, and He does give good gifts. He's in the benefits business!

How about you? Do you need a load of benefits? As you walk in His Word, begin to thank God for His goodness in your life and start thanking Him in advance for loading you with His benefits.

Read It! Proverbs 10:22

Speak It! "Father, I do believe that You are good and generous. I believe You want to perform Your Word in my life. I thank You for loading me with benefits daily, including today! I will begin to look to You expectantly, and I will be sure to thank You for each benefit—big and small. Thank You, Lord. In Jesus' Name. Amen."

DAY 249

(spiritual eating disorders)

"When your words came, I ate them; they were my joy
and my heart's delight..."
Jeremiah 15:16, NIV

Most of us are acquainted with the reality of regular eating disorders—the anorexic, the bulimic, the junk food junkie, the malnourished, the binge and over-eater, and other abnormalities. As a result, people experience ill health, loss of energy, disease, and sometimes death because of their eating issues.

The same is true spiritually. Multitudes of Christians don't have good spiritual eating habits and are suffering from the dramatic effects of (SEDs)—spiritual eating disorders. (This isn't an actual spiritual "clinical" diagnosis; I just made up this term to help illustrate a very real reality that many Christians experience.)

Here are a few types of Spiritual Eating Disorders (SEDs) and their similar effects:

- **Spiritual anorexics.** These are Believers who have been deceived into thinking they are more mature than they really are. They look in the mirror and see a spiritually fat person; so, they won't listen to anyone else and won't eat the Word, because they already "know it all." The truth is, they are not equipped to fight any faith battles, and onlookers can readily see the spiritual anorexic is spiritually shallow, thin and about two inches deep.

- **Spiritual bulimics.** These are Believers who vomit up everything they eat. They eat like crazy—listen to every sermon, subscribe to dozens of podcasts, read books galore—and then puke it all up! They won't embrace the Word and let it digest within them, allowing Its nutrients to provide the strength their spirit man needs to live a healthy Christian life of faith and power. The way they "vomit" is through a stream of doubt, unbelief, criticism, opinion and fear—everything but faith!

Yes, the good news is that there is a cure for SEDs!

Read It! Psalm 34:8

Speak It! "Father, I thank you for your health to eat the Word in a healthy balanced and nutritious way. In Jesus' Name. Amen."

DAY 250

(thanksgiving is good)

"It is good to give thanks to the LORD, and to sing praises to Your name, O Most High; to declare Your lovingkindness in the morning, and Your faithfulness every night..."
Psalm 92:1-2

Wanna do something good? Give thanks! It's a good thing to give thanks to the Lord. And, if you want to take it up a notch, bust out with a song of praise!

If you haven't said thank you to the Lord lately why not do so today? No need to wait for once a year to give thanks to God. Let's declare God's lovingkindness and His faithfulness right now.

It might seem like a small thing to say "thank you," but it must be a big thing to the Lord, because He sure seems to appreciate it. Perhaps it's a good thing because it's somewhat rare.

Think about your own life, for example. How often do you hear the word "Thanks"? It's refreshing when people say thanks and are grateful for whatever you've done for them. In the same way, God likes it when we don't take His goodness for granted, but rather we appreciate Him and are grateful for all that He has done and is doing for us.

Why is it a good thing to give thanks?

- **It's an interactive way to recall...**the reality of God's love, goodness, generosity and faithfulness. We are saying thanks to a real God, who has really touched our lives.
- **It's a proactive way to guard...**against an attitude of "entitlement" or becoming "spoiled" Christians. We get to acknowledge God's goodness and generosity and our dependence on Him.

Read It! Psalm 28:7, NIV

Speak It! "Father, thank You! Jesus, thank You. Holy Spirit, thank You. You are a good God, and I just want You to know that I appreciate all You are and all You have done for me. I want to declare Your lovingkindness; I have been a recipient. I want to praise You for Your faithfulness; I have been on the receiving end. It is a good thing to give thanks to You...so, thank You! In Jesus' Name. Amen."

DAY 251

(it takes one to know one)

"Every time you criticize someone, you condemn yourself. It takes one to know one. Judgmental criticism of others is a well-known way of escaping detection in your own crimes and misdemeanors."
Romans 2:1b, MSG

When I was in college, I remember this one guy who used to bug me! Every time he opened his mouth, I got irritated. There was just something about him that grated my nerves. One day the Holy Spirit spoke to my heart as plain as day and said, "The reason he bugs you so much is because you are just like him." I was mortified! It was true. The very things that irritated me about this guy were just a mirrored reflection exposing the yucky parts of my own personality.

This was the first time the passage in Romans 2:1 hit me. I started to take note. Anytime I was tempted to judge or criticize others, I had to look in the mirror and ask myself, "OK...what is it in my life that is irritating me so much in theirs?" It's easy to judge other people—their motives and behaviors. I was quite familiar with their faults because they were my faults, too. Yup, it takes one to know one! Let's just say, eventually, I got a clue and became a lot less judgmental. I discovered a verse that made my life a lot easier: "Love covers a multitude of sins," (1 Peter 4:8, NIV).

Ever been judgmental? Here are two reasons we should quit.

- **The Boomerang Effect.** It's true. The way we judge others is the way we'll be judged. We need to be rich in mercy toward others, so we can receive mercy! Let's do ourselves a favor. Let's not notice the speck in someone else's eye and miss the 2 x 4 in our own! *(Luke 6:37, 41-42, MSG)*
- **The "Who Are You?" Question.** We aren't qualified to judge others—after all, who do we think we are? Ever been on the brunt end of someone's judgmental comments? We have. In the early years of our ministry, people who didn't have the foggiest idea of what we had been going through—or were going through—felt free to judge us. We discovered a lot of "Well, if I was in their shoes, this is what I'd do" comments were being said about us. It was difficult. We learned a fresh lesson on the importance of *not* judging another man's servant. *(Romans 14:4, NIV)*

Today, if you are tempted to judge someone—show mercy and love them instead.

Read It! Matthew 7:1

Speak It! "Father, I ask You to forgive me for being judgmental toward others. I can see 'it takes one to know one,' and the very things I criticize in others are a reflection of my own faults. Help me to extend mercy and love to cover others' shortcomings. You are their Master and You are able to make them stand. In Jesus' Name. Amen."

DAY 252

("failure to thrive")

"Blessed are you who hunger now, for you will be satisfied."
Luke 6:21a, NIV

Years ago, a friend of mine delivered her first baby, diagnosed with what could only be labeled as an eating disorder. The baby wouldn't eat; she wouldn't nurse and wouldn't take a bottle. She just had no appetite. At first, the doctors were stumped. Naturally, all babies are born instinctively to eat; yet, this baby would not. Eventually, they diagnosed her with what the doctors called "failure to thrive." The food was available. The mother was ready to nurse; the doctors and nursing staff were on call to assist at a moment's   notice; so that as soon as the baby demonstrated hunger or thirst, she would be fed. Finally, when the baby did eat, she ate so sporadically and in very small amounts. As it turned out, the doctors discovered the baby's hips were broken during the birth process, and she associated eating with pain—so, she didn't eat. (Last I knew, this baby girl had grown up and, through God's grace and her loving parents, was able to cope with and overcome her many challenges.)

Similarly, thousands of Christians suffer from spiritual "failure to thrive." These are Believers who have no hunger for God and His Word. This SED is the most prevalent among Believers. They could take or leave reading God's Word and have no urge to pray or seek God. How is it that people can get born again, yet have no hunger for God? Why don't they have any desire to eat—to read the Word, to pray, to grow, to attend church and so on?

Why does this SED even exist? God's Word is available, standing by to feed hungry Christians. Pastors, teachers, and churches are on call, ready to assist at a moment's notice. Books, tapes, CDs, DVDs, Christian TV programs, Internet websites and podcasts are available in abundance. Everything God wants us to know about Him, His principles for successful living, and spiritual growth is there and available; yet, those with spiritual "failure to thrive" won't eat.

Hunger and thirst can be cultivated and stirred up. We create hunger and thirst by eating and drinking—on purpose. The more we eat and drink, the hungrier and thirstier we get? I can go all morning without eating and don't even notice. But, if I have a big breakfast early, by mid-morning, I'm starving again! It's the same way spiritually. We stir up hunger and thirst by eating and drinking more of God and His Word. The more time you spend with Him in honest, heartfelt communication, the hungrier and thirstier you will get.

Read It! Matthew 5:6, MSG

Speak It! "Father, I purpose in my heart to seek You, to eat Your Word, to spend time in prayer and to attend church. Lord, stir up a deeper hunger and thirst in my heart for You. In Jesus' Name. Amen."

DAY 253

(kum-ba-yah)

"May you be rooted deep in love and founded securely on love, that you may have the power and be strong to apprehend and grasp with all the saints [God's devoted people, the experience of that love] what is the breadth and length and height and depth [of it]; [That you may really come] to know [practically, through experience for yourselves] the love of Christ, which far surpasses mere knowledge [without experience]..."
Ephesians 3:17-18, AMP

The cry of everyone's heart is to truly experience God's love in a real, tangible way. We don't want Christianity or our walk with God to be the greatest-sounding theory we've ever heard; we want to experience it! We don't want our faith to be some clinical, theological thesis; we want to experience God.

We want kum-ba-yah moments! "Kum-ba-yah," a spiritual song from the 1930s that meant, "Come by here, Lord." In the 1960s it became a standard campfire song. The simple words go like this, "Someone's laughing (or crying, praying, singing), Lord, kum-ba-yah. Someone's laughing, Lord, kum-ba-yah. Someone's laughing, Lord, kum-ba-yah. O Lord, kum-ba-yah."

Whether we are laughing, crying, praying or singing, we want the Lord to *"come by here"* and touch us with the reality of His love. This is the deep cry of every-one's heart. We all want to apprehend, grasp and experience the breadth, length, height and depth of God's love. And...God also wants this for us! So, if God wants us to experience kum-ba-yah moments and we do, also, how can we do so in a greater and more tangible way? Here's one simple way, and the Lord encourages us to do this: Ask Him. Ask God to help you experience His love by praying this prayer below. Then, watch and see if you don't actually experience His love in a more real and practical way! (This prayer is taken from Ephesians 3:17-21 in the *Amplified Bible*.)

Read It! Romans 8:37-39

Speak It! "Father, may Christ through my faith [actually] dwell (settle down, abide, make His permanent home) in my heart! May I be rooted deeply in love and founded securely on love, that I may have the power and be strong to apprehend and grasp with all the saints [God's devoted people], the experience of that love, what is the breadth and length and height and depth [of it]; [That I may really come] to know [practically, through experience] the love of Christ, which far surpasses mere knowledge [without experience]; that I may be filled [through all my being] unto all the fullness of God [may have the richest measure of the divine presence, and become a body wholly filled and flooded with God Himself]! Now to Him Who, by (in consequence of) the [action of His] power that is at work within me, is able to [carry out His purpose and] do superabundantly, far over and above all that I [dare] ask or think [infinitely beyond my highest prayers, desires, thoughts, hopes, or dreams]... In Jesus' Name. Amen."

DAY 254

(jumper cables)

"He who speaks in a tongue edifies himself..."
1 Corinthians 14:4, NIV

Face it. At times, we all need a jump start or booster shot to our spiritual life. Living the life of faith, serving others, and seeking God's kingdom expends our spiritual energy and drains the battery dry. The next thing we know, too much time has lapsed in our prayer life or Bible reading schedule, and all our spiritual energy has evaporated. But, the good news is: God has a remedy. It's a supernatural charge!

The "jumper cables" God has given us to recharge our spiritual batteries is: speaking in tongues.

(Caveat: I know there have been all sorts of freakazoid ideas about speaking in tongues, and some people have thrown the "baby out with the bathwater." In the event you don't really understand the subject, just know there is a real experience of speaking in a spiritual language that God desires for Believers who are filled with His Spirit. If this topic interests you or if you have questions, I want to encourage you to study it out or feel free to check out our website for additional resources.)

Praying in tongues edifies our spirit—literally! When we speak or pray in tongues, it strengthens us in our inner man. It's like God hooks one end of the spiritual "jumper cable" to our hearts and the other end to heaven's battery. The results? We get some supernatural, spiritual juice to our weak battery, and we're refueled with high-octane God-energy! We not only get power in the battery, but we have energy to spare!

Today, pray in the Spirit. Sing in the Spirit. Yield to the Spirit and allow those rivers of living water to flow through you by speaking or singing in tongues in your private devotional life. Hook up to God's supernatural "jumper cables" and be refreshed and recharged!

Read It! 1 Corinthians 14:4 (Read it in both the NLT and the MSG!)

Speak It! "Father, Jesus, Holy Spirit...I need the refueling that only comes from You. I need a spiritual booster shot, Lord. I need to be filled with the Spirit, and I want to speak in the private prayer language that You give me. I am thirsty for more of You, Lord. My heart is filled with thanksgiving for all that You are. Jesus, I worship You. I exalt You. I bless Your Name. You are the Most High God, Creator of the ends of the earth. You are the Lord God Almighty, and I am going to yield to the Spirit now to pray and sing in tongues. (Do it!) Thank You for charging my spiritual batteries. In Jesus' Name. Amen."

DAY 255

(hotline to heaven)

"For if I pray in tongues, my spirit is praying,
but I don't understand what I am saying."
1 Corinthians 14:14, NLT

Batman had a great tool he used to his advantage—the Bat Phone! It was a direct hotline to the mayor of Gotham City, and no one else could hear or intercept their conversation. Whenever a crisis arose, the phone would ring, calling Bruce Wayne to leave civilian life and save the day.

In the same way, every Christian has their "hotline"—not to the mayor, or even the president, but to God Himself—with direct and uninterrupted access to the throne of God. What is our hotline to heaven? Praying in tongues.

For those who have never spoken, or prayed, in tongues, but desire to do so; perhaps, this analogy will be helpful. Think about a time when you were hungry for God and felt so much gratitude to the Lord, you couldn't help but belt out a shout of thanks! From the bottom of your heart-of-hearts, a song of praise or a "Praise the Lord" just came bellowing out! Praying in tongues is a lot like that.

Exercising our spiritual language in our private lives has many benefits. Not only does it strengthen us, but it also is a vehicle of prayer. It fully expresses all that is in our heart to the Lord. Through the language of "tongues," God gives us words that communicate the very depths of our hearts...directly to Him.

Every one of us has come to a time in our life where we just didn't know what to pray. Maybe the circumstance was more than we could bear, or we were confronted with a situation that was just over our head. We knew we had to pray, but didn't even know where to start. Enter...the Holy Spirit—our direct hotline to heaven!

It's in these times that we release the Holy Spirit to pray what we cannot. And guess what? God is on the other end of that hotline. Don't be afraid to use heaven's hotline. The Holy Spirit, in us, is the direct link—even if we don't know what we are praying or even saying. When we pray in tongues, we are always praying the perfect prayer for the situation! So, go ahead! Use your hotline!

Read It! 1 Corinthians 14:18, KJV

Speak It! "Father, thank You for filling me with the Holy Spirit. Now, I have a direct line to You that can help me when I don't know what to pray. I will pray in the Spirit and use my hotline to Heaven and believe You will be on the other end of my prayer, leading me to pray Your perfect will for my situation. Thank You, Lord, for this awesome tool. In Jesus' name. Amen."

DAY 256

(who me?)

"He made us accepted in the Beloved..."
Ephesians 1:6

You have been accepted! God approves of you. Because of Jesus, we've been accepted!

Many people struggle with a rejection complex. For many years, I did. In fact, it's common knowledge that nearly 90% of the population struggles with a low self-esteem. Why is that? It's the devil's plan. He doesn't want any of God's kids to be full of confidence, stability or a healthy self-esteem, so he sets up a vicious cycle of rejection that goes something like this...

Things happen: We sin. We feel guilty. We feel unworthy. We hear cruel comments. We're abused. We're abandoned. We're last to be picked. We get cut. We don't get asked. We lose. We look in the mirror. We feel ugly, fat, tall, skinny—unacceptable! We read into things. We think people don't like us. We compare ourselves. We become self-focused. We see our flaws. We don't think we are good enough. We get hurt...and then it happens...

We feel rejected, so we end up rejecting ourselves, others and even God Himself.

But there is a happy day...the day we surrender to Jesus Christ! When we accept His love, mercy and forgiveness and invite Him to be the Lord of our lives; instantly, we are accepted in the Beloved. That's when we realize God is not mad at us. He's forgiven us. He's given us another chance. He's not withholding from us. He's a giver. He's kind. He's good. He's patient. He approves of us. We are accepted.

Do you need that reminder today? Be encouraged—God accepts you. Yes, little 'ole you. Because of Jesus, He's not holding anything against you. He's for you. He's on your side. He wants you to be free from every sense of rejection and unworthiness. He wants you to be free to love...and be loved.

Think about it. If God accepts you, who can reject you?

Read It! Psalm 139

Speak It! "Father, I am so happy that You accept me in Christ! I am accepted in the Beloved. You aren't holding anything against me. It doesn't matter what anyone else thinks or says about me. You love me! You accept me! Thank You. Help me to experience this in a greater way in my life and help me to extend God's love, mercy, forgiveness and acceptance to others. In Jesus' Name."

DAY 257

(maximize your potential)

"Epaphras, who is one of you, a bondservant of Christ, greets you,
always laboring fervently for you in prayers, that you may stand
perfect and complete in all the will of God."
Colossians 4:12

Ever wondered why some people who are exceptionally gifted fail? Why so many gifted actors, athletes, singers, musicians, inventors, coaches, business-people, politicians and otherwise intelligent people end up blowing their potential? Why people called and gifted of God to raise up ministries, lead worship, preach, go on the mission field, start churches, pastor churches, teach the Word—end up doing something that costs them their ministry and/or their family? What about the shipwrecks of those God has gifted to be Involved in life-changing, earth-shaking, planet-rocking ministries?

For anyone to maximize their potential—and stay off the "has been" junk heap—there are two very important issues to consider:

- **Character Stamina.** There's an old saying that says: "Your gift will only go as far as your character will take you." Our giftedness will never go further than the level of our integrity. Our follow-through, faithfulness, ethics, self-discipline, endurance, perseverance, morality, honesty, humility and overall character can either send us soaring to new heights, or be a ceiling we can't get past.

  True character takes time and testing to develop and refine. But, some people are only wanting sloppy short-cuts to success. What they don't realize is that road usually ends with a lot of fender-benders and causalities. Their character is not developed; thus, their gifts are never maximized. Allowing the Lord to work in our lives, by developing a Christ-like character, is the only way for our gifts to take us further than we could ever imagine.

- **Prayer Power.** Some of us need to overcome a prayer deficit! We need to be prayer warriors and tap into God's power. Not only that, but we also need strong pray-ers who will pray for us. Epaphras was a prayer warrior who prayed for the church at Colossae to stand perfect and complete in all the will of God. And what was a big part of his prayer? That their character would develop into full maturity.

We all need an Epaphras in our lives—one who prays for our spiritual maturity and character development. Every person in the Body of Christ needs to flourish in their God-given calling. We can't afford any "blown-potentials," casualties, "has beens" or short-circuited careers. What's the key to reaching that maximized potential? Developing godly character.

Read It! Psalm 26:11 and Proverbs 23:7

Speak It! "Father, I want to grow and develop in Christian character and spiritual maturity. Lord, help me to maximize my God-given potential and the gifts you've given me so I can stand perfect and complete in Your will. In Jesus' Name. Amen."

DAY 258

(the power of Onesiphorus)

"May the Lord show special kindness to Onesiphorus and all his family because he often visited and encouraged me. He was never ashamed of me because I was in prison. When he came to Rome, he searched everywhere until he found me."
2 Timothy 1:16-17, NLT

I've always been intrigued by the relationship between Onesiphorus and the apostle Paul. I've come to the conclusion that every Christian leader needs an Onesiphorus, and every Onesiphorus needs a Paul.

The apostle Paul was mightily used of God. He wrote more than half of the New Testament, pioneered churches, taught the Word, preached to crowds, discipled Believers, traveled extensively on missions trips and faced intense persecution during most of his ministry. He was always in the "giving" mode and focused on ministering to others. However, near the end of his life when he was in prison for preaching the Gospel, he needed someone to "give" to him. That's when Onesiphorus showed up. Look at the way Onesiphorus ministered to Paul:

- **He often visited him.** How nice. Any leader will tell you that being at the "top" is wonderful, an honor and a privilege but also very lonely. Friends, like Onesiphorus, are a gift.
- **He encouraged him.** How refreshing. Paul was usually the "encourager," but in this relationship, Onesiphorus was the encourager.
- **He wasn't ashamed.** How courageous. Onesiphorus had guts. This imprisonment took place shortly before Paul was martyred. Onesiphorus didn't care that officials might associate him with Paul. He was willing to identify with Paul during some of the most difficult days of his life.
- **He searched for Paul.** How faithful. Paul was difficult to locate during this second imprisonment, but Onesiphorus searched for him and overcame any obstacles to find him. He wasn't using Paul for his own benefit; there was nothing in it for him, only a genuine love and care for Paul.

Are you an "Onesiphorus"? Is there a God-given desire in you to be a blessing to a Christian leader? Start by praying for them and trust the Lord to show you how to provide the type of "no-strings-attached" encouragement they need.

Are you a "Paul" and need an Onesiphorus in your life? Ask the Lord to bring them to you.

Read It! Proverbs 17:17, MSG and Colossians 4:12

Speak It! "Father, I'm willing to be an Onesiphorus. Show me how to encourage Your leaders. Father, I need an Onesiphorus in my life. I ask You to send one to encourage me as I fulfill Your will. In Jesus' Name. Amen."

DAY 259

(build that house)

"The wise woman builds her house, but the foolish pulls it
down with her hands."
Proverbs 14:1

Wow, there's nothing like a house full girls, is there? Moms, sisters, daughters and nieces...all together under one roof. When all of our extended family is together, all of us girls hang out together. The estrogen is flying! Between talking about God, our make-up, jewelry, clothes, shoes and perfume, we talk about our kids. Collectively, we have raised 14 of them—7 boys and 7 girls. Even though our work isn't done by a long shot, we have come to notice some common things a woman uses to build her house. Here are a few:

She, intentionally...

- **Imparts her love for the Lord into her children.** Ultimately, kids will have to choose Jesus for themselves. But, a wise woman is intentional about training her kids in the Lord. She talks about Him, shares her stories of faith, leads by example on how to pray and read the Bible, worships God and loves people.

- **Teaches her children to love others.** If you can get them to love their siblings, the rest is gravy! When we see our children reach out to others, hold open the door for an elderly person, offer up their seat to someone else, or just engage in a friendly conversation with a stranger, we know they are heading in the right direction.

- **Talks to and with her children.** No kid likes lectures, but they do like to talk and be taken seriously. A wise mom finds ways to draw things out of her children's hearts in healthy, fun, interesting ways. She asks questions they want to answer, and she makes communication a safe place. One night our 17-year-old wanted to talk to me—at 2 a.m! I was thrilled! Are you kidding? Anytime my teenage son wants to talk with me—I'm there!

- **Knows how to have fun.** It's true. Girls just want to have fun! (And so do boys!) A wise mom knows how to have a good time—even at random moments—with her kids. And don't forget to laugh at yourself—often.

- **Spoils them at times.** I don't know any kids who don't like gifts. Sometimes, a wise mom takes her kids shopping and buys them stuff—for no reason. It doesn't matter what it is, kids like to be blessed. Who doesn't?

Today, ask the Lord for some help to start "building that house."

Read It! Proverbs 31

Speak It! "Father, I want to be a wise mom (or dad), and I ask You for Your help in building my house and in raising my kids! In Jesus' Name. Amen."

DAY 260

(passion or apathy?)

"Upon this rock I will build My church;
and the gates of hell shall not prevail against it."
Matthew 16:18b, KJV

Jesus loves the Church, and He's busy building it. He declared it some 2,000 years ago, and His Words shall come to pass.

Satan hates the Church and doesn't want any church to grow or prosper. Why? Because the Church represents those who find, follow and exalt Jesus Christ. When people connect with Jesus and His Word, they are set free and empowered by God's Spirit—and the enemy hates it! He uses all sorts of tactics, strategies and rationale to come against the Church—from blatant anti-Christ spiritual attacks that are easy to recognize to the more subtle "anti-Church" attitude he perpetuates.

What about us? Are we passionately helping Jesus build His Church or are we operating apathetically or contrary to His purposes? Hopefully, we're ones who are being used to build His Church.

Sadly, some Believers can't say that. They've developed a great distaste or indifference toward the Church. We've heard many stories over the years—some sad and tragic; others, not so much. Those stories sounded like a broken record—somewhere along the way, they got hurt or offended by the pastor, the church leader or a church member; someone else sat in their seat, a sermon stepped on their toes, etc. Most of these offenses are the result of unintentional human error, and the enemy has used these little foxes to spoil the vine for them! We'll be the first to admit that there's no such thing as a perfect church—only a perfect Jesus! We, too, have been guilty of inadvertently offending people by not living up to their expectations.

If you've been in a "church funk," perhaps, it's time to kick the devil in the teeth or kick yourself in the rear—or both. But, make a decision to move on, get over it, call it water under the bridge, bury the hatchet, forget things that lie behind—and even...forgive. Let's get back to building what is front and center on Jesus' heart—His Church!

Read It! Psalm 92:13

Speak It! "Father, I believe Your Church is front and center on Your heart, and I choose to love what You love. I dedicate myself to building Your Church—through attending, praying, serving and giving. Lord, use me in whatever way You see fit. Help me to humble myself, so my gifts can be maximized for the building of Your Church. Forgive me for being offended or apathetic toward Your Church. I choose to forgive and move forward. In Jesus' Name. Amen."

DAY 261

("go to" people)

"Aaron and Hur held his hands up—one on one side, one on the other..."
Exodus 17:12b, NIV

Got any "go to" people in your life? Are you a "go to" person? Whose hands are you lifting? Who's lifting yours?

Take a minute to read the story in the **Read It!** segment. Moses was leading the Israelites into battle. When Moses operated in his God-given office and lifted his hands to heaven, the Israelites won the battle. When his hands fell, the Israelites began to lose the battle. In the midst of the battle, Moses got weary of lifting his hands and needed some "go to" people who would lift his hands—those he could count on and trust.

Aaron and Hur noticed Moses struggling, and they recognized the significant role he played in their victory. So, they went and held up his hands. Moses couldn't leave his post to micro-manage or babysit them. Aaron and Hur had to be trustworthy and able to be counted on to do an excellent job and not miss any details—and they were. They anticipated what Moses needed. They didn't create any problems or stress and brought solutions by engaging their creative minds and strong work ethic. They ended up putting a big rock under Moses and they held up his hands. The result? The Israelites, led by Joshua, won the battle!

I wonder how many leaders, business owners, pastors or spiritual leaders feel like Moses? They face what feels like constant spiritual battles on behalf of the people they lead. They need people they can count on who they can trust and who will hold up their hands...so victory can be won! Spiritual leaders, in particular, have a huge responsibility for leading God's people. They must take their place and "keep their hands up" to continually win battles. These leaders need "Aarons" and "Hurs" on their team.

Moses needed Aaron and Hur, and vice-versa. Each one played a part in the other's destiny. Today, let the "Aarons and Hurs" be looking for the "Moseses" to bring victory in every situation.

Read It! Exodus 17:11-13, NIV

Speak It! "Father, I feel like 'Moses.' I know You have called me to lead, but I am weary in well-doing, and I need some 'go to' people to hold my hands up. I ask You for divine connections. I pray You send me an 'Aaron' and/or 'Hur.' In Jesus' Name. Amen."

Or... "Father, I feel like an 'Aaron' or 'Hur.' I have a heart to help lift the load for the leaders in my life. Help me to see the needs, anticipate problems and find solutions. Show me what to do and how to help. In Jesus' Name. Amen."

DAY 262

(off the grid)

"Therefore we also, since we are surrounded by so great a cloud of witnesses, let us lay aside every weight, and the sin which so easily ensnares us, and let us run with endurance the race that is set before us."
Hebrews 12:1

Ever thought about things that weigh us down? Things that are...time stealers? Energy robbers? Trivial pursuits? Weights robbing us of time with God?

This talks about paring down our lives, like a runner, so we are spiritually aerodynamic and able to run our race without being tripped up or thwarted in our pursuit of God and His plan.

Notice the two categories here in this scripture: weights and sins. Weights are not necessarily sins. Sins are not necessarily weights. Of course, it's obvious that we should strip off every sin and run our race free from sin; but, what about weights? Weights are something that weighs us down and steals time that could be used for more important things. These things in our lives are not sins and are not bad in and of themselves; but, they may weigh us down in various seasons of life.

Let's look at a few examples: TV, Facebook®, Twitter®, YouTube®, eBay® or just the Internet, in general. In and of themselves, they're not bad. But, for those who spend unusual amounts of time entertaining themselves with them, they can become a weight and a distraction in their walk with God. What about sleep? Sleep is great and needed, but sleep can become a weight if we sleep our lives away.

The challenge to all of these is determining the point at which they become a distraction, time-waster or weight. I've been wondering what it would be like to be off the grid...at least for a few months anyways? What would it be like to "fast" Facebook® and Twitter® for 90 days? Not sure it's possible, but... What would life be like with the cell phone off for a week? How crazy would life or business or ministry be if we only checked and answered e-mail once a week? How possible would it be to detach from technology for a season? I suppose it's like everything else in life—moderation is the key.

Wanna travel light? Take time to pray about what weights or sins are in your life that are holding you down. Then, throw them off and run your race?

Read It! Proverbs 4:25, MSG, Proverbs 12:11

Speak It! "Father, I ask You to show me the things in my life that have become weights—robbing my time, stealing my relationship with You and ensnaring me in my race? Help me rid myself of any sin holding me back. In Jesus' Name. Amen."

DAY 263

(blind leap)

"Now faith is the assurance (the confirmation, the title deed) of the things [we] hope for, being the proof of things [we] do not see and the conviction of their reality [faith perceiving as real fact what is not revealed to the senses]."
Hebrews 11:1, AMP

Is faith a blind leap? No, it is not.

Faith is the assurance. Faith is the proof. Faith perceives.

A blind leap implies the unknown. It lends itself to hit or miss. Faith is not a blind leap. Faith is a fact. The God-kind of faith, that is.

The God-kind of faith takes God at His Word, because it has spent time with God to hear His voice, because it knows that God is not a man that He should lie, so if He said it, He must have meant it.

The God-kind of faith is fully persuaded that God is able to perform the very thing He promised because it knows that heaven and earth will pass away before God's Word will pass away.

The God-kind of faith trusts all of its weight on the living and active Word which is able to divide between soul and spirit and effectually work within us, knowing that God watches over His Word to perform it.

Faith is not a blind leap. Anything other than faith IS a blind leap...anything other than faith is a roll of the dice; it's a que sera sera; it's a 50/50; a fatalistic experience or a "gee-willy...I hope so" existence.

The Bible is clear: faith—the God-kind of faith—is a known commodity, not a blind leap.

Read It! 1 John 5:14-15, AMP and Romans 10:17

Speak It! "Father, I thank You for Your Word. I am so glad that living by faith in not a blind leap into oblivion, but it is the assurance and title-deed of things hoped for. Thank You for helping my faith to grow and be strong as I feed on your Word. In Jesus' Name. Amen."

DAY 264

(get your "ask" in gear)

"If you then, being evil, know how to give good gifts to your children,
how much more will your Father who is in heaven give good things
to those who ask Him!"
Matthew 7:11

God is a good Father. He's more generous than the very best human father we could ever think of. The Lord does not withhold, and He's not stingy. Let's get our mind renewed to this fact: God is love. Love gives. God is a giver. This is His very nature.

So, exactly who does God give these good gifts to? Simple. To those who ask!

Every parent loves it when their children ask for things. (Well, most of the time, anyway!) Face it. It's hard to resist that little girl who crawls up in her daddy's lap and starts in with, "Daddy, you are the best daddy in the whole wide world. I love you so much." Then, after she has him completely melted— bam!—the asking begins. "Daddy, can I have some ice cream tonight?" Of course, later in life, it's more like, "Hey, dad, can I borrow your car tonight? Me and the girls want to go to the movies?"

God's the same way as daddies! He likes it when His children crawl up and ask Him for good things. James tells us that because we don't ask, we don't have *(James 4:2)*. It's all in the asking! Perhaps asking puts us in a place of dependence on the Lord, rather than being self-sufficient or presumptuous. When we ask God for something, it's a humble acknowledgment that we're needy and He's our good and benevolent Father who's willing to give us the things we desire.

God is willing, ready and able to answer our prayers generously when we cooperate with Him in faith by asking! Don't feel guilty or selfish when asking God for things. When we ask for things according to His will, which is His Word, His desire is to give us things for His good pleasure.

Today, let's get our "ask" in gear! Let's spend some time in the Word and present our desires before the Lord by simply asking!

Read It! James 4:2, NIV

Speak It! "Father, I am going to spend some time in Your Word. I ask You to saturate my heart with Your Word and Your will. I have been negligent on 'asking,' so I am going to get busy 'asking' You for things! I believe You will be glorified and my joy will be complete! I thank You in advance for answering my 'asking.' In Jesus' Name. Amen."

DAY 265

(God's bad rap)

"Taste and see that the Lord is good..."
Psalm 34:8a, NIV

Isn't it sad that some people see God in a skewed light? They think He's a mean judge ready to slap them for everything, especially when they mess up. They think He's a taker. They think He's reluctant to give gifts. They think He's stingy and not fair.

There are so many bad raps about God, too many to mention in this entire book! Mainly, they are based on what religion has taught people, and not on the nature of God Himself.

Here are three very common ones—along with why they are not true:

- **Bad Rap #1:** *"If God knows what I'm going through, He'll just make sure all my needs are met."* Even though it sounds good, it's not necessarily true. Yes, God does know we need wisdom—and a host of other things—but there is a key that unlocks the door of receiving. It is called asking! *(Matthew 6:2 and James 1:5-8)*

- **Bad Rap #2:** *"God is only concerned with spiritual things."* Really? That's not what Jesus said. Jesus said if we remain in His Word, and His Word lives in us, then we can have anything we ask, according His will. The way we discover His will and desire is by spending time in His Word. We might be surprised to find that the Lord will put all kinds of interesting and fulfilling desires in our hearts when we delight in Him. *(John 15:7 and 1 John 5:14-15)*

- **Bad Rap #3:** *"God can just do whatever He pleases."* While it is true that God is sovereign and has the ability to do whatever, whenever; it is not always how He works. Jesus talked about how the power of agreement—two or three agreeing on something—can move God to action. When someone asks, in the name of Jesus and according to the Word, things happen. Jesus says that we hold the keys to the kingdom and the authority to bind and loose things on the earth like they are in heaven. *(Matthew 18:19-20; John 16:23-24; Matthew 16:19)*

Let's live the life that dispels the bad raps and show the world just how good our God is!

Read It! Psalm 145:9, NLT

Speak It! "Father, I thank You, today, that You are a good God. Thank You for loving me unconditionally. I know Your desire is for my good. Thank You that You have given me the authority in Jesus' name to come before You, today, boldly to get the help I need. In Jesus' name. Amen."

DAY 266

(God's HR—everyone)

"Now you are the body of Christ, and members individually."
1 Corinthians 12:27

God is the smartest CEO. He's the superior HR Manager. He's the quintessential Administrator. He's the best Executor. He knows how to start, pioneer, grow, manage, maintain and expand every aspect of His kingdom—particularly His most prized operation—The Church.

The Lord sets people in the Church...as it pleases Him. There is great freedom in knowing and understanding this. We don't choose where we want to be on His Org Chart—He chooses. The Lord knows the gifts, passions, callings, talents, capacities, potential and divine destiny He has ordained for each and every person. In light of His foreknowledge, He predestines us to serve in His Church. Based on His foreknowledge and predestination, He appoints each of us to perform various functions in the Body of Christ.

Let's take a quick look at this:

- **Everyone.** He has given EVERYONE a gift and has called EVERYONE to do something! *(Ephesians 4:7 and 1 Peter 4:10)*

- **Some.** He gives SOME people a leadership gift and calls SOME people to lay foundations, pioneer works, teach, preach, equip, build up and oversee the Church. *(Ephesians 4:11-12 and 1 Corinthians 12:28, KJV)*

It's true, SOME people are called to leadership in the Church; but EVERYONE has a role to play in assisting the leaders. Everyone has something to do in God's kingdom.

Where's the best place for us? Right slap-dab in the middle of where God has placed us! Everybody has a gift. Everybody has a job. Everybody has place. Let's find it, fill it, and watch God bless everything we put our hand to!

Read It! Romans 12:4-6

Speak It! "Father, I thank You for the gifts You have given me. If I am called to the ministry of helps, help me to serve with a fresh passion, zeal and excellence to provide the relief and assistance my church leaders need to fulfill Your vision for the Church. If I am called to lead, teach and preach to build up Your Body, help me to serve with a fresh passion, zeal and excellence to provide the leadership those in the ministry of helps need, so we can fulfill Your vision for the Church. In Jesus' Name. Amen."

DAY 267

(what is your theme?)

"My heart is overflowing with a good theme..."
Psalm 45:1a

We have all prayed, "God, what's Your will for my life?" or, "Lord, help me find my destiny!" What we need to realize is God's will (or theme) for our lives (our season) may be closer than we think! Of course, we may feel that life is just a series of detached, disconnected, and insignificant events. But, that's not true! God really does have a theme!

So, how do we identify this theme? Simple. It overflows out of our hearts. Spending time with the Lord and His Word gives us confidence that our heart is full of God's good theme for our lives. No more scratching our heads, wondering what the plot of life is supposed to look like. We don't need to figure it out; we just need to identify what is already in our hearts.

Over the past 30 years of walking with the Lord, I've noticed a few reoccurring themes that have filled my heart: the desire to please the Lord, the desire to be a good wife, mom and friend; the desire to write, speak, laugh and sing to the Lord (which I find very funny); the desire to find creative and innovative ways to reach the lost and help people "get a grip" on the basics of God's Word. There are others, but these themes are ever-present in my heart.

One thing I have found to be true is that life is more congruent, efficient, calm, purposeful and productive when we know the theme God intends! Once we identify the things that overflow from our hearts, then we need to take practical steps toward fulfilling them. One way is to see what the Bible says about them.

What Scriptures fit the theme of our lives? The next step is getting our mouths in gear by reciting those verses to God and praying for wisdom to walk them out. Taking the time to find out God's purposes and theme for our lives is the beginning of living the full life God originally intended for us to live!

Read It! Psalms 37:4

Speak It! "Father, thank You that You have a 'theme' for my life! How comforting to know that You don't want my life to be a disorganized, confusing, disconnected mess. Rather, You have filled my heart to overflowing with the theme You have for me. Help me to identify the reoccurring themes You have planted in my heart and help me find the scriptures and practical steps I need to walk them out. In Jesus' Name. Amen."

DAY 268

(good angels)

"For He shall give His angels charge over you, to keep you in all your ways."
Psalm 91:11

This is just a friendly reminder that we are not alone! Thankfully, the Father, Son and Holy Spirit are always with us. Our Father is Omnipresent, and He will never leave or forsake us. Jesus is with us always, and The Holy Spirit lives in us and is ever-present.

But, that's not all!

God is so good that He has also sent His angels to be with us—to take charge over us. Truly, we are not alone!

Although we don't usually see the angelic realm, they are there. The Bible says they are sent to minister for Christians—the heirs of salvation. They obey the Lord's Word and visit mankind, speak, open doors, remove chains, give directions, enter rooms, stand by, protect and much more. Here are just a few things the Book of Acts tells us about God's angels at work on the earth:

- **Opened prison doors.** *"But at night an angel of the Lord opened the prison doors and brought them out..." (Acts 5:19)*
- **Gave directions.** *"Now an angel of the Lord spoke to Philip, saying, 'Arise and go toward the south...'" (Acts 8:26)*
- **Appeared in visions.** *"About the ninth hour of the day he saw clearly in a vision an angel of God coming in and saying to him, 'Cornelius!'" (Acts 10:3)*
- **Gave instructions.** *"And he told us how he had seen an angel standing in his house, who said to him, 'Send men to Joppa, and call for...Peter.'" (Acts 11:13)*
- **Brought deliverance.** *"Now behold, an angel of the Lord stood by him, and a light shone in the prison; and he struck Peter on the side and raised him up, saying, 'Arise quickly!' And his chains fell off his hands... And when Peter had come to himself, he said, 'Now I know for certain that the Lord has sent His angel, and has delivered me...'" (Acts 12:7,11)*

The Bible also says that you just never know; a stranger who comes across your path today just might be an angel in disguise. Whether it's a stranger on the corner or the Angel of the Lord you will never see, be encouraged. You are not alone today!

Read It! Acts 27:23-24

Speak It! "Father, I thank You that I'm not alone. Those that are with me—in the angelic realm—are more than those that are against me. I thank You for the work of the angels of God in my life as they do Your bidding! In Jesus' Name. Amen."

DAY 269

(not-so-good angels)

"...for Satan himself masquerades as an angel of light."
2 Corinthians 11:14, NIV

Where there are good angels, there are also not-so-good angels. We need to be aware of their deceptive ways. Satan, himself, is described as an angel—an angel of light. What does this mean?

A couple of things...

First, he can look radiant, much like a good angel. He talks the talk, says all the right things and makes people believe that his way is okay. Then, before you know it, his real motives and character show through.

Secondly, he produces a blinding light. It's not the light of glory, but the light of deception. Everything looks good. Everything will be okay. He assures, *"Nobody will ever know..."*—and, once again, his true colors are revealed and devastation follows.

Just as heaven sends angels to earth, so does the devil. They are counterfeit angels called demons. They try to mimic God's angels but are easily recognized by those who know the Word of God. Everything they say and do contradict God's revealed Word.

Psychics, mediums, fortune-tellers and the like—those who do not profess the Lordship of Jesus—are not being motivated by the Holy Spirit or God. They are being motivated by not-so-good angels led by their leader, Satan. Oh, they can look good and enticing; but we shouldn't fall for every thing that looks "spiritually good!" Anything that's labeled as "spiritual," you need to check it out first. Make sure it agrees with the Word, or the door to darkness will be opened. That's exactly why the Bible tells us to be wise as serpents.

Remember this. Just because someone says they've been "touched by an angel," doesn't necessarily mean it was an angel sent from God Almighty. It might have been a not-so-good one!

Read It! Galatians 1:8

Speak It! "Father, I thank You for Your protection and wisdom today. I realize there are angels of light out to bring destruction and calamity to my life. I believe today that I will discern what is good and what is bad. I will judge everything according to Your Word and will not follow anything or anyone that is contrary. Thank You for leading me today. In Jesus' name. Amen."

DAY 270

(if you build it...)

"For every house is built by someone, but God is the builder of everything."
Hebrews 3:4, NIV

God is the builder of everything!

What do you need built? What do you need to build? A new house? Your family? Your marriage? Relationships? Your faith? Your confidence? A church?

Every house IS built by someone. In the natural, we have our part to play. We can't just sit back in the Lazy Boy® and wish upon a star for a house, church, marriage or any other thing to be magically built. Every house is built by SOMEONE.

That means, if you're building a home, you may need to study and scrutinize blueprints. If you're building a family, you may need to put extra effort into focusing on the needs of each member. If you're building a marriage, you may need to figure out what tools and materials to use. If you're building your faith, you may need to lay a stronger foundation in the Word. If you're building your confidence, you may need to get up to speed on all the permits of your identity in Christ. If you're building a church, you may need to multi-task with all the contractors and subs.

But, ultimately, God is the builder of everything! We do our part; but if we'll put our "building project" in the Lord's hands, He is the builder of everything. Think about that. We do the natural, but God adds the "super"—and we get...the SUPERNATURAL!

Be inspired today. You're not building things all by your lonesome. God is the builder of everything. Say that about a 100 times and be encouraged!

Read It! Psalm 127:1, KJV

Speak It! "Father, I am so thankful that You are the builder of everything! I thank You that as I do my part—the natural—I am confident You will do Your part—the supernatural; and You will build a supernatural building in my life! *(Now, be specific and ask the Lord to build the things you need to fulfill His will and purposes.)* In Jesus' Name. Amen."

DAY 271

(red)

"He replied, 'When evening comes, you say, 'It will be fair weather, for the sky is red,' and in the morning, 'Today it will be stormy, for the sky is red and overcast.' You know how to interpret the appearance of the sky, but you cannot interpret the signs of the times.' "
Matthew 16:2-4, NIV

Jesus said it was easy for us to interpret the indicators and predict the weather. Shouldn't we be able to do the same with the signs of the times?

The most amazing thing, to me, has been the way news headlines have confirmed these signs of the times! The economic collapse of banks and credit markets around the world is a recent indicator. The technological boom and the 5,000 day-old Internet have changed everything forever. Only God knows what the next 5,000 days look like as the Information Age continues to explode. The increase of famine, potential for pandemics and rise in earthquakes around the world is evident—just do a few Google® searches. The threat of a nuclear war between Israel and Iran is real. The coalition between Russia, Iran and other nations is building.

It's apparent that our national security, social culture, family structure, values and very freedoms are at stake in these days. Persecution of Christians in many nations is another sign of the times. In the midst of all of this, there is a great revival happening around the globe. People are coming to Christ in record numbers. People without Christ in the Middle East are having Damascus Road experiences with visions and dreams of Jesus Christ. God is pouring out His grace in every land—Australia, Middle East, China, Iran, Zimbabwe, South America— even Las Vegas! If there was ever a time to know God, this is that time! All of these things were predicted by the Bible thousands of years ago and are leading up the next big event on God's calendar—the Rapture.

Jesus doesn't want us to be ignorant about the signs of the times. Let's be as wise in recognizing the indicators of the times as we are in—understanding the indicators of a "red sky at night" or a "red sky in the morning."

Read It! Matthew 24

Speak It! "Father, I'm so glad I know Jesus. I'm thankful to have the Holy Spirit— the Greater One—living in me. He gives me great peace, comfort and courage. In these days, help me to recognize the indicators all around. Help me to have understanding of the times. Help me to reach out to others with the Gospel and live my life in such a way that Jesus is seen as Lord. Most importantly, help me to know You—my God. In Jesus' Name. Amen."

DAY 272

(initiate a mid-life crisis)

"If you fall to pieces in a crisis, there wasn't much to you in the first place."
Proverbs 24:10

For some of us, it's that time of life—mid-life! And for the rest of you young peeps,...well, your time will come! You know you're in mid-life when you look in the mirror and see your mother instead of Julia Roberts, Anne Hathaway or Jada Pinkett-Smith. You know you're in mid-life when your upper arms jiggle, liver spots suddenly appear on your hands and your lipstick bleeds. (Yeah, not a look we are going for!) You know you're on the cusp of a potential mid-life crisis when you have a meltdown because you can no longer get fit at Forever 21; when the barber spends more time trimming your ear hair instead of your head hair; when you actually *want* to buy a 3-wheel bike; when being a mall-walker is your idea of a good time.

For some people, it happens when their last child moves out, when a close friend or co-worker their age dies or when they start to feel regrets about what "coulda, shoulda, woulda." Unfortunately, for many people, a mid-life crisis "happens" unexpectedly and ends up rocking their world and self-esteem. If mishandled, it can destroy a marriage, a family, a child, a friend or a vibrant life.

Why not avoid the mid-life "crisis" by initiating your own "mid-life metamor-phosis"? Don't wait for the straw that broke the camel's back or an epiphany. Get ahead of the curve and make your mid-life crisis happen now! Hey, you only get one life! The clock is ticking. It won't be long, and you'll be old and gray...with regrets.

Have you always wanted to do something? When are you going to give your-self permission to do it? Maybe a red Corvette isn't so wrong for you? Maybe running that marathon isn't out of the question? Maybe it's time you took that missions trip. More importantly, think about God's plan and purpose for your life, family and relationships—it's not too late to fulfill it! If you're not careful, you'll wish you had romanced your husband more, laughed with your kids more. You'll wish you had done something to help others in a significant way. You'll wish you had given to the poor and lonely. You'll wish you had written that book, learned to dance, played the piano, studied Japanese, traveled to Rome or bungee jumped off a bridge. You'll wish you'd led more people to the Lord. So, don't wish... Just do it!

Read It!   Philippians 3:13

Speak It!   "Father, I want to maximize my life. I thank You for the wisdom and courage I need to live the life You've called me to live. I don't want to wait for a mid-life crisis. I want to create a mid-life 'metamorphosis' and live a life that honors You. In Jesus' Name, Amen."

DAY 273

(what to do when you feel blue)

"A cheerful heart brings a smile to your face;
a sad heart makes it hard to get through the day."
Proverbs 15:13, MSG

Feeling blue? Down in the dumps? God has the remedy...

Rejoice. Smile.

Sing. Shout.

Whistle. Laugh. Jump.

- **If you need a little more joy—shout for it!** *"Be glad in the LORD and rejoice, you righteous; and shout for joy, all you upright in heart!" (Psalm 32:11)*
- **If you need a little more gladness—will it!** *"I will be glad and rejoice in your love, for you saw my affliction and knew the anguish of my soul." (Psalm 31:7, NIV)*
- **If you need a little more cheer—sing it!** *"A miserable heart means a miserable life; a cheerful heart fills the day with song." (Proverbs 15:15, MSG)*
- **If you need a little more joy—whistle, laugh and jump for it!** *"I'm whistling, laughing, and jumping for joy; I'm singing your song, High God." (Proverbs 9:2, MSG)*

Read It! Psalm 27:13, NIV

Speak It! "Father, I believe. I would have lost heart and thrown in the towel, but today I choose to believe. I believe that I will see Your goodness while I am alive on Planet Earth. I thank You for moving heaven and earth, opening and closing doors and making a way where there is no way, so I can see Your goodness. In Jesus' Name. Amen."

DAY 274

(God's eye contact)

"I will instruct you and teach you in the way you should go;
I will guide you with My eye."
Psalm 32:8

Did your mom have eyes in the back of her head? God does, too. In fact, God's eyes search to and fro throughout the whole earth to show Himself strong on the behalf of those whose hearts are fully devoted to Him. God has eyeballs on everyone and everything. We can be encouraged by that. We have not been forgotten or overlooked. He sees you. He's given us some promises that we can take to the bank regarding this fact.

If you're in a season and you don't know what to do or which way to go, take comfort in knowing the Lord will instruct you and show you the way to go—if you'll listen to His Word. Not only that, He promises to guide us with His eye.

Think about that. Ever been in the store and looked down the aisle to see your kids misbehaving? Did you give them the "eye"? They knew exactly what to do when they saw your "eye," didn't they? How about making eye contact with your spouse? Ever been at a party and your spouse "guided" you with his or her eye? Maybe those eyes said, "Let's go," or "Hey, when we get home, let's have some fun!" You didn't need words did you? You knew exactly what those eyes were saying! Maybe you winked at your friend, son or daughter before their big game, and that wink told them you were praying and rooting for them. Eyes can tell us a lot.

How cool that God guides us with His eye! Maybe we need to take better note of the "eye contact" God is making with us. There is just one problem. In the natural, we can't see His eyeballs, so we need supernatural help. We need God to open up the "eyes of our hearts" so we can see His eyes. Thankfully, this is something He will do. The apostle Paul prayed this very thing for the Believers in Ephesus. Take a look at his prayer in the **Read It!** segment.

Today, pray that the Lord will enlighten the eyes of your heart, so you can see His eyes guiding you into the hope to which He has called you.

Read It! Ephesians 1:18, NIV

Speak It! "Father, I thank You that You will instruct me and teach me in the way I should go. I am so glad that You guide me with Your eye. I pray You will open the eyes of my heart, so I can discern the 'eye contact' and guidance I receive from You. In Jesus' Name. Amen."

DAY 275

(make a decree)

"You shall also decide and decree a thing, and it shall be established
for you; and the light [of God's favor] shall shine upon your ways."
Job 22:28, AMP

The power of words. Most of us have not even scratched the surface of this powerful truth. God has endowed man with one of the most amazing gifts and honors—the ability to speak words that have the power of life or death! We know God's words have power; they created the world! But, often, we've forgotten that He's given us the power to frame our world with our words. Whether we believe it or not, we are living in a world that has been largely created by words we have decreed over the years. A man will be satisfied—or not—by the fruit of his mouth *(Proverbs 12:14)*. Our words establish things in our lives. When we constantly say, "I am so stressed...," or, "I am so depressed...," and then we wonder why we're feeling stressed or depressed, it's just proof that we've decreed and established things with our own words.

Why not speak God's blessings, according to His Word, over our life and family, instead of cursing them? Let's prime the pump and decree some "in Christ" realities and blessings right now!

I decree that Jesus is the Lord of my life. I live to please the Lord and know Jesus more intimately. I decree that Jesus is my Redeemer. He has redeemed me from sin to eternal life; from sickness to health and healing; from poverty and lack to abundance and blessing. I decree that the favor of God surrounds me like a shield. God causes people to like me, and I like them. I decree that I am filled with peace. I am easy-going and patient. I decree that I am accepted in Christ. God loves me, and He's made me righteous in His sight—without any sense of guilt, inferiority or shame. I decree that I can do all things through Christ who strengthens me. I can do all that God asks of me. I decree that my spouse and kids are blessed. We are a family mightily used of God. I decree that the joy of the Lord is my strength. I am happy and full of joy and laughter. I decree that I am blessed to be a blessing, and that I am a blessing going somewhere to happen.

May it be established!

Why not decide to walk in the light of God's Word and continually decree the things His Word has declared belong to us in Christ?

Read It! Psalm 107:2 and Proverbs 18:21

Speak It! "Father, I decide to walk in the light of Your Word and make decrees that are consistent with Your Word. I thank You that in due season, they are established in my life. Thank You that I am 'in Christ' and an heir to all of God's promises. I decree it. In Jesus' Name. Amen."

DAY 276

(don't hate me because I'm beautiful)

"A heart at peace gives life to the body, but envy rots the bones."
Proverbs 14:30, NIV

Meet two, evil twins—Envy and Jealousy. They ruin relationships, teams, families, and churches. Even though they are similar in nature, each one has different, unique characteristics about them. So, allow me to introduce you to Envy and Jealousy. **Envy** wants what others have and resents seeing others blessed. **Jealousy** is hostility toward a rival, never wanting others to have success.

When my youngest sister and I were in our early 20's, we visited the home of a very successful surgeon which had every bell and whistle. We muttered under our breath, "Wow, are we jealous or what?" He heard us and said, "Don't ever be jealous of another Christian brother or sister. Be happy for them, knowing you are standing in the same line." At first, we thought, "That's easy for you to say, Mr. Millionaire. Guess it's time for us to leave and drive back to our duplex in our beat up Honda CVCC. Mind if we take a handful of peanuts for the road?" But, then, we pondered his statement, and the light bulb went off for us: "Hey, that's right! We are in the same line—the line of faith and obedience—and in time, if we rejoice with others and stay faithful to God, we'll get our turn." Turns out, he was right.

- **The Seeds of Envy and Jealousy.** Accolades—a great sale, achievement, message or worship—are great, but they will do us in if we're not careful. What if other people start getting more kudos than we do? If we are not careful, the seed of Envy and Jealousy can begin to take root in our hearts.

- **The Fruit of Envy and Jealousy.** Distress and oppression usually accompany Envy and Jealousy. We can never rejoice with someone else's successes. Why? Because they become a threat to our success; and we feel as though we have been overlooked, not celebrated.

- **The Price of Envy and Jealousy.** The two evil twins could take everything we so dearly cling to—including our anointing from God! Fear and Insecurity are also their offspring. Jealousy and Envy can warp our minds so much, that we desire others to fail; just so we can feel superior in our own identity.

Today, let's kick Jealousy and Envy out by walking in God's love. Remember, what God has done for someone else, He can do for anyone who will believe. Don't be jealous or envious. Instead, rejoice, because we are all in the same line!

Read It! 1 Samuel 18:5-16

Speak It! "Father, forgive me for being so selfish and filled with envy and jealousy toward others. I am kicking these evil twins out of my life today, and I ask You to bless, encourage, increase, favor, anoint, use, open doors for and promote them. In Jesus' Name. Amen."

286

DAY 277

(high praises)

"Let the high praises of God be in their mouth,
and a two-edged sword in their hand."
Psalm 149:6

What a great combo...the high praises of God in our mouths and a two-edged sword of His Word in our hand. If you need to feel empowered today, this is the way to do it. This psalm is one of triumph, a prediction of victory over enemies and a great source of encouragement if you're facing any type of battle. My *PC Study Bible* commentary notes, *Barnes' Notes,* gives a bit more insight:

- **"Let the high praises of God be in their mouth..."** "In the very work of executing the purposes of God on his enemies, there should be the feeling and the language of praise. Their hearts should be full of confidence in God; they should feel that they are engaged in his service; and while they defend themselves, or inflict punishment on the enemies of God, they should chant His praise. ... Perhaps the Hebrew word rendered 'high praises' may imply more than mere praise. It may embrace anything that is lofty and exalted, and may mean here that they would have the consciousness that they were engaged in high and lofty aims; that they were carrying out the great designs of God; that they were executing purposes more momentous than their own could be—even the eternal purposes of the Most High. This would give an importance, a dignity, an elevation to their conduct which could spring from no other source."

So, get your praise on! There is NO God like our God! Everything about His purposes and His specific purpose for your life is high, lofty and dignified and deserves nothing less than your highest praise! If you need some inspiration to jump-start your praise life, the Lord has raised up some great worship teams to lead God's people into the high praises.

- **"...and a two-edged sword in their hand."** "This represents a literal sword—a sword made for piercing, as well as striking." Spiritually, we know this represents the Word of God. The living active Word of God pierces and strikes! In addition to reading your own Bible, if you need some ammunition; God has raised up many preachers and teachers of the Word to help equip you! The list of anointed, faith-filled preachers is too large to even begin a list; but if you need a booster shot for your faith, first, listen to your pastor and as needed, find Word-loaded teachers and soak up their messages until your heart is filled with the Word.

Start lifting up the praises of God with your mouth and wielding the sword of the Word. What God has spoken in His Word and His spoken "rhema," word to you, He will perform!

Read It! Psalm 149 (yes, the whole thing!)

Speak It! "Father, I am going to get the high praises in my mouth and the two-edged sword of the Word of God in my hand! Thank You for leading me in triumph and victory over all the works of the enemy in my life. In Jesus' Name. Amen."

DAY 278

(slammed)

"Heaven and earth will pass away, but My words will never pass away."
Matthew 24:35, NIV

Ever caught any flack for believing the Bible? Is it because Christian leaders haven't done a good job of esteeming the Word, and so many church-goers don't really believe it like they should? Is it because it's programmed in our DNA to be rebellious, and people don't want to submit to anyone or anything—much less a book written 2,000 years ago? Is it because when the light of God's Word shines on the dark areas of our lives, people get uncomfortable, sometimes combative? When someone's only reference point is human knowledge, rather than revelation knowledge, they often resort to insults or arguments in an attempt to diss those who believe God's Word. When we take some heat for believing the Bible, we can be encouraged. God gave us some good advice in His Word. Take a minute to read the **Read It!** segment.

So, is the Bible still relevant? Is it naïve to believe the Bible these days? Jesus said His Word would never pass away *(Matthew 24:35).* That's enough evidence to settle the relevancy question. However, He has given us even more proof.

For those who like to study the historic, archeological and scientific proofs regarding the authenticity and infallibility of the Bible, I recommend: *The Case for Faith* and *The Case for Christ* by Lee Strobel; *Mere Christianity* by C.S. Lewis and *Evidence That Demands a Verdict* by Josh McDowell. All of these scholarly books give great details on the inerrant Word of God.

But, for those looking for something beyond the academic approach, there is a better proof for the truth of the Bible—a changed life! Knowing Jesus and living by God's Word changes a person's life. Millions will testify that when they finally decided to live by the Word, it absolutely, unequivocally filled their heart with great joy and changed their life for the better! *(Jeremiah 15:16)* How can you dispute a changed life? You can't. The proof for the Bible's relevancy is in the pudding—the evidence is the fruit.

If you've been catching some flack for being a Jesus-loving, Bible-thumper, just smile. Be gracious to your critics, walk your talk and rejoice that you are in good company!

Read It! Colossians 2:8, NLT and MSG (Read it in both translations!)

Speak It! "Father, I believe You. I believe the Bible is still relevant. My life has been changed through knowing Jesus and living by Your Word. No matter what the critics say, Your Word is true and a joy to my heart. Lord, I pray for those who criticize me and Your Word, I pray You will open the eyes of the hearts of those who don't know what they don't know (name them: _____). In Jesus' Name. Amen."

DAY 279

(99 bottles of beer on the wall)

"Leaders can't afford to make fools of themselves, gulping wine and swilling beer, lest, hung over, they don't know right from wrong, and the people who depend on them are hurt."
Proverbs 31:4-6, MSG

So, should a Christian drink alcohol? Is there anything wrong with a beer, wine or a martini? In this party culture, we're asked that question a lot. Several years ago, playing Bunco with some girls, one of the gals asked me, "What do you believe about drinking?" Suddenly, the room got very quiet and every eye in that margarita-laden room was fixed on me, awaiting my response. I told her it was quite the loaded question, but three things made sense to me:

- **The real issue.** God seems to be more concerned with drunkenness, than drinking. It's my personal opinion and experience that very few people have the self-control to drink and not get drunk. Back in my drinking days, the goal *was* to get blasted. Today, we know many people who have a drinking problem, but would deny it vehemently. Clearly, they think they have self-control, but actually the alcohol is controlling them.

- **Real versus counterfeit.** The Bible actually tells us that drinking is a counterfeit. God said not to drunk with wine, but to be filled with the Spirit (Ephesians 5:18). Being "filled with the Spirit" is God's idea of getting loaded! Getting drunk on alcohol is a counterfeit, because God has something better. The Lord knew we needed a little "intoxication" to get through this life; and when we are "under the influence" of the Spirit, we get all the benefits of being intoxicated: relaxed, carefree, uninhibited and bold—all without the adverse side effects of hangovers and regrets.

- **Not for leaders.** While it may be okay for a Believer to have a beer or a glass of wine as long as they don't get drunk, the Bible said it wasn't for kings—leaders—to drink, since they are held to a higher standard and set an example for people to follow. They need to be sober-minded at all times in order to help others in a time of need or crisis. Jesus, our example in leadership, turned water in wine and ministered to drunks, gluttons, prostitutes and lost people every day; but there is no record that He ever drank with them to be more relatable. As leaders, what kind of example are we setting for those who truly have a drinking problem? If someone is trying to overcome drinking, how are they supposed to get set free from that addiction when their leaders are doing the same? Leaders can't afford to be a stumbling block to others or cheapen their witness for Christ.

If you're unsure or haven't settled this issue in your own heart, why not pray and ask the Lord about it?

Read It! Proverbs 20:1, KJV

Speak It! "Father, I seek Your direction on this topic in my life. In Jesus' Name. Amen."

DAY 280

(God is God)

"The LORD is in His holy temple; the LORD is on His heavenly throne.
He observes the sons of men; His eyes examine them."
Psalm 11:4, NIV

God is God. He is on His Throne. God is God, and most of the eternal fruit that happens in and through our lives has very little to do with us. Be encouraged by this truth.

Have you ever interviewed for a job and thought you totally bombed it, only to be offered that job the very next day? Have you ever sang what you thought was an Grammy award-winning song, only to find out people thought you sounded flat? Have you ever tried to encourage someone else and felt like your words were hollow and empty, only to discover that something you said turned out to be their key to victory? Have you ever tried to make a sale and thought your pitch was worthy of a signed order, only to find out your potential customer went with your competitor? Have you ever preached a message that was so boring, even you couldn't wait until you were done, only to find people raving about it?

When we give God our best effort, song, encouragement, pitch, sermon, article, design or idea, He is still God. When we feel like it was our worst performance, concert, advice, sales call, speech, project or suggestion, He is still God.

Bottom line: God is God.

We've seen it time and again. It never fails; when we think a church service was a total train wreck—crazy audio issues, funky lights, flat worship and a disjointed message—people seem to have these life-changing, Jesus-visitation encounters! On the other hand, when we think a church service has been amazing and everything worked like clockwork, people seem just ho-hum about it. We figure that's God way of reminding us that it's not about us, our great works or our great failures—it's about Him!

If you've failed in a big way or had what looks like grand success; remember, God is God...thank God!

Read It! 1 Chronicles 29:11, NLT

Speak It! "Father, I am so glad You are God. I am thankful the universe doesn't depend on my good days or bad days. The world is held together by Your Word. You are on Your throne, and I am going to rest in that today. In Jesus' Name. Amen."

DAY 281

(pray for leaders)

"I urge, then, first of all, that requests, prayers, intercession and thanksgiving be made for everyone-for kings and all those in authority, that we may live peaceful and quiet lives in all godliness and holiness."
1 Timothy 2:1-2, NIV

The whole world seems to be in a pivotal time. Every nation needs prayer. The best way to pray for the world is to pray for its leaders—not only the current leaders, but the future leaders: spiritual leaders, business leaders, media leaders and, most certainly, political leaders. Let's pray for God's hand to raise up divinely-appointed leaders for every sphere of life. Let's pray now for the next season and the next generation of leaders.

Who does the Lord want in power around the world? In our own country? State? Territory? Province? Cities? Villages? Let's pray and seek Him on these very things! How should we pray? The Bible gives us some help on how to pray...

- **Pray for the leaders called to God's purposes for such a time as this.** We may or may not know their names, but the Lord does. Pray that these people would be strengthened in their inner man and that they would be strong in the Lord and the power of His might. Pray that no weapon formed against them would prosper and every tongue that rises in judgment against them would be put down. Pray for the anointing of the Lord to be strong on and in them.

- **Pray for God's divine protection, favor and witty-ideas.** The Lord knows how to raise up one and put another down. Promotion doesn't come from the east or the west; promotion comes from the Lord. Ask the Lord for divine angelic protection and pray that the Lord speaks to them in the midnight hour to give them divine strategies, favor and witty-ideas for their role as a leader.

- **Pray for God's wisdom to flow in and through them:** Ask God to give them the spirit of wisdom and revelation in the knowledge they need. Pray that their mind and heart is clear and uncluttered and able to receive God's wisdom, direction and guidance. Pray that they lead and govern in such a way that their followers are able to lead quiet and peaceable lives in all godliness and holiness. Pray for them to have courage and boldness and ask the Lord to give them wisdom that their adversaries cannot refute.

If the Lord puts particular people on your heart; then pray for them and follow the Holy Spirit's unction. Let's get ahead of the prayer curve in this season and pray for those in authority.

Read It! James 5:16, AMP

Speak It! "Father, I pray You continue to raise up leaders for Your purposes. Anoint them in every way, in every relationships and in every environment. I pray You protect and surround them with favor and wisdom. In Jesus' Name. Amen."

DAY 282

(single...and not loving it?)

*"Search from the book of the LORD, and read: not one of these shall fail;
not one shall lack her mate. For My mouth has commanded it,
and His Spirit has gathered them."*
Isaiah 34:16

If you're single and not loving it... If you're single, and the desire of your heart is to get married... If you're single and want some encouragement on how to believe God for the mate of His choosing, be encouraged.

When I was single and really desiring to get married and meet the person God had for me, I was inspired by the passage above in Isaiah 34 and made it a part of my prayer life. You can, too!

- *"Search from the book of the Lord..."* Get into the Word and let the Lord talk to your heart from the Scriptures about your mate. You'll find prayers you can pray and verses you can stand on and believe for. Search the Book and see what the Lord says. *(Psalm 119:105, KJV)*

- *"...not one shall lack his or her mate..."* If the desire of your heart is to be married and have a mate, God will honor that. If we delight ourselves in the Lord, He will give us the desires of our hearts. Rest in the fact that as you keep the Lord as your first love, He will make sure you don't lack the desires of your heart. *(Psalm 37:4, NIV)*

- *"...My mouth has commanded it..."* God is not a man that He should lie—if He said it, He'll do it! When God commands something you can count on it. *(Numbers 23:19)*

- *"...His Spirit has gathered them."* Trust the Lord that, by His Spirit, He is gathering you to your mate; and He is gathering your mate to you. He will order your steps, and you will be in the right place at the right time. God knew how to bring Eve to Adam, and He can surely bring your mate to you. *(Psalm 37:23, NLT)*

A God-ordained marriage is a true blessing. When we patiently wait for the mate the Lord has for us and allow Him to gather us together, we will enjoy His best plan for marriage and all that goes with it. For now, until you are "gathered" to your mate, search the Book and invest your time in praying the Word for your future spouse and marriage. None shall lack his or her mate!

Read It! Genesis 2:18-24, NLT

Speak It! "Father, I thank You that as I delight myself in You—You will give me the desires of my heart. I desire a mate. I will search Your Book to find scriptures that apply to my future spouse. I am thankful that none shall lack his or her mate; Your mouth has spoken it and I believe it. I know and trust that by Your Spirit You will gather me to my spouse. I thank You now, in advance, for a marriage made in heaven! In Jesus' Name. Amen."

DAY 283

(pump it up)

"For physical training is of some value (useful for a little), but godliness (spiritual training) is useful and of value in everything and in every way, for it holds promise for the present life and also for the life which is to come."
1 Timothy 4:8, AMP

OK, so is it time again? You know,...to get back into the workout routine? Eat more than Milk Duds® and Sonic® lime-aids for lunch? Jump on the treadmill? Lift some weights? Is it time to get up early and work out? It is.

Physical training is of some value—useful for a little. A training routine gives us a better quality of life while we are on earth; but once we leave our bodies and head to heaven, the physical realm has no more value. So, in the short run, physical training gives us a little profit.

Sure, working out gives us more energy, better fitness and added strength. We seem to have a better disposition and outlook on the day when we get to work out—especially when we invite the Lord to join us. It helps to center our hearts and minds with the Lord.

Godliness and spiritual training are useful and of value in everything and in every way! Pursuing spiritual disciplines benefit us in this present life and in the life to come. When we purpose to seek the Lord and do the hard work of "praying through" and exercise diligence in studying His Word, we get huge benefits. His presence and His Word are eternal, and the revelation knowledge He gives us will profit us in this life and in the life to come.

What is your training plan for the next month? Three months? Six months? Year? Five years? How will you work some physical training into your schedule? Where do spiritual disciplines fit in your daily regiment? It might be difficult to be in a regimented workout routine during vacation times or holidays, but when life is normal, let's be sure to get serious about physical—and godly—training.

Read It! 1 Corinthians 9:24, NLT

Speak It! "Father, I ask You for Your wisdom and assistance as I put together my monthly, weekly and daily routines. I want to have regular times for working out and for engaging in spiritual training. I ask You for grace to help me do it. In Jesus' Name, Amen."

DAY 284

(rescued)

"Christ has rescued us..."
Galatians 3:13, NLT

Ever seen a movie on the IMAX? Wow! What a difference the big screen and honkin' subwoofers make! Yeah, it's impressive, but not as impressive as God's eternal, big-time production. There's no superhero, special effect or action film like the all-time, award-winning classic: "Rescued!" starring: Jesus! Do you remember your life without Christ? Let's rewind the "Rescued" movie...

- **Scene 1:** We were deceived. We sinned. We got slammed. Our sin separated us from God, and we became slaves, yoked to a Joker—the harsh taskmaster. We were promised freedom and satisfaction through the pleasures of sin...only to discover that every temptation was a baited lure.

- **Scene 2:** We never got free. The wages of sin was death. So, we just despaired. We learned to live with emptiness. We expected fear, anger and depression. We tried religion, but it just made things worse.

- **Scene 3:** Our hearts were darkened and, like little marionettes, we marched to the beat of the god of this world, pretending to be happy, but really...we had no hope of eternal life—only guilt, remorse, shame. We had no hope for true love, real joy, lasting peace—only rejection, disappointment and agitation. We were doomed and didn't know there was any other option...UNTIL...

(SET CHANGE AND LOUD SUBWOOFING SURROUND SOUND...)

- **Scene 4:** Jesus Christ came to rescue us...to redeem us...to open the prison door!

- **Finale:** Christ HAS redeemed us from the curse of the Law. He is the only Redeemer authorized to set us completely free, now and forevermore! He rescued us!

- **Grand Finale:** On the horizon...when Jesus returns for the Redeemed and we live forever with Him as King of kings and Lord of lords!

Have you been rescued? Redeemed? The Bible says, "Let the redeemed of the Lord say so...," so, let's do it!

Read It! Isaiah 53

Speak It! "Jesus, thank You for rescuing me! You have redeemed me spirit, soul and body. Whoever You set free is free indeed! I say it! I am redeemed from sin and death to life eternal! I am redeemed from poverty and lack to abundance and prosperity. I am redeemed from sickness and disease to wholeness and health. I am redeemed from rejection and emptiness to love and peace. Help me to walk in all that redemption includes to a greater degree. I am Yours and You are my Redeemer! Thank You so much for setting me free. In Jesus' Name. Amen."

DAY 285

(we blinked)

"And the Child grew and became strong in spirit,
filled with wisdom; and the grace of God was upon Him."
Luke 2:40

There was time in my life where I couldn't listen to Martina McBride's "In My Daughters Eyes" or Steven Curtis Chapman's "Cinderella" song without becoming a boo-hoo mess—especially on the day we took our oldest child, Annie, to college. Talk about bittersweet! It was the day we had prepared for—and dreaded—for almost 18 years.

We blinked and she grew up.

No one hands us an Owner's Manual when our children are born, do they? We just have to trust God and figure it out as we go. As parents, there are many things we've done wrong, but one thing we did right was help our kids come to know Jesus, personally, for themselves. As pastors' kids (better known as "PK's"), we've tried to make it clear to them that they were not under any pressure to be perfect—and neither was God requiring perfection.

Of course, our kids have not been perfect—neither has anyone else's! And neither have we! But, to see their walk with God makes it all worth it! Not only do we love our kids and the people they are becoming, we even like them! There is a great sense of peace in knowing that they are in a good place with God; that, indeed, they are growing and becoming strong in their spirits; they are being filled with wisdom, and they are being empowered by the grace of God that is upon them.

Letting one of those "babies" fly away from the nest is not easy! But, be encouraged. They are in God's hands. Continue to trust the Lord and put Him and His priorities first. He is faithful to reward our efforts—and our kids—with growth, strength, wisdom and grace.

Read It! Luke 2:40

Speak It! "Father, I lift up these children to You _____ (name your kids or children you know) and I ask You to help them to grow and become strong in spirit. I pray You fill them with Your wisdom. I ask You to pour Your grace out upon them—anoint them, empower them and strengthen them to live a life that pleases You. Help them to become independently, dependent upon You, Lord. In Jesus' Name. Amen."

DAY 286

(God's health care)

"Those who are planted in the house of the LORD shall flourish in the
courts of our God. They shall still bear fruit in old age; they shall be fresh
and flourishing..."
Psalm 92:13-14

God has a health care plan that surpasses anything man can come up with. He offers health care that covers the natural and the supernatural. In the natural, we know the Lord gives insight, discovery, innovation and inventions to scientists, researchers and doctors to provide the best possible health care for humanity. In the supernatural, we know Jesus is the same today, as He was when He walked this earth. He still heals those who are sick or oppressed by the devil. He is the Great Physician. Here are a few of the benefits He offers and the conditions for receiving His coverage:

- **Health and healing.** *"If you will diligently hearken to the voice of the Lord your God and will do what is right in His sight, and will listen to and obey His commandments and keep all His statutes, I will put none of the diseases upon you which I brought upon the Egyptians, for I am the Lord Who heals you." (Exodus 15:26, AMP) "You shall serve the Lord your God; He shall bless your bread and water, and I will take sickness from your midst." (Exodus 23:25, AMP) "Praise the LORD, O my soul, and forget not all his benefits—who forgives all your sins and heals all your diseases..." (Psalm 103:2-3, NIV)*

- **Long life and prosperity.** *"My son, do not forget my teaching, but keep my commands in your heart, for they will prolong your life many years and bring you prosperity." (Proverbs 3:1-2, NIV) "Because he loves me, says the LORD, I will rescue him; I will protect him, for he acknowledges my name. He will call upon me, and I will answer him; I will be with him in trouble, I will deliver him and honor him. With long life will I satisfy him and show him my salvation." (Psalm 91:14-16, NIV)*

- **Eternal life.** *"In order that everyone who believes in Him [who cleaves to Him, trusts Him, and relies on Him] may not perish, but have eternal life and [actually] live forever! For God so greatly loved and dearly prized the world that He [even] gave up His only begotten (unique) Son, so that whoever believes in (trusts in, clings to, relies on) Him shall not perish (come to destruction, be lost) but have eternal (everlasting) life." (John 3:15-16, AMP) "And this is the testimony: God has given us eternal life, and this life is in his Son. He who has the Son has life; he who does not have the Son of God does not have life. I write these things to you who believe in the name of the Son of God so that you may know that you have eternal life." (1 John 5:11-13, NIV)*

Read It! Psalm 103:1-5

Speak It! "Father, I thank You for Your health care plan that costs me nothing, but cost Jesus everything. Help me to appropriate all of the benefits You have so generously provided. In Jesus' Name. Amen."

DAY 287

(go!)

"Then I heard the Lord asking, 'Whom should I send as a messenger to my people? Who will go for us?' And I said, 'Lord, I'll go! Send me.'"
Isaiah 6:8, NLT

I was a junior in college, eager to graduate from Boston University. That's when God challenged me. I attended Campus Crusade's Christmas conference, and one of the guest speakers challenged those of us who were juniors to take one year off from college to go on the mission field. The program was called "Stop Out," and the mission field was Guam. He talked about the lost condition of the world and the eternal difference we could make by focusing on missions work for one year.

Immediately, I said to myself, "No way." Then, I heard the Lord speaking to my heart: "Will you go?" I wrestled with the Lord, telling Him all the reasons I couldn't take a year and "stop out" of college. I never heard another word the guest speaker said because I was arguing with the Lord. After the speaker's session, I went to my hotel room mad, frustrated and feeling guilty. I spent the rest of the afternoon talking to the Lord and trying to convince Him that He really should ask someone else to go to Guam. I was so close to getting my degree, and it just wasn't a convenient time for me to go into missionary work. Interestingly, the only words the Lord ever said to me were, "Will you go?" (I've learned that the Lord doesn't argue.)

Finally, I said, "OK, fine. Lord, if You want me to drop out of college for a year and go to Guam, I'll go. It's not what I want to do; but if it's what You want me to do, I'll do it." I felt some relief and was trying to figure out how to tell my parents I was moving to Guam. That's when I felt like the Lord spoke to my heart and said, "OK, good. You don't have to go to Guam. I just wanted to see if you were willing." As it turned out, I didn't go to Guam; but I did pass the "willingness" test.

How about you? Has the Lord asked you to be His messenger? Can you say, "Here am I, send me"? One thing I've learned as I've served the Lord is that the best place on earth is in the center of His will! The issue is: willingness!

Many friends of ours, whom we respect greatly, have answered the call to go around the world with the Gospel. They have a real passion for the Lord and are willing to be His messengers wherever He sends them. But, God is still asking the question, "Who shall I send as a messenger?" Are you willing to go?

Read It! Mark 16:15, NLT

Speak It! "Father, here am I; send me. I'll go where You want me to go. I'll do what You want me to do. I'll say what You want me to say. In Jesus' Name. Amen."

DAY 288

(the whole city!)

"On the next Sabbath almost the whole city came
together to hear the word of God."
Acts 13:44

So, imagine the world's stadiums packed with people hungry to hear the Word of God! If 61,500 people can show up to Solider Field to watch the Chicago Bears play football, I wonder if we can expect a whole city—or more—to come worship Jesus and hear His Word? I know it will happen one day—when every knee bows and every tongue confesses that Jesus is Lord *(Romans 14:11)*. But, could it happen before then? Is a day coming when multiplied thousands of people are so hungry for the living God that they pack stadiums to hear the Word of the Lord?

When people get desperate enough to hear from heaven, they will go anywhere to hear the Word of God. I think we are coming into that season. The world is growing darker and darker, and people are searching for hope. When churches of all denominations lift up the Name of Jesus, hear from Heaven and preach a "now" word from the throne of grace, they will be an oasis in a desperate world without answers.

We can learn something from a prophetic passage in the Word about Jerusalem that speaks to the days we are living in, as well. God predicted it long ago. A dark day is coming to the earth, but the glory of the Lord will arise on His people and those in darkness will run to the light! *(Isaiah 60:2)*

Read It! Isaiah 60:2-3, NIV

Speak It! "Father, I pray for the day when whole cities come to hear the Word of God. I thank You for continuing to build Your Church around the world. I pray You strengthen pastors, raise up leaders, build buildings and continue to draw people to Jesus and Your Word. In Jesus' Name. Amen."

DAY 289

(the church I see)

"When they said, 'Let's go to the house of God,' my heart leaped for joy. "
Psalm 122:1, MSG

Jesus is the Light of the World and He is shining through His Body—the Church! I love the inspiring word Pastor Brian Houston from Hillsong Church in Sydney, Australia delivered several years ago. It's his vision for his church, but I believe it's also God's vision for the Church of the living God. Let your heart ponder these words today:

The Church I See

The Church that I see is a Church of influence. A Church so large in size that the city and nation cannot ignore it. A Church growing so quickly that buildings struggle to contain the increase.

I see a Church whose heartfelt praise and worship touches heaven and changes earth; worship which influences the praises of people throughout the earth, exalting Christ with powerful songs of faith and hope. I see a Church whose altars are constantly filled with repentant sinners responding to Christ's call to salvation.

Yes, the Church that I see is so dependent on the Holy Spirit that nothing will stop it nor stand against it; a Church whose people are unified, praying and full of God's Spirit. The Church that I see has a message so clear that lives are changed forever and potential is fulfilled through the power of His Word; a message beamed to the peoples of the earth through their television screens.

I see a Church so compassionate that people are drawn from impossible situations into a loving and friendly circle of hope, where answers are found and acceptance is given. I see a people so kingdom-minded that they will count whatever the cost and pay whatever the price to see revival sweep this land.

The Church that I see is a Church so committed to raising, training and empowering a leadership generation to reap the end-time harvest that all its ministries are consumed with this goal. I see a Church whose head is Jesus, whose help is the Holy Spirit and whose focus is the Great Commission.

Yes, the church that I see could well be our church, and it could well be your church.

-Brian Houston, Senior Pastor
Hillsong, Sydney, Australia

Read It! Matthew 16:18

Speak It! "Father, help me to see the Church that You see. In Jesus Name. Amen."

DAY 290

(who's your daddy?)

"And I will be your Father, and you will be My
sons and daughters, says the Lord Almighty."
2 Corinthians 6:18, NLT

Everyone needs a dad—that's how we're wired. We all need a father who will provide for us, throw is arms around us, give us assurance, confidence, tell us that he's proud of us and love us unconditionally. Thankfully, we have such a father—our Heavenly Father.

If you were fortunate to have a great earthly father, you are blessed. If you were not so blessed to have had a good earthly father, or if your father died when you were young, you may long for a father. If your father was non-existent, abusive or self-absorbed, you probably have a hard time connecting the dots of God as a good Father. But, God is our loving, Heavenly Father who wants to reveal Himself to us. This is what the Word says about a good Father, in particular, our Heavenly Father. A good father...

- **Pours His love on us.** God doesn't keep His love a secret. *(1 John 3:1, NIV)*
- **Knows what His kids need.** God knows what we need, because He's paying attention to our lives. *(Matthew 6:8-9, NLT)*
- **Is a "more than enough" giver.** God is generous and giving. He gives more than enough in every way. *(Matthew 7:11, NLT)*
- **Is compassionate and full of mercy.** God is the God of all mercies. *(Luke 6:36, NLT)*
- **Longs for His kids.** God isn't satisfied to be separate from His children; He's watching and ready to love and embrace His kids. *(Luke 15:20-21, NLT)*
- **Is comforting.** God pours out comfort and mercy when we are facing troubles. *(2 Corinthians 1:3-4, NLT)*
- **Gives good gifts to His kids.** God is not stingy or cheap; He's a Father who pours out all kinds of good gifts. *(James 1:17, NIV)*
- **Wants to spend time with His kids.** God enjoys our fellowship. *(1 John 1:3-4, NIV)*
- **Tells His kids He's proud of them.** God lets us know He's pleased with us. *(Matthew 3:17, NLT)*

Today, ask the Father to reveal Himself to you in a greater way.

Read It! Romans 8:15, KJV

Speak It! "Father, I want to know You and Your love in a fresh way. You are my Father and I am Your child. I know You are a good, 'more than enough' type of Father. I pray You reveal Yourself to me as my Father in a greater way. In Jesus' Name. Amen."

DAY 291

(taking a flying leap)

"Jesus was matter-of-fact: 'Embrace this God-life. Really embrace it, and nothing will be too much for you. This mountain, for instance: Just say, "Go jump in the lake"—no shuffling or shilly-shallying—and it's as good as done.'"
Mark 11:22-23, MSG

Faith is a leap. It's not a blind leap...but it is a leap. Faith is taking God at His Word. It's letting go of the trapeze bar and trusting the Lord will catch you. It's getting out of the boat and believing God will enable you to walk on water. It's jumping out of the natural realm of the five physical senses and into the realm of the spiritual reality of God's Word.

Have you taken a flying leap lately? Have you jumped out on God's Word? When we take God at His Word, He has authorized us to speak words of faith! Not only can we take a leap of faith, we can "tell things" to take a flying leap.

Have you told the mountains in your life to "jump in the lake"? Jesus said we could! When we embrace the God-life—and all that goes with it—He empowers us with His authority and nothing is impossible.

Today, make a decision to take a flying leap of faith—on the authority of His Word—and tell those mountains in your life to jump in the lake, too!

Read It! Matthew 17:20, KJV

Speak It! "Father, I believe You! I embrace Your God-life and I choose to live the 'faith leaping' kind of life. Thank You for authorizing me to tell the mountains in my life to jump into the lake. With You, nothing is impossible. In Jesus' Name. Amen."

DAY 292

(the steeple and creative people)

"Look, I have chosen Bezalel son of Uri, grandson of Hur, of the tribe of Judah. I have filled him with the Spirit of God, giving him great wisdom, intelligence, and skill in all kinds of crafts. He is able to create beautiful objects from gold, silver, and bronze. He is skilled in cutting and setting gemstones and in carving wood. Yes, he is a master at every craft! And I have appointed Oholiab son of Ahisamach, of the tribe of Dan, to be his assistant. Moreover, I have given special skill to all the naturally talented craftsmen so they can make all the things I have instructed you to make."
Exodus 31:1-6, NLT

God calls artsy people to do incredible things! Isn't that great?

In this story, the Lord had called Moses to lead His people, and He had given him a divine blueprint for getting God's plan done. The problem was that Moses couldn't do it by himself. He needed help! God specifically called and anointed two creative people—Bezalel and Oholiab—to help Moses. It was their job to use the creative skills God gave them to breathe life into the vision God had given Moses.

I have no doubt God is still calling "Bezalels" and "Oholiabs" to help "Moses"-types further His plans! We have a lot of creative people on our staff, and they are fun to be around! Recently, I was talking with one of the gals on our staff who serves in the design/set design and lighting areas of ministry. She is definitely called to be an "Oholiab." She is very creative and it's her passion to use her gifts to help us and our church in advancing the kingdom of God. It's evident that God has anointed her to do so and her gifts are a huge blessing to thousands of people!

I wonder how many other "Bezalels" and "Oholiabs" are out there? We are in an era where people in the Church seem more open to the creative expressions of God and the power of the arts than ever before. There is no reason the Church shouldn't be absolutely loaded with creative gifts—artists, writers, painters, musicians, singers, video editors, directors, producers, set designers, graphic artists, lighting designers, web designers, upholsterers, woodworkers, craftsman and metal workers. Hollywood, Broadway, Disney® or Ikea® shouldn't have anything on the Church!

Read It! Exodus 35:35, NLT

Speak It! "Father, I thank You for anointing creative people to fulfill Your purposes. I pray that You continue to raise up 'Bezalels' and 'Oholiabs' to help advance Your Church and help them follow Your plans to maximizing their gifts. In Jesus' Name. Amen."

DAY 293

(creative juice)

"And the LORD God formed man of the dust of the ground, and breathed into his nostrils the breath of life; and man became a living soul."
Genesis 2:7, KJV

God, the Master Creator, formed Adam out of the dust of the ground. That same creative ability is on the inside of us. So, the question is: what are we going to do with it?

Do you have an artistic bent? Do words, songs, images, stories, colors and "out of the box" thoughts fill your mind and heart? It may be that the Lord has given you a special skill or aptitude to be like Bezalel or Oholiab, like we talked about yesterday.

What should a creative person do to utilize their gifts? Often, by their very nature, creative people struggle with structure and focus. This weakness can limit their effectiveness in maximizing the use of their creative gifts—thus the term: "starving artist" exists! If you've been anointed in the creative arts arena, here are some things that will help you harness those gifts and flourish:

- **Seek God's heart.** Keep your heart centered on the Lord. Seek first His kingdom, and He will give you all the things you need to succeed in your creative anointing.

- **Stay humble.** Sometimes, because you are so creative and see things differently and in such random and unusual ways, you can get frustrated with people who don't see things that way. In fact, you can get bugged by those who lean toward a more administrative or organizational bent. If you're not careful, you can get puffed up with pride and start to resent the organizational and strategic people sent to help you flourish.

- **Serve a "Moses."** It's very likely that God has gifted you to help a "Moses" fulfill a God-given vision. God gives the "Moses"-types the ability to see both sides of the coin—the creative side, as well as the administrative side. They are gifted to lead from a spiritual platform and through a strategic blueprint and game plan; they mobilize people to accomplish His purposes. A good "Moses" will bring the administrative/organizational people together with the creative artists to fulfill a God-ordained vision!

If God has anointed you with creative gifts, seek after God's heart, stay humble and serve a "Moses"—and then watch God multiply your creative gifts for His eternal purposes.

Read It! Genesis 1:1, KJV

Speak It! "Father, I thank You for anointing me with gifts and skills to use for Your kingdom. I ask you to continue to stir up the creative ideas in me and help me to relay them effectively to the Body. I make myself available to You to do Your and fulfill Your purpose. In Jesus' Name. Amen."

DAY 294

(you won't pop)

"Enlarge the place of your tent, and let them stretch out the curtains of your dwellings; do not spare; lengthen your cords, and strengthen your stakes. For you shall expand to the right and to the left."
Isaiah 54:2-3a

Have you ever blown up a balloon for the first time? That's always the hardest. Once it's been blown up and the air has been let out, it's easier to blow it up the next time. Have you ever blown up a balloon until it popped? All of these things describe the idea of "enlarging and expanding."

Sometimes, we are the balloon, and God is the One blowing us up to enlarge and expand us to our maximum capacity! When the Lord wants to take us to the next level of growth, impact or influence—He has to enlarge our capacity for EVERYTHING! He has to expand our capacity for stress and pressure; for dealing with multiple, simultaneous issues, problems, deadlines and challenges; for endurance, perseverance and not for popping!

The first time God begins to blow up our balloon to expand our capacity, it's hard. We feel stretched to the gills and almost as if we are going to blow a gasket! We wonder if we can take any more pressure. We can—because God is faithful, and He will never expect more of us than we are able to handle; although at times, it can feel that way. When the Lord starts to inflate our balloon, He's at work expanding our ability to do more, to handle more, to lead more, to fulfill more, to impact more and to influence more for His purposes. The Lord has to stretch us to the point of "almost" popping because He knows that, in real life, we'll never actually get to that point. We'll probably operate at an 80-90% level of our absolute full capacity or "popping" potential. But, once He's enlarged and expanded us to the 100% level over and over again, operating at 80-90% is a piece of cake!

So, how about you? Felt like the balloon lately? Have you sensed the Lord stretching you lately? Stretched to the gills? If so, be encouraged; He's preparing you for what He's prepared for you! You won't explode! You're heading into a season of greater impact and influence. He's enlarging your capacity for big things!

Read It! 1 Chronicles 4:10, AMP

Speak It! "Father, expand and enlarge my capacity! I know that I can do all things through Christ who strengthens me. I thank You for grace for the pace. I thank You that You will never give me more than I can handle, but You are preparing me for what You are preparing for me. I believe it and I trust You. In Jesus' Name. Amen."

DAY 295

(who's your source)

"Yet for us there is [only] one God, the Father, Who is the Source of all things and for Whom we [have life], and one Lord, Jesus Christ, through and by Whom are all things and through and by Whom we [ourselves exist]."
1 Corinthians 8:6, AMP

There is something liberating about making God our source. When we do this—it takes the pressure off all other relationships. When we look to the Lord to meet our needs—our eyes are on Him and our expectation is in Him.

Think about how freeing this is for us and others when we don't:

- **Get hurt when others don't live up to our expectations.**
- **Get offended when someone doesn't meet a need we have.**
- **Put unrealistic pressure on others.**
- **Lay guilt trips on people for not measuring up.**
- **Manipulate relationships to accommodate our needs.**
- **Become bitter or resentful because of what people did or didn't do.**
- **Get angry at people for being insensitive, uncaring or disinterested.**
- **Have to go without when people don't live up to our expectations; we can expect the Lord to meet all of our needs according to His resources in Christ.**

If you think about it, it's really not fair to expect others to meet the needs we have. No other human being has the spiritual, emotional, mental, financial or physical resources to be our source. Besides, what if those we are placing demands on are going through their own personal challenge, and they need help? What if they need from us the very things we need from them—a word, encouragement, a hug, help, finances or prayer? It's a cycle of unmet needs and disappointment. However, when we love people without expecting anything in return and without making them our source, we get to see the Lord go to work as our source. We get to experience true freedom! And...guess what? The Lord is able to do exceedingly and abundantly above and beyond all that we could ask or think! When we make the Lord our source; we free people up—and by faith, we get to watch the Lord meet our needs and exceed our expectations in a personal, customized and godly way.

Read It! Philippians 4:19

Speak It! "Father, I have made my spouse, my family, my friends, my pastor, my boss or _____ (fill in the blank) my source, and I realize I have set people up for failure and myself up for disappointment. Forgive me for expecting people to do and be what only You can do and be for me. You are the source of my life. My expectation is in You! In Jesus' Name. Amen."

DAY 296

(be the enforcer)

"And the God of peace will crush Satan under your feet shortly.
The grace of our Lord Jesus Christ be with you. Amen."
Romans 16:20

Newsflash: Satan is defeated!

Today, be encouraged to enforce Satan's defeat in your life. Jesus completely whipped the enemy and made an open show of him by triumphing over him on the cross. When Jesus went to the cross, the devil thought he'd won a mighty victory; he thought he had killed the Lord of Glory—the Redeemer and only hope for the salvation of mankind. Hell was rejoicing...for a few days.

Can you imagine Satan's surprise when hell began to tremble and the power of the Holy Ghost quickened Jesus' mortal body, and He was raised from the dead? That's when God got the last laugh!

One day, there will be a grand finale, and Satan and his evil hosts will be judged and cast into the Lake of Fire for eternity! Until that time, we have been given authority to enforce Satan's defeat, to rule and reign in this life. Jesus has given us the armor of God, the Name of Jesus, the Word of God, the blood of Jesus and the mighty power of the Holy Ghost!

We don't have to fight the devil; Jesus already did—and won! We have to fight the fight of faith by appropriating God's Word, enforcing Satan's defeat and laying hold of all that belongs to us in Christ.

Be strong in the Lord, today. Be the enforcer, in Jesus' Name.

Read It! Colossians 2:15, NLT

Speak It! "Father, I thank You for the victory You have given me in Christ. You have made me more than a conqueror. Today, I appropriate Your Word, the Name of Jesus, the blood of Jesus and the power of the Holy Ghost to enforce Satan's defeat in my life. Jesus is the Lord of my life, my family, my body, my finances, my mind, my time and my destiny. Lord, be exalted in my life today. In Jesus' Name. Amen."

DAY 297

(c'mon, get happy)

"God blesses those who are persecuted because they live for God, for the Kingdom of Heaven is theirs. God blesses you when you are mocked and persecuted and lied about because you are My followers. Be happy about it! Be very glad! For a great reward awaits you in heaven. And remember, the ancient prophets were persecuted, too."
Matthew 5:10-12, NLT

When people persecute and hate you because of your faith, what should you do? When people mock, lie and twist the truth about you because you follow Jesus, how do you respond?

Unfortunately, there will always be people in the world with the negative, anti-Christ disposition. Jesus predicted it. He said if people in the world don't accept Him, they won't accept His followers. Jesus made it clear that those who hate Believers...hated Jesus first. Those who listen to Jesus...will listen to those who follow Jesus. Those who don't know God...will hate those who do know God. It's that basic.

So, what's a Christian to do when family, friends, co-workers, neighbors or complete strangers—those who don't know God—hate you? Say evil things about you? Exclude you? Mock or curse you? Two things:

- **Be happy about it!** God will bless you, and there is a great reward awaiting you in heaven.
- **Keep teaching and preaching.** Keep spreading the message of Jesus as Savior, Lord, Healer, Redeemer and Soon Coming King!

Our primary example is Jesus. In spite of the spiritual attitudes of some people, the Bible says He was still moved with compassion and went about the towns and villages healing all the people. *(Matthew 9:35-38, NIV)*

Listen, we can't afford to pay any attention to the world—the misled, ungrateful, antagonistic, nay-saying, mocking, lying, hating, persecutors. We have to keep going after the plentiful harvest of those who do have ears to hear the good news about Jesus Christ! Now, that's something to get happy about!

Read It! John 15:18-22, NLT

Speak It! "Father, I'm thankful for the great reward that awaits me in heaven for the persecution, hatred, mockery, criticism and lies that have been thrown against me. While those who don't know You may hate me because of my faith in Jesus, help me to keep a tender heart toward the plentiful harvest of people who are lost and helpless and longing to know You. In Jesus' Name. Amen."

DAY 298

(this is a test; this is only a test)

"My brethren, count it all joy when you fall into various trials, knowing that the testing of your faith produces patience. But let patience have its perfect work, that you may be perfect and complete, lacking nothing."
James 1:2-4

My husband and I and four other couples spent a week riding motorcycles in the Smokey Mountains of North Carolina. We rode the infamous "Tail of the Dragon" with 318 tight turns within 11 miles. Talk about a faith test! All of us girl bikers were a little "iffy" on taking on the challenge—especially me! I'm a newbie, and I faced a serious test the morning when I got to the starting point.

I had no choice. I "fell" into a trial, and had to "count," "know" and "let" instantly! That day, we rode the "dragon" and then spent the next three hours riding in the mountains in pelting rain, wind, fog and 9% inclines and declines. I had to "count" this challenge as a joy, "knowing" the test would produce good things. Instead of bailing on the ride, I had to "let" patience have its perfect work! Man, oh man... I was "counting" on the exhilaration I knew we would all feel once we had tamed the dragon! I was "knowing" the test of 318 turns would produce new skills and confidence in me. I was "letting" patience work as I prayed, sang to the Lord, prayed some more, paid attention to the road, followed my leaders...and kissed the ground when we got back to camp. In the end, I was "lacking nothing"—and got the t-shirt! That ride challenged me to the core; but the test actually made me a better, more "perfect and complete" motorcycle driver and gave me new reference points and confidence.

- *"Count it all joy when you fall into various trials..."* You can count on God! He's up to something in your life, so count it a joy when you face a big trial.
- *"...knowing that the testing of your faith produces patience..."* When your faith is tested, patience is being produced, and that produces good things.
- *"...let patience have its perfect work, that you may be perfect and complete, lacking nothing."* In the end, you'll be perfect and complete, lacking nothing— so go ahead and let patience do its thing.

Are you facing a big test? Trial? Faith challenge? It's not always easy, but I encourage you to "count," "know" and "let." This principle works—not just on motorcycle trips, but in whatever trial or test you're in. And, in the end, you win!

Read It! 1 Peter 1:7, NLT

Speak It! "Father, I trust You. I'm facing a big trial right now, and my faith is being severely tested; but I count it all joy! I rejoice because You are up to something good in my life! I know it's producing patience in me, so I'll let it have its perfect work! Thank You, Lord, for Your faithfulness to me. In Jesus' Name. Amen."

DAY 299

(cold shoulder)

"Turn your back on evil, work for the good and don't quit.
GOD loves this kind of thing, never turns away from His friends.
Live this way and you've got it made..."
Psalm 37:27, MSG

What do you do when you want to return evil for evil? When you want to give people a piece of your mind? A taste of their own medicine? What do you do when you want to quit? When you've had it with difficult people?

You continue to work for good.

You don't quit.

You stay in the game.

You pursue a righteous cause.

You set your face like flint.

You give evil the cold shoulder.

You stand still and see the salvation of the Lord.

Remember, God loves this kind of thing; and He will never turn His back on you! Keep living this way. Be wise, walk in love, speak the truth and always do good—and you've got it made.

If God is for you, who can be against you? *(Romans 8:31, NIV)*

Read It! Psalm 118:6-8, AMP

Speak It! "Father, I thank You for the grace, wisdom, strength, faith and love to turn my back on evil. I will work for the good, and I won't quit. I thank You, Lord, that You love this kind of thing, and You won't turn Your back on me. Because of You, I've got it made! In Jesus' Name. Amen."

DAY 300

(the party's over)

"You've already put in your time in that God-ignorant way of life, partying night after night, a drunken and profligate life. Now it's time to be done with it for good. Of course, your old friends don't understand why you don't join in with the old gang anymore. But you don't have to give an account to them. They're the ones who will be called on the carpet—and before God Himself."
1 Peter 4:3-5, MSG

At some point, everyone has to cross the line—the "I want my friends to like me; I don't want to seem judgmental; I want to keep a foot in both worlds" line AND the "I want to please the Lord; I want to be free from my old life; I want to be on -fire for God" line. The sooner we cross that line—the better.

There's no getting around it. If we want to be a friend of God, we can't be friends with the ways of the world. We can still love the people in the world; but we can't hang with them. If you've become a Christian and are still feeling the tentacles of the old party life trying to pull you back, cut those ties! Seriously— cut the ties...today. Make a decision to say good-bye to your old life. That means: your house is no longer party central, you need to flush the pot, throw out the paraphernalia, empty the vodka bottles, throw out the beer cans, burn the nasty magazines and books, pitch out a few ungodly CDs or DVDs, kick the live-in boy or girlfriend out and be done with your old life for good!

And...know this... Some of your old friends won't understand. They won't. It's a fact. They'll think you've gone off the religious deep end; they'll call you a "Jesus freak." They'll diss your Christian life, friends, church, Bible and Jesus. They'll try to woo you back to that immoral, party life with all sorts of reasons why you don't need to be so 100% Christian. Don't fall for it! Stay strong in the Lord. Your life in Christ will far surpass all of the best days of your old life put together! Many have been deceived into thinking they can live a completely godless life, pray for God's blessings and then die one day and just waltz into heaven as if they've known the Lord and served as an altar girl or boy their whole lives. That's not how it works. One day, there will be a very sad and rude awakening for a lot of people who have not surrendered to the lordship of Jesus! That's why it's important for you to leave that old life, stay strong in the Lord and blaze a trail for your friends to follow and find Christ. Love them, but don't get entangled with their way of life any longer. Stay committed to the Lord and His Word. Over time, your friends will observe God's blessings in your life and see your personal witness and hopefully they will be drawn to follow Jesus!

Read It! 2 Peter 2:20, NLT

Speak It! "Father, I cross the line today. I'm done with that old immoral, wild, addictive party life. Jesus is the Lord of my life. Help me to be strong in the Lord and let my life in Christ be a light for my friends. In Jesus' Name. Amen."

DAY 301

(nurture the nature)

"So God created man in His own image; in the image of God He created him; male and female He created them."
Genesis 1:27

God knew what He was doing when He created mankind to be male and female.

Raised in a house full of girls, my mother raised me and my three younger sisters. When I got married, I had two daughters. God made females to be uniquely female. Like it or not, our DNA makes us female. I get the "female, girl-thing"—the connection, emotions, hormones, attitudes; the need to talk; the ability to communicate without saying a word. We have a tendency toward being spiritually intuitive; deal with weight and body issues; have good and bad hair days; know how to multi-task and want to fulfill a destiny by expressing domestic skills, leadership skills, creative intuition, administrative talent, a teaching gift, a heart for serving, a bent toward nurturing or building relationships—and a host of other female things.

Later, I had two sons and learned about a whole new world—the world of boys. Now that our daughters are in college, I'm living in a boys' world, and I have to say, I love it. Boys are easy. They have so many God-given qualities that are uniquely male.

We live in a culture that is so gender-confused, but God is not. People debate whether our sexual identity and even sexuality is nature- or nurture-driven. How about both? We don't have to be confused or conflicted. He made us to be either male or female, so, let's nurture the nature of the person God created us to be. If you're a girl, be one; God made you that way. Don't be a man. You may be a frilly-girl or a "tom-boy" girl, a domestic girly-girl or an athletic tough-girl, a follower or a leader. No matter what "version" of female you are, enjoy being female. Or, if you're a boy, be one; God made you that way. Don't be a girl. You may be a strong-leader-type guy or a creative-caring-type guy, a powerful communicator or a protective provider, an aggressive risk-taker or a more laid-back, steady-eddy. No matter what "version" of male you are, enjoy being male. There are unique benefits, blessings and challenges that go with each gender, so cultivate the expression of being female or male.

Read It! Psalm 139:14, KJV

Speak It! "Father, I thank You for making me to be a_____ *(declare who God made you to be—male or female).* You didn't make any mistakes. I celebrate the unique blessings, gifts, benefits and challenges that go with the gender You've made me to be. Help me enjoy the full purpose and expression You intended in making me male or female. In Jesus' Name. Amen."

(Satan's worst nightmare)

*"The Lord gives the word [of power];
the women who bear and publish [the news] are a great host."*
Psalm 68:11, AMP

It might be hard to believe that Satan—the ultimate nightmare—has a worst nightmare of his own! Yep, and it might surprise you what it looks like! It's an army of women turned loose to teach and preach the Word of God. That makes sense, since research proves that women have a need to speak three times as many words a day as men. Think about what would happen if millions of women—who *all* love to talk—were allowed to preach, teach, and lead? Just the thought probably makes hell tremble!

Even though the Bible says this is true, it hasn't always been widely accepted.

I remember my first experience with a person who didn't believe in women preachers. My husband, Jeff, and I were pioneering our church in Kalamazoo, MI. We had only been there for about 10 months, and a woman who served as our lead teacher in children's ministry came up and boldly told me, "I just want you to know that we're leaving the church." I was stunned! I asked her, "Really? Why?" "Because of you," she said. "Me? What did I do?" She looked at me and said, "My husband doesn't believe in women preachers," and with that, she turned and walked away. I was surprised and deeply saddened. What made matters worse was, at that time, my "preaching" only amounted to teaching the "Get a Grip" foundations class. Little did I know then, how controversial this topic could be!

I was raised as a Catholic with priests and nuns; therefore, I didn't have much experience with the "controversy" over women preachers and the two Scripture passages that send many people into a theological tailspin. However, I quickly learned some familiar phrases that I'd come to hear often:

> *"How can you, a woman, teach the Bible? Doesn't the Bible say women should be quiet in the church, and that they cannot teach, preach or lead?" Or, "OK, fine you can teach the Bible, but only to other women—not to men—because you are supposed to be submissive and not have any authority over men."*

I'm glad I followed what the Bible says! If women joined together as a force to preach and proclaim the name of Jesus, hell would be trembling in its shoes!

Read It! Acts 18:26

Speak It! "Father, thank you that you created women in a special way, to be used in the kingdom of God. I ask that you help every women fulfill their God-ordained purpose on this earth and realize their gifts and calling. In Jesus' Name. Amen."

DAY 303

(the great divide)

"There is neither Jew nor Greek, slave nor free, male nor female,
for you are all one in Christ Jesus."
Galatians 3:28, NIV

I suppose there will always be a theological divide on the topic of women in ministry. While experts debate it, let's look at the fruit. It's hard not to notice that God has raised up some powerful female voices. Here are three instances, for starters:

- **Joyce Meyer.** One of the most widely-read, listened-to and well-known Bible teachers in the world today. She's reaching millions through TV, radio, books and her vast overseas missions trips and relief efforts.
- **Darlene Zschech.** This native Australian, acclaimed all over the world as a singer/songwriter, worship leader and speaker, is known for spearheading the worship music from Hillsong Church, notably for writing *Shout to the Lord.*
- **Yoido Full Gospel Central.** The largest church in the world, located in Seoul, Korea. With a 2006 membership of 800,000 members, it has been built largely by women in leadership through cell groups, according to a report making reference to Pastor David Yonggi Cho. Check this out:

  "Cho then went on to devise his plan to minister to the people through a network of home cells and using the people to lead them. He took this plan to the deacons, but they said no. He then took the idea to the deaconesses and they accepted it. They realized that the biggest problem with this was going to be for the men to come under the authority of women leaders... They overcame this problem by having the women wear caps to signify that they were under Cho's authority. Using the women as leaders, they started with 20 home cells. This quickly grew to 150 groups."

The Lord gave the Word and great was the company of women who proclaimed it. So, girls, if you have "the preach," talk to the Lord and the godly men in your lives. Then, be wise, humble, faithful and go for it! It was prophesied of you many, many years ago.

Read It! Acts 2:17-18, NIV

Speak It! "Father, I pray for the women I know who are called to teach, preach and publish Your Word. I pray You give them Your wisdom, confidence, boldness, humility and approval as they fulfill Your calling in their lives. Lord, I pray for the men who are called to teach, preach and publish Your Word. I pray You give them Your wisdom, confidence, boldness, humility and approval as they fulfill Your calling in their lives. I pray for men and women to work together in love and unity as they teach, preach and publish Your Word. In Jesus' Name. Amen."

DAY 304

(your days of labor)

"Servants, do what you're told by your earthly masters. And don't just do the minimum that will get you by. Do your best. Work from the heart for your real Master, for God, confident that you'll get paid in full when you come into your inheritance. Keep in mind always that the ultimate Master you're serving is Christ. The sullen servant who does shoddy work will be held responsible. Being Christian doesn't cover up bad work..."
Colossians 3:22-25, MSG

Work is a blessing! To have a job is a gift from God. As Believers, we need to give the Lord and our employers our very best. We should work hard. Be diligent. Give 110%. Have fun. Get a lot done. Exceed expectations. Be known for an exceptional work ethic. Produce great fruit and expect favor, promotion and prosperity!

Remember, we're serving the Master Jesus in all that we do. He knows everything, sees everything. He knows who's carrying their weight and who's slacking. He's up on those who are serving Him from their heart and who's just trying to make a good show for the boss.

So, since we are working for Jesus and our earthly masters, here are some things NOT to do:

- **Arrive late for work.**
- **Leave early from work.**
- **Take extra long lunch breaks.**
- **Chat with co-workers on non-work-related topics for extended periods.**
- **Spend excessive personal time on Facebook®, Twitter® or other social networks or texting on your cell phone.**
- **Handle personal issues.**
- **Make personal copies on work copiers.**
- **Use office supplies for personal use or taking them home.**

Today, determine to give God and your employer your very best and remember the joy of the Lord is your strength.

Read It! Ephesians 6:5-9, AMP

Speak It! "Father, help me to be a good employee. Help me to work heartily, diligently and with excellence as if I were serving You. Forgive me for any of the areas where I have NOT fulfilled Your Word and the things You expect of me. Help me to make things right. I want to serve You as I serve my employer and I know that You will reward me with favor, promotion, prosperity and good fruit. In Jesus' Name. Amen."

DAY 305

(running the show)

"And masters, treat your servants considerately. Be fair with them.
Don't forget for a minute that you, too, serve a Master—God in heaven."
Colossians 4:1, MSG

Running the show—owning a business—is not for the weary. With the responsibilities of managing employees, making schedules, setting short-term and long-term goals, and keeping up with inventory and cash flow, dealing with the human factor of business ownership can get a little hairy at times. Attitudes, different personalities, various gifts, talents and skills of employees—they can sometimes cloud our purpose for even having a business—to further the kingdom and provide blessing for our life and our family.

If you own a business, God can use your business to bless others through it. In this instance, I'm referring to your employees. God has entrusted people to your care to help you accomplish the goals and vision for your business. But, He has also given you a mandate by which to follow concerning how to treat them.

Like employees, God also sees what we do and what we say, how we deal with individuals and how we treat them on a daily basis. We have the opportunity to sow good seed into our employees that bring a harvest of profit in the end. Here are a few things NOT to do as a godly employer:

- **Be overly demanding.**
- **Under-pay your staff.**
- **Don't set the pace or lead by example.**
- **Put an unfair burden on your employees.**
- **Ask your employees to do unethical things.**
- **Don't value their skill sets and gifts.**
- **Don't acknowledge extra effort or factor in special circumstances that deserve a reward, day off, bonus or appreciation.**
- **Use violence, abusive words or intimidation to motivate.**

Today, if you're an employer, make a decision to be fair, generous and considerate to your employees. Remember, the joy of the Lord is your strength, too!

Read It! Ephesians 6:9, KJV

Speak It! "Father, help me to be a good employer. Help me to be kind, fair, considerate and generous to my employees. Forgive me for any areas where I have NOT fulfilled Your Word and the things You expect of me. Help me to make things right with each and every employee. I thank You that together—as I do my part as the leader/employer—our staff can work together in serving and honoring You. I know that You will reward our organization with favor, promotion, prosperity and good fruit. In Jesus' Name. Amen."

DAY 306

(is your God too small?)

"Who has scooped up the ocean in His two hands, or measured the sky between His thumb and little finger, who has put all the Earth's dirt in one of His baskets, weighed each mountain and hill?"
Isaiah 40:12, MSG

You can tell a lot about people by looking at the things they create; they reveal a lot his/her creativity, ingenuity, imagination, excellence and attention to detail.

Just the same, you can tell a lot about God from all of His works. From the farthest star to the most delicate flower to the smallest cell—He's an amazing Creator! Here are a few facts to remind us how very big and amazing our God is!

- **Light.** In the beginning, God said *"Let there be light..."* and light has been being ever since! Light travels at 186,282.397 miles per second, 671 million miles per hour, 5,878,630,000,000 miles per year—and has been doing so ever since God commanded it to exist! It takes about 1.3 seconds for light to reach us from the moon. Light travels around the earth 8 times in one second. The nearest known star (other than the sun), is called the Proxima Centauri and is about 4.22 light-years away. (Remember light travels 5,878,630,000,000 miles per year.)
- **Earth.** God can put all of Earth's dirt in a bucket. To put it in perspective, it would take 1,000,000 Earth's to fit inside the Sun. If Earth were the size of a dime, Jupiter would be the size of a dinner plate! They say, 1,300 Earths could fit inside Jupiter and over 926 Jupiters could fit inside the Sun.
- **Universe.** No one knows the exact size of the universe. We only know this—God made the universe. *(Hebrews 1:2-3, NLT)* The nearest galaxy to our Milky Way is the Andromeda galaxy which is 2 million light-years away. The visible universe (what man has been able to actually see) is 28 billion light years in diameter.

Get the idea? He's a big God! He's not boring. He's not predictable. Nothing is too difficult for Him. Nothing is impossible with God. All things are possible to him who believes. No matter what you are facing, you have a big God! Take some time today to magnify Him. Put the magnifying glass on God and see how big He really is!

Read It! Isaiah 40:12-14, MSG

Speak It! "Father, I take time today to magnify You! I see You for who You really are—a mighty big God! I'm so glad You are the Creator of the ends of the earth and in Your love and mercy, You reach down to Planet Earth to know, care for and help me. Today, I need You to be big in my life in this area: _____ *(Ask the Lord for His help!)*. I thank You for injecting my life and circumstances with the power of Your bigness! In Jesus' Name. Amen."

DAY 307

(free bird)

"And you shall know the truth, and the truth shall make you free."
John 8:32

Ever been in a funk and didn't know why? It's not like you're in gross sin or blatant rebellion; you're just a bit disappointed, discouraged or detached—in a spiritual funk? Has it been hard to put your finger on "the issue"?

We all face seasons like this. We have an enemy who wants to derail our faith. We live in a world where the "gravity" of this culture's mindset, attitude and disposition can contaminate our minds and hearts and get us off center. Sometimes, we don't even realize these things are happening. Without notice—we end up in a funk. But, Jesus said the truth would set us free, so we need to get reconnected to the truth about whatever funky issue we are facing.

I remember a time when I found myself feeling a bit detached from the Lord. I knew the Lord loved me, and I loved Him; yet, I was very disappointed about some things and felt detached from the Lord. I couldn't put my finger on why was I feeling so discouraged and didn't know what to do about it?

One day, while driving in my car, I had some heart-to-heart time with the Lord and asked Him to help me. Instead of talking, I listened. That's when He asked me, "Do you trust Me?" I said, "Do I trust You? So, THAT was the issue?" In an instant, I realized the Lord had hit the funk "nail on the head." All of the sudden, I could see that a series of things had eroded my trust in the Lord to a degree, and the disappointment, discouragement and detachment I had been feeling was the result. Instantly, I started to cry...a lot. (I am not normally a crier.) Then, I said, "Yes, Lord, I trust You." I can't explain it, but the "truth" of getting to the root of things, set me free; and I felt the disappointment, discouragement and detachment melt away. He began to speak to me about my life and reminded me of the scripture in Proverbs 3:5-6. Even though I'd known this passage for years, when God spoke these words to my heart at that time, it was a living word (a.k.a: a "rhema" word) from God's heart to mine—and literally, His truth set me free from the funk!

So, if you're in a spiritual funk—feeling disappointed, discouraged or detached—it's the truth that will set you free. Get some face time with the Lord and listen to His voice. He knows what the issues are; and when He speaks the truth to your heart, it will set you free.

Read It! Proverbs 3:5-6, NIV

Speak It! "Father, I ask You to help me. I've been in a spiritual funk and need You to speak to me and reveal to me the truth and root cause of the disappointment, discouragement or detachment I've been experiencing. In Jesus' Name. Amen."

DAY 308

(church hoppers, sheep stealers & other crazies)

"...you will know how people ought to conduct themselves in God's
household, which is the church of the living God,
the pillar and foundation of the truth."
1Timothy 3:15, NIV

Jesus is building His Church, but sometimes, we get in His way and mess every-thing up. Our culture doesn't know how to conduct themselves in the Church of God, because they don't know much about respecting, honoring or esteeming Jesus and His Church. However, when we cooperate with God and seek first His kingdom, He adds everything else we need in life *(Matthew 6:33, KJV)*.

The problem is that we, as leaders, have been guilty of abdicating our responsi-bilities to lead and feed the sheep. Instead of walking in love, teaching the Word and reaching lost sheep; some have resorted to dissing other churches, teaching man's opinions and stealing another pastor's sheep to build their ministries. As a result, we have confused, self-focused, "feed me/bless me" Believers/sheep who don't know much about what the Word says about commitment, honor, sacrifice or seeking His kingdom first. A pastor will pack the house when teaching a prosperity series and welcome a whopping 8 to 10 people for prayer. America's churches are full of Believers still wearing diapers, when they should be wearing the armor of God and taking territory from the enemy. Sadly, many haven't grown up enough to understand that, when it comes to the Church, it's not about them; it's about serving the Lord—and that's not always easy. When pastors/shepherds and Believers/sheep don't know how to conduct themselves in the Church of the living God, the Body suffers and ends up with major issues: stolen sheep, burnt-out pastors, church splits, maverick sheep trying to be shepherds, spiritual babies who never grow up; whiners, instead of winners; church hoppers, defeated and dysfunctional Believers and church families with ministerial integrity out the window. It's crazy in the church world!

The Bible says a lot about how we are to conduct ourselves in the Church. It starts with having His heart. Let's look at one Church 101 biggie:

- **Jesus loves the Church—everything else is peripheral!** The Church is Christ's body, through which He speaks and acts. The Church is not peripheral to the world; the world is peripheral to the Church. We should esteem the Church, never minimize it—God doesn't. He loves the Church, and so should we. The Church—filled with Believers who have His heart—is truly the hope of the world, not the government, education, business, or money.

Read It! Matthew 6:33

Speak It! "Father, help me to love, respect and esteem Your Church in the same way You do, so Your plans can be fulfilled. In Jesus' Name. Amen."

DAY 309

(need directions?)

"Your word is a lamp to my feet and a light to my path."
Psalm 119:105, AMP

We were talking with some friends recently about the Lord's perfect will—getting His direction and finding the sweet spot of God's plan. Living in the center of God's will is always the safest, most stable and uniquely blessed place to be. Being in God's will in the middle of the North Pole is better than being out of God's will on the finest beaches of Hawaii. There's just something about being in the perfect will of God. Everything works better. There's grace for the pace, faith to move mountains, anointing to break yokes, weapons to tear down strongholds, divine favor so things fall into place like clockwork and the ability to live in peace and joy. Operating outside of God's will is a continual experience of frustration and disappointment. It's like sledding down a dirt hill; being a day late and a dollar short; ending up on the short end of the stick...a lot; and being continually overlooked, underpaid and out of the loop.

How do we discover God's perfect will and specific direction for our lives? Thankfully, He's made it easy. His Word is a lamp for our feet and is full of general directions—things like *"I know the plans I have for you...plans to give you a hope and a future...," (Jeremiah 29:11).* These are great; but often we need more than general direction—we need specific direction. Jesus said, *"Man does not live on bread alone, but on every word that comes from the mouth of God," (Matthew 4:4).* That means, we can take God at His Word and follow the direction that the lamp of His Word gives us.

We've seen it work time and time again throughout our entire Christian lives. When we need the Lord's direction, our first stop is His Word. We spend extra time in the Word listening for His voice. I could tell you story after story of how the Lord has led us by His Word all of these years. When we have allowed His Word to be the lamp for our feet, we have always landed in His sweet spot.

Need specific direction in your life? Spend some extra time in His Word and allow it to be the lamp you need.

Read It! Romans 12:2, KJV

Speak It! "Father, thank You that Your Word is a lamp to my feet. Help me to have eyes to see and ears to hear Your voice and specific direction as I seek You and spend time in Your Word. In Jesus' Name. Amen."

DAY 310

(you are a gifted child)

"As each of you has received a gift (a particular spiritual talent, a gracious divine endowment), employ it for one another as [befits] good trustees of God's many-sided grace [faithful stewards of the extremely diverse powers and gifts granted to Christians by unmerited favor]."
1 Peter 4:10, AMP

You are a gifted child! That's right...a gifted child of God. In the same way that we, as parents, see the unique gifts in each of our own children, God sees the gifts He has given to each one of us. So, it's time we see those gifts and start using them. God wants us to identify and use our gifts, to be good stewards over the particular spiritual talent or divine endowment He has given us. What are your gifts? Have you been able to locate them? Look at the next verse: *"Whoever speaks, [let him do it as one who utters] oracles of God; whoever renders service, [let him do it] as with the strength which God furnishes abundantly, so that in all things God may be glorified through Jesus Christ (the Messiah). To Him be the glory and dominion forever and ever (through endless ages). Amen (so be it)." (1 Peter 4:11, AMP)*

Our gifts can be divided into two main categories: "communication gifts" or "serving gifts." Most people are gifted in one of these categories, some possibly in both. Here's a little help in discerning the way God has gifted you.

- **Communication Gifts.** Do you have a gift for communicating? Speaking? Writing? Singing? Writing songs? Giving instruction? Teaching? Preaching? Explaining? Use your gift to glorify God, to encourage others and to spread the good news of the Gospel. Don't waste your time on frivolous pursuits; maximize your gifts to bring attention to Jesus and the Gospel and in producing eternal fruit.

- **Serving Gifts.** Do you have a gift for serving? Lifting the load? Helping others? Working behind the scenes? Cooking? Building? Creating? Designing? Organizing? Administrating? Helping? Developing? Managing? Making music? Graphics or video creation? Understanding computers? Running audio? Directing traffic? Use that gift to help others. Those who serve behind the scenes enable those who communicate to do the job they are called to do.

When we all work together using the gifts God has given us, His purposes are fulfilled. Be encouraged. God has given you a gift(s), but He expects you to use it/them for His glory. Don't squander what He's given you. Don't minimize or despise the gifts God has given you; they are tied to your destiny.

Read It! Proverbs 18:16

Speak It! "Father, thank You for giving me a talent(s) and/or divine endowment(s). Help me discern and recognize them and be a good steward of your grace. I want to use them for your glory. Help me to do so! In Jesus' Name. Amen."

(what would Jesus Twitter®?)

"Yes, I try to find common ground with everyone so that I might bring them to Christ. I do all this to spread the Good News, and in doing so I enjoy its blessings."
1 Corinthians 9:22-23, NLT

I love the question a pastor friend of mine, Blaine Bartel, posted on his Facebook® wall a few weeks ago. He asked, "What would Jesus Twitter®?" Then he had some fun with it and imagined what Jesus might tweet: "Headed to Philippi with My staff team and thinking about changing Simon's name to Peter. Always good to shake things up a bit..."

Would Jesus use Twitter®? Facebook®? YouTube®? I think so. Back in the day, He was relevant to His culture and communicated with people in the venues of the day—the synagogues, hillsides, seashore—anywhere a crowd could gather. I believe Jesus is still relevant to His culture, and He's quite aware of the explosion of technology and today's venues for communication. I'm sure Jesus would know how to balance the use of technology for Gospel purposes, while avoiding the snare of wasting time with these toys. That is the big challenge, isn't it? Using technology for God's purposes, rather than being used by technology! Finding common ground with people on social communities and business networks is wonderful. Sharing the latest status update, funny link, preaching clip on Facebook,® Twitter® or YouTube® can be a great source of encouragement. Being able to have real-time conversations with people halfway around the world via the Internet is truly remarkable and has such great potential for the Body of Christ! We just have to walk in God's wisdom to manage and balance it all.

Recently, the Lord spoke to one of the teens in our youth group and gave Him an interesting exhortation on keeping his priorities straight in the midst of our hyper-technology world. The Lord spoke to Logan's heart and said, "Quit texting and get into My Text. Quit Facebooking and get your face in the Book. Quit watching television and tell people about My vision." Now that'll preach on a Monday morning, eh? If you're a Crackberry addict, a Facebook® junkie, in a Twitter® hypnosis, a YouTube® or Vimeo® groupie or a blog, RSS or iTunes® cult member—beware! Ask the Lord to help you find His balance. In the meantime, have fun using technology for His purposes and continue to find common ground with everyone, so you might bring them to Christ.

Read It! Ephesians 4:29, KJV

Speak It! "Father, thank You for the opportunity to connect with family, friends and co-workers through Internet social networks. Thank You for the ability to communicate the Gospel through modern technology. Help me manage my time and use technology for Your purposes. In Jesus' Name. Amen."

DAY 312

(Uzziah, the good boy)

"...as long as he sought the LORD, God made him prosper."
2 Chronicles 26:5

There was a 16-year-old boy who became king. His name was Uzziah. He reigned in Jerusalem until he was 68 years old. Royalty was not new to him; he grew up in the house of a king—his father, Amaziah. He sought the Lord, and God prospered him. Destiny was on Uzziah, as long as...

...he sought the Lord!

To seek the Lord in this context means: to "frequent" something. If people "frequent" a restaurant, it means they go there a lot. Uzziah "frequented" the Lord; He followed, pursued and searched for God. Apparently, God liked it, and caused Uzziah to prosper!

The word "prosper" in the case of Uzziah comes from the Hebrew word "tsalach" which means "to push forward." The idea is that because Uzziah spent frequent time with God, the Lord caused him to push forward in life, to break out, and be profitable! And it worked. Just look at his resume:

God blessed him with military genius. He started and won wars against his adversaries. He built defense towers in the city to gain the visual and military advantage. He was a strategic and organized commander who led a team of 2,600 military officers, each overseeing their own combat unit made up of over 300,000 prepared men, armed ready to fight. He was innovative in weaponry development and invented some of the first military machines—catapults on towers that shot arrows and rocks. *(2 Chronicles 26:11-15, KJV)*

In addition to his great military accolades, Uzziah was also an urban real estate developer, gifted in agriculture and blessed with great wealth and fame.

Wow! It sounds like a life of blessing to me! And why? One simple reason: because Uzziah sought the Lord.

Read It! 2 Chronicles 26:1-10

Speak It! "Father, I seek You. My heart cries out to know, pursue and follow You. I want to 'frequent' You in my thoughts, prayers and choices in everyday life. I need, require, crave and desire You. I know the result of seeking You will be the same as it was for Uzziah. You will cause me to prosper and push forward in life as it pleases You. I thank You for that. In Jesus' Name. Amen."

DAY 313

(Uzziah, the bad boy)

"But then the strength and success went to his head.
Arrogant and proud, he fell."
2 Chronicles 26:16

Pride always comes before a fall. How many preachers, actors, politicians or others who have achieved a degree of success have found it going to their heads—right before their big, public fall? We've seen that story played out in the headlines time and time again. It must be easy to do. In fact, it must be something we have to intentionally guard against. If some of the best have easily fallen into this trap, let's not presume we are immune.

Uzziah was the to take over his life. All of a sudden, he was "the man," but he wasn't for very long. Just like his prosperity had an anatomy, so did his fall. Let's take a look to see what we can learn from his demise.

- **Success went to his head.** Seeing all of his accomplishments, Uzziah started to feel invincible. A word to the wise: don't ever believe your own press. None of us are *that* good! Any success we've ever had is because of God's grace and the help of a lot of other people. Don't ever forget that.

- **He quit seeking God.** At one time, Uzziah sought the Lord continuously; it was the key to his success. But, he began to despise the Lord. Why, we don't really know, but we have to guard against this, too. We cannot get offended at God if He doesn't answer a prayer like we think He should. We need to keep our hearts pure and turned toward Him, no matter what the situation.

- **He intruded into another's office.** Uzziah was the king, not the priest. Yet, he intruded into the priest's office, which he was not anointed or qualified to fulfill. God took that seriously—and still does today. Azariah and 80 other priests went in after him, but his prideful heart wouldn't let him listen to them. This same scenario happens today. God anoints someone to serve in the office of a pastor (priest), and then other leaders (kings) are compelled to intrude into that office. Next thing you know, they are telling him how to run the church. Don't ever intrude into an office you are not called into by God. It can be the beginning of the end! *(2 Chronicles 26:16-20)*

Tragically, Uzziah was struck with leprosy right where he stood. He faced a life of pain and died in isolation. The lesson to learn is this: we should always guard our heart against pride and follow Uzziah's "good boy" pattern instead—depending on God and walking in His abundant blessings!

Read It! 2 Chronicles 26:16-23

Speak It! "Father, forgive me if I've been prideful or had rebellion in my heart toward You. I know You have my best interests in mind. Help me be true to my own calling and keep a humble heart toward You. In Jesus' Name. Amen."

DAY 314

(nothing could make me happier)

"I have no greater joy than to hear that My children walk in truth."
3 John 4

Parents, is there any greater joy than to know your kids are walking in the Truth? I don't think so. There's just something about the peace and joy that comes with knowing our kids are in a good place with God. I love how *The Message Bible* translates this verse, *"Nothing could make me happier than getting reports that my children continue diligently in the way of Truth!"*

When we are confident that our kids "own" their personal walk with the Lord, what a happy day it is! When our kids embrace Jesus and His Word as truth, our hearts enter a rest, and we know everything will be okay. Sure, our kids may still make some mistakes; but when they walk in the Truth and embrace God's Word, we know that the Lord will pick them up and correct, guide, lead, help, direct and instruct them. What a great relief and a great joy this is for any parent.

To the contrary, it's heartbreaking for any parent to watch a child who wanders aimlessly without a compass, without direction, without boundaries, without the guidance of the Truth.

Note to Kids: If you're reading this devo, you can do something today to change your life and bless your parents. Today, embrace Jesus Christ as your Lord and start walking in the Truth of His Word. Get serious about the Lord and His plan for your life. Make hard decisions and obey God. Do what He's called you to do. Here's what you can expect: God will bless your life and fill your parents with an unspeakable joy!

Read It! Proverbs 22:6, KJV

Speak It! *(Parents, say this:)* "Father, I pray for my children today. I ask You to continue to reveal to them the power of walking in the Truth! Help them to embrace Jesus Christ and Your Word as the ultimate authority in their lives and help them to walk in obedience to it. Help them make hard decisions, today. Help them to choose Truth, today. I have no greater joy than to hear that my children are walking the Truth. Thank You, Lord, for working this into their hearts today! In Jesus' Name. Amen."

(Kids, if you've been away from what you know is right, then say this:) "Father, I repent. I have been running away from You, away from the Truth and away from my parents. I want to live by the Truth. I choose to embrace Jesus Christ and Your Word. I will make the hard decisions I need to make to obey Your Truth and this will result in blessings for me and great joy for my parents. In Jesus' Name. Amen."

DAY 315

(the fine line)

"But let every person carefully scrutinize and examine and test his own conduct and his own work. He can then have the personal satisfaction and joy of doing something commendable [in itself alone] without [resorting to] boastful comparison with his neighbor."
Galatians 6:4, AMP

- **The Ugly Side of Pride.** Sometimes pride can look like humility. When pride puts on a "humility" show, so it looks humble, it's really still pride. When pride is disguised as humility and nobility and says, "I'm just a lowly, ugly worm...an unworthy, old sinner...," while completely rejecting that the Word says, "I can do all things through Christ because He has made me His righteousness," it's really still pride.

  Sometimes pride is just ugly pride. When pride makes us think more highly of ourselves than we ought, it's just ugly pride. When pride gets its feathers ruffled when someone tells us the truth, it's still ugly pride. When pride thinks it's overly important, superior to others or the smartest person in the room, it's really ugly pride. *(Romans 12:3, AMP)*

- **Beauty of Humility.** Sometimes humility can look like pride. When we humble ourselves under the Word and believe and speak what the Bible says instead of going with our feelings or circumstances, it can sound arrogant or overly confident; but it's actually humility. When humility rates his or her ability as they actually are, not thinking more highly or more lowly of itself than it should, it can look like pride; but really, it's true humility. *(Galatians 6:3-4, AMP)*

Sometimes there is a fine line between pride and humility.

So, what does all this mean? Simply, stay small in your own eyes. Don't compare yourselves to others. Don't be proud of being humble. Believe the truth about yourself—don't inflate it and don't underestimate it. Remember, unbelief and not taking God at His Word is pride; while living by faith, believing and speaking the Word is true humility. Sometimes, it's a thin line. Let's do our best to stay on the humility side of life!

Read It! Proverbs 11:2, NIV

Speak It! "Father, I thank You for helping me to make any adjustments I need today in the areas of pride and humility. Help me to scrutinize, examine and test my own conduct and work—so I can have the personal satisfaction and joy of doing something commendable without boastful comparison with others. Help me to not estimate or think of myself more highly than I ought or to have an exaggerated opinion of my own importance, but to rate my ability with sober judgment, according to the degree of faith You have given me. I believe Your Word is the final authority on all things, so I choose to humble myself under Your mighty Word. I will believe and speak the things I find in Your Word, regardless of my own feelings or circumstances. In Jesus' Name. Amen."

DAY 316

(grow up!)

"Instead, speaking the truth in love, we will in all things grow up..."
Ephesians 4:15, NIV

The truth hurts sometimes. It can feel like the meanest enemy or our best friend. One thing is for sure, though, the truth spoken in love causes us to grow up.

If the truth be told, sometimes, I don't want the truth. There are times I want to live in the fantasy world I have created. I don't want to hear the truth about myself—how people perceive me, how I act, how my hair looks, what people think of my preaching, how tired I look, how spiritual I am or ain't, how I communicate, how I cook, how I decorate...and on it goes. But, if I want to grow up in all things, I need to hear the truth.

I've found that once I hear the truth and embrace it, the Lord goes to work in my heart and mind and helps me to change, improve, eliminate and tweak whatever is necessary, so I can grow up. In the end, it's always for the best.

I have observed three ways the truth comes to us:

- **We can speak the truth in love—to ourselves.** When we're honest and speak the truth in love to ourselves, it can be brutal. Taking a personal assessment of our spiritual condition—our hunger, maturity, prayer life, Word-life, depth, passion for eternal things and commitment to growth and sacrifice—can be a bitter pill at first. However, it's a pill worth taking, and it will make us grow.

- **Someone else can speak the truth in love—to us.** When people we respect love us enough to tell us the truth, it may be tough to hear; but a wise man accepts those loving rebukes. When people we don't respect give us a spoonful of "truth medicine," it can almost cause us to gag; but if we have the maturity to receive it, we will grow.

- **The Holy Spirit can speak the truth in love—to our hearts.** When the Holy Spirit speaks to our hearts through the Word and in those still small voice moments, He shines the truth light on areas of lives that need attention. While it's painful at times, there is a sweet sense of relief. We know He only speaks the truth in love for our benefit, so we grow up in all things.

If someone—you, others or the Holy Spirit—speaks the truth in love to you, don't resist, rebel, get defensive, make excuses or go into a depression. Just take an honest inventory, and let the Lord use it to help you grow up.

Read It!   John 8:32, KJV

Speak It!   "Father, thank You for helping me to speak the truth in love to myself, to others and let the Holy Spirit speak the truth in love to me, too, so I can grow up into all that You want me to be and do. In Jesus' Name. Amen."

(be healed)

"When evening had come, they brought to Him many who were demon-possessed. And He cast out the spirits with a word, and healed all who were sick,... 'He Himself took our infirmities and bore our sicknesses.'"
Matthew 8:16-17

Jesus, the Great Physician, is still in the healing business today! He is the same yesterday, today and forever. I love the various pathways Jesus uses to bring His healing, restoring, recovering, strengthening power to the scene. Here are a few pathways:

- **God-initiated.** At time, God, exercises His Sovereignty to initiate a healing for people, based entirely upon His will. Sometimes those who are healed say, "I can't believe it!"—proving it wasn't their faith that pulled on God's healing power; it was God's divine will and mercy in action to fulfill His purposes. Often, God does this as a "sign and wonder" for unbelievers or baby Christians.

- **Faith-initiated.** In the majority of healings that took place during Jesus' ministry, it wasn't Jesus' faith that healed people; it was THEIR faith. Over and over, Jesus said, *"Your faith has made you whole,"* or, *"Be it unto you according to your faith."* Thank God that if He doesn't initiate a sovereign act of healing for us, we can still use our faith in Him and His Word to appropriate His Word and lay hold of His healing power by faith. (Study the woman with the issue of blood in Mark 5. She's a great example of a person who was healed by using her faith.) It seems the Lord expects Believers to grow, develop and use their faith to access His healing power.

- **Wisdom-initiated.** In addition to a God-initiated or faith-initiated healing, it seems that many times the Holy Spirit will guide us into God's divine health and healing through a wisdom-initiated approach. That is, the Holy Spirit may lead us to a particular doctor, clinic, treatment, therapy, surgical procedure, medicine, lifestyle change, nutrition or exercise regime or other option, so we can obtain His healing power in our lives through both supernatural and natural means. For example, I once knew a Christian orthopedic surgeon who noticed a constant rash on his hands. As a surgeon, this was not a good thing. He believed in God-initiated healings and in faith-initiated healings, but as he sought the Lord regarding the rash, the Holy Spirit spoke to his heart and said, "Quit using the soap at the hospital; it's causing a reaction." So, he quit using it, and the rash went away. This doctor didn't need a miraculous healing; his cure was in what wisdom provided.

Whatever pathway the Lord leads you to follow, know that Jesus is still in the healing biz; He took our infirmities and bore our sicknesses, so we wouldn't have to!

Read It! Isaiah 53:5, KJV

Speak It! "Father, thank You that Jesus took my infirmities and bore my sicknesses. Today, I appropriate Your healing power in my body, so I can walk in Your divine health and healing. In Jesus' Name. Amen."

DAY 318

(the Rock)

"From the end of the earth I will cry to You, when my heart is overwhelmed;
lead me to the rock that is higher than I."
Psalm 61:2

Feeling overwhelmed? Over your head in stress, pressure and trials? Be encouraged. No matter where you are, where you live, the negative reports you've been given, the natural circumstances you face, the demands that are pulling on you, the deadlines staring you down, the checklist that keeps growing, the challenges that never end or the obstacles the enemy throws in your path, there is a ROCK that is higher than you!

There's an old hymn that goes something like this:

"Where do I go, when there's no one left to turn to? Who do I talk to, when no one wants to listen? Who do I lean on, where there's no foundation stable? I go to the Rock. He's more than able. I go to the Rock."

That old hymn is still true! When our heart is overwhelmed, we can cry to the Lord; and He will lead us to the Rock. Jesus is that Rock, and He is far above anything—and everything—you or I could possibly face. Somehow, when we get to the Rock and hide under the shelter of the Almighty, seated with Christ far above all principalities and powers in heavenly places, things don't look or feel so overwhelming.

Have you cried out to the Lord lately? One of the best ways I know to cry out to the Lord and allow Him to lead us to the Rock is through worship. If your heart is overwhelmed today, find a quiet place and a quiet moment to listen to a few worship songs that "take you there" to that secret place with the Rock that is higher than you! In just a few moments, the weight of the world can fall off your shoulders, and you can rest in the shelter of the Almighty.

Read It! Psalm 3:3-4, NLT

Speak It! "Father, I cry out to You today. My heart is overwhelmed with so many things. Lead me to the Rock that is higher than I. You are a shield around me...the glory and the lifter of my head. Because of my Rock, I know I am strong in the Lord and the power of His might, and I can do all things through Christ who strengthens me. I thank You for Your help today. In Jesus Name. Amen."

DAY 319

(wicked)

"'O my God,' I prayed, 'don't forget all the evil of Tobiah, Sanballat,
Noadiah the prophetess, and all the other prophets who have
tried to discourage me.'"
Nehemiah 6:14, TLB

God keeps good records. Don't ever forget it. If you've had a wicked Tobiah, Sanballat or Noadiah come against you or your God-given assignment with evil plans, comments, deceptions or discouragement, just know this: in the end, God will have the final word—and the wall will be finished. *(Nehemiah 6:15, TLB)*

The Tobiahs, Sanballats and Noadiahs never win. (Read the book of Nehemiah and you'll see.) These people are definitely wicked—even though they may not see themselves that way. They are often self-righteous, and they usually have big mouths. They live passive-aggressive lives, use intimidation to get their way, lie through their teeth and mock everything that is godly. Eventually, they are found out, kicked out, voted out...or they die out. In due season, they will reap what they've sown *(Galatians 6:7)*. God's plan will prevail. His purposes will be fulfilled. Jesus will build His Church. The wall will go up!

Vengeance is the Lord's. So, if a wicked person or group has tried to get you down, just stay steady and keep building the wall. Keep moving forward in God's plans and purposes. Keep preaching the Word. Keep exalting Jesus. Keep telling the truth. Keep building His Church. Keep walking in faith and love. Keep seeking first the kingdom of God. And, in the end, you and the Lord will prevail!

Got a Tobiah, Sanballat or Noadiah on your case? No worries... God keeps good records! For all the evil they've caused you, they'll get theirs. (Unless, of course, they repent and fall on their face before the King of kings and Lord of lords... then they can get saved—and apologize.)

Read It! Nehemiah 6:1-16, NIV

Speak It! "Father, I will not be moved, intimidated, duped or discouraged by some wicked, self-righteous, loud-mouthed, passive-aggressive, intimidation-filled, lying, mocking, evil-doer. I have set my face like flint to do Your will in the face of the Tobiahs, Sanballats or Noadiahs in my life. Jesus is Lord! As I stay in faith and walk in wisdom and love, His plan will prevail. The wall will go up! In Jesus' Name. Amen."

DAY 320

(victory newsflash)

"But thanks be to God, Who gives us the victory [making us conquerors]
through our Lord Jesus Christ."
1 Corinthians 15:57, AMP

Just in case you need a reminder today, God—through Christ—gives us the victory and makes us conquerors. I don't know how He does it, but He has a way of moving mountains, raising valleys, making crooked ways straight, making a way where there is no way, overcoming the world, opening or closing doors, giving favor, always leading us in triumph and giving us the victory!

Here are a few more victory verses for your day:

- **Our faith gives us the victory.** So, let's stay in faith. *"For whatever is born of God is victorious over the world; and this is the victory that conquers the world, even our faith. Who is it that is victorious over [that conquers] the world but he who believes that Jesus is the Son of God [who adheres to, trusts in, and relies on that fact]?"* (1 John 5:4-5, AMP)

- **He always leads us in triumph.** Keyword: always. *"But thanks be to God, Who in Christ always leads us in triumph [as trophies of Christ's victory] and through us spreads and makes evident the fragrance of the knowledge of God everywhere..."* (2 Corinthians 2:14, AMP)

Read It! Psalm 41:11, NLT

Speak It! "Father, I thank You that You give me the victory through my Lord, Jesus Christ. Today, I ask You for Your Word and all the promises to provide the favor, knowledge, wisdom, insight, discernment and discretion I need to overcome. I thank You for Your mighty hand, divine power and all of heaven's help that is at work on my behalf according to Your purposes! In Jesus' Name. Amen."

DAY 321

(it's already yours)

"...he said to him, 'Son, you are always with me, and all that I have is yours.'"
Luke 15:31

Ever been a little jealous or irritated with the prodigal son? Ever thought the prodigal son got all the press, all the attention, all the kudos, while the older son was stuck being the invisible good boy?

In Luke 15, Jesus tells the story of a prodigal son and an obedient son. Most of the time, when that story's told, the prodigal son is the hero. He "comes to himself" and repents; then, his loving father welcomes him back home with open arm and throws him a big party. Woo hoo! Everyone talks about the prodigal son. No one ever talks about the older son—other than to criticize him for being jealous and irritated with all the attention his brother is getting.

Kinda makes you feel for the older son, doesn't it? Are you the older son? Have you faithfully served the Lord? Been obedient to God? Been a "good Christian," yet felt a little overlooked? Maybe you've been there when the back-slidden, pot-smoking, wild-living, party-going, immorality-loving prodigal finally repents, gives his testimony about God's mercy and grace reaching him in the deepest pit—and the crowd goes wild! Then, you share your testimony—a story of obedience and faithfulness to God and the crowd yawns...cricket...cricket. If you've thought about back-sliding just to get some attention. Don't do it!

Listen, the "prodigal son repents" testimonies are a dime a dozen. But, your testimony of staying faithful and obedient to God in the midst of temptations is the REAL testimony the world needs to hear. The "Good Christian"—didn't rebel, backslide, get wasted or sleep around and don't have a lot of baggage—testimony is a REAL testimony. Thank God for His mercy on the prodigals, but praise God for His keeping and blessing power on the faithful.

And that's not all... If you're the "older son," don't miss the point of the prodigal son's story. As you read it, watch what the Father said to the older son. He said, "Son, you are always with me, and all that I have is yours." Did you read that? You don't need to backslide, run from God or live a life of sin to have God love you, bless you or throw you a big party. All that God has is ALREADY yours. Everything. By faith, ask, receive and appropriate it...right now!

Read It! Mark 11:24, KJV

Speak It! "Father, I'm sorry for being a jealous or irritated with the attention prodigals get. I can see You've always loved me and wanted me to be blessed with all that You have. I'm glad to be Your child, to know You, to live for You and to serve You faithfully. Everything I need, I receive it now in Jesus' Name. Thank You for being a good Father to me. In Jesus' Name. Amen."

DAY 322

(shamah, shamah, keys to my Honda®)

"A person who speaks in tongues is strengthened personally in the Lord..."
1 Corinthians 14:4, NLT

Need to be strengthened in your inner being? Do you need to be refreshed beyond what you can get from a good night's sleep? Need to be revived beyond the benefits of a week's vacation?

Pray in tongues.

If you haven't gotten into a quiet place alone with the Lord and purposefully prayed in tongues lately, I encourage you to do so. One of God's best gifts to Believers is the ability to be filled with the Spirit and pray in a language given by the Spirit.

I don't know how it works; I just know that it *does* work. When we set aside time to pray in the Spirit (pray in tongues), He builds up our spirit. Our mind may not understand what we are praying about, but our spirit—the real us—is praying directly to the Lord, and we are charged by God's power in our inner man. *(1 Corinthians 14:2, NIV)*

If you've been burning the candle at both ends, pray in tongues. If you're running out of gas, pray in tongues. If you're tired and feeling weary...you got it! Pray in tongues. *(1 Corinthians 14:4, NIV)*

I know, speaking in tongues can seem weird, like a waste of time, a dumb thing to do—and even foolish. Sometimes people have made fun of speaking in tongues with the "shamah, shamah, keys to my Honda..." humor. But, for whatever reason, God seems to take pleasure in using the "foolish things" to confound the wise *(1 Corinthians 1:27-29, NIV)*.

I hope you'll be desperate enough, hungry enough, bold enough and humble enough to forget what other people think and get alone with the Lord to speak in tongues and be strengthened inwardly. If you've never prayed in tongues, but you desire to do so, I encourage you to simply ask the Holy Spirit to come upon you and fill you with His power. He will do it! Then, simply yield to the Spirit and begin to speak the language the Spirit gives you. Your mind may not understand it, but your spirit will be praying directly to the Lord and the Lord will personally strengthen you in your inner most being.

Read It!   1 Corinthians 14:14-15, NIV

Speak It!   "Father, today, I ask You to fill me with Your Spirit. Help me yield to the Spirit and pray in tongues, offering up my heartfelt prayers to You; so I may be strengthened inwardly. Thank You for this great gift. In Jesus' Name. Amen."

DAY 323

(love never fails)

"Love never fails..."
1 Corinthians 13:8, AMP

Been stretched lately? Need a challenge? Tired of the easy, cake-walk Christian life? Think "love" is for wimps? In case your Christian life's been a bed of roses lately and you're looking for the ultimate challenge, here's a reminder that Jesus has called us to live the love life. If you haven't taken the "love test," try it! Say 1 Corinthians 13 out loud by saying *your* name every place you see the word "love." Yeah,...and then just see how many times you cringe. Go ahead... Take the test for yourself:

> "**_Love_** *endures long and is patient and kind;* **_love_** *never is envious nor boils over with jealousy, is not boastful or vainglorious, does not display itself haughtily. It is not conceited (arrogant and inflated with pride); it is not rude (unmannerly) and does not act unbecomingly.* **_Love_** *(God's love in us) does not insist on its own rights or its own way, for it is not self-seeking; it is not touchy or fretful or resentful; it takes no account of the evil done to it [it pays no attention to a suffered wrong]. It does not rejoice at injustice and unrighteousness, but rejoices when right and truth prevail.* **_Love_** *bears up under anything and everything that comes, is ever ready to believe the best of every person, its hopes are fadeless under all circumstances, and it endures everything [without weakening].* **_Love_** *never fails [never fades out or becomes obsolete or comes to an end]." (AMP)*

Don't know about you, but when I take the test, I cringe so many times! Sometimes I wonder if I'm even a Christian! Apparently, God's work in me isn't done. How about you? If you had to cringe more than once when you confessed it, pray it this time.

Read It! Proverbs 10:12

Speak It! "Father, I need Your help! I ask You to forgive me for my failure to walk in the God-kind of love. I ask for Your continued grace, so I can love according to 1 Corinthians 13. I pray I may endure long and be patient and kind; that I'm never envious or boiling over with jealousy, am not boastful or vainglorious or do not display myself haughtily. I pray that I'm not conceited (arrogant and inflated with pride), am not rude (unmannerly) and do not act unbecomingly. I pray Your love in me will flow, so that I don't insist on my own rights or my own way. I pray that I am not self-seeking, fretful or resentful; that I take no account of evil done to me, and I pay no attention to a suffered wrong. I pray for Your help, so I don't rejoice at injustice and unrighteousness; but I rejoice when righteousness and truth prevail. I pray that Your love in me is so strong, I can bear up under anything and everything that comes. I pray I'm ever ready to believe the best of every person. I pray Your love in me causes my hopes to be fadeless under all circumstances, so I endure everything [without weakening]. I know Your love never fails [never fades out or becomes obsolete or comes to an end]. In Jesus' Name. Amen."

DAY 324

(revive me)

"My soul clings to the dust; revive me according to Your word."
Psalm 119:25

Ya know, when we need that morning jolt, a skinny triple cappuccino has a way of "reviving" us...temporarily.

Well, if you need a real, long-lasting revival, there is one sure way to get it—the Word. If you read Psalm 119, you'll notice the phrase "revive me" mentioned 9 times. David needed a big shot of God's reviving power during a particular season of his life, and he asked the Lord to revive him according to the Word. There is something about the reviving power of God's Word—the Bible—that is unlike anything else.

God's Word is living and active and has the power to effectually work within us. I don't know how the Lord does it, but I have experienced the tangible, reviving power of His Word.

How about you? Because the Lord loves us, He wants to revive us. It's one of those little nuggets worth reviewing.

I remember one season in my life when I needed a personal revival. I was driving to speak at a church and had a long trip in my car—just me and the Lord. I decided to listen to the Bible on tape. Five hours later, I had practically listened to the whole New Testament and was revived and ready to preach to the cows!

Need a revival? Spend some extended time reading, listening and meditating upon God's Word and ask Him to revive you...according to His Word.

Read It! Psalm 119:40

Speak It! "Father, I thank You that You revive me according to Your Word. I ask You to speak to me in and through Your Word and revive my spirit, soul and body. In Jesus' Name. Amen."

DAY 325

(blast off)

"For the Lord Himself will come down from heaven, with a loud command, with the voice of the archangel and with the trumpet call of God, and the dead in Christ will rise first. After that, we who are still alive and are left will be caught up together with them in the clouds to meet the Lord in the air. And so we will be with the Lord forever..."
1 Thessalonians 4:16-18, NIV

One day, it's gonna happen. There will be a grand blast-off when millions of Jesus-loving Believers all over the face of the earth vanish in the twinkling of an eye. No, this is not sci-fi; this is Bible fact! There is a big event on the horizon for Christians. It's called the Rapture. All of the signs of our times indicate that this event is getting closer and closer to becoming a reality.

Perhaps you've read the fiction series, *Left Behind*, or Joel Rosenberg's novels that started with, *The Last Jihad*, and you've gotten a taste of how things could play out. It's exciting! While it's true, no one knows the day or hour of Jesus' return and the Rapture of the Church, we can see the signs of the times and get clues. It doesn't matter to me whether the Rapture happens in the "pre-trib" or "mid-trib" or "post-trib" time frame...or whether everyone is dividing the semantics of the "catching away of the Church," the "appearing of the Lord" or the "Day of the Lord" perfectly. I'm just excited that Jesus is Lord and is coming again...soon!

One day, Jesus will appear in the sky and every eye will see Him. Those who love His appearing will hear His command, and a loud trumpet blast will sound. Then, those, who are alive at that time, will be caught up together with the Lord to meet Him in the air...and so we will forever be with the Lord.

The Lord told us to encourage one another with these words. So, listen, if you're having a down day, an overwhelming week, a stressed-out month or the year from hell, keep things in perspective. Be comforted. One day all of these temporal troubles will be swallowed up in a glorious Rapture, and you will enjoy an eternity with the Lord that will be full of joy unspeakable—not to mention, no more tears or pain or sorrow, streets of gold, custom-built mansions, no limits of time or space, relationships full of God's love and sweet, eternal fellowship with God, the Father; Jesus and the Holy Spirit!

Read It! Matthew 24:36-44, NIV

Speak It! "Father, I am so thankful for one of the next big events on Your calendar—the Rapture. I look forward to the day when we see Jesus face-to-face, and we blast off into an eternity with You. In the meantime, help me to be effective in reaching people with the Gospel and being busy with Your business. In Jesus' Name. Amen."

DAY 326

(are you hot?)

"I know your works, that you are neither cold nor hot. I could wish you were cold or hot. So then, because you are lukewarm, and neither cold nor hot, I will vomit you out of My mouth."
Revelation 3:15-16

I always thought these verses seemed a little harsh. How about you? But the other day, I had a God-inspired, light bulb moment...and it all made sense.

Here's what I saw:

- **Hot people.** I saw that God loves people who are passionate for Him and His purposes. He likes people who are hot for Him and on-fire for the things that He is. He's merciful, even if—and when—these people mess up. There are plenty of Bible characters, modern-day Believers and preachers who have messed up royally—still, the Lord is rich in mercy and so willing to forgive and restore those who are on-fire for Him. Sometimes, people throw stones and giant rocks at well-known Believers or preachers who have had a big fall; but I saw that because they were "hot" for the Lord at one time, He is so willing to be gracious, patient, merciful and full of forgiveness toward them when they repent.

- **Cold people.** I saw that while He doesn't want people to be "cold" toward Him, He respects cold people. At least, they aren't being hypocritical about their faith. They clearly don't believe in Jesus, and they live accordingly. Although they are lost and will spend eternity in hell, God respects their right to choose to be cold.

- **Lukewarm people.** I saw that these people really disappoint God. They are in the "disgusting" and "abomination" category. They are Christians in name only, but there isn't very much Christian about their lives. They are religious, but lack a hot relationship with the Lord. They have a form of godliness, but it lacks power. Often, they are "dignified" in their powerless faith and are completely clueless that the Lord is not amused. Their hypocritical lifestyle does a disservice to the cause of Christ. Their critical and judgmental attitude toward the "hot people" adds insult to injury. Their apathy toward the things of God displeases the Lord. Their lack of passion for the Gospel and their lack of action towards His purposes make Him want to vomit them out of His mouth.

Let's not be "cold" or "lukewarm," but "hot" for the Lord and His purposes.

Read It! Matthew 24:12, NIV

Speak It! "Father, I want to be hot for You and Your purposes! If I have been lukewarm, today, I repent. I am sorry for displeasing and dishonoring You by a form of godliness that lacks Your blessing and power. I choose to step over the line today. From now on, You can consider me a radical, on-fire, Jesus-loving Believer, fully committed to Your cause. If I have been cold toward You, I repent, and I invite Jesus to be the Lord of my life today. In Jesus' Name. Amen."

DAY 327

(got pray-ers?)

"Through your faithful prayers and the generous response of the Spirit of Jesus Christ, everything He wants to do in and through me will be done."
Philippians 1:19, MSG

There's nothing like having people who pray for you. The thing I most value in any friendship or relationship is prayer. I believe in the power of prayer. I have experienced the absolute, tangible, life-changing power of prayer.

How about you? I'm sure you feel the exact same way. Isn't it a wonderful thing when the Holy Spirit prompts people to pray for things according to His will?

I have been on both ends of the prayer spectrum. I've been led by the Lord to pray for others, and I've been the recipient of the prayers of wonderful pray -ers! During some difficult days, we have needed and requested the prayers of others, and we've been so thankful for the people who have been so willing to sacrifice their time to pray for us!

I love how the *Amplified Bible* lays out this Philippians 1:19:

> *"For I am well assured and indeed know that through your prayers and a bountiful supply of the Spirit of Jesus Christ (the Messiah) this will turn out for my preservation (for the spiritual health and welfare of my own soul) and avail toward the saving work of the Gospel."*

Between the faithful prayers of dear-hearted, Jesus-loving people and the supply of the Spirit, the Lord preserves and empowers us to do His will and to preach His Gospel. What a blessing!

If you are a pray-er, may the Lord reward you mightily for the prayers you have sown into the lives of others. May He empower and lead you to keep praying and making tremendous power available for others!

If you need prayer, may the Lord raise up pray-ers to lift you up to the Lord, and may He answer in tangible ways for your spiritual health and welfare.

Read It! James 5:16, NLT

Speak It! "Father, I thank You so much for those who have prayed for me, for those who have sacrificed their time, sleep and personal life to lift me up to You. I thank You for answering those prayers. Today, I pray for them, and I ask You multiply every prayer they have prayed back to them and reward them mightily. Father, I ask You to help me be a pray-er for others. Help me listen to the voice and promptings of the Holy Spirit, so that I pray for those You lay on my heart. In Jesus' Name. Amen."

DAY 328

(pray it through)

"Likewise the Spirit also helps in our weaknesses. For we do not know what we should pray for as we ought, but the Spirit Himself makes intercession for us with groanings which cannot be uttered. Now He who searches the hearts knows what the mind of the Spirit is, because He makes intercession for the saints according to the will of God."
Romans 8:26-29

If you feel like you have a big "frustration" living in the middle of your heart, you need to pray it through! If you feel like you're on the verge of tears, you need to pray it through! If you're facing a situation where it looks like there's no way out, you need to pray it through!

We have the best prayer partner in the world. Don't let another day go by where you live with an internal frustration, weakness, anxiety, burden, heaviness or where you're on the verge of tears. Take some time to pray. Get in a quiet place. Go for a drive. Shut your door. Get under your covers. Whatever you need to do to pour your heart out to God, do it!

Like you, I know from experience, the best thing in the world to do when frustration, anxiety, burdens, heaviness or tears try to take over, is to pray it out... and pray it through. In practical terms, that means get to a place where you can hook up with the Holy Spirit and pray out loud, shout, cry, declare, decree the Word, pray in tongues and groanings and put your spiritual stakes in the ground. Yield to the Spirit and trust Him to help you pray according to His Word and His perfect will. He knows the perfect will of God. When we yield to Him and pray/say whatever thing He puts in our spirit and mouth, He helps us pray according to God's will.

Are you ready? Pray from your heart—or your guts—not from your head. Pray the Word of God. Say, "It is written...," and believe it! Pour out your heart and stay in it until you get to the end. Some things take time in prayer. You might have to stay in there for an hour or two and pray it through. When you get to the "end," you will know it because a sense of victory and lightness will fill your heart and mind. You will sense that peace that passes all understanding filling your heart! You may start laughing or singing. When you get to the place of knowing you have the victory, you have prayed it through! Then, after you've prayed it through, you'll know that all things will work together for good for those who love God and are called according to His purpose!

Read It! James 5:16, NIV

Speak It! "Father, I will set aside time to pray...to pray it through. I thank You that the Holy Spirit is my Helper, and He will help me pray according to Your perfect will. In Jesus' Name. Amen."

DAY 329

(you are bigger on the inside)

"Therefore we do not lose heart. Even though our outward man is perishing, yet the inward man is being renewed day by day. For our light affliction, which is but for a moment, is working for us a far more exceeding and eternal weight of glory, while we do not look at the things which are seen, but at the things which are not seen. For the things which are seen are temporary, but the things which are not seen are eternal."
2 Corinthians 4:16-18

Be encouraged. If you are doing your best to follow the Lord, keep up with your family, kids, friends, job, house, bills, volunteering...while at the same time fighting the fight of faith for yourself and others...while at the same time being a source of encouragement for those who are weary...while at the same time getting by on very little sleep...while at the same time feeling like your output is more than your input...while at the same time resisting the devil, know this: though your outward man is getting tired and weary, God is strengthening your inner man. Your spirit is getting stronger, your capacity is being enlarged and your life is producing eternal fruit. *(Isaiah 54:2, NIV)*

These light afflictions are nothing compared to the glories that will be revealed one day. Stay strong. Don't quit! See yourself as a strong, spiritual giant internally. You are strong in the Lord and in the power of His might *(Ephesians 6:10)*. You are more than a conqueror *(Romans 8:37, NIV)*. You are victorious in Christ. Greater is He that is in you than he that is in the world *(1 John 4:4, KJV)*.

I pray for you today. I pray God will make a way to give you rest and refreshing; that the Lord will quicken your mortal body, so you can stand perfect and complete in all the will of God. I pray you see that the eternal fruit will be well worth any temporary challenges or afflictions you may face.

Read It! 1 Chronicles 4:10, NIV

Speak It! "Father, I thank You for strengthening me in my inner man today. I thank You that these light afflictions are nothing compared to the eternal glories that are to be revealed. I am strong in the Lord. I am an overcomer through my faith in Jesus. In Jesus' Name. Amen."

DAY 330

(crooked places)

"Every valley shall be exalted and every mountain and hill brought low;
the crooked places shall be made straight and the rough places smooth;
the glory of the LORD shall be revealed, and all flesh shall see it together;
for the mouth of the LORD has spoken."
Isaiah 40:4-5

Today, trust in the Lord.

Here's a short and simple exhortation. Remember, the Living God is on the job!

Got a valley? It shall be exalted.

Facing a mountain? It shall be brought low.

Dealing with something or someone who is crooked? It shall be made straight.

Facing some rough places? They shall be made smooth.

The result? The glory of God shall be revealed and everyone will see it!

God said it. We can believe it!

Read It! Luke 3:5, KJV

Speak It! "Father, I believe it. My valleys will be exalted. My mountains will be brought low. The crooked ways shall be made straight, and the rough places shall be smooth. I thank You that You will be glorified! You said it, and I believe it. In Jesus' Name. Amen."

DAY 331

(thanks ain't always easy)

"Therefore by Him let us continually offer the sacrifice of praise to God, that is, the fruit of our lips, giving thanks to His Name."
Hebrews 13:15

Giving God thanks is often a sacrifice. It's not always easy to be thankful when you are in a hard place, but it is possible.

Today, think about this:

- **"Let us continually..."** That means...all the time. Don't quit.
- **"...offer the sacrifice of praise to God..."** It's a sacrifice, especially when our feelings aren't in the thankful mode or our circumstances are looking bleak. Offer it. Sacrifice it.
- **"...the fruit of our lips..."** Simply, the power of our words. There are many things that God can give to Himself, but the fruit of our lips isn't one of them. He won't twist our arms; we get to choose to give Him praise and thanks. That fruit can come from our lips.
- **"...giving thanks to His Name..."** Give thanks. We can start giving thanks by looking around and being thankful for what we have now. What do we have? Give thanks to Him for it, today.

Read It! Hebrews 13:15, NLT

Speak It! "Father, I choose to thank You today. I choose to continually offer the sacrifice of praise to You. I praise You for who You are. I praise You that You are these things to me: _____. I give You the fruit of my lips by giving thanks to Your Name. I thank You for what You have done for me. I am thankful today for these things: _____. In Jesus' Name. Amen."

DAY 332

(whoever and whatever)

"For assuredly, I say to you, whoever says to this mountain, 'Be removed and be cast into the sea,' and does not doubt in his heart, but believes that those things he says will be done, he will have whatever he says."
Mark 11:23

Talk about some big words: "whoever" and "whatever."

Jesus had just demonstrated the amazing power of faith. Having walked by a fig tree in the previous verses and not finding any fruit on it, He told that fig tree it would not produce fruit ever again. Jesus talked to a fig tree! The disciples heard Him. The next day, as the disciples were walking by, they noticed that this fig tree had dried up from its roots! Jesus spoke words to a tree and the tree obeyed! The disciples marveled, and Jesus explained what happened. He explained a basic faith principle—the law of faith—and told His disciples—and us—how to operate by faith!

What Jesus didn't say was, "Well, now little disciples, you should not try this at home. I am Jesus, and I am the only One who talks to trees."

- **Whoever.** Jesus said that "whoever" could have faith in God could talk to a tree, a mountain or anything else standing in their way, and it would have to change! Notice, Jesus said that "whoever" could talk to a mountain. He didn't say talk to God about your mountain, and He didn't say talk *about* your mountain; Jesus said "whoever" could talk to the mountain—directly! Are you a whoever? Have you talked directly to the mountains in your life lately?

- **Whatever.** Then, notice that Jesus said we could have "whatever" we say! What does "whatever" include? It includes "whatever" the Bible promises us! Have you gotten into the Word lately to see "whatever" it says about your life and the mountains you face?

If you are *whoever,* you can speak words to your mountain; and if you don't doubt in your heart, but believe the things you say will be done, you can have *whatever* you say! That's the way faith works!

Read It! Luke 17:6

Speak It! "Father, this is almost too good to be true. I believe I am a 'whoever' and I ask You to show me the 'whatevers' in Your Word. I want 'whatever' Your Word has promised me...and especially as it relates to me speaking to the mountains in my life! Lord, I ask You to continue to give me the revelation I need to have faith in God and be a 'whoever' who has 'whatever' I say. In Jesus' Name. Amen."

DAY 333

(new levels, new devils)

"For a great and effective door has opened to me,
and there are many adversaries."
1 Corinthians 16:9

Whenever the Lord opens up big doors, there's also big opposition. As Joyce Meyer puts it, "New levels, new devils." The apostle Paul also dealt with these adversaries during his ministry (*1 Corinthians 16:9 and 2 Timothy 3:12-13, MSG*).

When we built our "mega" church building, we experienced more opposition than at any other time in the history of our ministry. Our church had faithfully served our region for almost 18 years; but from the unrelenting attacks we received—even from those in our community—you would've thought we were building a torture chamber! It was very disappointing and, strangely, almost comical. BUT! The gates of hell could not prevail against the house that Jesus built!

Jesus, as our Redeemer, has completely defeated the devil and every adversary! Think about it this way. When the devil motivates people to oppose the progress of the Gospel or the kingdom life, we should really consider it a compliment from the devil and a sign that great things are ahead! Remember when Peter was inspired by the devil to say words contrary to God's will to Jesus? Jesus had to rebuke the devil by speaking to Peter saying, *"Get thee behind Me, Satan,"* (*Matthew 16:23*).

If you're facing opposition and adversaries, be of good cheer. God is working on a massive testimony; and in the end, you win! As one person put it: "No test. No testimony!" You might be facing some unprecedented, puzzling, vicious and bewildering opposition right now. God may have even opened a door for you, but it seems all hell has come against you and attacks are coming from all directions. Be encouraged today. You can make it! Stand strong and trust the Lord to bring you through!

Read It! Luke 21:15, NIV

Speak It! "Father, I thank You for a great and effective door. I thank You that Jesus is Lord and is the final authority on all things. He has already defeated the enemy; and through the power of Jesus' Name, we enforce the defeat of every adversary. Jesus is the light of the world, and the darkness can never put out the light. He will build His Church, and the gates of hell will not prevail against it. The Lord God Almighty will continue to open up great and effectual doors for church leaders around the world and for Believers in every land. They will proclaim the Gospel with a greater anointing, boldness, and more eternal fruit will be produced than ever before! In Jesus' Name. Amen."

DAY 334

(peace, baby)

"And the peace of God, which transcends all understanding, will guard your
hearts and your minds in Christ Jesus."
Philippians 4:7, NIV

Living in peace is...well...peaceful. Ever noticed?

Sometimes, we get so used to living in God's peace, we forget how wonderful
it is...until we lose our peace. When we start to allow our hearts or minds to
feel unsettled, uneasy, agitated, worried, frustrated or anxious, we know the
peace of God has left the building.

When we yield to God's peace, it acts as a guard over our minds and hearts.
Peace is more than a warm feeling or freedom from fear and anxiety; it's a
spiritual force that helps us to stay in faith. Peace adds courage, strength,
calm, balance, stability and temperance to our lives. Peace is not moved by
bad news. Peace is not easily angered. Peace is not full of anxiety. Peace rests
in God and His Word. Peace is a beautiful thing.

Been agitated or unsettled lately? Stressed out, angry and frustrated? You
need peace, baby! God tells us to pursue peace...so it must be possible to
pursue and catch peace. The Bible actually tells us how to receive peace in
multiplied measures.

When we grow in the full, personal, precise and correct knowledge of God and
Jesus...He automatically multiplies in our hearts and minds. What does that
mean? It means...go after the knowledge of God and peace will be multiplied
to you! Read the Word to get more knowledge. Spend time with God to get
more knowledge.

Today, may your personal knowledge of the Lord increase and may you
go after the precise and correct knowledge of His Word...and may peace be
multiplied to you!

Read It! 2 Peter 1:2, AMP

Speak It! "Father, I thank You for Your peace, today. Thank You that it guards my
heart, my thoughts, and my life. As I seek You today, and obtain knowledge, thank
You that Your peace is growing in my life. I will not be stressed, angry, frustrated,
or full of anxiety because I am filled with Your peace. In Jesus' name. Amen."

DAY 335

(calling good evil)

"Woe to those who call evil good and good evil, who put darkness for light and light for darkness, who put bitter for sweet and sweet for bitter. Woe to those who are wise in their own eyes and clever in their own sight."
Isaiah 5:20, NIV

Now there's a verse that accurately describes our culture! It used to be good to pray in public schools—now it's considered evil. It used to be evil to commit adultery and immoral acts—now it's considered good, acceptable. It used to be evil to kill innocent, unborn people—now it's considered a good thing. We used to call leaders, actors, politicians, athletes and preachers who were honest, upright, honorable, ethical, prayerful and faithful to their spouses good role models. Now, we call those who are cruel, mean-spirited, vulgar and profane...those who lie and then get caught and then apologize...those who diss God and those who cheat on their spouses good role models.

- **The evil will get their reward.** *"Evil men will bow down in the presence of the good, and the wicked at the gates of the righteous." (Proverbs 14:19, NIV) "If a man pays back evil for good, evil will never leave his house." (Proverbs 17:13, NIV) "Many are the sorrows of the wicked..." (Psalm 32:10, AMP) "...the LORD turns his face against those who do evil; he will erase their memory from the earth." (Psalm 34:16, NLT)*

- **Vengeance is the Lord's; good overcomes evil.** *"Never pay back evil for evil to anyone. Do things in such a way that everyone can see you are honorable. Do your part to live in peace with everyone, as much as possible. Dear friends, never avenge yourselves. Leave that to God. For it is written, 'I will take vengeance; I will repay those who deserve it,' says the Lord. Instead, do what the Scriptures say: 'If your enemies are hungry, feed them. If they are thirsty, give them something to drink, and they will be ashamed of what they have done to you.' Don't let evil get the best of you, but conquer evil by doing good." (Romans 12:17-21, NLT)*

Woe to those who call evil good and good evil! Keyword: woe. But, no worries. God always settles the score; and in the end, good prevails over evil.

Read It! Isaiah 5:21, NIV

Speak It! "Father, thank You that good always triumphs over evil; light overcomes darkness. Vengeance is Yours. With Your help, I will conquer evil by doing good. In Jesus' Name. Amen."

DAY 336

(who taught the sun where to stand?)

"For by Him all things were created that are in heaven and that are on earth,
visible and invisible, whether thrones or dominions or principalities or powers.
All things were created through Him and for Him."
Colossians 1:16

The first verse of the song *Redeemer* by Nicole C. Mullen says: "Who taught the sun where to stand in the morning? Who told the ocean you can only come this far? Who showed the moon where to hide 'til evening? Whose words alone can catch a falling star?" There's something about God's creation that makes us stand in awe!

While we were in the process of building our new sanctuary, we got a little taste of "creating." Every week, we'd have a lengthy meeting with our contractor, going over numerous checklists and literally thousands of details—just for one little 'ole building! One week, we brought our daughter, Annie, into the meeting. She was blown away of how intricate all of the fine details were. We spent nearly an hour just to finalize the welcome center kiosks! The height of the finished cabinets and counters, the direction of the wood laminate, the size of pipe to hold the plasma screens...and more. After all of our discussions, we did our weekly walk through making even more detailed decisions on the fly!

One thing we have learned: details aren't often noticed when done right, but are always noticed when done wrong! When details are ignored or not communicated, people get frustrated, make mistakes and things go wrong. Fortunately, God is very into communication and the creative, structural, organizational and logistical details!

When God created the heavens and the earth, He actually "fabricated" them into being with meticulous craftsmanship and attention to details! Just take a look around. A blade of grass. The ecosystem of a lake. A daylily. The workings of a cell. The synchronization of seasons, tides and cycles. They are all the reflection the meticulous Creator.

Creators are known by their creations. All of creation tells us a lot about our amazing Creator and God! Today, let's not make the mistake of worshiping the created things; rather than our Creator, God, who is to be praised forever! He's the One who taught the sun where to stand in the morning.

Read It! Romans 1:20, NLT

Speak It! "Father, I just want to say, 'Thank You,' for all the designing, fabricating and creating You have done in the heavens and on Earth! Thank You that I get to experience and enjoy all of the beauty, aromas, tastes and sounds You have created. In Jesus' Name. Amen."

DAY 337

(the performance)

"I will cry to God Most High, Who performs on my behalf and rewards me
[Who brings to pass His purposes for me and surely completes them]!"
Psalm 52:7, AMP

God is a performer!

He shows up and shows off on the behalf of those who love Him. His eyes are searching to and fro throughout the whole earth to show Himself strong on the behalf of those who are fully devoted to Him.

Be encouraged today. Are you longing for God to perform something amazing in and through your life? He is all about bringing to pass His purposes in your life!

When we embrace God and His Word—specifically this passage—we can rest and trust God to perform things on our behalf. Of course, we have a responsibility: to listen to His voice, be led by His Spirit and obey His promptings. But, He has already obligated Himself to do the hard stuff—the performance part. When God puts on a performance, watch out! When His fingerprints are on something, it's obvious to everyone that the Lord God Almighty is in the house!

God is a performer. Think about that. He performs things on your behalf. Say this a dozen times: "Father, I thank You that You perform on my behalf! I thank You that You perform on my behalf!"

He will perfect whatever concerns us *(Psalm 138:8)*. He will complete what He has started. The living God is on the job and quite the performer! Whatever the Lord has told you, believe that there will be a performance and you'll be blessed!

Read It! Philippians 1:6, KJV

Speak It! "Father, I do believe there will be a performance of the things You have spoken to my heart. I cry to You, the Most High, and I know You will perform on my behalf. You will reward me and bring to pass and complete Your purposes for me. In Jesus' Name. Amen."

DAY 338

(don't have to like 'em, just gotta love 'em)

"We know that we have passed from death to life, because we love the brethren. He who does not love his brother abides in death. Whoever hates his brother is a murderer, and you know that no murderer has eternal life abiding in him."
1 John 3:14-15

Ok, are you struggling with some of the relationships in your life? A family member? Your boss? Co-worker? Friend? A neighbor? Be encouraged. You don't have to like everyone, but you do have to love 'em!

How? With God's love. The minute Jesus comes into our lives, we pass from death to life, and God's love is poured into our hearts. Literally, God infuses us with His unconditional love; and with that love in our hearts, it's impossible to hate people. When God's love fills our hearts—even if someone irritates us, disses us, cheats us, hurts us or mistreats us—we cannot hate them. I'm not saying we don't dislike them, don't get angry with them or don't feel like slapping them. I'm not saying we don't feel like giving them a taste of their own medicine and making their life miserable. I am not even saying we don't get hurt and frustrated with people, at times. BUT! Nonetheless, because of God's love deep within us, we cannot hate them.

Here's the good news: we don't have to like 'em, but we do have to love 'em! I realize some people aren't very likeable. We don't have to like mean-spirited people. We don't have to like our enemies or our critics or liars and abusers. We don't have to like incompetent, manipulative sweet-talkers. We don't have to tolerate being mistreated. We don't have to like what certain people represent or stand for, what they do, what they say or how they behave; but we do have to love them with God's unconditional love.

Somehow, when we yield to the Lord, the love of God bubbles up inside of us, and God's love in us ultimately wants God's best for people—even our enemies. God's best for people is that they repent, surrender and come to know Jesus! It's His best when people He goes to work in their lives renewing, convincing, convicting, changing, rearranging and transforming them. God's love in us wants that for everyone. The caveat: when we love others, not only is it good for them; it's very good for us. The flow of God's love through us washes away anger, bitterness and resentment and fills us with great joy, freedom and peace!

Read It! Romans 13:8, NIV

Speak It! "Father, I've been really frustrated with these individuals (name them). Right now, I don't like them very much, but I choose to love them. I pray You draw them to Jesus and help them become the person You have called them to be. In Jesus' Name. Amen."

DAY 339

(grace and peace...bring it on!)

"Grace to you and peace from God our Father and the Lord Jesus Christ."
Ephesians 1:2

Ever noticed that every epistle in the New Testament starts with some variation of these words, *"Grace to you and peace from God..."*? Most of them end with something like this: *"The grace of our Lord Jesus Christ be with you..."* Romans, 1 and 2 Corinthians, Galatians, Ephesians, Philippians, Colossians, 1 and 2 Thessalonians, 1 and 2 Timothy, Titus, Philemon and Hebrews—even James, and 1 and 2 Peter—bestow "grace and peace" on the reader in the first and last chapters. The Book of Revelation—the last book in the Bible—has as its last words: *"The grace of our Lord Jesus Christ be with you all. Amen,"* (Revelation 22:21).

You kinda get the idea that the Lord wanted His people filled with grace and peace. Perhaps, "grace and peace" are more than nice-sounding platitudes or modes of greeting? Maybe these salutations and benedictions carried more weight than we've originally thought. Rather, they held the power to empower and bless Believers.

- **What is grace?** Grace—from the Greek word "charis"—is a multi-faceted word. The Bible refers to "saving grace," "standing grace," and "serving grace." Grace is the tangible expression of God's favor, joy, delight and His divine influence upon the heart. My favorite meaning of "charis" is from Thayer's Greek Lexicon: "...charis is used of the merciful kindness by which God, exerting His holy influence upon souls, turns them to Christ, keeps, strengthens, increases them in Christian faith, knowledge, affection, and kindles them to the exercise of the Christian virtues..." When "grace" is bestowed on us, we receive God's favor, joy, divine influence in our hearts and His inner strength and ability to do all that is set before us. Wow! Bring it on!

- **What is peace?** Peace—from the Greek word "eirene"—implies prosperity. Peace refers to that tranquil state, quietness, rest. It speaks of harmony between individuals and peace with God. Thayer's Greek Lexicon says this, "...according to a conception distinctly peculiar to Christianity, the tranquil state of a soul assured of its salvation through Christ, and so fearing nothing from God and content with its earthly lot..." The thing so remarkable about peace is that sometimes it's more noticeable when it's gone! A lack of peace is a life of turmoil, anxiety, unrest, rage and frustration. God must've wanted His people loaded with peace of heart and mind at all times. When we receive peace, we enjoy a quiet, tranquil, fearless heart full of confidence, assurance and rest in the God with whom we have peace. His peace acts like a bodyguard—only it guards our minds and hearts in the midst of trouble and fear. Wow! Bring it on!

Read It! 2 Peter 1:2, KJV

Speak It! "Father, I agree with Your Word. I ask for grace and peace from You, the God and Father, and from my Lord Jesus Christ. In Jesus' Name. Amen."

DAY 340

(got soul?)

"He restores my soul..."
Psalm 23:3

Need some refreshing? Need an emotional, mental and personal reset? Thank God; He restores our soul! We are a three-part being—spirit, soul and body.

Just as a reminder, our spirit (or heart)—the part of us that contacts God and is born-again—is the real us. Our soul consists of our mind, emotions and will. Our body is the vehicle we live in in order to have the legal right to live on the earth! At times, the "soulish" part of us—our mind, emotions and will—needs a booster shot!

In some seasons, our spiritual gas tank can be full, and our physical gas tank may be strong; but our soul is weary, tired, drained, overwhelmed and overloaded. In those times, we need the Lord to restore our soul—our mind, emotions and will!

In life, we all experience "drainers" and "replenishers." Certain people or things drain us and certain people or things replenish us. If you are in a season where many people, things, deadlines, emergencies, duties and responsibilities are draining your soul, it's time to find out what refreshes you; and let the Lord fill your soul tank!

Sometimes, the Lord can restore our soul with something as simple as an ice cream cone! My mom and I had a chance to drive to the beach a few weeks ago to look at the sand and water...and eat big ice cream cones. It was simple, yet refreshing!

What refreshes your soul? Hitting a bucket of golf balls? A new tube of lipstick? Coffee with a friend? A date night? A walk in the park? A motorcycle ride? Laying in the sun? Alone time with a book? Gardening? Fishing? What is it for you?

Today, may the Lord give you an opportunity to refresh and open up doors to restore your soul!

Read It! Psalm 23:3, MSG

Speak It! "Father, I am so glad that You restore my soul! I ask You to help me identify the things that refresh and restore my soul, and I thank You in advance for making a way for my soul—mind, will and emotions—to be refreshed and restored, today. In Jesus' Name. Amen."

DAY 341

(throw Jonah overboard)

"Then they said to him, 'What shall we do to you that the sea may be calm for us?'—for the sea was growing more tempestuous. And he said to them, 'Pick me up and throw me into the sea; then the sea will become calm for you. For I know that this great tempest is because of me.' ... So they picked up Jonah and threw him into the sea, and the sea ceased from its raging."
Jonah 1:11-12, 15

Facing a storm? Winds blowing? Waves beating? Facing emotional turbulence? Mental rage? Physical storms? Financial typhoons? You might have to kick a Jonah off your boat!

Most people know the story. God told Jonah to do something, but he ran...from God! He wouldn't obey the Lord. Jonah ran, went to the port and jumped on some stranger's boat. As soon as he got on board, a huge storm started beating against that boat so much, they thought they were all going to die.

Is someone like Jonah on our boat? Have we noticed the constant storm of confusion, strife and frustration in our lives? Could it be associated with the presence of a Jonah? Sometimes, people who are running from God decide to hop on our boat—our emotional, mental, company, financial, staff, church, family or friend boat—and they are the cause of the big storms and difficult seas in our lives!

If you've got a Jonah on board, they've gotta go! Sure, we have to love everyone, but we don't have to everyone access to our lives. Notice the phrase, *"What shall we do to you that the sea may be calm for us?"* Sometimes, it takes more than prayer, reading the Word and fasting. Sometimes, we have to *do* something...if we want the seas to be calm for us. It takes courage to dump a co-dependent or toxic personality; but in the end, it's the best for him or her, too—just like it was for Jonah. Once he found himself in the belly of a giant whale, he finally repented and obeyed God. For those on the boat, the storm waters calmed.

If we want calm to be restored to our lives—spiritually, emotionally, mentally, financially and/or physically—throw Jonah overboard and don't allow him to have access to our life, time, mind, emotions and sphere anymore. It's not always easy to do; but if we want calm waters, we must do it!

Read It! 2 Corinthians 6:14, NLT

Speak It! "Father, my life has been full of turmoil, strife and storms, and I want the seas to become calm for me. I make a decision now to throw Jonah overboard, and I will not give him/her access to my spiritual, mental, emotional, physical, financial or any other boat any longer. In Jesus' Name. Amen."

DAY 342

(this is your wake-up call)

"...'The ground of a certain rich man produced a good crop. He thought to himself, "What shall I do? I have no place to store my crops." Then he said, "This is what I'll do. I will tear down my barns and build bigger ones, and there I will store all my grain and my goods. And I'll say to myself, 'You have plenty of good things laid up for many years. Take life easy; eat, drink and be merry.' But God said to him, 'You fool! This very night your life will be demanded from you. Then who will get what you have prepared for yourself?' This is how it will be with anyone who stores up things for himself but is not rich toward God."
Luke 12:16-21, NIV

This is the big wake-up call parable. It's all about investing in the right things. You get the story, right? This guy was successful and wealthy, and he was great at investing in himself, his family, his company, and his life! He probably drove a nice donkey, his wife shopped at the best markets and had a sweet weaving machine, his oldest son was on a full-ride to Jerusalem U and his youngest daughter was an all-star on the "kick the stone" travel team. His business was going through the roof, and he was in the midst of a big expansion... Then, then suddenly...he had a wake-up call!

God called him a fool and let him know his life was ending that night! Everything he had poured himself into was for naught. He had spent his whole life investing—in all the wrong things! He never had the time or desire to invest in the things that really mattered. He wasn't rich toward God.

How about you? Are you a good investor? Are you rich toward God? The world might call you a great success, but will God call you a fool?

Read It! Luke 12:16-21, NIV

Speak It! "Father, this is a wake-up call. I have been rich toward myself, my family and my kids...but not towards You and Your priorities. I ask You to forgive me. I don't want to be a fool and gain the whole world—all the success and personal perks—and totally miss investing in the most important, eternal things. I repent. In Jesus' Name. Amen."

DAY 343

(the happiest place on earth)

"...How happy your men must be!"
2 Chronicles 9:7, NIV

We asked our staff one day, "Where on earth can people go to experience genuine love, joy, peace and life?" We came to one conclusion: the Church! At least, that's how it's supposed to be. When Jesus is the Head of a church and the Spirit is flowing freely, it should be the happiest place on earth—a place of great joy, freedom, life, gladness, excellence, service and a major, "Wow!" for everyone who enters.

Other than Disneyland, where can you experience this type of thing for an extended period of time? Education can't offer it. The government can't offer it. Many families don't offer it. Most jobs don't offer it. Disney shouldn't have anything on the Church. The Church has an amazing opportunity to be marked by God's very presence, and in His presence is fullness of joy! When there's an open heaven over a church, the Lord pours out His Word, His Spirit, His love, His freedom and His life. He fills a place with an atmosphere of happiness, warmth, excellence, friendliness, care, prayer, worship and genuine love.

Read the whole story of the Queen of Sheba. She went to the happiest place on earth at the time, and her experience took her breath away. She was absolutely amazed. That's how our churches ought to be, right?

"When the queen of Sheba heard of Solomon's reputation, which brought honor to the name of the LORD, she came to test him with hard questions. She arrived in Jerusalem with a large group of attendants and a great caravan of camels loaded with spices, huge quantities of gold, and precious jewels. When she met with Solomon, they talked about everything she had on her mind. Solomon answered all her questions; nothing was too hard for the king to explain to her. When the queen of Sheba realized how wise Solomon was, and when she saw the palace he had built, she was breathless. She was also amazed at the food on his tables, the organization of his officials and their splendid clothing, the cup-bearers and their robes, and the burnt offerings Solomon made at the Temple of the LORD. She exclaimed to the king, "Everything I heard in my country about your achievements and wisdom is true! I didn't believe it until I arrived here and saw it with my own eyes. Truly I had not heard the half of it! Your wisdom and prosperity are far greater than what I was told. How happy these people must be!" (1 Kings 10:1-8, NLT)

Read It! Psalm 35:18, Psalm 22:22

Speak It! "Father, I agree that Your Church should be the happiest place on earth. A place full of friendly people, joy, warmth, freedom and love. Help me to do my part so that my church is a place like that. In Jesus' Name. Amen."

DAY 344

(three things to do in a storm)

"He calms the storm, so that its waves are still. Then they are glad because
they are quiet; so He guides them to their desired haven."
Psalm 107:29

Facing a storm? In my life, the Lord has often given me a heads-up about a
coming storm in my life or ministry through dreams. I could always see the
Lord's mercy and precise wisdom in giving me His strategy to stand and/or overcome any storm. Sometimes, I could do nothing to avert the storm; and He was
just showing me things, so I could stand in faith until it blew over. Other times, it
was because He wanted me to do something by obedience or faith to stop or
calm the storm. If you're facing a storm, here are three things you can do:

- **Repent and obey.** Sometimes, storms come because we're running from the
  Lord. Anytime we decide to rebel or disobey the Lord, we might as well prepare
  for a great wind; we are asking for a storm. Remember Jonah? God told him to
  go to the people of Nineveh and preach the Gospel, but instead Jonah ran away.
  (Jonah 1:3-4, NIV) The mariners eventually threw him overboard. Jonah finally
  repented from inside the belly of a whale, got vomited out and finally obeyed
  God. Listen, if God has called you to go preach or get out of a toxic relationship
  or get off drugs...do it! You're only asking for serious storms if you run from
  Him.

- **Rebuke in faith.** Sometimes, storms come because the enemy wants to distract,
  hinder or stop us from following our God-given mission. Jesus and the disciples
  were in a boat on a mission to get to other side of the lake when a big storm
  arose. The enemy knew if he could take out that boat, he would have destroyed
  Jesus and all His preachers. Jesus woke up and rebuked the storm. Immediately,
  it grew calm. *(Mark 4:37-40)* Notice, God didn't send this storm—otherwise,
  Jesus would have been rebuking Himself. Sometimes, we need to take authority
  over a storm that's hindering the Gospel from going forth, or trying to hinder or
  destroy us. Jesus expects us to exercise the authority He's given us in His Name.
  We can use the Name of Jesus to rebuke any storms that come against us.

- **Believe God.** Sometimes, we are smack dab in the center of God's will and find
  ourselves in the midst of a storm. The apostle Paul was a prisoner on a big ship
  and facing the storm of his life, because the people around him didn't listen to
  his warning. *(Acts 27:9-10)* The ship smashed into the rocks and was destroyed,
  even though everyone's life was spared.

When we face a storm, it's important to listen to the Lord and believe what He
says. It will be just as He says. When we follow Him, He will calm the storm!

Read It! Psalm 34:19

Speak It! "Father, thank You for divine strategies to get through any storm. You
always bring me through as I follow You and Your Word. In Jesus' Name. Amen."

DAY 345

(don't be hating)

"I tell you, her sins—and they are many—have been forgiven,
so she has shown me much love. But a person who is forgiven
little shows only little love."
Luke 7:47, NLT

People who have been forgiven much...show much love to Jesus! People who have been healed aren't afraid to get their praise on. People who know God's goodness...are free to worship. Fellow Believer, don't be hating on these people!

I've heard a few too many Christians say something like this, "I don't like the way So-and-So worships...they are so exuberant," or, "I don't like it when So-and-So says, 'Amen,' during the sermon...," or, "I don't like all that 'hands in the air' worship stuff...," or, "I don't understand why So-and-So gets so excited about God...," or, "I don't like the way that preacher snorts and shouts and spits...,"—and on and on.

Listen, if you have been forgiven for a lot, you can't help but be thankful for God's mercy to you! If you have been healed from a terrible disease, you can't help but praise God! If you really know the Lord, and His goodness is real to you, you can't help but shout, sing, preach, snort and lift your hands to praise Him!

Sure, there are some who may put on a "worship show" just to draw attention to themselves, but that's between them and the Lord. It's not our job to criticize those who are free to worship the Lord; we have no idea what the Lord has done for them!

In fact, we may be the ones with the problem; and our lack of showing love for the Lord may be more of a commentary on our lukewarm status than we realize. Regarding those who show their love for the Lord—God likes it! Take a minute and read the **Read It!** segment about David's worship. He loved the undignified way King David praised Him, but He was very displeased with his wife, Micah, when she dissed on his style of worship. She ended up being barren for the rest of her life.

Don't be a Micah...be a David. Love the Lord...much!

Read It! 2 Samuel 6:14-16, 20-23, MSG

Speak It! "Father, I'm so thankful You've forgiven all my sins and healed my body. I want to show You my love—no matter what others think. I'm not ashamed to praise You and thank You for Your goodness to me. I have been forgiven much, and I love You much! In Jesus' Name, Amen."

DAY 346

(bite the bullet)

"'Bring all the tithes into the storehouse, that there may be food in My house, and try Me now in this,' says the LORD of hosts, 'If I will not open for you the windows of heaven and pour out for you such blessing that there will not be room enough to receive it. And I will rebuke the devourer for your sakes, so that he will not destroy the fruit of your ground, nor shall the vine fail to bear fruit for you in the field,' says the LORD of hosts, 'And all nations will call you blessed, for you will be a delightful land,' says the LORD of hosts."
Malachi 3:10-12

The world's finances are shaking. God's economy is as stable as ever...have you jumped into His plan yet? If not... Have you had enough financial pain yet? Struggled enough? Tired of living paycheck to paycheck?

Get yourself into God's economy! Quit fighting it, making excuses and trying to do it your way. Just follow God's financial plan and start tithing. Really, for your own benefit, you should do it! Malachi 3 is the one passage in the Bible where God says, "...try Me now in this..." In other words, the Lord is says, "C'mon, prove Me now in this," or "Test Me in this and see." If you haven't done so yet, you really should "bite the bullet" and prove God!

Tithing in God's economy is like "Start" in the game of Monopoly. You're not even in the game until you start! Tithing is entry level Christianity—"The Blessed Life 101." It's one of the first doors we need to walk through, if we want to live a supernatural, God-touched life. Sadly, many rationalize why they can't or won't tithe. They decide they'd rather use their own wisdom to live on 100% of their income, rather than giving God His 10% and letting Him bless the 90%. Unfortunately, the result of being the "lord" of your own finances is being disqualified from the blessings that belong to the tither. The windows of heaven aren't opened. The devourer isn't rebuked. Nations aren't calling you blessed. Instead, you end up with the thing they're trying to avoid: continued financial struggles, lack, a burden of debt, a steady stream of "unexpected" things that devour your finances.

The price is too high to not tithe! Prayerfully consider stepping out in faith—give God His 10% and trust Him to bless and multiply your 90%. Bite the bullet and prove Him!

Read It! Malachi 3

Speak It! "Father, You are my source. I trust in You, not uncertain riches or my own wisdom. Thank You for proving Yourself to me in the area of finances, as I take the needed steps to obey You. In Jesus' Name. Amen."

(home sweet home)

"[Put first things first.] Prepare your work outside and get it ready for yourself in the field; and afterward build your house and establish a home."
Proverbs 24:27, AMP

This verse in Proverbs sounds a lot like what Jesus said in Matthew 6:33, *"But seek first the kingdom of God and His righteousness, and all these things shall be added to you."* Jeff and I came to understand that these passages to mean that we were to focus on building His church, and THEN the time would come to focus on building or establishing our own home.

Now, 30 years later, we can honestly say that we have seen these scriptures prove out to be true! When we are faithful to God and His Word, He is always faithful to fulfill His Word for us!

So, what does it mean to *"prepare your work outside and get it ready for yourself in the field"*? Here's what some of the words in this passage refer to:

Prepare = to erect, stand perpendicular
Work = ministry, deputyship
Outside = outside, outdoors
Get it ready = prepare
Field = land, country, ground
Build = begin to build, obtain children, repair
House = family, place, home

If you've been helping a ministry to stand—working and serving in ministry outside of your "8 to 5" job, or as your "8 to 5" job—preparing and getting things ready, volunteering hours into the kingdom of God, you're putting His house first. You qualify for God's promise to meet all of your needs, to take care of your family, and to help you build and establish your own home.

When you put first things first, the Lord will see to it that all the things you need will be added to you—particularly, that your homes and families are built!

Read It! Psalm 92:13, NIV

Speak It! "Father, I am going to put first things first. I choose to seek first Your kingdom, Your priorities, Your Church and Your purposes. I thank You for Your wisdom and grace to balance the responsibilities You have given me. One thing I know for sure, when I seek first Your kingdom in a way that pleases You, Your hand of blessing will be on me as I build my home. I thank You for great blessings in both arenas of my life. In Jesus' Name. Amen."

DAY 348

(what's your problem?)

"Jesus replied, 'Your problem is that you don't know the Scriptures,
and you don't know the power of God.'"
Mark 12:24, NLT

Anyone ever asked you, "What's your problem?" Ever asked yourself, "What's my problem?" If we've got problems, Jesus has the answer! Jesus nailed it in this passage. He identified and told us the root of most of our problems: we don't know the Scriptures...or the power of God.

- **If we don't know the Scriptures...**then we don't have access to God's wisdom, will, strategies or solutions; because that's where we'll find them. Too many of us don't know what we don't know, and we don't realize that from the Lord's point of view, it's a problem! No wonder the Lord said, *"My people perish for a lack of knowledge," (Hosea 4:6).* What we don't know can hurt us! God wants us to know the Scriptures. No matter what we may face in life—in any area of our lives—the Lord has given us answers for every problem in His Word.

- **If we don't know the power of God...**then, we don't have access to God's supernatural intervention on our behalf. God's power is released by faith through the working of the Holy Spirit and in line with the Scriptures. When God's power comes on the scene, everything changes! If we're not experiencing that life-giving, life-changing power that raised Jesus from the dead, then that's a problem. The Almighty is still distributing His power these days!

Can you imagine how disappointing it would be to live in a "smart" house and not know it? You know, the ones that have power lights, window shades and music; remote-controlled everything! Major security, high-tech electronics and appliances that are networked and connected to the wireless Internet that was available in every room of your house. Wouldn't that be incredible!? But, if you didn't *know* you lived in a "smart" house, you would resort to old-fashioned ways of doing things and would create more work for yourself than was necessary.

That's exactly what happens when we don't know the power of God. We create a lot of work for ourselves. Ready to fix your problems? It's guaranteed; if we'll spend time in the Word of God and spend time in conversation with the Holy Spirit, God will fill us with His wisdom and a supernatural power to overcome any problem!

Read It! Proverbs 2:6, NIV

Speak It! "Father, I can clearly see what my problem is. I need to know the Scriptures and the power of God more—a lot more! Help me set aside time to read and study Your Word and to converse with the Spirit so I know what I know and walk in Your power. In Jesus' Name. Amen."

DAY 349

(trick questions)

"Jesus saw through their hypocrisy and said, 'Whom are you trying to fool with your trick questions?'"
Mark 12:15, NLT

Don't be duped by people who want to impress, intimidate, irritate, dissuade, mislead or stop you. At times, we all have to interact with dishonest, insincere, hypocritical people who try to thwart God's plan by fooling us, pulling the wool over our eyes and tricking us with their questions.

Jesus faced it, too. He was here on a heavenly assignment, completing God's mission and fulfilling His purpose and—try as they might—the human powers that be could not stop Him! Maybe they thought He was naïve or too loving to call them on the carpet, but they were wrong! Jesus saw right through the trap these leaders were setting, so He wowed them with His wisdom and left them speechless.

These things still happen today. Jesus is still here on a heavenly assignment, completing God's mission and fulfilling His purposes through His people! No one and nothing—not even the gates of hell—are going to stop Him or His Church *(Matthew 16:18)*. Nonetheless, on occasion, people in positions of power or influence try to take advantage of Christians because they mistakenly think they are naïve, weak, spineless people who don't know how to recognize and stand up to a trap or trick.

I love how Jesus beat them at their own game—every time! Is someone trying to push you around? Are you being unfairly harassed or hindered in your God-given purpose by anyone in a power position? Anyone setting traps or trying to trick you with their deceitful questions?

Be like Jesus and see right through the hypocrisy. Wow them with godly wisdom! Listen to the Holy Spirit, and He will help you play "the games" and win!

Read It! Isaiah 54:17

Speak It! "Father, thank You that in Christ, I win! No weapon formed against me will prosper. I am here on a heavenly assignment, completing Your mission and fulfilling Your purpose. I am not going to lay down and be duped by trick questions or hypocrisy. Thank You for filling me with Your wisdom to win! In Jesus' Name. Amen."

DAY 350

(the 1,000-yard stare)

"We are hard pressed on every side, but not crushed; perplexed, but not in despair; persecuted, but not abandoned; struck down, but not destroyed."
2 Corinthians 4:8-9, NIV

Are you battle-weary? Been facing unrelenting stress? Feeling detached? Got the "1,000-yard stare" going? According to *Wikipedia*, the 1,000-yard stare is a phrase originally coined to describe the limp, unfocused gaze of a battle-weary soldier. The stare is the result of combat stress. One soldier, Corporal Joe Houle, described the 1,000-yard stare when he arrived in Vietnam in 1965. He said he saw no emotion in the eyes of his new squad: "The look in their eyes was like the life was sucked out of them."

Sometimes, we can get weary in the Christian life, especially when we are in the heat of battle and are facing constant trials, tribulations, persecutions and opposition. The enemy loves nothing more than to press, perplex, persecute and strike at any Believer who's making a dent on his kingdom. He'd love to make God's soldiers battle-weary by sucking the life out of them and sending them into the 1,000-yard stare.

If you're weary, be encouraged today. You will not be crushed, abandoned or destroyed. Jesus is still Lord, and He will strengthen you today! I encourage you to meditate and saturate your heart in these verses of Scripture and be strengthened in your inner man.

"But those who wait on the Lord shall renew their strength; they shall mount up with wings like eagles, they shall run and not be weary, they shall walk and not faint." (Isaiah 40:31)

"So let's not allow ourselves to get fatigued doing good. At the right time we will harvest a good crop if we don't give up, or quit." (Galatians 6:9, MSG)

Read It! Hebrews 12:2-3, MSG

Speak It! "Father, my eyes are fixed on You and the things that matter. I know these hard times are small potatoes compared to the coming good times. I will pray constantly and never quit. I will wait on You, and You will renew my strength. I set my eyes on the finish line and dig my heels of faith into You and Your Word. Thank You for shooting 'adrenaline' into my soul! In Jesus' Name. Amen."

DAY 351

(are you kidding me?)

"...'Man shall not live by bread alone, but by every word that proceeds from the mouth of God.'"
Matthew 4:4

Many of the significant events in my life are referenced not by dates on a calendar, but by scriptures in the Word. If we will live by the Bible, the Lord will literally give us words to live by! Here are some examples:

Years ago, I was living in California to help out a friend. Unfortunately, they weren't very receptive, and my words fell on deaf ears. When I sought the Lord about staying there in Cali or moving back home to Michigan, this is the Scripture I read: *"And when they had performed everything according to the Law of the Lord, they returned to Galilee, to their own city of Nazareth," (Luke 2:39).* Bingo! I got the word I needed, so I loaded up and moved back home, just like the Bible said! And, God blessed me in that move.

At another point in my life, I was working in a good job, but I wasn't fulfilled. My desire was to go to Bible school in Tulsa, OK. So, again, I asked the Lord for direction, just knowing I would hear, "Yes, Beth! This is My ordained will for you. Be blessed and learn!" Ummm, not quite. Again, while reading my Bible, I came across this scripture: *"...dwell in the land and cultivate faithfulness," (Psalms 37:3).* I thought, "What? Are you kidding me? Dwell here? In Michigan? Be faithful? This must be the devil talking!"...but I knew it was the Lord, so I stayed and worked on being faithful; and the Lord blessed it.

By year's end, I was offered my "dream job" as Creative Art Director for a large greeting card company. Again, I asked the Lord about it and read it in the Word: *"You have dwelt long enough at this mountain. Turn and take your journey...," (Deuteronomy 1:6,7).* Which way should I turn? Greeting cards or Bible school? Again, I got into the Word and read: *"Then Samuel left for Ramah...," (1 Samuel 15:34).* I did a double-take! Ramah? Are you kidding me?" The Bible school I really wanted to attend was "Rhema." Was it a fluke coincidence or God? I sensed God's peace in my heart, and I took my journey to Rhema! It was the right move. God blessed me beyond my wildest imaginations!

The Word is full of specific direction for our lives; and as we spend time in His Word, He will give us words to live by!

Read It! Matthew 4:4

Speak It! "Father, I trust You with everything I am, and everything I will be. You know my life, inside and out. Today, help me to hear You in Your Word. I believe that as I read, You will speak directly to my life and give me specific direction today. Thank You for loving me! In Jesus' name. Amen."

DAY 352

(the currency of the kingdom)

"But without faith it is impossible to please Him,
for he who comes to God must believe that He is,
and that He is a rewarder of those who diligently seek Him."
Hebrews 11:6

Faith is the currency of God's kingdom! It pleases the Lord when we are loaded with faith. It pleases Him when we appropriate our faith and partake of His goodness and rewards.

In the natural world, money is the currency of the earth's kingdoms, right? Financial wealth is what gives us purchasing power in the world. But, in God's kingdom, faith is the currency. Faith is what gives us the "purchasing power" to obtain, access and walk in the abundant life.

I love this because by making faith the currency of the kingdom, the Lord leveled the playing field. It doesn't matter what language you speak, what nation you live in, what color your skin is or what gender you are—faith is an option for whosoever will.

How do we know that faith is the currency of God's kingdom? Listen to what Jesus said, *"If you can believe, all things are possible to him who believes," (Mark 9:23).* He didn't say "all things are possible to him who is a millionaire..." Jesus said all things are possible to those with faith. So, if you are not a financial tycoon, be encouraged. You can be rich in faith and when you are loaded with faith—all things are possible!

We can't buy the truly blessed, successful life with the currency of money; however, we can use the currency of faith and access an extremely blessed, successful and servant-hearted, fruitful life that pleases the Lord.

So, what's the bottom line? Get rich in the currency of faith. You don't have to beg for it, pray for it or work for it. There is only one way to get more faith: *"Faith comes by hearing and hearing by the Word," (Romans 10:17).* The more you hear God's Word, the more faith you get! If you want to be rich in faith, get into God's Word and get loaded in faith! God will be pleased!

Read It! Mark 11:24, NIV

Speak It! "Father, I want to please You by operating in faith. I can see that, in Your kingdom, the currency is faith. Help me spend more time in Your Word, so I am rich in faith. I want You to be magnified as I access the blessed, successful, servant -hearted and fruitful life! In Jesus' Name. Amen."

362

DAY 353

(my magnificat)

"My soul magnifies the Lord, and my spirit has rejoiced in God my Savior."
Luke 1:46-47

Mary burst out with what is known as "Mary's Magnificat"—or Mary's Song. When she experienced God's favor and goodness in being selected to carry Jesus, the Son of God, she magnified the Lord and rejoiced in God her Savior. Keep in mind that when Mary sang her song, the only "evidence" she had of being pregnant with Jesus was God's Word spoken to her by the angel Gabriel. By faith, she believed and rejoiced!

Have you had a "magnificat" lately? Has the Lord promised you some mighty things? Has the Lord done mighty things for you? Today, why not break free with a song of praise—an exclamation of rejoicing!

Grab onto a few verses and start priming the magnificat pump:

"Not to us, O LORD, but to You goes all the glory for Your unfailing love and faithfulness." (Psalm 115:1, NLT)

"This is the LORD's doing, and it is marvelous to see. This is the day the LORD has made. We will rejoice and be glad in it." (Psalm 118:23-24, NLT)

"And my soul shall be joyful in the LORD; it shall rejoice in His salvation. All my bones shall say, 'LORD, who is like You...'" (Psalm 35:9-10)

"Shout joyfully to the LORD, all the earth; break forth in song, rejoice, and sing praises." (Psalm 98:4)

Today, pour out your heart to the Lord and give Him your "magnificat!"

Read It! Psalm 34:3, KJV

Speak It! "Father, I rejoice in You! You have been good to me; You have been a faithful God. I praise You for Your mercy, grace, favor and blessings! You are the great God above all and over all. You are the Most High God. Jesus, You are exalted over all the earth; Your Name is above every name. At Your Name, every knee will bow; and every tongue will confess that You are Lord. You are the Lord of glory, my good Shepherd, my Healer, my Redeemer, and my dearest Friend. Holy Spirit You are the greater One. You are my Helper, my Counselor, my Strengthener—and so much more. I worship You; all glory and honor goes to You, Lord God Almighty! You are the exalted One, the Creator of the ends of the earth. You are before all things, and in You all things consist. You are the first and the last, the beginning and the end; the Alpha and the Omega, the Author and the Finisher. You have done great things. May You be honored, recognized, respected, admired and lifted up in every way, every day. In Jesus' mighty Name. Amen!"

DAY 354

(the credits)

"This was the Lord's doing; it is marvelous in our eyes."
Psalm 118:23

Do you ever sit through the credits at the end of a movie? It's amazing how many people are involved in making a film, isn't it? It takes dozens of people working behind the scenes to put a few actors on the big screen; and after all their hard work on the production, they get to be mentioned and recognized in the credits.

So, at the end of the various scenes and the grand finale production of our lives, who's getting mentioned in the credits? Of course, we can—and should—give honor to whom honor is due; that is, the various people God has used to help enrich and bless our lives. But, ultimately, Jesus should get the highest honor in "the credits" of our life. Any good thing in our life is the Lord's doing and quite marvelous. When the credits roll, Jesus should be seen and recognized.

If we aren't careful, we can start to take the credit, forgetting that apart from Christ, we can do nothing. When we really stop and think about it, what credit can we take for anything? Someone might say, "I've worked hard to accomplish all of these things! I deserve the credit." That may be true, but who gave you the strength to work so hard? Someone might say, "It was my idea! I deserve the credit." Really? Who gave you the creative mind? Someone might say, "I am the one who paid for it. I deserve the credit." Yeah, but who gave you the power to get wealth? Someone might say, "I started it. I stopped it. I brought it. I took it. I created it. I invented it. I stayed up late. I got up early. I built. I sold. I finished. I grew. I inspired. I wrote. I sang. I led. I drew. I designed. I carried. I lifted. I negotiated. I healed. I represented. I taught. I preached. I trained. I worked. I prayed. I cried. I laughed. I cooked. I cleaned. I cared. I comforted. I called. I held. I stood. I served. I deserve the credit!" Is that right? Who gave you the power to see, hear, taste, touch, smell, think, create, get up, lie down, walk, talk, imagine, move and...breathe?

Let's just admit it. Apart from Christ, we can't do anything! We need to keep things in perspective. While He may use us to do any number of things, He gets the glory; and we get the joy of being used by Him. He gets the credit, and we get the benefit!

Read It! Revelation 4:11

Speak It! "Father, I thank You for all the good things You are doing in and through my life. Today, I remember that it is not by my might or power, but it is Your power and blessing in my life that enables me to do anything of worth. I give You all the credit! The blessings in my life are the Lord's doing and they really are marvelous in my eyes. In Jesus' Name. Amen."

DAY 355

(the fruit speaks)

"A tree is identified by its fruit. Make a tree good, and its fruit will be good.
Make a tree bad, and its fruit will be bad."
Matthew 12:33, NLT

A tree is known by its fruit. This little truth answers a lot of life's questions.

People can say all kinds of amazing things or all kinds of terrible things about a particular tree—a person, a church, a family or an organization—but if you really want to know what that person, church, family or organization is like, just look, listen and taste the fruit! The fruit will tell you all about the tree! If you bite into a juicy peach, you can be 100% sure that the tree is indeed a peach tree. If you bite into a bitter crab apple, there's no doubt about it—it's a crab apple tree.

If you've ever thought, "I wonder what that person, church, family or organization is really like?"...just look at, listen to, and taste the fruit! Does the consistent, overall fruit of a person, church, family or organization sound, look and taste like: love, joy, peace, patience, kindness, gentleness, goodness, faith, generosity, sweetness, grace, mercy, truth, honesty, integrity, humility, victory and success? If so, you can be 100% certain the tree is good. That is a fact. You can fake a lot of things...but you can't fake fruit!

On the other hand, if the consistent, overall fruit of a person, church, family or organization sounds, looks and tastes like: hate, anger, bitterness, depression, agitation, impatience, mean-spiritedness, cruelty, harshness, criticism, unbelief, doubt, selfishness, greed, dishonesty, immorality, pride, complaining, grumbling, negativity and defeat...you can be 100% certain that the tree is bad!

Today, why not quit listening to everyone's opinions, the latest polls, news media, editorials, blogs, or gossip about every person, church, family or organization. Be smarter than that. Just look, listen and taste the fruit. Remember, a tree is identified by the kind of fruit it produces.

Read It! Luke 6:43-45, NLT

Speak It! "Father, I thank You for making things so simple. I want to be a good tree that produces good fruit. Forgive me for judging people, churches, families or organizations based on anything other than their fruit. Give me discernment to recognize good fruit and good trees and to have the wisdom to stay away from bad fruit and bad trees. In Jesus' Name. Amen."

DAY 356

(seven things God hates)

"There are six things the Lord hates, seven that are detestable to him:
haughty eyes, a lying tongue, hands that shed innocent blood, a heart that
devises wicked schemes, feet that are quick to rush into evil, a false witness
who pours out lies and a man who stirs up dissension among brothers."
Proverbs 6:16-19, NIV

God is love, but what about the things He hates? Seems a bit oxymoronic,
doesn't it? It's not! Actually, *because* God is love, He hates these things!

- **Haughty eyes.** This is the person who has a proud look; thinks more highly of
  themselves than they ought, and more lowly of others than they ought.
  Arrogant eyes are revealed in their looking down their nose and condescending
  air. Humble those eyes!

- **A lying tongue.** Liars are fryers! God hates lying. Jesus said the devil was a liar
  and the father of lies; so liars are not keeping good company. Honesty is the
  best policy. Some people can smile and look you right in the face while telling
  you a bold-faced lie. People usually lie to cover their tracks or for selfish gain;
  but in the end, it always backfires. Tell the truth.

- **Hands that shed innocent blood.** God never condones those who justify hurting
  the innocent—those in the womb, infants, children, teens or those who are old
  and unaware. If God hates it, then we should hate it. Defend the innocent.

- **A heart that devises wicked schemes.** This would include manipulators, cheats,
  smooth-talkers and double-tongued people who talk out of both sides of their
  mouth. They only have their own best interests in mind. God hates this.

- **Feet that are quick to rush into evil.** God hates evil. People who call good evil and
  evil good and those who make evil prevail are not friends of God. Run from evil.

- **A false witness who pours out lies.** Today, people feel they have the right to say
  anything they want about anyone—true or not. God hates it. Thankfully, He
  knows the truth and will vindicate the righteous and judge the liar.

- **A man who stirs up dissension among brothers.** This is the one who enjoys those,
  "I'm just telling you this, but don't tell anyone," conversations to spread untruths
  and undermine their relationships, friends, co-workers, boss, or church. They
  think they're getting away with it, but "the little birdy" always finds them out. God
  hates those who sow discord. Be a unifier!

Let's live our lives in such a way as to experience the goodness of the Lord,
instead of finding ourselves on the "severe" side of the Lord.

Read It! Romans 11:22

Speak It! "Father, I'm sorry for participating in any things You hate. Help me to
live in a such a way to do the exact opposite of those things. I want to live in Your
goodness. In Jesus' Name. Amen."

DAY 357

(everyone has a story)

"The Spirit of the Lord GOD is upon me, because..."
Isaiah 61:1, NASB-U

The Spirit of the Lord is upon us *because...* Because of what?

Because He wants to minister "to us" and "through us."

Everyone has a story, a story that God wants to touch, heal and bless. Everyone has a story that the Lord wants to use to help others. In order to do that, He often has to minister "to us" and then "through us" in order to help others.

The Lord knows all about "our story" and all the things we have been through. He knows the toll that sin, this fallen world and cruel human beings can take. Jesus knows the pain of abuse, rejection, disapproval, loneliness, illness and human cruelty. The Lord is aware that these things often bring us to a place of brokenness, emptiness and utter dependence on Him. Don't despair. No matter how bad or sad, God can redeem our story.

Whether we have experienced these things in a huge way or in a small measure, we've all been scathed by the world in which we live. When we cry out to the Lord, He will minister "to us" and heal our broken hearts. He'll set us free. He'll restore our lives and fill us with joy, strength and purpose. Then, the Lord will minister "through us," so we can help others with their story.

Today, be encouraged and allow the Lord to minister "to you," so He can also minister "through you" to help others.

Read It! Isaiah 61:1-4, NASB-U

Speak It! "Father, I thank You that You will use my story for Your glory. Thank You for the anointing of the Holy Spirit that ministers 'to me' and 'through me.' Help me to be patient as You work in me and as You prepare to work through me. In Jesus' Name. Amen."

DAY 358

(dislocated?)

"But now God has set the members, each one of them,
in the body just as He pleased."
1 Corinthians 12:18

I remember jumping off the diving board and seeing little Eddie in his bright orange life jacket. He darted out to the middle of the pool just as I starting flying through midair! When I hit the water, all the parts of my body plunged below the surface—except for my little finger! My pinkie got caught on Eddie's life jacket strap. When I popped up out of the water and saw my little finger bent at 90 degrees, I knew I had a problem!

Did you know that many members of the Body of Christ are just like my finger was? They are dislocated from their God-intended position and intended purpose. The Lord has designed a perfect fit for every one of us in each season of our lives, but being "dislocated" from the Body makes it very difficult to fulfill the role God has ordained for us!

We need to always ask the Lord what "body part" He desires us to be?

He knows where we all fit. Even if we do become "dislocated," He knows what other parts of the Body to connect us with. All we need to do is get quiet, humble ourselves before the Lord and ask Him where we are to function. Don't tell Him...*ask Him*! Find out what pleases Him—the Great Shepherd. Then, follow His orders and take the necessary steps to become a fruitful part of a local Body (a.k.a. a local church) under the leadership of a local under-shepherd (a.k.a. a pastor).

Read It! Ephesians 5:30, KJV

Speak It! "Father, I will follow You. It's no fun to be dislocated from Your Body. I ask You to set me in the Body as it pleases You. Maybe I have been trying to figure out what job to take, what neighborhood to live in and what school to attend—when the real question ought to be: 'Lord, what church do you want me to be a part of; what role do You want me to play in the Body?' I know that when I'm connected to Your Body in a healthy way, all of the other things in my life will fall into line. Jesus, You are the Chief Shepherd of the global Church. Help me follow You as I do my part in a local church led by the under-shepherds/pastors You have ordained. In Jesus' Name. Amen."

DAY 359

("they" don't know squat)

"Where is the wise man? Where is the scholar? Where is the philosopher of this age? Has not God made foolish the wisdom of the world?"
1 Corinthians 1:20, NIV

Ever been intimidated, silenced, put down, ridiculed or scoffed at by "they"? Are you ready to stand up to "they"? Here's a pep talk to put things in perspective. "They" are...

- Usually one or two people who are outspoken, not an entire nation; so don't back down.
- Often "wanna-bes" who don't have a lot of success in their own lives, so they spend their energy telling you why you can't do something.
- Usually too timid or spineless to talk to you face-to-face, so they act like a mouse with a megaphone, as they criticize you and your success.
- Generally impressed with themselves and their own knowledge or importance, but don't understand things of eternal value and are often unknowingly motivated by the evil one and pushing his agenda.

It's time we stood up to "they"—so, be strong and courageous! What have "they" said to you? What have "they" tried to talk you out of? Here are a few things "they" tried to talk me out of:

- Told my sisters and me that kids from broken homes don't amount to much, but God said he had a plan for our future to prosper us! *(Jeremiah 29:11, NIV)*
- Told us God could never bless or grow a church with a woman co-leading; but God said He wouldn't only use me, but that I would be effective! *(Acts 18:24-26, NLT)*
- Told me to be quiet, but God said for me to speak out and not be afraid! *(Acts 18:11, NLT)*
- Told us pastors' kids turn out to be rebels, but God said they would choose the right path and serve the Lord! *(Proverbs 22:6, NLT)*
- Told us you can't build a mega-church in a small little community, but Jesus said the gates of hell couldn't stop it! *(Matthew 16:18)*
- Told all of us, "You can't do that," but Jesus said all things are possible if we only believe! *(Mark 9:23)*

Get it? "They" don't know squat! Keep listening to the Lord and obeying His Word. God delights to make foolish the wisdom of "they."

Read It! 1 Corinthians 1:27, KJV

Speak It! "Father, thank You that I don't have to listen to 'they,' because 'they' don't know squat. I believe what You say in your Word! In Jesus' Name. Amen."

DAY 360

(clickage)

"Behold, how good and how pleasant it is for brethren to dwell together in unity! ... For there the LORD commanded the blessing..."
Psalm 133:1, 3

Our paraphrase goes like this: "How good and pleasant it is when you have clickage with others...for there the Lord commands the blessing..." There is something to be said about the intangible "clickage" factor when it comes to relationships, teams, staffing and group dynamics.

Bill Hybels, founder of Willow Creek Church, believes to accomplish anything of significance in God's kingdom, we must be surrounded by people who have the 3 "C's"—Competence, Character and Chemistry. We totally agree. So much so, that we added another one—Communication. Whether you are a leader, manager, pastor, team-member, or volunteer, these 4 "C's" are crucial to make your team reach their maximum potential.

- **Competence.** Every team must have competent people who are knowledgeable, skilled, talented and wise in maximizing their God-given gifts. Charisma will only take us so far. Without competence in a given area, a team member will thwart his or her long-term effectiveness and even damage to the entire team.

- **Character.** Businesses and ministries have paid a high price by having immature, ungodly people with loose morals on their teams. People who have matured in their walk with God and know how to exercise character traits like honesty, integrity, morality, humility and self-control are worth their weight in gold.

- **Chemistry.** This is what we call "clickage." After all, if we are going to spending at least 8 hours a day together, it's important that we all click and get along at some level. Chemistry and clickage are such tangible intangibles. We don't always know at first if we have it; but we definitely know if we don't. Clickage makes the whole team more creative and productive.

- **Communication.** If people are going to have any sense of team, they must communicate. In our experience, we can't over-communicate. People want and need to know what's expected of them and how well they are doing. Leaders need to constantly speak the vision. Nothing will ruin a team's momentum or dynamic any quicker than a lack of communication or communication that is confusing or hard to follow.

We have found that when these 4 C's are working in our leadership team, we have fun, experience creativity and freedom, and see great fruit. When we work together in unity, *there* God commands His blessing!

Read It! Acts 4:32, KJV

Speak It! "Father, I thank You that You know what team I need to be on at work, at church and in other areas of my life. Help me to function effectively in all 4 C's and flow well with others. In Jesus' Name. Amen."

DAY 361

(the red line)

"Then, because so many people were coming and going that they did not even have a chance to eat, He said to them, 'Come with Me by yourselves to a quiet place and get some rest.'"
Mark 6:31, NIV

Been living on the red line? Red line living is fun, fast and exciting...no doubt about it. But, living on the red line cannot be sustained—nor should it be. The red line is for overdrive seasons. If you've been burning the candle at both ends, working a 24/7 schedule and carrying the weight of the world—take a break!

Jesus approves and recommends it. How to detach from the red line:

- **"Come with Me..."** Take a break with Jesus. Hang out with Him. Go shopping with Him. Read a book with Him. Take a walk with Him. Sing with Him. Golf with Him. Lay in the sun with Him. Stare at the mountains with Him. Be with Him.

- **"...by yourselves..."** Being with a group is great, being in church is great, being with our spouses, kids and friends is great; but we all need time by ourselves with Jesus. Get alone with God.

- **"...to a quiet place..."** Silence is good. Tune out the noise, clutter and commotion of this world. Find your quiet place. Some versions state the passage this way... *"Come ye yourselves apart into a desert place,"* (vs. 31, KJV)—a sure sign that Palm Springs is God's will. *"And they departed into a desert place by ship privately,"* (vs. 32, KJV)—a definite confirmation you need to go on a cruise.

- **"...to get some rest."** Keyword: rest. That means unplug. Turn off the cell phone. Don't do work on your laptop. Sleep. Eat. Laugh. Wind down the turbines. Forget the schedule. Rest the mind, body, emotions and spirit.

We have seasons of living intensely on the red line—working 80+ hour weeks, late nights and early mornings, living under crazy pressure and opposition and carrying a lot of extra weight. In some ways, it was fast, fun and exciting; yet, we've also known it could not be sustained, nor would God want it to be. It was an appointed season. We do something really smart during these red line seasons. We make plans to take several breaks at the end of the red line—to get with Jesus, by ourselves, to a quiet place and rest and recharge.

Is it time to detach and get some rest? Find pockets of time to seek the Lord and get your battery recharged and your tank re-fueled.

Read It! Psalm 62:1, NIV

Speak It! "Father, thank You for the grace and joy of those red line seasons and the eternal fruit they produce. Tank You for the opportunity to get alone with You, by myself, in a quiet place to get some rest. I ask You for Your strategies to do this. In Jesus' Name. Amen."

DAY 362

(run, baby, run)

"God-devotion makes a country strong;
God-avoidance leaves people weak."
Proverbs 14:34, MSG

What makes a great nation? God-devotion. What brings a nation to downfall? God-avoidance. What's the difference? We are! It's time for Christians—Christ-followers, true-blue Believers—to wake up, rise up, stand up and run, baby, run! That's right—run for office.

How will the world around us know anything about Jesus if we keep Him locked up inside the four walls of the church? They won't! Why do Christians seem to think that being involved in their political landscape is not "spiritual" or something God would approve of? The truth is, we were put here on this earth to make a difference—in every arena.

Maybe when we get tired of ungodly agendas and personal ambitions dominating our schools, cites, states, and countries, we will do something about it. It's time for us to hear the direction of the Lord and then go for it. Run, baby, run! Run for township positions. Run for School Board slots. Run for City Council. Run for Mayor. Run for State Representative. Run for the Senate. Run for Governor—even run for President! Don't be afraid. Be encouraged by what the Bible says about Godly leaders and authorities:

- **Good leaders are called and appointed by God.** *(Romans 13:1-2)*
- **Good leaders are called to help their constituents.** *(Romans 13:4, NLT)*
- **Good leaders have a good moral compass.** *(Proverbs 16:12, MSG)*
- **Good leaders speak the truth.** *(Proverbs 16:13, MSG)*
- **Good leaders invigorate others.** *(Proverbs 16:15, MSG)*
- **Good leaders don't lie.** *(Proverbs 17:7, MSG)*
- **Good leaders are good at heart.** *(Proverbs 19:12, MSG)*
- **Good leaders are honest and effective communicators.** *(Proverbs 22:11, MSG)*
- **Good leaders are competent.** *(Proverbs 28:16, MSG)*
- **Good leaders have self-control, know right from wrong.** *(Proverbs 31:4-5, MSG)*

If we meet the standards and qualifications for godly leaders, and if God is leading us in that direction, then here is the word for today: Run, baby run!

Read It! Psalm 33:12, TLB

Speak It! "Father, I'm willing to do whatever You ask of me. I seek You Lord, and I know that the only way for evil to increase is for good men and women to do nothing. I submit myself to You and I ask for Your direction. In Jesus' Name. Amen."

DAY 363

(the sweet spot)

"Your word is a lamp to my feet and a light for my path."
Psalm 119:105, NIV

There's nothing better than living in the perfect will of God. Everything just works better. There's grace for the pace, faith to move mountains, anointing to break yokes and divine favor at every turn. Things fall into place like clockwork and life is full of joy and peace. I like to call it, living in the sweet spot of life.

Golfers know about the sweet spot. It's the one place right in the middle of the club that, if you can hit it, makes everything work perfectly. The sound it makes when it hits that little, white ball is like none other! And when that little ball takes off, all of the sudden, the person who hits it feels like Tiger Woods! (That is...until they shank the next one!) Even some golf club makers advertise: "Our clubs have a larger sweet spot!"

Oh, to live in that exact place, every day.

Of course, trying to live outside God's will is not so sweet. Believe me, I've been there! There is continual frustration and disappointment. It's like sledding down a dirt hill; being a day-late-and-a-dollar-short; ending up on the short end of the stick... You get the picture.

So, how do we find that sweet spot? Thankfully, He's made it easy! His Word is a lamp to our feet. God says, *"I know the plans I have for you...plans to give you a hope and a future...," (Jeremiah 29:11).* How do we know the "plans" God has given each of us? Jeff and I have seen time and time again that when we need the Lord's direction, our first stop is His Word. We spend a little extra time there, listening for His voice and direction. And guess what? Every single time, God has met us there with a specific path or leading to take.

Jesus said we cannot live—or survive—by bread alone. It's by His Word we live, move, and have our existence. Find that sweet spot, and live life to the fullest—just like God planned it!

Read It! Matthew 4:4

Speak It! "Father, I thank You that you have a perfect plan and place for me. Before the world was even formed, You knew all about me. Thank You for revealing Your plans and purpose for my life today. I will walk in Your Word, listen to Your voice, and live in my sweet spot starting today! In Jesus' name. Amen."

DAY 364

("give me a 'v'")

"But thanks be to God! He gives us the victory through our Lord Jesus Christ."
1 Corinthians 15:57, NIV

On May 13, 1940, in his first speech—known as "Blood, Sweat and Tears"—Prime Minister Winston Churchill uttered these words to the House of Commons, "You ask, what is our aim? I can answer in one word: It is victory, victory at all costs, for without victory, there is no survival." Less than one month later, he gave his famous "we will fight them on the beaches" speech to encourage the British Empire to fight for victory during World War II.

The same battle cry should be heard for every Christian: "Victory, victory at all cost!" The good news is that Jesus has won the battle and given us the victory!

For the first few years of my Christian life, I lived in defeat. I loved the Lord but still suffered from a roller-coaster Christian experience. One day, I felt God's presence and was full of joy; the next day, I was discouraged and down-in-the-dumps. I never knew I could life a consistent, victorious Christian life! My battle cry was more of a battle-whine, "Oh Lord, why is this happening? Oh God, life is so hard and the enemy keeps coming against me. There are so many burdens to bear. Dear God, I am so scared...so mad...so depressed... Oh, Jesus, give me grace to endure my defeated life."

Then one day, I got off the spiritual roller-coaster. I heard that I could actually believe the Bible and live like it was true! I found all the verses that were "in Christ," "in Him" and "in Whom" and I purposefully began to identify with those truths. I found my identity "in Christ"—not in my feelings, circumstances, others' opinions, successes or failures. I renewed my mind with the truth of who I was in Christ; and over time, I was transformed!

When we live "in Christ," we have a rich inheritance that is accessible in this life! We don't have to wait to get to heaven! This inheritance includes so many things—a great salvation, mercy, redemption, peace, acceptance, restoration, strength, grace, the Holy Spirit's power, authority, joy, wisdom, understanding, discernment, healing, abundance, the power to witness, favor to be an influence for Christ, and all kinds of blessings.

The life of victory is available to every Christian...today! Stand up and say: "Give me a 'v'!"

Read It! 1 John 5:4-5, 2 Corinthians 2:14, Romans 8:37

Speak It! "Father, thank You for providing the victorious Christian life for me. Help me obtain the revelation knowledge of who I am 'in Christ,' so I may appropriate the victory and all that You have provided for me. In Jesus' Name. Amen."

DAY 365

(be congruent)

"Let your light so shine before men that they may see your moral excellence
and your praiseworthy, noble, and good deeds and recognize and honor
and praise and glorify your Father Who is in heaven."
Matthew 5:16, AMP

I love to be around people who act like Christians. Strange thing to have to say, isn't it?

Jesus had a lot to say about hypocrisy among Believers. He got in the face of religious people who said one thing and did another. He wasn't big on people wearing religion as a badge and never playing the part in real life. He didn't like the idea of putting on a show that wasn't consistent with one's life. He expected His followers to live in a way that was congruent with their faith.

We all know "Christians," in name, who don't act like Christians, right? To hear them talk, cheat, swear, lie and curse others is a bit incongruent with the Christian life.

We had an instructor in Bible school who cautioned all of us zealous students to make sure we love people, not just crowds. He noted his experience with ministers who loved to stand before a crowd and preach; but off the platform, they were impersonal, unfriendly and rude toward people. That's incongruent. It's incongruent to be a Christian and never talk about Christ; to be a Believer and doubt most of the Bible; to be a follow of Christ and never submit to His lordship. It's oxymoronic. We should be the same person in public that we are in private. If we lead people to the Lord from the pulpit, we should be proactive about leading people to the Lord in our private lives, too. If we pray tear-filled, passionate prayers in leading the prayer meeting, we ought to pray the same way in our private prayer closet. If we praise the Lord and lead worship from the stage, it should be obvious that we praise and worship off stage. If we tell everyone else to tithe and give to the Gospel, we should be leading the charge by tithing and giving as much—or more. If we quote the Bible to others, we need to live by the Bible in front of others. Right?

There's nothing more detrimental to Christianity than a "schizo-Christian"—one who puts on the church-face and makes a big hallelujah show for the public, but is hypocritical and carnal in private. If we're going to be Christians—then, let's be Christians. Let's be congruent.

Read It! Matthew 23:25, NIV

Speak It! "Father, I want my life in Christ to be congruent. Shine Your spotlight on areas of my life that are incongruent with Your Word. I want my public and private life to be consistent and honoring to You. In Jesus' Name. Amen."

Beth Jones

Beth Jones is a Bible teacher, author, wife and mother of four children. She is passionate about helping people get a grip on the Word of God by sharing relevant, humorous and down-to-earth insights.

She is a sought-after speaker and the author of the popular *Getting a Grip on the Basics* series, which has been translated into over a dozen foreign languages and is being used by thousands of churches in America and abroad.

Beth has also written the *Bite-Sized Bible Study* series and *The Question Series* of mini-books. Beth writes the free, daily "Jump Start" e-Devo for over 5,000 subscribers and hosts the www.bethjones.org website.

She received her B.S. in Communication from Boston University, Boston, Massachusetts. Beth and her husband, Jeff, founded and serve as the senior pastors of Valley Family Church a growing and influential church in Kalamazoo, Michigan.

Beth can be reached @ either...

www.valleyfamilychurch.org

www.bethjones.org

INKED

"Aha! I get it!" There are moments when everything becomes clear and the light bulb in our understanding goes on. We all have those times when a new concept or truth turns into more than just words on a page, but becomes revelation inked in our heart. In *Inked: Marked Moments*, Pastor Beth Jones shares 10 specific truths that will transform your life when you allow God to "tattoo" them on your heart. Once we are "inked," God turns our very lives into beautiful art where everyone can see the life of God revealed in and through us. Are you looking for a breakthrough? Need to put your faith into action to live in victory everyday and release fears and guilt that are weighing you down? Then *Inked: Marked Moments* might be the series that gives you the epiphany you've looking for!

LOST

Got a passion and a heart to reach the lost in your world? This passionate and inspiring series—loosely based on the TV show, "LOST"—will give you a fresh fire and compassion to reach out to people you know with the good news of Jesus Christ. Discover how to effectively reach the "LOST" in your world with this 4-part series by Pastor Beth.

BENNIES

Bennies. Blessings. Would you like to know about the rest of the benefits in your inheritance in Christ? *Bennies* is a 3-part series by Pastor Beth Jones. In this series, you'll discover how to appropriate the 6 benefits in Psalm 103.

RED

There are signs all around us! God doesn't want us in the dark on future events; He wants us to discern the times in which we live. In this 3-part series, *RED.* we'll take Jesus' words to heart: "You have a saying that goes, 'Red sky at night, sailor's delight; red sky at morning, sailors take warning.' You find it easy enough to forecast the weather, so why can't you read the signs of the times?" How do we discern the times, world events and national headlines? Join Pastor Beth as we look into God's Word to see what's next on God's calendar.

LIVING ON A PRAYER

Almost everyone wishes they had a better prayer life, but few know how to improve it. In Beth's series, "Living on a Prayer", she explains not only how to pray, but when to pray and what to pray. You won't want to miss a moment of this exciting series as you discover how to enjoy the freedom and blessings that come from living in conversation with God.

for more resources available from Beth...

visit her @ bethjones.org

CPSIA information can be obtained at www.ICGtesting.com
Printed in the USA
LVOW071723310512

284116LV00010B/28/P

9 781933 433172